THE COMPLETE IDIOT'S GUIDE® TO

Psychology

Fourth Edition

by Joni E. Johnston, Psy.D.

ALPHA

A member of Penguin Group (USA) Inc.

This book is dedicated to my brother, Mike, who grew from a little brother into a big-hearted man.

ALPHA BOOKS

Published by the Penguin Group

Penguin Group (USA) Inc., 375 Hudson Street, New York, New York 10014, USA

Penguin Group (Canada), 90 Eglinton Avenue East, Suite 700, Toronto, Ontario M4P 2Y3, Canada (a division of Pearson Penguin Canada Inc.)

Penguin Books Ltd., 80 Strand, London WC2R 0RL, England

Penguin Ireland, 25 St. Stephen's Green, Dublin 2, Ireland (a division of Penguin Books Ltd.)

Penguin Group (Australia), 250 Camberwell Road, Camberwell, Victoria 3124, Australia (a division of Pearson Australia Group Pty. Ltd.)

Penguin Books India Pvt. Ltd., 11 Community Centre, Panchsheel Park, New Delhi—110 017, India

Penguin Group (NZ), 67 Apollo Drive, Rosedale, North Shore, Auckland 1311, New Zealand (a division of Pearson New Zealand Ltd.)

Penguin Books (South Africa) (Pty.) Ltd., 24 Sturdee Avenue, Rosebank, Johannesburg 2196, South Africa

Penguin Books Ltd., Registered Offices: 80 Strand, London WC2R 0RL, England

International Standard Book Number: 978-1-59257-891-7
Library of Congress Catalog Card Number: 2008943865

12 11 10   8 7 6 5 4

Interpretation of the printing code: The rightmost number of the first series of numbers is the year of the book's printing; the rightmost number of the second series of numbers is the number of the book's printing. For example, a printing code of 09-1 shows that the first printing occurred in 2009.

Printed in the United States of America

Note: This publication contains the opinions and ideas of its author. It is intended to provide helpful and informative material on the subject matter covered. It is sold with the understanding that the author and publisher are not engaged in rendering professional services in the book. If the reader requires personal assistance or advice, a competent professional should be consulted.

The author and publisher specifically disclaim any responsibility for any liability, loss, or risk, personal or otherwise, which is incurred as a consequence, directly or indirectly, of the use and application of any of the contents of this book.

Most Alpha books are available at special quantity discounts for bulk purchases for sales promotions, premiums, fundraising, or educational use. Special books, or book excerpts, can also be created to fit specific needs.

For details, write: Special Markets, Alpha Books, 375 Hudson Street, New York, NY 10014.

Publisher: *Marie Butler-Knight*
Editorial Director: *Mike Sanders*
Senior Managing Editor: *Billy Fields*
Acquisitions Editor: *Tom Stevens*
Development Editor: *Michael Thomas*
Senior Production Editor: *Megan Douglass*
Copy Editor: *Nancy Wagner*

Cartoonist: *Steve Barr*
Cover Designer: *Kurt Owens*
Book Designer: *Trina Wurst*
Indexer: *Tonya Heard*
Layout: *Ayanna Lacey*
Proofreader: *Mary Hunt*

Contents at a Glance

Contents

Foreword

If your mind came with an owner's manual, what would it say? *The Complete Idiot's Guide to Psychology, Fourth Edition*, offers you just that glimpse. Why your moods change, what motivates you and those around you, why you feel what you feel, and what turns you on and what turns you off are just a few of the questions for which you can expect to find answers.

As psychologists, we help people every day to find the solutions to some of their most haunting problems. Those answers can be complex and difficult. The beauty of *The Complete Idiot's Guide to Psychology, Fourth Edition*, is that it puts so many theories at your fingertips and then simplifies them in a way that helps you to apply this crucial information to your life.

The Complete Idiot's Guide to Psychology, Fourth Edition, is certain to give you insight into your career choices, family relationships, and love relationships. How your brain works is a fascinating adventure that has never been more understandable. To the extent that you can see how your mind and body work together to produce stress, your unique formula for bringing the stresses of everyday living under your own control will become far more understandable. Even more important, you will learn in simple and clear terms about the things that make you anxious, along with tips for overcoming your anxiety. If you or someone you know is depressed, it could be invaluable to gain insight into the nature of depression and how it is treated in state-of-the-art terms. Addictions, eating disorders, and sexual dysfunctions are stripped of their stigma and put into perspective.

You will understand the causes of and treatment for personality disorders as well as the more severe mental illnesses. Until now, it was extremely difficult to find so much research and bottom-line explanation for the many aspects of that vast and mysterious subject of human psychology in one place. *The Complete Idiot's Guide to Psychology, Fourth Edition*, gives you all the important information that you would expect to find in the finest introductory psychology textbook, without drowning you in the details or the trivia. The examples given are both user friendly and highly applicable to your life. In addition, you will learn much about the field of psychology itself: its history, the pioneers, and even some of the contemporary leaders of the field whose work continues to evolve today. This plethora of information is easy to find and fun to use.

So get ready for a wonderful adventure into who you are and how you became that way. On this incredible journey, be prepared to learn things that will help you now and in the future as well as clarify for you what may have been going on at some time in the past. You will meet many people along the way who are presented as case studies that you will highly identify with, or recognize in those people who are or have been a part of your life. Whether you are reading this book as a manual to under-standing yourself, as a primer on the field, or as a study aid, enjoy your journey!

Michael S. Broder, Ph.D., and Arlene Goldman, Ph.D.
Authors of *The Secrets of Sexual Ecstasy*

Introduction

If you're into immediate gratification, then psychology is for you. What other subject can you instantly apply to every aspect of your life? And it's practical. Learn about human nature and you can't help but understand and improve your own.

The purpose of this book is to give you a quick and comprehensive overview of psychology. Although I've tried to stay off my soapbox, I'd be less than honest if I didn't tell you that my own "psychology" may at times color this book. Obviously, a book of this length can't cover everything, and you'll notice I spend more time talking about psychological disorders than psychological theory. And you'll certainly encounter my optimistic bias about human resilience (I never recovered from *The Grapes of Wrath*). However, you now hold in your hands a good place to start, a road map for your journey into the human psyche. Here's how it looks:

Part 1, "Putting It in Perspective," sets the stage for our human drama. In these chapters, we'll meet the major players in psychology and visit the various schools they started. We'll then shift to various theories of evolution—how psychology as a science evolved, how human behavior evolved, and how individual behavior evolves.

In **Part 2, "Wake Up and Smell the Coffee,"** we'll explore how we make sense of the world, starting with our ability to touch, taste, hear, see, and smell. We'll investigate how information from the world around us becomes grist for our psychic mills, and how we raise our consciousness and all the ways we alter it. We then turn to the fascinating subjects of learning and memory—how we profit from experiences and the peculiar ways we remember them, and how we organize things in our minds.

Part 3, "The Forces Are with You," unleashes the forces that drive human behavior. We'll look at motives, drives, emotions, and all the other things that rouse us to action. We'll look at our hunger and sex drives in depth, and then switch gears to examine the power of language to shape our lives. And we'll wind up with an exploration of stress—what people do when the forces in their lives get out of control.

While the first three parts look at qualities that we all share, **Part 4, "All for One and One for All,"** dares to be different. In this section, we'll cover all the characteristics that make each person unique, starting with the formation of our identity and ending with our individual brand of psychic self-defense. In between, we'll explore personality development, how other people influence us (even when we think they aren't), and the difference between quirky personality traits and mental illness.

Part 5, "Just What Is Normal, Anyway?" serves up the meat of clinical psychology—the ability to distinguish between what's normal and what's not. The first chapter in this section takes a close look at the pros and cons of psychological diagnoses, why we have them, and who decides what they are. The next chapter looks at a relatively new branch of psychology—positive psychology—and some of the tools that can move us from surviving to thriving.

The chapters in **Part 6, "Between a Rock and a Hard Place,"** take a look at the latest weapons in the battles against mental illness, dissect the major psychological disorders, and tease out, based on scientific evidence, what psychological treatment works best for what problem.

Extras

In addition to the main narrative of *The Complete Idiot's Guide to Psychology, Fourth Edition*, you'll find the following other useful types of information:

Psychobabble
Anecdotes or information that is too bizarre, interesting, helpful, or juicy to leave out.

def•i•ni•tion

Short summaries that define psychological terms in a fun and comprehensible way.

Insight

Quick points or observations that shed light on a confusing topic or provide a bit of useful self-help advice.

Brain Buster

Brief tidbits that debunk popular myths and misconceptions or warn you away from common errors or problems.

Acknowledgments

Hillary Clinton once said it takes a village to raise a child. Well, it also takes a village to write a book, or, I should say, for *me* to write a book. Here's where I get to say thanks to all the people who worked in my writing "village" and raised me (sometimes, it seemed, from the dead) while I was writing this book:

- ◆ To my literary agent, Evan Fogelman (a.k.a. Hercules), who has the patience of a saint and the heart of a lion.

- ◆ To Jessica Faust, for giving me the chance to talk about psychology and then actually liking what I had to say.

- To the talented Nancy Gratton, Eric Heagy, and Jennifer Moore, for turning my literary lemons into lemonade.

- To Zach, Zane, Zhanna and Zaylin, who inspire me every day to try to master the art of motherhood (and who have motivated me to learn more than a few stress-management strategies).

- To my sister, Julie, a master in the psychology of sisterly love.

- And to my editor-in-chief, husband, and best friend—Alex Tsakiris—for everything.

Special Thanks to the Technical Reviewers

The Complete Idiot's Guide to Psychology, Fourth Edition, was reviewed by two experts who double-checked the accuracy of what you'll learn here, to help us ensure that this book gives you everything you need to know about psychology. Special thanks are extended to Michael S. Broder, Ph.D., and Arlene Goldman, Ph.D.

Michael S. Broder, Ph.D., and Arlene Goldman, Ph.D. are psychologists, husband and wife, and co-authors of *Secrets of Sexual Ecstasy.* Dr. Broder's other books include *The Art of Living Single, The Art of Staying Together,* and *Can Your Relationship Be Saved?* They live and practice in Philadelphia, Pennsylvania. Visit Dr. Broder at DrMichaelBroder.com.

Trademarks

Part 1

Putting It in Perspective

The study of psychology is as complex as its subject—the human psyche. So it's no surprise that the development of the discipline took a lot of twists and turns to get to where it is today. In these first few chapters, you're going to trace the paths of the various schools of psychology and see how we humans study ourselves. From there, it's on to a discussion of how human behavior, and the behavior of individuals, has evolved.

A Little Psychological Insight

In This Chapter

◆ Understanding psychology

◆ A day in the life

◆ Psychology's major players

◆ Ways psychologists "do" psychology

◆ Psychology's many points of view

Psychology has come a long way, baby. Way back when, in the nineteenth century, much of what passed for psychological practice was based on guesswork, informed by the social prejudices of the day. But over the years, the contributions of a great many careful researchers and deep thinkers have given birth to the modern science of psychology—and every day, new insights are still being achieved.

This chapter explains what psychology is and what it is not. You'll meet the major players in the development of the science and understand the tools psychologists use to figure people out. By the time you finish reading this chapter, you'll be well on your way to thinking like a shrink!

What Is Psychology?

Psychology is the science of human nature. It's all about studying the human mind and behavior so that we can figure out why people think, feel, and do what they do. How do we fall in love, communicate with each other, solve problems, and learn new things? Psychologists are constantly asking questions, developing theories, and conducting experiments to better understand human nature and improve our lives. Whether they're therapists, professors, or researchers, psychologists are constantly trying to reach four goals:

♦ To describe what people do

♦ To explain why we think, feel, and act the way we do

♦ To predict what, when, and how we will do it

♦ To change the parts of human behavior that cause us pain

Let's take a look at each of these goals.

Telling It Like It Is

The first goal of psychology, describing human behavior, sounds easy: just watch what someone is doing and describe it. But that's tougher to do than you might think because no matter how hard we try not to, we see each other through the filters of our prior experiences, our cultural values, and our beliefs.

For example, if you've just been dumped by the love of your life, it would be pretty hard to jump into a new relationship with complete optimism. You might try to protect yourself by watching closely for any sign of rejection. In fact, you might be so worried about getting hurt that you'd overlook evidence that your new love cares about you. Your mental filter has a worthy goal, to prevent more heartache, but it's still blinding you from seeing the world the way it really is.

Insight

Want to start applying psychology to your life right now? Use what you learn in this book to solve just one real problem in your life—or, at least, to understand it better.

Here's another example of how expectations and beliefs can cloud one's vision: when asked to describe their newborns, parents of daughters will describe them as softer, smaller, and weaker than parents of sons, even when there is no actual difference in size, shape, or health. Even at birth, parents are "seeing" their children with eyes that reflect their expectations about gender.

Psychologists also have their share of biases, expectations, and prejudices, which, whether doing therapy or research, they're constantly trying to keep out of their work. That's why therapists consult with their peers: to make sure they're keeping their own "stuff" from interfering with their sessions with their patients. "Telling it like it is" is no easy task!

Why, Oh Why, Oh Why?

Any mystery novel buff will tell you the motive in the whodunit is as important as who did it. Like mystery writers, psychologists often focus on the motives driving a person's behavior. They look for connections between things that happen and how people respond to them. Why do some—but not all—abused children become abusive adults? How does a brain tumor affect someone's personality? Does watching violent television lead to violent behavior? These are examples of the kinds of relationships psychologists try to explain.

Explanations are also useful in everyday life. People often seek therapy to make sense out of a painful situation such as a divorce or a loss. Even if we can't change what has happened to us, understanding the reason it happened gives us a sense of comfort and control, a sense that maybe we can prevent it from happening again.

The Exception to the Rule

Understanding why something happened is helpful, but being able to predict that something is going to happen gives us more options. For example, consider this psychological fact of life: when it comes to human beings, the best predictor of future behavior is past behavior. So how can we use this fact in our day-to-day lives?

Well, let's say you've been dating someone for six months and are starting to get serious. During a romantic dinner, your new love interest suddenly confesses he's been married four times. This information might change your prediction about the odds of the two of you turning gray together. You may be tempted to pull out your little black book of former loves and make a few calls. And you'd have good reason to do so—your

Brain Buster

Research shows that a psychologist is likely to overestimate the likelihood that prisoner Joe will become violent even after extensively interviewing and testing him. Asking a psychologist what a single person will do is like asking a physicist to predict what will happen to a particular drop of water in the ocean.

dinner companion's past behavior suggests that, when it comes to long-term commitments, he's *not* a reliable candidate.

Or at least, that's the obvious conclusion to draw. But let's look at a real-life example: well-known writer Harlan Ellison. By 1985, he had married four times, each time for less than four years before the marriage ended in divorce. Statistically speaking, the odds of a successful fifth marriage surviving beyond his four-year-itch would seem very low. However, Ellison, apparently an eternal optimist, married again in 1986—and is still married to the same woman!

For better or worse, the best predictor of human behavior isn't always accurate. As a profession, psychology has an abominable track record for predicting what any one person will do. Real life doesn't always cooperate with what theory says should happen—especially when we're dealing with what a single individual might do in a given set of circumstances.

When it comes to predicting behavior within a group, psychology does much better. For example, what if you wanted to predict the relationship between intelligence and success? Whether a smart individual will live up to her potential will be determined by many variables—maybe she is lazy, has a serious medical illness, or can't get along with others. A psychologist can't easily predict that intelligence in this *particular* person will result in success in life. But psychologists *can* accurately predict that intelligent people, taken as a group, are more likely to be successful than their unintelligent counterparts.

Brain Buster _____

Using groups to predict individual behavior has its downside. Since 9/11, racial profiling—the use of demographic statistics—to justify restrictive government activity has increased. And historically, many African Americans have complained that they've been stopped by law enforcement for nothing more than "DWB"—driving while black.

Becoming the New, Improved Model

Human beings are always trying to improve, do better, or feel better, so it should come as no surprise that psychologists want to do more than understand human behavior. They want to shape it, mold it, and generally help people run their lives more effectively. The heart of all psychological treatment is teaching a client how to move his behavior in the desired direction—to stop drinking, to communicate more effectively, or to cope with the memories of a painful childhood.

A Day in the Life of a Shrink

If you take a psychologist to the movies, he or she may watch the audience instead of the show. Shrinks are always trying to figure out who people are and why they think, feel, and behave as they do. But they go about their work in many different ways.

The Couch Trip

Most people picture a psychologist sitting behind a couch or desk and listening to people's problems all day. They visualize Robin Williams in *Good Will Hunting* or Barbra Streisand in *The Prince of Tides*. These are images of clinical psychologists, the branch of psychology that trains clinicians to deal with people's emotional and behavioral problems. However, although clinical psychology is the most popular area of specialization, most clinical psychologists aren't in private practice; most of them work in clinics, hospitals, or universities.

They're Everywhere, They're Everywhere!

And they do much more than provide therapy. They teach; they promote mental and physical health; they help businesses run more smoothly; and they conduct research. You can find psychologists in just about any place you'd find human beings—courtrooms, campuses, locker rooms, hospitals, or boardrooms.

And then there are the other branches of psychology, which not only study individual behavior but also the relationships between individuals and anything they may do or influence. Social psychologists study how people influence one another. Environmental psychologists work with architects and city planners to improve the "relationship" between human beings and their workspaces and living quarters. Believe it or not, there's even a group, called human factors psychologists, who look at the relationships between workers and their machines!

Insight _____

For a comprehensive list of psychology disciplines, go to www.en.wikipedia.org/wiki/List_of_psychology_disciplines.

There are many ways to study human beings. Astrologists use the moon and the stars; philosophers apply logic and reasoning; and psychics consult tea leaves and crystal balls. Psychology got *its* start when great philosophers began thinking about human nature.

How They Used to Do It

For hundreds of years, philosophers thought a lot about people, but most of them thought human nature was a spiritual matter that they could not study scientifically. Fortunately for us, in the seventeenth century, a philosopher by the name of René Descartes had the radical view of the mind as a distinct and knowable entity that could be understood through meditation and contemplation.

It wasn't until the end of the nineteenth century, though, that people went beyond just *thinking* about human nature and started *studying* it. In 1879, Wilhelm Wundt founded the first psychological laboratory at the University of Leipzig in Germany, and psychology as an academic discipline was born. This transformed psychology from philosophy to a science and forever changed the study of human behavior.

Instead of using logic and common sense, researchers now had to look at objective, outside evidence that either confirmed or disproved their ideas about human beings. Psychologists developed a "show-me" attitude.

Psychology Today

In today's scientific climate, valid research questions about human behavior are those that are testable and replicable. They should be answerable through someone's first-hand experience, with no reliance on "experts," hearsay, or religious dogma. If I want to know whether studying before a test lowers test-taking anxiety, I'll research the question by finding students who hit the books before an exam and see whether they're less nervous than their less-studious counterparts.

def•i•ni•tion

The **scientific method** is a way of answering questions that helps remove bias from the study. First, form your question into a statement that can be disproved; then test it against observable facts. Other researchers who doubt your findings can duplicate your test and see whether they get the same results.

Then, if you, too, are curious about the link between anxiety and studying, you can ask the same question, do the same research, and see if you get the same answer I did. That's the *scientific method*.

Experimental psychologists are always checking up on each other's findings. After scientists publish results, their colleagues try to shoot holes through them, offer alternative explanations, and see whether they can get the same results. This asking, theorizing, predicting, testing, and retesting forms the basis of what we know about human psychology today.

But not everything can be directly observed in a laboratory or field test. Many human activities, such as reasoning, creating, or dreaming, are private; we assume they happen, but we can't see them. Psychology as a science draws its conclusions about such activities by observing what a person does, when he or she does it, and how he or she does it.

Through their careful observations of human behavior, psychologists make inferences about the mind. However, any judgments about thoughts or feelings must be checked out—after all, appearances *can* be deceiving. For example, if I greet my husband and he ignores me, I might immediately assume he's mad at me. If I ask him about it, however, I might learn that he wasn't giving me the silent treatment on purpose. Maybe he was preoccupied with work or, more likely, was temporarily hard of hearing after watching three football games at maximum volume!

Methods to Studying Madness

Science gave psychologists some pretty clear guidelines for studying human behavior:

- Be skeptical.
- Keep your values and opinions separate from your ideas and beliefs.
- Only ask questions you can answer yourself.
- Show other people your results, and make sure they can check your answers.

Psychology as a science dictates what kinds of questions we can ask—they must be objective and replicable. But how do we decide which questions to ask? Think *theories*, my dear Watson. A theory is a set of related principles used to explain or predict something.

Because human beings are so complex, psychologists have theories for just about everything from learning to child development, from memory to mental illness. Personality theories try to explain why human beings are the way they are; development theory looks at how children become grownups. Different theoretical perspectives about what parts of human nature are important influence the questions we can ask.

If for instance, we theorize that mental illness is a result of painful childhood experiences, we start to wonder what particular kinds of painful childhood experiences cause the most damage. Or we may ask if the age at which the experience happens makes a difference.

def•i•ni•tion

A **theory** is a set of assumptions about a question. A **hypothesis** is an answer to the question, based on theoretical assumptions that we can test to see whether the answer can be proven wrong.

Next, we start to generate *hypotheses*, predictions about what we would expect to happen if our theory were true. If we believe that a person's childhood has a major impact on his or her adult life, for example, we might expect abused children to have some problems when they grow up. To test our hypothesis, we would conduct a study using one or more scientifically appropriate research methods, chosen to suit the kind of question we are asking. The most common research methods are *descriptive studies, correlation research*, and *experiments*.

Delving into the Descriptive

If the question starts with "How often," "How much," or "How many times," then a descriptive study is the way to go. In this method, the researcher describes the behavior of a person or group of people. For example, we might ask how much violence the average child sees on television. Or we might survey people to see what percentage of the population has been treated for depression. Or if we're assessing a person's assertiveness, we might count the number of times he or she speaks up in a group.

Is There a Relationship?

Descriptive studies give us a good idea of what we're looking at, but they don't tell us what it all means. The level of violence a child sees on television might not matter if it doesn't lead to aggressive behavior. Correlational research tries to assess the relationship between two aspects of human behavior.

Researchers must always remember a golden rule: correlation does not equal causation. *Huh?* In other words, just because two things are related (for example, they happen around the same time or they always seem to go together) doesn't mean one caused the other. For example, kids who watch violent TV may be more aggressive, but this doesn't mean shoot-'em-up shows *cause* punching and kicking; maybe both are caused by a third factor, such as the lack of parental supervision.

Let's assume we're doing a study on TV violence and aggressive behavior in children, beginning with the theory that there is a link between watching violent television and expressing aggressive behavior. Our hypothesis is that children who watch violent television are more aggressive than those who watch little or no violent television.

> **Brain Buster**
>
> By allowing us to see pictures of the brain in action, functional magnetic resonance imaging has done for brain studies what the diving bell did for ocean studies. But even the best technology can be used erroneously, as evidenced by the recent trend to over-rely on neuroscientific explanations for voting behavior while ignoring the research-backed logical reasons that sway voters.

Right away, it gets complicated. How are we going to measure aggression? This sounds simple but it's not. We might count the number of times a child is sent to the principal's office, but that could be misleading: some teachers run a tight ship, whereas others may be real slackers. We might rely on the number of times a sibling complains about a shoot-'em-up-show-watching child's hitting and shoving. However, depending upon tattletales introduces all kinds of problems, such as loyalty, sibling rivalry, and even the possibility of bribery. All these extra issues can make our measurements unreliable.

One way to overcome such problems is to give the children's parents some kind of behavior-rating scale that clearly defines aggressive behavior. We'll be equally clear in defining what we want to count as exposure to violent television: do we measure the number of violent incidents in any show or just the number of violent shows? Does yelling count as violence? Do shoot-'em-up cartoons rate the same as live news coverage of terrorism?

Once we have measured both behaviors, we compare the results. If children who watch violent television are rated as more aggressive than children who watch tamer fare, we have some support for our theory. If on the other hand, children who watch violent television are less aggressive, we'd have to look for another explanation. And we'd have a new hypothesis to test: perhaps watching violent television serves as a safe outlet for children's anger and aggression and actually reduces the odds of their acting violently.

The Experimental Experience

To tease out the cause and effect between two things, the researcher changes one and sees what effect this change has on the other. The thing the experimenter changes is the *independent* variable; the thing that is influenced by the independent variable is called the *dependent* variable.

> **Psychobabble**
>
> The American Psychological Association (APA) in Washington, D.C., is the largest scientific and professional organization representing psychology in the United States and is the world's largest association of psychologists, with more than 148,000 members and 54 subspecialties.

If we want to find out whether exposure to violent television causes children to be more aggressive, we might show children violent television one hour this week, ten hours the next, and five hours the week after that. Each week, we'd see how changing the TV-watching time (the independent variable) affects aggression levels (the dependent variable).

But our experiment may still fail to give us clear-cut results. That's because of *confounding variables*—things that aren't supposed to be a part of the experiment but creep in anyway and influence the results.

In our example, parental expectations might confound the results. If parents knew the amount of violent television their children were watching each week, they might unintentionally rate their children as being more aggressive during weeks of heavy viewing because they expected that behavior. We can try to safeguard against this by leaving the parents in the dark about the actual amount of their child's exposure to violent television during the period of our observations (but, of course, we'd get the parents' permission for this at the outset of the experiment).

Keeping "Junk Science" Out of Your Mental Closet

"Junk science" is a term used to describe research based on faulty, insufficient, unreliable, twisted, dredged-up, or biased data. It often has a hidden agenda: the personal-injury attorney trying to win money for his or her client, the scientist seeking personal fame, the corporation trying to sell its product, or the political activist seeking to support his or her political agenda. However, being able to separate the scientific wheat from the chaff is an important skill; it might influence whether or not you start a certain diet, get help for a child with a learning disability, or make a life-saving phone call to your physician.

So how can you tell what's bunk from what's breakthrough? Start by asking the following questions:

- **Says who?** Hundreds of newspaper stories between 1993 and 2001 encouraged new parents to permanently boost their babies' I.Q. by playing Mozart's music to them. However, the original study that spawned this myth (and two self-help books) was conducted with *college students* and found only a *temporary* increase in the ability to perform a specific task while listening to a Mozart sonata. The moral of this story is to make sure you know who was involved in the study, how they were selected, who did not respond or participate, and how the study population matched—or didn't—the claims.

- **How did they ask "why"?** Claims based on a single or a few observations aren't data, and statistics don't prove cause and effect. Mice aren't humans, and exposure doesn't mean toxicity. Make sure you know the limits to the methods the studies used to back their claims.

- **What's the alternative?** A study claims that a new French language program is superior to its three competitors; the evidence is the superior results of a French test given to four groups, each of whom has received three months of French instruction using one of the four products. Are you convinced? Not yet, I hope. What do you know about the four groups? What if the new French language program was tested on Harvard seniors while the three competitors were given to college dropouts?

Multiple Perspective Disorder

If you've ever seen the movies *Sybil* or *Three Faces of Eve*, then you're aware of the condition we used to call multiple personality disorder, a rare mental illness in which a person develops different personalities to cope with severe childhood trauma. Psychologists have their own version of this disorder, which has haunted the field of psychology since its early years. I call it multiple perspective disorder.

Imagine setting out to become the world's authority on elephants by studying only their legs. You can tell a lot about an elephant from its legs—the texture of its skin, the climate in which it lives, maybe even its travel patterns. On the other hand, you would be clueless about its mating habits, eating rituals, or defense strategies. Even if you studied for years, the best you could do is become the leading expert on elephant legs. It'd be ludicrous to claim you truly understood elephants.

Yet for years, that's exactly what some psychologists did. Some groups studied the mind, while others focused on human behavior. Some believed that childhood influences were the key to our psyches and spent their time analyzing dreams and unlocking childhood memories. Others believed it was the here and now that mattered. Seven different perspectives emerged during the twentieth century, and most of them claimed to be *the* right way to study human nature. At times, battles became pretty heated over whose perspective was right.

Fortunately, psychologists today value the unique contribution of *each* psychological perspective. While some psychologists might still tell you that their beliefs about human nature fall in line with one particular perspective, in practice they are likely to apply whichever perspective best deals with the problem at hand. For, as you shall see, each perspective offers valuable insights into human nature. The seven perspectives most prevalent today include the following:

1. The biological perspective

2. The psychodynamic perspective

3. The behaviorist perspective

4. The humanist perspective

5. The cognitive perspective

6. The sociocultural perspective

7. The evolutionary perspective

I Was Born This Way

The biological perspective looks to the body to explain the mind. Biological psychologists look at the influence of hormones, genes, the brain, and the central nervous system on the way we think, feel, and act. How much of our personality is inherited? Is there a gene for suicide? Does mental stress cause physical illness? Do the brains of schizophrenics function differently than those of normal people? In the endless "nature versus nurture" debate of human behavior (see Chapter 3), biological psychology clearly sides with nature.

Biological psychology has been instrumental in the development of medications that effectively treat depression, anxiety, bipolar disorder, and schizophrenia. It has reawakened our awareness of the mind/body connection and given us specific ways to measure, and conquer stress. Through its identification of the physiological components of many mental illnesses, it has helped tear down the false dichotomy between illnesses of the mind and illnesses of the body. This has helped remove the stigma associated with mental illness—a development that has been as beneficial to people's mental health as any technique developed in the last 20 years!

Insight

Your genes may be causing your blues! We now know depression runs in families and chemical changes in the brain coincide with clinical depression. Medications, psychotherapy, and other treatments can adjust these changes and chase depression away.

It's Only the Tip of the Iceberg

The psychoanalytic perspective (psychoanalysis is the technique, not the theory) views behavior as driven by powerful mental conflicts locked deep within the subconscious. Sigmund Freud, the father of psychoanalysis, thought most people were riddled with conflicts between their own needs and society's demands.

Freud thought an adult's mind was like the tip of an iceberg; he believed that conflicts arise and are pushed down when we are children. Because of this, we have little insight into the motives that drive our behavior as adults. We do, however, get clues through dreams, *slips* of the tongue, or sudden, unexplainable behavior. Freud believed unconscious conflicts were the source of his patients' pain and frequently led them to behave in an irrational manner.

Freud also believed that children are naturally sexual and aggressive but that society was not willing to accept these natural urges in youngsters. He specifically pointed the finger at parents who, he claimed, often became upset when faced with a child's erection or natural interest in bodily functions and often punished the child for expressing natural urges.

def•i•ni•tion

A **Freudian slip** is a mistake or substitution of either spoken or written words. Freud believed such "slips" come from unconscious wishes that pop up unexpectedly through unintentional words. By analyzing these "slips," a person might get some clues into his or her inner thoughts or "real" intent or wishes.

Thus Freud explained the beginnings of psychological and behavioral problems. To survive the threat of parental punishment, the child quickly learned to push these natural urges out of sight and out of mind. Freud attributed much of human discomfort to the ongoing battle between our own individual needs and desires and society's rules and norms, a battle that continues long after we pass through childhood.

Freud was perhaps the first to stress the influence of traumatic childhood events on shaping our personalities and worldviews. He was the first to recognize that human behavior is not always rational or easy to explain. He was also one of the first to see the healing that occurs when a client revisits, and works through, the trials and tribulations of childhood. Last but not least, Freud certainly had a way with words; he gave us many words that are now a common part of our lingo: Oedipal complex, penis envy, id, ego, and superego.

Psychobabble

Most of Freud's specific theories, like his Oedipal complex and stages of psychosexual development, have fallen out of favor with today's practicing psychotherapists. However, he is still credited with being the first to popularize the idea that someone could solve his problems simply by talking about them, an idea unheard of in the nineteenth century.

We're Just Rats Caught in a Maze

The behavioral perspective all started with rats. After spending many years watching rats race through mazes, a psychologist named John Watson realized he could accurately predict where a rat would run if he knew where it had found food on previous trials. He was impressed with the amount of information he could learn about rats just by watching their behavior and understanding the environment in which it occurred. And he found he could change the rat's behavior pretty quickly by putting the food in a different place.

Maybe, he thought, people aren't much different. Maybe we aren't as complicated as we think, and maybe all that mental mumbo jumbo, like thoughts and feelings, doesn't matter. Maybe, he proposed, human behavior is as simple as *ABC*:

*A*ntecedent	The environmental trigger
*B*ehavior	The behavioral response to the environmental trigger
*C*onsequence	What happens next

Watson believed psychology should seek to understand people by studying what happens to them and how they respond. His focus was firmly on the bottom line: behavior. He theorized that behavior usually started as a response to an environmental event. From this he went on to reason that the consequences of that response would determine whether that behavior would increase over time or become less frequent.

Insight

You can (and probably already do, sometimes) use behaviorism in your daily life. Any time you use praise or rewards to get the kids to do their chores, you're acting like a behaviorist!

Let's say that every time the phone rings, your new love interest is on the line. Chances are you'll start racing for the phone at the first ring. On the other hand, if bill collectors often give you a jingle, you might ignore the telephone no matter how many times it rings.

Behaviorism ruled the psychological roost for almost 50 years and contributed many practical tools and ideas. For one thing, it shifted the focus of psychological research from generating insights onto behavior change. It gave us behavior modification, a process of shaping someone's behavior by consistently rewarding the desired actions, thus earning the eternal gratitude of countless parents, teachers, and savvy spouses! And it gave us some pretty powerful weapons against irrational fears and phobias (see Chapter 18).

I Think, Therefore I Am

Cognitive psychology is the study of people's ability to acquire, organize, remember, and use knowledge to guide their behavior. Cognitive psychologists think we're much more than a bunch of rats. Yes, they say, we react to our environment, but we also act upon it: people solve problems, make decisions, and consider options and alternatives before we act.

The cognitive perspective assumes that connections exist between what people perceive, think, feel, and do. Unlike the behaviorists, cognitive psychologists think that what goes on inside someone's head is of critical importance. In fact, they believe that a lot of how we feel and what we do starts with what we're thinking, not with some impersonal stimulus from the environment. They would argue, for example, that someone who sees a cancer diagnosis as a meaningful personal challenge is likely to approach his or her treatment very differently than someone who views it as a death sentence.

Although the cognitive perspective focuses on the mind, it doesn't rely on introspection or intuition to study it. Cognitive psychologists study human behavior and then make inferences about the mind from their observations. For example, Swiss psychologist Jean Piaget gave children a series of problems to solve and then documented the mistakes they made and their reasons for their answers. After testing many children at varying ages, he formed his theory about how children develop their ability to reason.

Cognitive researchers develop theories about the mental processes that influence what we do. They test those theories by creating situations in which people would be expected to behave in one predictable way if the theory were true or in another way if the theory were not true. Through the influence of cognitive psychology, we understand more about decision making, creativity, and problem solving than ever before. We've also learned how to do them better.

The influence of cognitive psychology is everywhere today; we see it in the numerous self-help books that proclaim the power of self-talk and in the concept of attitude adjustment. When someone says, "When life gives you lemons, make lemonade," he is speaking from a cognitive perspective.

It's a Dog-Eat-Dog World

You're probably familiar with Darwin's "survival of the fittest" idea. Darwin basically thought that the creatures whose inherited characteristics were best adapted to the environment were the ones that survived and reproduced. If a duck with a wide beak can get more food than a narrow-beaked duck, the wide-beaked duck will survive. Over time, all ducks will have wider beaks.

def•i•ni•tion

Natural selection is the Darwinian principle that says the best-adapted traits are the ones that will pass along from one generation to another in a species. Creatures with less-well-adapted traits will die out before they can reproduce, so their poorly adapted traits will eventually disappear from the population.

Evolutionary psychology applies that same principle of *natural selection* to human behavior. It holds that human beings, as a species, have acquired innate problem-solving tendencies that promote their survival and reproduction. Evolutionary psychologists study behaviors that are common among all humans and try to figure out how those behaviors helped us become top dog of the animal kingdom. They believe that a key to understanding human nature is in the behavior of our ancestors; if we can reconstruct the problems our ancestors dealt with, then we can understand the problem-solving tendencies that helped them survive and thus became a genetic part of being human.

For example, all human beings hate, love, and get angry. Evolutionary psychologists would say we inherited the ability to express our feelings from our ancestors because the ability to communicate feelings and intentions helped them survive. Once we know how our emotions evolved, we can be more aware of, and therefore control, these natural tendencies.

Of course, who, what, or when any one human being will love is much more complicated; we must also look at his or her culture, life experiences, genes, and personality. And we still must contend with the here and now. A man might blame his having an affair on an ancestral legacy that called for men to ensure maximum reproduction by mating with multiple partners. But he's still going to face his wife's wrath, and, possibly, the consequences of his behavior in court!

> **Psychobabble**
>
> Evolutionary psychologists have identified 26 behavior traits that all humans on our planet share. Just a few of the more interesting ones are: deception, detecting emotions, gossip, humor, perception of status/rank, and romantic love.

No Man Is an Island

Why do eating disorders only occur in countries like the United States, where "thin" is the beauty ideal? If aggression is a human instinct, why is the rate of violence so different from country to country? A sociocultural psychologist would tell you that if you want to understand such human behaviors, you must start with the culture in which people live.

All human beings have minds, but each culture produces a different version. The sociocultural perspective focuses on the differences among people living in various cultures as well as the ways a people's culture influences their thoughts, feelings, and behavior. From this perspective, our culture influences how we think, feel, and act. Culture teaches us about the roles we play and gives us informal rules about what is, and what is not, socially acceptable. If you've ever visited another country, you've encountered the sociocultural perspective up close; it can be quite a shock realizing that what's "normal" is suddenly different!

Even psychology has cultural biases. In the United States, a country that values self-sufficiency and individualism, the focus of therapy is often on individual behavior change. In many Asian countries, where fitting into the group is a highly valued trait, therapy would emphasize the understanding and acceptance of ourselves and the people around us. And in some Latin American cultures, where the family unit is *numero uno*, it would seem absurd to treat someone without including the whole family; behavior we would describe as healthy and independent might be viewed as selfish!

Looking on the Bright Side

Undoubtedly, the stereotype of the "touchy-feely" psychologist started with a humanist. As a backlash against the doom and gloom of the psychoanalytic perspective and the behaviorist's robotic view of humankind, the humanists looked on the bright side of human nature. People are naturally good, the humanists said, and if left to their own devices, they will strive to become the best they can be. Problems only come up when other people get in their way.

According to this view, a parent or teacher might criticize a child's natural attempt to grow. If this happens often enough, such criticized children begin to doubt their own thoughts and feelings. They begin to see themselves as incapable and, as a result, start mistrusting their own judgment. As adults, they may not take charge of their own lives because they no longer believe they are capable of doing so.

> **Psychobabble**
>
> One of psychology's new kids on the block is positive psychology, the view that psychology should devote more attention to what makes people happy and well-adjusted and find more ways to help people flourish.

With this theoretical viewpoint, it's not surprising that regaining a positive self-concept is a major therapeutic goal. The self-esteem movement started with humanists; in addition to their emphasis on promoting positive self-concepts, the humanists encourage therapists to look at their clients' psychological reality—the way they perceive their experiences—rather than focusing on the experiences themselves. From the humanist perspective, a person's view of his or her life is much more important than what actually happened—understand her perspective and you'll know why she thinks, feels, and acts the way she does.

Psychology in Action

Different psychological perspectives offer different explanations for the same behavior. Consider this fictional scenario:

> Janine, a straight-A college student and track star, lined up to compete at the NCAA 5,000-meter regional finals—held later on the same day that she had to take her MCAT. Having spent the night studying for that all-important exam, Janine was operating on three hours of sleep. As the runners took off, Janine got off to a slow start and fell behind. Suddenly, she veered off the track, scaled an 8-foot fence, and jumped off a 45-foot bridge. Her injuries ended her running career and indefinitely postponed her dream of medical school.

Now take a look at how each perspective might try to explain why Janine acted as she did:

A Potpourri of Psychological Perspectives

Perspective	Burning Questions	Possible Answers
Psychoanalytic	What forces drove Janine so hard that she "snapped"?	Maybe her parents pushed her too much; perhaps she overcompensated for feelings of inadequacy by "winning" and panicked at the thought of failure.
Behaviorist	What have been the previous consequences for Janine when she lost a race? In the past, did she usually lose when she fell behind?	Maybe past losses were followed by painful consequences (criticism or derision), and Janine was trying to avoid experiencing them again.
Humanist	Was Janine's self-image such that she only felt loved and respected if she won?	Maybe she was trying to change the basis of her self-worth or trying to test her friends' and family's love for her.
Cognitive	What was Janine thinking during the race? How did these thoughts lead her to act the way she did?	Maybe her fear of failure interfered with her ability to think rationally and thus impaired her judgment.
Sociocultural	What has American culture taught Janine about winning and the price of failure? How would she expect others to treat her if she lost the race?	Maybe Janine's behavior was so desperate because of the social consequences she anticipated if she failed; maybe she took "winning isn't everything, it's the only thing" to the extreme.

continues

A Potpourri of Psychological Perspectives   (continued)

Perspective	Burning Questions	Possible Answers
Biological	Did Janine have an undetected medical condition that was aggravated by the running? Maybe she had a predisposition toward impulsive behavior?	Maybe Janine had an untreated chemical imbalance; maybe she had a brain tumor or some other physical problem that caused her to act out of character; maybe the physical effects of sleep deprivation were a factor.
Evolutionary	Was Janine's behavior an example of adaptive behavior gone awry?	Maybe Janine perceived her fear of failure like our ancestors perceived threatening predators and was trying to flee from them.

Each perspective approaches the scenario from a different set of assumptions (theoretical position) and therefore, comes up with a different question to answer. Each question has a certain amount of validity, but it's clear that no single perspective asks, or answers, every question the scenario raises.

Psychology's Report Card

As we approach 2010, what progress has psychology made over the 135 years it's been in existence? What grade would you give the school of psychology? Of course, the grade you give will depend upon your own psychology—your values, beliefs, personal history, and so forth. Some of the brightest minds in the world have pondered this question over the past decade—and the reviews have been mixed. While I don't put myself in the "brightest minds" category, here's my score:

◆ Psychology's progress has not been constant or steady—but we've made good progress. We're no longer drilling holes in the heads of mentally ill people to release evil spirits or blaming their symptoms on an excess of phlegm or bile.

◆ American kids are the most heavily medicated in the world. They are three times more likely to be prescribed psychiatric medication than children in Europe.

◆ When it comes to mental illness, we're still better at treating symptoms than in understanding causes. However, we're getting pretty good at treating the symptoms; today's psychiatric medications have fewer side effects and are prescribed with more knowledge and understanding by psychiatrists.

In the following chapters, we look more closely at how insights from all these psychological perspectives have contributed to the development of the science of psychology as we know it today.

Straight from the Lab

Get Back on Track   Historically, there has been a rift between clinicians and researchers. A new research study, however, aims to bridge the gap between how psychotherapy is studied in research settings and how it is actually conducted in real-world clinical practice. By carefully tracking a patient's symptoms before, during, and after treatment, and then applying specialized statistical analysis, psychologists and psychiatrists can conduct perfectly sound case studies out of their offices.

Back to the Future   Major Gen. Antonio Taguba's report on the conditions at Abu Ghraib describe a prison that was the perfect Petri dish in which the culture of guard violence could flourish. Phillip Zimbardo, the researcher behind the Stanford prison experiments that led to unexpected abuse by college "prison guards," cited the weak leadership, cloud of secrecy, and lack of resources as the perfect environment for violence and abuse.

Sensitive Periods of the Psyche   New research suggests that there may be critical times during which we are more vulnerable to psychological trauma than others. One of these is during the transition from high school to college. Being a new drinker during the first year of college significantly increases the likelihood of physical victimization, and increased drinking during the first year increases the risk of physical and sexual assault.

Psychologists Extend the Couch to Outer Space   As NASA begins preparing astronauts for longer and tougher trips, psychologists are helping to develop computer programs that will aid explorers in handling the emotional challenges.

The Least You Need to Know

◆ Psychology is the scientific study of human behavior and mental processes.

◆ Psychologists wear many different hats: they research why people think, feel, and act the way they do. They help people solve their problems, and they use their knowledge about human behavior to help courts, companies, schools, and sports teams run more efficiently.

◆ Because psychology is a science, the questions it raises must be objective and testable, and research must be theory based, systematic, and replicable.

◆ Predicting the behavior of groups is much easier than predicting the behavior of individuals. Applying statistical information about groups to one individual can be misleading and hurtful.

◆ Today, psychology has seven major psychological perspectives: biological, psychodynamic, sociocultural, evolutionary, cognitive, humanist, and behaviorist.

◆ Each of the perspectives psychologists employ has contributed important insights into the how and why of human nature.

2

Bio Psycho What?

In This Chapter

- ◆ The biology of psychology
- ◆ The best communication system ever invented
- ◆ The true meaning of "getting on your nerves"
- ◆ Left-brained vs. right-brained
- ◆ Recycling the plastic brain
- ◆ Brain booboos

"Let's brainstorm." "Watch it, you pea brain." "She's the brains behind it." When we listen to the words we use, it's clear we know who rules the roost when it comes to human behavior: the brain. But we're still mystified by how it doesn't always listen to what we think we're telling it.

After reading this chapter, you'll be up to speed on the biological hardware that programs human behavior as we explore the parts of the brain that cause us to think, feel, and do the things we do. We also explore how they do it, how different parts of the brain communicate with each other and the rest of the body, and how hormones and other chemicals influence human behavior. So let's get started at the real beginning of psychology—our brains.

You Are What You Think

For hundreds of years, the Greeks thought the heart and blood were the CEOs of human beings. And who can blame them? Weighing in at around three pounds, the human brain looks like a wrinkled, gray cantaloupe. Even in the most vibrant human being, it appears to be sitting around doing nothing. Contrast this with a fiery red, pulsing heart, and you'll understand why the Greeks made the heart our chief executive organ.

> **Psychobabble**
>
> Phrenology was a pseudo-science in the nineteenth century that tried to use bumps on the skull as indications of intelligence and character. No wonder Ambrose Bierce defined phrenology as "the science of picking the pocket through the scalp"!

To understand human nature, we must first understand the nature of the brain because, in essence, psychology is the study of what the brain does. There's a biological counterpart to every thought or feeling we have. And as you'll see, physical changes in the brain can produce dramatic changes in human behavior.

It's Evolutionary, My Dear Watson

We're all winners from an evolutionary perspective. The very fact that we exist means our ancestors possessed favorable characteristics that enabled them to adapt and flourish in their natural environment. They passed these advantageous traits on to the next generation, who passed them on to their children, and so on, until here we are. We're the "fittest" in the "survival of the fittest."

Adapting to Changes

Have you ever felt like you finally figured out the rules of life and then someone changed them? So did our ancestors. Here they were, trying to adapt to their environment as best they could, and suddenly nature decided to play a joke or two. Resources became scarcer, or the average temperature suddenly skyrocketed. These environmental shifts could drastically change which organisms were favored.

A rise in temperature, for example, might select against the animals with the heaviest fur. Scarcity of resources sharpens the competitive edge and speeds up the natural selection process. Think about the competition on Donald Trump's *Apprentice*, and you'll know what I mean!

In terms of human evolution, two environmental adaptations assured us the highest place on the totem pole, and of course, all humans share these things today. These adaptations were bipedalism, the ability to walk upright, and encephalization, the development of a larger brain.

On Your Feet, Big Head!

Bipedalism, which occurred between 5 and 10 million years ago, freed our hands. It made us better able to explore and manipulate our environment than other species and to relocate when needed. When the going got tough, human beings were the first who were able to get going.

Human evolution really took off a couple of million years ago, when our brains got bigger. Encephalization gave us more "head room" for thinking and ultimately led to our increased ability to reason, remember, and plan.

From a psychological standpoint, though, we're more interested in what our evolutionary path means for brains living here and now. How do our brains help each one of us solve our problems, remember birthdays, and plan our future? To answer these questions, let's take an inside look at the human brain.

Psychobabble
A neuropsychologist is a psychologist specially trained in the assessment and rehabilitation of brain damage. Neuropsychological assessment includes observation, a detailed personal history of the patient, and many specialized tests for memory, intelligence, and other functions. Unlike a CT (computerized tomography) or an MRI (magnetic resonance image), which give us a picture of what the brain looks like, a neuropsychological assessment tells us what a person can do after injury or disease strikes.

The Headquarters of Human Behavior

The brain contains more cells than there are stars in the universe. And each part works together to produce, direct, and choreograph what we think, feel, and do.

A Living Record of Time Travel

One of the stories our brain tells us is the story of human evolution. From the neck up, it's structured in the order in which it evolved. The brain stem, the bulb where the brain meets the spine, is the oldest part of the brain; the midbrain and higher brain evolved on top of it in much the same way newer buildings are constructed on the old foundations of an ancient city.

As with your brain's structure, so developed the behavior each part of your brain controls. They, too, go from primitive to most sophisticated. The lower brain is responsible for aggression, territoriality, and rituals. The midbrain holds the limbic system, the seat of powerful emotions, sexual instincts, and the sense of smell. Over the top arches the cerebral cortex, the part of the brain that regulates higher levels of cognitive and emotional functioning. This is the site of reasoning, planning, creating, and problem solving, and it is the part that makes us human.

Psychobabble

We share the lower part of our brain with all reptiles. Now you know where the expression "giving in to your baser instincts" comes from.

Hello Central!

The bottom-up approach reveals the human brain's structural evolution inside each of us. Human behavior evolved from base instincts to thoughtful planning. From a psychological standpoint, you can see why it can be challenging to use your reasoning and self-control to keep from acting on powerful feelings or strong desires. After all, those desires have been around much longer than your logic!

If the brain is the headquarters of human behavior, the cerebral cortex is unquestionably the commander in chief. Not only does it make up two-thirds of your brain, its job is to coordinate all the brain's units and strategically channel your resources in ways that will give you the best chance to survive and flourish in your environment. When we say "use your brain," the cerebrum is the part we're talking about.

Getting Your Brain Organized

Because our cerebrum plays such a big role in human behavior, the lower and middle portions of the brain often get overlooked. However, these more primitive parts of the brain are the foundation on which our mental houses are built. You couldn't survive long without them.

A quick rundown of the parts of the brain will give you a good sense of the way cognitive tasks are parceled out. Each part is a specialist:

- **brain stem** Regulates the internal physiological state of the body

- **medulla** Regulates breathing and the beating of the heart

- **pons** Regulates brain activity during sleep

- **reticular formation** Arouses the brain to attend to new stimuli even during sleep

- **thalamus**   The relay station between senses and the cerebral cortex

- **cerebellum**   Organizes physical balance and movement

- **limbic system**   Regulates motives, drives, feelings, and some aspects of memory

- **hippocampus**   The key player in long-term memory

- **amygdala**   The tough guy, with roles in aggression, memory, emotion, and basic motives

- **hypothalamus**   Regulates eating, drinking, sexual arousal, body temperature

- **cerebrum**   Regulates higher levels of thinking and feeling

- **cerebral hemispheres**   Each half mediates different cognition and emotions

Left Brain, Right Brain

Do you prefer geometry or English? Would you rather be a painter or a writer? Are you creative or logical? Depending on how you answered, popular psychology would classify you as "right-brained" or "left-brained."

Psychobabble

This "left brain/right brain" craze started with the discovery that the two sides of the cerebrum are not created equal. The two halves of the brain have different processing styles: the right half sees things holistically, while the left is more logical. In addition, they divide up the work. Some functions are more under the control of the right hemisphere and some are more under the control of the left.

Left-Leaning or a Rightward Slant?

For most people, the left brain is more involved in language and logic. The right half of the brain handles visual patterns and spatial relationships. Hence, painters are thought to be more "right-brained" and writers are thought to be more "left-brained."

Sports psychologists have put the "right brain/left brain" concept to good use. By teaching athletes to use both sides of the brain, they help them improve their performance. For example, tennis players naturally exercise their left brain every time they swing their tennis rackets. The series of steps that form a backhanded swing is a left-brain activity. However, players can also use their right brain to play tennis: lying awake at night, they can mentally practice their game. Tennis players who visualize the perfect swing in their mind's eye and practice it are making creative use of the right hemisphere's holistic processing. And it works!

This division of labor holds true for our feelings as well. The left hemisphere is associated primarily with positive emotions while the right hemisphere is responsible for negative emotions like anxiety and depression. Given that painters and sculptors use their right hemisphere so much, maybe there's something to the idea of a tortured artist!

Partners for Life

In reality, though, the popular left brain/right brain distinction is overly simplistic. These two halves of your brain are partners; they constantly talk to each other through a huge bundle of fibers that connect the two hemispheres, the *corpus callosum*. They also work in sync. For example, when you run into an acquaintance, your left hemisphere remembers his name and your right hemisphere recalls his face.

Oddly enough, the left cerebral hemisphere controls the movement on the right side of the body and the right hemisphere controls the left. When you write your name with your right hand, your left hemisphere is actually doing the work. Specifically, your left parietal lobe is busy—which brings me to the next topic of conversation: the four lobes that make up each hemisphere.

Meet the Mother Lobes

You have more lobes than the ones you hang your earrings on. Each half of your brain has four lobes—a parietal lobe, a temporal lobe, a frontal lobe, and an occipital lobe.

Front and Center

The frontal lobes, which sit just behind your forehead, are the newest additions to the human brain. They're considered the "executive" part of the brain—the seat of purposeful behavior. They plan, make decisions, and pursue goals. They also inhibit or override more primitive behavior. This is the part of the brain that keeps you from calling your boss an idiot—even when he deserves it!

Temporally Speaking

Your temporal lobes sit directly behind your ears—convenient, since their job is to make sense of what you hear. The left temporal lobe enables you to understand speech. Your right temporal lobe helps you to understand music, the ringing of the telephone, and other nonverbal sounds. In neuropsychological terms, telling someone that she has an ear for music translates into excellent right temporal lobe functioning.

> ### Brain Buster
>
> Chronic pain is bad for your brain. In a healthy brain, when one region is neuronally active, the others are quiet. But the brain in constant pain, firing in a frontal cortex area associated with emotion, gets stuck on full throttle, wearing out—and even killing off—neurons, and altering their connections to each other.

Parietals Rule

Your parietal lobes sit at the top of your head and integrate sensory information from the opposite sides of your body: your left parietal lobe makes sense of information coming in from the right side of the body, and your right parietal lobe takes care of the left side. These lobes help you understand what you're touching. When you reach into your purse or pocket, for example, your parietal lobes help you distinguish between a quarter and a dime just by the way they feel.

An Occipital Complex?

If you cup your hand on the back of your head, you are hugging your occipital lobes, which make sense of what you see; their primary job is to process visual information. See? You do have eyes in the back of your head!

The left occipital lobe controls the right visual field in both your eyes, while the right occipital lobe controls the left visual field. To see how this works, hold your hands out in front of your face so that your palms are facing you. Now, draw an imaginary vertical line down the middle of each hand. The right visual field is the right half of each hand; the left visual field is the left half of each hand.

New research also suggests that we all have double vision, or at least two visual systems.

> ### Insight
>
> Read Oliver Sacks's *The Man Who Mistook His Wife for a Hat* for a close look at the impact of brain disorders on everyday life. The title of this book comes from one of Dr. Sacks's patients, whose inability to recognize faces caused him to mistake his wife's head for a hat; as a result, he attempted to pick it up off her shoulders!

The visual system that shows you a coffee cup sitting on your desk isn't the same one that guides your hand to pick it up. The first system, called vision-for-perception, enables you to recognize objects and build a "database" about the world. The other, less-studied, vision-in-action system provides the visual control you need to move about and interact with objects.

These systems are completely separate. Brain scans have located the vision-for-perception system deep in the cerebral cortex near the memory and language areas. This system is more interested in the identity of an object than in its orientation in space. In contrast, the vision-for-action system, located toward the top of the cerebral cortex near the motor and touch areas, is more interested in the object's orientation than its identity. Patients with damage to the perception system can't recognize an object by looking at it but can accurately reach out and grasp it. Conversely, patients with damage to the action system have a hard time "finding" an object even though they can still "see" it.

> ### Psychobabble
>
> Do you wish your boyfriend could read your mind? Maybe he can—if he's a scientist. In a recent study researchers were able to predict what subjects were viewing from just four spikes of neuronal activity. This study also found that some of our neurons respond to specific people or objects; some subjects' brains only fired to photos (and even the letters in the name!) of Jennifer Aniston, others to Halle Berry, others to places such as the Sydney Opera House.

Viva la Recycling: The Plastic Brain

Twenty years ago, we thought that once neural networks were wired, they were permanent. But as it turns out, our brains are capable of *plasticity*—that is, they are flexible, adaptive plastic, which can come in handy in the event of disease, injury, or disorder.

def•i•ni•tion

Brain **plasticity**, also known as neuroplasticity refers to the brain's ability to rewire itself, rerouting information or processing functions to different brain areas and/or neural networks to compensate for damaged brain pathways and lost functions.

A brain trauma patient who has spent 19 years in a minimally conscious state of coma suddenly wakes up … a stroke victim regains the use of her left arm … how are these events possible? Their plastic brains built new neural pathways and evolved new anatomical brain structures to re-establish functional connections.

Our brains don't have to be damaged for plasticity to occur, though. Plasticity also occurs with learning. You've heard the old expression "practice makes perfect"? Studies of musicians and athletes have shown that repetition (rehearsal) solders in permanent, optimized neuronal connections in specialized brain areas that are responsible for "fine" movements of the hands. Even repeatedly thinking about doing something can forge these connections.

Our brains are also more flexible when we're younger and become more specialized as we mature. This helps explain why children who injure a large part of one brain area tend to recover well, often completely.

> **Psychobabble**
>
> Unfortunately, our brain's flexibility only goes so far. The largest known ingestion of ecstasy pills—40,000 over a nine-year period—was recently reported. Known as Mr. A, this gentleman hasn't taken X for seven years but still suffers from memory problems, paranoia, hallucinations, and depression.

Working with Half a Brain

Once psychologists realized that different hemispheres did different jobs, they started wondering what one would do without the other. What would happen if the two halves couldn't communicate back and forth? Would they fight with each other? Would they get along?

Researchers Roger Sperry and Michael Gazzaniga found some amazing answers to these questions. They studied patients whose *corpus callosum* (which connects the two hemispheres of the brain) had been cut in order to reduce the severity and frequency of their epileptic seizures. On the surface, these patients seemed fine; they walked normally, had no drop in their I.Q., and could carry on a good conversation. But when information was presented to just one visual field, they behaved as if they had two separate minds.

In their experiments, Sperry and Gazzaniga flashed pictures of common objects on a screen and asked the subject to identify them. When the objects were flashed to the right, the person would look at the researchers as if they were complete idiots and say, "It's an apple."

> **Psychobabble**
>
> Could you really live with just half a brain? More than 50 epileptic children are successfully doing so. These children had severe, uncontrollable seizures confined to only one hemisphere; as a last-ditch measure, a hemispherectomy—the removal of one half of the brain—was performed. All are expected to lead normal lives.

However, when the picture was flashed to the left, the subject would either deny that an object had appeared or would make a random guess.

When subjects were next asked to reach under a barrier and touch the object that had just been flashed, they could reliably identify the object with the left hand but not the right! The right hemisphere could remember the feel and shape of the apple but couldn't produce the word for it. If you never forget a face but never remember a name, you can relate!

What was going on? Remember that the right hemisphere controls sensation and movement from the left half of the body and vice versa. Remember, also, that input from the right visual field goes first to the left hemisphere and vice versa. And recall that, in most people, the left hemisphere controls language, and the right dominates spatial perception (faces, pictures, geometry).

No matter how "smart" your brain is, if the different parts aren't communicating effectively, they don't work as well. And in the experimental subjects, the connection that let the hemispheres communicate had been cut. The information simply couldn't get where it had to go to be processed!

In a way, you might say that the brain's parts are like relationships—they need communication in order to thrive. Unlike relationships, however, the brain can call upon some superpowered equipment that virtually guarantees good communication. Let me introduce you to the fastest communication system in the world—your nervous system.

You've Got a Lot of Nerve

Your nervous system is a choreographer; it constantly sends and receives messages that coordinate the stage show of human behavior.

def•i•ni•tion

A **nerve** is bundle of sensory or motor neurons that exist anywhere outside the central nervous system. When someone is getting on your nerves, you have 43 pairs for the person to get on—12 pairs from the brain and 31 pairs from the spinal cord. A **neuron** is a nerve that specializes in information processing.

The Internet has nothing on your nervous system— it's a huge network of more than 100 billion nerve cells that rapidly relays messages to and from the brain. These *nerve* cells, called *neurons*, are specialized cells that receive, process, or relay information to other cells within the body. The fastest of these messengers can send electrical impulses at a rate of up to 250 miles per hour.

The nervous system has two substations: the central nervous system (CNS) and the peripheral nervous system (PNS). The CNS is made up of all the neurons in the brain and the spinal cord, whereas the PNS is made up of all the neurons forming the nerve fibers that connect the CNS to the rest of the body.

If the body were an army, the brain would be the general, synthesizing and coordinating all bodily functions, interpreting all the messages coming in from the body, and sending strategic commands appropriate to the environmental situation. The spinal cord, a trunk line of neurons that connects the brain to the PNS, would be the lieutenant.

All the messages directed to the CNS are sent and received through the spinal cord. Damage to the spinal cord disrupts the brain's ability to send and receive messages and, if the spinal cord is severed, the brain can no longer receive important messages from its limbs about what they are experiencing. So for instance, you wouldn't feel pain even if a toe was roasting in the fireplace. Without the lieutenant, the general can't send commands for the body to protect itself. Your foot soldiers—your sense organs—would be completely disabled.

Psychobabble
It's hard to believe that wisdom comes with age when you realize you lose almost 200,000 neurons each day. Fortunately, you start out with so many that even after 70 years you've still got more than 98 percent of your original supply. Besides, it's the connections between the neurons that count. Albert Einstein had no more brain cells than you or I, but allegedly he had incredibly dense connections between the various parts of his brain.

Speedy Delivery

Neurons are the basic unit of the nervous system and are of three types: sensory neurons, motor neurons, and interneurons. Sensory neurons carry information in from the senses toward the central nervous system. When someone steps on your toes, the sensory neurons get excited and send the scoop to the brain.

Psychobabble
A new class of brain cells has recently been discovered. Tagged "mirror neurons," they fire both when we perform an action and when we watch one being performed. Some scientists speculate that a mirror system in people forms the basis for social behavior, for our ability to imitate, acquire language, and show empathy and understanding.

Motor neurons carry messages from the central nervous system back to the muscles and glands. Since sensory neurons rarely communicate directly with motor neurons, the interneurons act as brokers, relaying messages back and forth between the two and, occasionally, communicating with other interneurons.

Doing the Neuron Dance

So how do neurons do their thing? All neurons have a soma, dendrites, and an axon. The soma contains the nucleus of the cell and the cytoplasm that supports it. At one end of the soma are the dendrites, a bunch of branched fibers that receive messages from other neurons or sense receptors. The soma integrates the information from the dendrites and passes it on to a single, extended fiber called an axon.

The parts of a neuron.

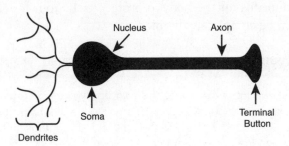

The axon's job is to carry electrical impulses, called action potentials, from the cell body to other cells. A neuron's message lies in the number of action potentials that move down the axon. In Morse code, the message lies in the number and sequence of taps; with neurons, it lies in the speed with which electrical impulses are produced. The axon conducts these electrical impulses along its length until they literally reach the end of their rope—swollen, bulblike structures called terminal buttons that lie at the end of the axons. Action potentials trigger the release of chemical substances called neurotransmitters from each terminal button.

When a neuron is stimulated by another neuron's impulses or by sensory stimulation, it fires off its own electrical impulse. The neural impulse travels the length of the neuron along the axon, finally arriving at the terminal buttons.

Synaptically Speaking

Here's where it gets a little tricky because there is no direct physical contact between a terminal button and the impulse's next destination. Instead, there's a gap at the near junction of two nerve cells—we call this gap a *synapse*. The traditional view of neurotransmission has been that, when an impulse leaps the gap from a terminal button to the next stage in its journey, a small packet holding neurotransmitters (a synaptic vesicle) moves to the inner membrane of the terminal buttons.

The vesicle ruptures, spilling its neurotransmitters into the synaptic gap, and neurotransmitters attach themselves to the dendrites of neurons on the other side of the gap. If the neurotransmitter inputs are sufficiently stimulating, the receiving neuron will either fire or be prevented from firing, relaying the impulse message from cell to cell.

However, new research suggests that neuronal firing does not occur exclusively at the synapse. Rather, neurons may release neurotransmitters along the entire length of the axon, exciting neighboring cells. Whew! It's even more complicated than we thought!

White Matter Matters!

Surrounding the neurons is white matter, which contains axons and ancillary cells—cable ducts—that link the left and right hemispheres of the brain. Since the white matter contains no dendrites or synapses, we might not expect neurotransmission to occur. Yet researchers have recently discovered that it does, revolutionizing the way we've viewed neural communication for the past 100 years. When an electrical impulse travels through an axon cable, tiny bubbles containing the neurotransmitter glutamate travel to the axon membrane and release their content into the brain.

Researchers believe that glutamate guides cells in the white matter known as oligodendrocytes, "insulating cells," to produce myelin, a fatty layer that surrounds the axons and ensures rapid retransmission of signals. Axons travel through the cable ducts in the white matter to the brain's grey matter, where the message is relayed at the synapse to receptor dendrites, but also to other areas in the gray matter which do not contain synapses. The axon not only excites receptor dendrites but also other surrounding nerve cells as well.

With all this firing going on, it's no surprise that there are often tiny leftover "sputtering" releases of neurotransmitters, even up to a few minutes after the main firing event. And these leftovers can lead to neurological chaos.

> **Brain Buster**
>
> Too much glutamate can be hazardous to these insulating cells. During an epileptic seizure, for example, nerve cells fire rapidly and fiercely, sending a torrent of impulses through axons and releasing too-high doses of glutamate that damage the oligodendrocytes.

Enter complexins, small proteins that act as gatekeepers, preventing neurotransmitters from releasing prematurely. But if there's a breakdown in this gatekeeper mechanism, spontaneous mini firings can occur unchecked, rewiring neural pathways and spurring massive amounts of synaptic new growth. MIT researchers believe this chaos may be the culprit behind neurological disorders such as schizophrenia. And controlling this area may one day allow us to rewire brain areas involved in neurological disorders and disease.

> **Psychobabble**
>
> A new study reveals that cognitive decline in normal aging may be caused by a breakdown of neural crosstalk. Age slowly degrades white-matter nerve axons that act as communication conduits between different brain regions—for example, between the network that processes information from the outside world and our internal "default network," which kicks in when we muse to ourselves.

Blame It on Your Hormones

Remember all the weirdness you went through in your teens? Hair sprouting in different places and body parts growing at different speeds? How about those mood swings? Blame it all on your hormones.

Your nervous system gets most of the press, but another communication system can pack a powerful punch in terms of what you think, feel, and do. It is your endocrine system, and its messengers are your hormones.

The endocrine system, controlled by the hypothalamus in the midsection of the brain, produces and secretes hormones into the bloodstream. These chemicals are involved in many different bodily functions, from your sexual development to your arousal, mood, and metabolism. Your endocrine communication system helps you regulate everyday alertness and mood. It also helps you respond to emergencies. The most famous hormone is adrenaline, an energizer that responds to emergencies by preparing you for "flight or flight."

Adrenaline Alert!

When something frightens you, your heart may pound; your muscles tense; and you may break out in a cold sweat. That's your endocrine system preparing you to respond to a life-threatening situation. In fact, long after the danger passes, you may still feel your endocrine system doing its job.

Brain Booboos

Imagine that your spouse is diagnosed with a brain tumor. After the initial shock, you and he discover that the tumor is nonmalignant and, although large, quite operable. During surgery, the tumor is removed, recovery goes well, and your spouse is pronounced completely cured.

Except that he's not. Ever since his surgery, you feel like you've been living with a different person. Your sweet, patient, adoring spouse now seems moody, impatient, and short-tempered. Although your well-meaning friends and family are telling you both how lucky you are, inside you feel increasingly confused, frustrated, guilty, and scared. And you're no longer sure you want to stay married to the stranger your spouse has become.

Given the interlink between our minds and our brains, it's not surprising that physical injuries to our brains can do a number on our psyches. The severity and type of personality change usually depends on the part of the brain that's been injured. For example, because the frontal lobes often serve as "the brakes" in controlling our emotions, impulses, and instincts, a person with frontal lobe damage may have difficulty inhibiting inappropriate behavior. This person may be particularly prone to saying and doing things that may appear insensitive or irritable.

The survivor of a brain injury may become a more exaggerated type of the person he or she was before the trauma. My great-aunt Bess, who died from Alzheimer's disease, was a quiet, rather pessimistic person for as long as I knew her. As her dementia progressed, she would go for days without talking and developed considerable suspicions about the people around her. This exaggeration of pre-existing personality traits can make a progressive neurological illness difficult to diagnose, especially in the absence of physical symptoms.

Insight

Boost your brain—and help ward off Alzheimer's—with exercise! Researchers have found that regular exercise controls the expression of genes in an area of the brain important for memory and maintaining healthy cells in the brain; this maintenance breaks down with Alzheimer's.

You can see that much of what goes on in our brain is outside our conscious awareness. You can also see that we're discovering new things about—and developing more respect for—our brains every day; take a look at just a few of the cutting edge research that's just emerged.

The mind may be more of an interpreter than a leader; although it gives us rational explanations for our behavior, it may not always be in the driver's seat. In the next chapter, we explore two areas that influence how well we drive: nature and nurture.

Straight from the Lab

Those Traveling Brain Cells!   When our brains are damaged, they make new ones. New research shows that these future neurons (baby brain cells) are born in the forebrain, then migrate to the olfactory bulb (which processes smells), maturing into neurons along the way. As a result, the loss of smell may be one early sign of neurodegenerative diseases such as Alzheimer's and Parkinson's.

Robots R Us   Researchers have developed a robot with a biological brain formed from cultured neurons. As the robot nears an object, signals stimulate electrodes in its brain, driving its wheels so that it will attempt to avoid hitting objects. Fun aside, the robot is helping us to understand how our brain learns and memorizes its experiences.

Does Brain Damage Drown the Baby and the Bathwater?   Individuals with damage to certain parts of their frontal lobes tend to lack empathy and compassion in social situations. New research finds that this brain damage—and the resulting emotional disconnection—may significantly influence moral reasoning ability. When research subjects were confronted with the hypothetical option to either kill a person or risk future harm or death to many, normal subjects either waivered or said they couldn't. In contrast, the brain-damaged people regularly showed a willingness to bring harm to an individual.

The Least You Need to Know

- The human brain evolved into its present form because it contained features that enabled our ancestors to thrive.

- The brain's structure reflects our evolutionary history: the old brain governs the most primitive human behavior; the midbrain is the seat of human drives and emotions; and the newer cerebral cortex guides the most complex thinking and feeling.

- The cerebral cortex—divided into two hemispheres and eight lobes—is the headquarters of human behavior.

- The human nervous system, which sends messages to and from the brain through electrical impulses, is the best communication system in the world.

- ◆ Medical tests can define damaged areas of the brain, but a neuropsychologist can assess how well a person is able to function after an injury or disease.

- ◆ Natural hormones keep our bodies and brains in balance and also prepare us to deal with life's emergencies.

Chapter 3

The Chicken or the Egg?

In This Chapter

- ◆ The nature-nurture debate
- ◆ Getting into your genes
- ◆ What flips the switch?
- ◆ Just what *are* you born with?
- ◆ You're *so* mature
- ◆ Establishing one's attachment style

Are you the way you are because of your genes or because of your life experiences? This nature-nurture debate has a long, tedious, and politically influenced history.

In the nineteenth century, for example, educated people widely believed that "biology is destiny." Sir Francis Galton did a study showing that eminent people (of which, not coincidentally, he was one) produced eminent heirs while a study of the infamous Jukes family revealed that seven generations had cost the state $1.5 million dollars through various types of crimes. In the 1900's, many psychologists considered infants blank slates, waiting to be written on by their parents and teachers.

Today we know it's not so cut and dried. Whether studying personality, intelligence, or our susceptibility to mental disorders, psychologists are still trying to tease out how much our genes contribute to who we are and how much we're molded by our environment. In this chapter, we take a look at this "chicken or egg" debate, at why we have the genes we have, and at the role our environment plays in nurturing our nature.

Brain Buster

There's danger in making overly simplistic explanations for something as complex as human behavior. Over-reliance on "nature" explanations has led to justifications of racism. Over-reliance on the "nurture" side can lead to neglect of real, physical causes of mental disabilities, such as chemical imbalances or genetic abnormalities.

Dancing with Wolves

In 1801, a 12-year-old boy was discovered in the woods outside Aveyron, France. Apparently raised by wolves, he nor anyone else knew where he came from, and he acted more like a wolf than a human being. A French doctor named Jean-Marie Itard renamed the boy "Victor" and took on the challenge of teaching him to be human.

Taming the Wild Child

As Jean-Marie began an intensive training program with Victor, initial results seemed promising. Fairly quickly, Victor became affectionate and well-mannered and could utter a few words. After five years, however, he could learn no more. Although he lived to age 40, Victor never became a fully functioning human being. From Jean-Marie's perspective, his experiment had failed.

Looking Beneath the Surface

But was it nature or nurture that failed? The good doctor had no information about Victor's genetic makeup; perhaps the boy had been abandoned because he was developmentally disabled to begin with. Perhaps no training program would have worked. Alternatively, maybe Jean-Marie's training program was off the mark, and Victor could have whizzed through a different one. Or maybe Victor could have learned the lessons of human nature at one time but had outgrown his receptivity to language by age 12.

Nature or Nurture?

For the past 200 years, scholars have argued over whether we are the product of genetic Russian roulette or our environment. It all started with a debate between two philosophers: John Locke and Jean-Jacques Rousseau.

The Great Debate, Philosophically Speaking

British philosopher John Locke formed the nurture camp. Babies, he argued, are born without knowledge or skills and enter the world as blank slates upon which experience writes. He believed the stimulation received through experience and education directed human development.

However, French philosopher Jean-Jacques Rousseau thought this idea was hogwash. Human beings, he argued, are hardwired from birth with all their predispositions and abilities. Sure, we're unsophisticated when we enter the world, but we're also innocent and good. We're born "noble savages."

When it comes to nature versus nurture, the issue is often more complex than it seems. Take Victor the wolf boy, for example. If his training program had produced a fully functioning, "normal" human being, it would have offered strong evidence that nurture is powerful. The fact that it didn't, however, doesn't prove the opposite. Since we have no information about Victor's genes, we can't say that Victor's stunted growth potential was due to nature *or* nurture.

Taking the Middle Road

In reality, both our biological inheritance and our life experiences shape complex skills and behaviors. Our heredity gives us our potential, but our experience determines how—and how much of—that potential we realize.

In fact, environmental factors play a huge role in turning genes "on" or "off." For example, studies show that physical aggression in children comes from their genes and the environment they grow up in. A study of seven-year-old twins revealed that the genetic disposition to physical aggression was more likely to express itself when children were exposed to physically aggressive friends.

And some types of aggression, like social aggression, (e.g., spreading rumors or ignoring other children) seems to be more heavily influenced by environmental factors than genetic ones. In fact, peer modeling only seems to promote the specific type of aggression kids see; hanging around with snobbish friends, for example, isn't likely to make a child more physically aggressive.

Asking the Right Questions

A common mistake made in the nature-nurture debate is asking the wrong questions; for example, asking how much of one's intelligence was a gift from his parents and how much was acquired by the sweat of his brow is, if taken literally, silly. In some respects, both nature and nurture contribute 100 percent. After all, if a person didn't have any genes at all, he wouldn't be alive. And one's mother's womb was his first environment—he wouldn't be alive without that, either. No environment, no person—no person, no intelligence.

Psychobabble
To guard against a repeat of how biased and inaccurate views of heredity have historically been used to justify horrible deeds (think Holocaust or Rwanda), a multi-disciplinary group at Stanford University has proposed ten principles to guide human genetic variation research, the core of which states that there is no scientific basis for hierarchical categories of race or ethnicity and that, when it comes to complex human behavioral traits (e.g., I.Q., violent tendencies, or athletic talent), to leap to genetic conclusions to explain group differences is folly.

The real nature-nurture question is whether differences in a trait among a *group* of individuals are due more to differences in their genes or to their environment. In other words, why are some people smarter than others? Why do some people graduate from high school and others drop out? The nature-nurture question helps us look at groups of people and explain or predict their differences; it's not very good at helping us predict why one individual does the things she does.

Differences in intelligence may be due to genes for one set of people and environment for another. If you were raised in a loving family and I in solitary confinement, I.Q. differences are more likely to be due to environment. If we were raised in similar homes, though, differences in our genes might have more influence.

> **Psychobabble**
>
> Each child growing up in the same family can experience that environment very differently; for example, a baby with an irritable temperament can elicit different reactions from caretakers than a baby blessed with an easygoing one.

G × E = Me

There's a new research design in town: G × E. G × E, which is designed to test the interaction between genes (G) and environmental factors (E), may help us finally resolve many nature vs. nurture debates.

A Notre Dame study of male adolescents in a Russian juvenile detention center investigated whether a gene associated with dopamine interacted with negative maternal parenting styles to predict depression. Researchers assessed aspects of maternal rearing such as physical punishment, hostility, lack of respect for the child's point of view, and unjustified criticism in front of others. While neither factor alone predicted depression, the boys who had especially rejecting mothers plus a specific form of the dopamine transporter gene were at higher risk for major depression and suicidal ideation. Nurture, in the form of psychosocial interventions, could help fight those blue mood genes.

What Twins Tell Us

Heritability is the degree to which variation in a particular trait within a certain group stems from genetic differences among those members as opposed to stemming from environmental differences.

If a trait can be passed down from parent to child, we would expect relatives to be more similar in that trait than people who are not related. So if we have smart parents, we should see smart kids, and, assuming our kids don't marry dummies, smart grandkids.

The catch, of course, is that relatives often live together. The fact that brothers and sisters have more similar I.Q.s than unrelated people does not, by itself, tell us whether it's the egg (the genes) or the chicken (the home) that's responsible. That's where the twins come in. Identical twins have virtually identical genes, while fraternal twins and other siblings share only about 50 percent of their genes.

For example, comparing the I.Q. scores between identical twins reared in the same home and identical twins adopted by different families at birth enables us to look at the influence of environment on intelligence. Since identical twins are genetically alike, we can feel pretty confident attributing any I.Q. difference to the different environments in which they were reared. On the other hand, if identical twins reared miles apart from each other have more similar I.Q. scores than fraternal twins who shared a bedroom since birth, nature pretty much wins the debate.

When it comes to intelligence, nature is the winner. Identical twins consistently have more similar I.Q. scores than fraternal twins *regardless of the environment in which they are raised.* Anatomy, however, is not destiny. A surprisingly small relationship exists between intelligence and success, suggesting that smart genes may give us a jump start in life, but our intelligence can't help us that much if we don't use it.

Flip That Switch!

In the brain, some genes are only expressed or "turned on" in response to environmental influences. Like light switches, genes must receive electricity to turn on and express their particular proteins. Without environmental help, genetic predispositions never have a chance to realize their potentials.

> **Psychobabble**
>
> Autism is a strongly genetic disorder but is thought to be tied to brain changes that occur during critical development periods when the brain is highly susceptible to environmental influences. By identifying which genes are apt to switch their expression patterns in response to nurture, researchers can potentially isolate the ones that may be implicated in developmental disorders.

For instance, people who share the same genetic makeup but live in different environments may have different expression profiles. Respiratory genes are turned on more frequently in urban populations than in rural populations. That's logical, since urban dwellers must contend with greater pollution that can contribute to diseases such as asthma and bronchitis.

There also seems to be critical periods of necessary exposure for some genetic tendencies to express themselves. When one eye is deprived of sight during a critical period of brain development, that eye becomes (and remains) permanently blind, even after it's uncovered. Synapses for the covered eye, deprived of environmental stimulus (nurture), shrivel up or get reassigned to other functions.

Give Your Genes a Little Culture

Do you ever notice that people from some countries seem a little more reserved than people from other ones? To determine the extent to which sociability is universal across *cultures*, Salk Institute scientists came up with a clever way to sort nature from nurture. Parents from both countries rated their child's social behavior, i.e., the child's tendency to approach others, ability to remember names and faces, eagerness to please, and tendency to empathize.

"Normal" American and Japanese children were compared with children of both cultures who had Williams syndrome, a genetic condition characterized by significant medical problems as well as an extremely social personality. Social norms, even for children, are vastly different for these two countries; in the United States, the squeaky wheel gets the grease while, in Japan, the nail that stands out may get pounded down.

Interestingly, the sociability ratings of normal American kids (by their parents) was about the same as Japanese Williams syndrome kids, whose social behavior, we should point out, would be considered out of bounds in Japan! While the ratings differences among Williams' kids in different countries may be a result of cultural influence dampening a genetically determined expression of sociability, it may also, of course, be a result of the stigma Japanese parents felt over having a "different" child. Either way, score one for nurture.

def•i•ni•tion

Culture is a system of shared ideas about the nature of the world and how to behave in it which shape how we learn and behave. You may be genetically hard-wired to learn language, but the fact that you're reading this sentence in English is a direct result of your culture, not your genes.

Family Genes and Other Heirlooms

Research with twins does seem to tell us that smart parents make bright children and dumb parents don't have many children in graduate school. But how does all this genetic passing down work?

When dad's sperm and mom's egg unite, the new cell it creates is a zygote. This zygote contains the full human complement of 23 paired chromosomes, with one member of each pair coming from each parent. The zygote grows up and becomes you. Because each sperm cell is different from each egg cell, each zygote is different from any other.

The fact that genes come in pairs helps geneticists calculate percent relatedness, the amount of genes you share with another human being. You may be the spitting image of your dad, but you've inherited 50 percent of your genes from each parent.

The difference between the actual amount of genetic material you share with your parents and the way you physically look illustrates the difference between your genotype and your phenotype. Genotype refers to the entire set of genes you inherit, your biological potential. Phenotype refers to the observable properties of your body and your behavioral traits.

Dominating Genes

Your genotype may be predetermined, but your phenotype is a control battle between your genes. The most dominant genes win. A dominant gene is one that will produce its observable effects if it is present in either parent; a recessive gene will show up only if both parents possess it.

Jeepers, Creepers, Where'd You Get Those Peepers?

There are more brown-eyed people than blue-eyed ones because the gene for brown eyes is dominant; if one parent contributes blue-eyed genes and the other contributes brown-eyed genes, the child will have brown eyes. But we all know a few blue-eyed children whose parents are both brown-eyed. How can that be? Simple—sometimes brown-eyed parents have a recessive gene for blue eyes lurking in the background, and those are the ones that got passed along to form the blue-eyed child's zygote. Because blue eyes are recessive, both parents must have contributed blue-eyed genes in order for them to show up in their offspring.

You Can't Get Lost with This Map

A *genome* is an organism's complete set of DNA (deoxyribonucleic acid), the chemical compound that contains the genetic instructions to make that organism. Thanks to the Human Genome Project (HGP), we now have the complete mapping of all human genes. The full sequence was completed and published in 2003.

We learned some pretty interesting things from this international research project. For one thing, we humans have about 30,000 distinct genes residing on our 23 chromosome pairs.

We also learned that, in order for an organism to survive, the genome must remain stable, a matter which is handled by a sister act of matched chromatids— the pairs of the double helix DNA molecule that exist during chromosome duplication—and a helpful enzyme known as acetyltransferase.

def•i•ni•tion

The term **genome** refers to the full complement of an organism's genetic material—in other words, a blueprint for building all the structures and directing all the processes for the lifetime of that organism.

Too Much Information?

The HGP is a basic owner's manual that may help us find and fix faulty parts before they cause problems; for example, we've already started identifying specific genes that contribute to cystic fibrosis, mental retardation, and some forms of cancer.

But we will also face new ethical dilemmas and, for some of us, some tough personal choices. What will health insurers do if they know a person has a high likelihood of developing cancer? Would you still get pregnant if you knew your child would have a 25 percent chance of developing Parkinson's disease? Would you take a test to determine if you're likely to develop Alzheimer's disease?

Anatomy is not destiny, and yet knowing that we are at high risk for a debilitating illness could literally rob us of a quality life, long before we had the chance to see if our grim genetic potential became a reality.

Psychobabble

We're a lot like chimpanzees, sharing about 98.7 percent of our genetic code with these adorable creatures. And the difference between you and Albert Einstein, genetically speaking, is less than 1 percent!

Don't Blame Your Genes

If you were a smart kid, thank your parents for your good genes. If you dropped out of school to flip burgers and now regret that you never lived up to your potential, blame yourself. Your genes aren't responsible for your behavior.

The influence of our genes on our behavior is indirect. Their main task is building and organizing the physical structures of the body, including the brain. These structures interact with the environment to produce behavior. Good genes give us resources for coping with our environment, but a bad environment can challenge even the most resilient genes.

Growing Up on the Wild Side

Take, for example, a child growing up in an extremely violent neighborhood. Evidence suggests that the stress of living under these conditions may stimulate the development of the part of the brain that responds to threatening stimuli and organizes aggression. The child may, as a result, be more aggressive, because the environment in which he lives encourages the aggression centers of the brain to become more developed.

Over time, a high-crime environment might naturally select more aggressive individuals; as a result, genes that promote the development of the brain's aggression center could be passed down to future generations. But be careful about the conclusions you draw from this; there's a big leap between inheriting a predisposition for aggression and actually committing a crime. We might be predisposed toward violence to help us survive a bad neighborhood, but our genes don't pick up a gun and shoot it.

The same is true for all human behavior. Natural selection has bred us to be better at doing whatever we needed to do to survive and thrive in our environment. As a result, certain behavioral mechanisms have evolved, including our capacity for language, our ability to learn and remember, and our problem-solving skills.

What About the Suicide Gene?

A couple of years ago, I heard a radio announcer proclaim the discovery of "the suicide gene." To hear him talk, you'd think some of us have a time-bomb lurking in our DNA that would, without warning, compel us to jump out of a high window or chug a bottle of sleeping pills.

Fortunately, we aren't peas in pods just waiting to be manipulated by a single gene. Common, complex disorders are genetically influenced but not genetically determined. Many genes are involved in complex psychiatric disorders. Genes work like risk factors, increasing or decreasing risk for a disorder; they're not master puppets pulling our strings.

Genetic information can help us take more control over our lives by helping us identify our individual susceptibility to certain problems and clarify the specific factors that interact with this susceptibility to produce certain behaviors or diseases.

Psychobabble

Genetic information may also provide guidance for targeted screening efforts; for example, people who have a first-degree relative with a history of depression are more likely to develop an affective disorder themselves, particularly in response to an environmental stressor. Screening these individuals for major depression six months after the loss of a loved one is likely to be much more effective than screening all bereaved people.

Typical Human Behavior

Did some human behaviors evolve to give our ancestors an environmental edge? How, for example, did talking help human beings survive or get along better in the world?

Understanding our genes can help us understand our own behavior. Functional psychology tries to explain behaviors in terms of the purposes they serve for the individual. Evolutionary psychologists look at the bigger picture and try to understand why human beings, as a species, act the way they do. In essence, they study universal human behaviors and try to figure out what caused these behaviors to evolve.

Evolutionary psychologists are particularly interested in species-typical behavior—behaviors so common among members of a species that they can be used as identifying characteristics. Barking, four-legged walking, and pooping on front lawns pretty much sums it up for dogs. Two-legged walking and talking are species typical for humans.

Vive la Différence!

Species-typical behavior does not mean that human beings are all alike. Not all human beings feel happy eating chocolate ice cream, nor do all of us cry when we're afraid. In humans, species-typical behavior means that we are biologically prepared for that behavior. But exactly when, how, and why each human experiences and expresses his unique feelings is a complicated jumble of biology, life experience, and cultural legacy. Species-typical behaviors identified by psychologists include …

Insight

Seven basic emotions appear to be universal among human beings: surprise, fear, disgust, anger, happiness, contempt, and sadness. When you're feeling sad, it can be comforting to know that every other human being has felt this way, too.

- Living in communities
- Male violence

- Nepotism (favoring kin)
- Marriage contracts

Evolutionary Theory Gone Awry

The application of evolutionary theory to psychology has stirred up a jumble of emotions, not to mention some pretty dark ulterior motives. Instead of explaining behavior through evolution, evolutionary psychology has, at times, been used to justify it.

Mother Nature's Morality

One misuse of evolutionary psychology is the naturalistic fallacy. According to this error in logic, nature is guided by a moral force that favors what is good or right. If male mammals in the wild dominate females through force, well, that's the way it "should be." British philosopher Herbert Spencer, a contemporary of Darwin, used this argument many times to justify the most extreme abuses of nineteenth-century capitalism. Of course, his biggest fans were those in power at the top of the industrialist ladder.

I Just Couldn't Help Myself!

A second misuse of evolutionary psychology is the deterministic fallacy or the genetic version of "the devil made me do it." According to this viewpoint, our genes control our behavior, and we can do nothing about it. If natural selection teaches me to fight for my territory, can I help it if I slug the man who took my parking space?

Or maybe it's cultural. No matter how aggressive my nature, if I grew up among the Amish, I may be less likely to react violently because of the cultural taboo in my environment. On the other hand, if I was raised by gang members in a tough part of town, I may slug the man over a parking place just to fit in with the crowd.

In reality, neither genes nor social pressure influence our behavior in a way that's beyond our control. We can control—or rebel against—our environment, and we can learn to control ourselves.

Baby Builds on Blueprints

But even after taking into account the genes that your parents gave you and the environment you're born into, there's still something more to be reckoned. And that "something more" is the unique, the individual, the personal *you*. You came into the world prepared to take your inheritance and grow with it and, from birth, you've been hard at work.

Babies come into this world with some pretty sophisticated equipment and some pretty strong preferences. Even while still in the womb, they're moving around, listening to their mother talk and preparing for their grand entrance into the world. When they're born, they are already biologically prepared to seek food, protection, and care.

For example, from birth, babies establish a relationship with people who can take care of them. They start out preferring female voices and, after just a few weeks, they can recognize their caregiver's voice. By seven weeks, they've learned to scan their caregiver's face and start to make eye contact when she talks. If Locke and Rousseau had spent any time around babies, they would have quickly given up the "blank slate" or "noble savage" descriptions. "Preprogrammed friendly computers" is a better description of newborns.

> **Psychobabble**
>
> Our early years are very important. Our brains grow 50 percent larger in the first 12 months after birth, and by our second birthday, our brains are 80 percent larger than the brains we were born with. This growth eventually tapers off, and, by age 12, we're pretty much stuck with the brains we have.

As early as 12 hours after birth, babies show distinct signs of pleasure at the taste of sugar water or vanilla and aversion to the taste of lemon or the smell of rotten eggs. Days-old infants quickly learned to anticipate dessert when researchers stroked their foreheads and then fed them sugar water. Not only did babies turn their heads in the direction of sugar, but they also cried when the goods weren't delivered. From birth, it seems, we feel pain when a reliable relationship breaks down.

Is "Normal" Just a Setting on the Clothes Drier?

Genetic inheritance gives a baby a jump start on life, but he still has a lot of growing to do. After birth, a child's physical growth and abilities follow a genetically based timetable. This genetic blueprint is responsible for the appearance of certain behaviors at roughly the same time for all human beings, taking into allowance cultural variations. And as you're about to see, the following of this timetable, from a *maturation* standpoint, makes us "normal."

def•i•ni•tion

Maturation refers to the process of growth typical of all members of a species who are reared in the usual environment of that species.

Oh, Grow Up!

If anyone ever said that to you, they were giving you a clear message that you weren't living up to their expectations of how a person your age should behave. But how do we know how we're supposed to behave at what age? We know by looking at the human process of maturation, the timely and orderly sequence of developmental changes that takes place as a person gets older.

For example, by four months most babies sit with support. Between five and six months, they stand holding on to something, and at about a year they start walking. If a baby can't do these things, parents start worrying.

Walking follows a fixed, time-ordered sequence that is typical of all physically capable members of our species. In cultures where there is more physical stimulation, children begin to walk sooner. However, contrary to many parents' beliefs, babies do not require any special training to learn to walk.

The Parental Part of the Equation

While baby's doing his developmental thing, part of a parent's emotional growth is learning to relax and trust her baby to develop at his own pace. That's because the parent's role in the process is to provide the emotional security that is necessary for her child's physical growth. Physical and emotional development go hand in hand.

What's Your Attachment Style?

The way we attach to our earliest caregivers can set the pattern for our relationships for the rest of our lives. To see how you tend to relate to others, put a check beside the self-descriptions that you most agree with:

1. _____ I am somewhat uncomfortable being close to others; I find it difficult to trust them completely, difficult to allow myself to depend on them. I am nervous when anyone gets too close and often love partners who want me to be more intimate than I feel comfortable being.

2. _____ I find it relatively easy to get close to others and am comfortable depending on them. I don't often worry about being abandoned or about someone getting too close to me.

3. _____ I find that other people are reluctant to get as close as I would like them to. I often worry that my partner doesn't really love me or won't want to stay with me. I want to get very close to my partner, and this sometimes scares people away.

If you selected (1), you're expressing an avoidant, insecure attachment style. About 25 percent of us have this attachment pattern. Twenty percent of us will choose answer (3), which represents an anxious-ambivalent, insecure style. Fifty-five percent of us are lucky enough to answer (2), which suggests that we attached securely to our parents and are secure in our attachment to others.

Growing Up Emotionally

If you watch a baby learn to walk, you aren't just witnessing physical development, but you're witnessing emotional growth, too. From birth, our minds and bodies are intertwined.

Psychobabble

While there may be "sensitive periods" during which children need nurturing in order to be able to form attachments, the upper age limit for these sensitive periods may be much older than the previously believed first year of life. Studies show that children adopted before age four tend to bond well with their parents, while children adopted after age four are more likely to experience problems attaching to their caretakers.

As a baby begins to physically explore his world, he depends on his parents to make him feel safe. Time and time again, toddlers go back and forth between venturing out into the world and returning to check in and make sure Mom or Dad is still around should things move a little too fast. What does this pattern mean for a child's development? Children who don't trust their parents to be there when they get back often don't venture out to explore.

Studies of infants reared in institutions have clearly demonstrated the criticalness of the parent-child attachment to social and physical development. Infants who were isolated for the first eight months of life rarely tried to approach adults later on, either to hug or caress them or to get reassurance when in distress. And not surprising, this social impairment led to other developmental delays—such children failed to utter a single word by the first year of life.

Fortunately, few babies ever face the trauma of living in isolation for the first few months of life. However, most of us have experienced at least one occasion when a parent couldn't be there for us. What impact does this have?

Psychologist Mary Ainsworth studied young children and their relationships with their primary caregivers. By placing them in novel situations where they were briefly separated from their parent, she identified three different attachment styles—one secure style and two insecure styles. And each of these attachment styles influenced the child's physical development.

Ainsworth discovered that securely attached children felt closer to and safer with their caregivers. As a result, they were more willing to explore or tolerate novel experiences. They were confident they could cry out for help or reunite with a caregiver if needed.

Insecurely attached children, on the other hand, reacted to separation and new situations with avoidance, anxiety, or ambivalence. Anxious or ambivalent children sought contact with their caregivers but were fearful and angry when separated from them. These children were also difficult to console when reunited with their parents.

Children with an avoidant attachment style, on the other hand, didn't seem to care whether their primary caregivers left and showed little emotion when they returned. Dr. Ainsworth hypothesized that these children were victims of long-term rejection and had given up on their efforts to have a consistent, caring caregiver. In reaction to an abusive or neglectful environment, these children developed an unhealthy protective shell around their hearts. In extreme cases, they became adults with little concern for anyone but themselves.

Nature? Nurture? It's Both!

In a way, we're back where we started with nature versus nurture and the chicken and the egg. Children who aren't loved don't grow. Children who have irritable natures may be harder to nurture. Intelligence is in our nature, but success depends on nurture. When it comes to human beings, nature and nurture are inseparable. Given the amazing ways children develop, which we discuss in Chapter 4, perhaps that's the way it should be.

Straight from the Lab

You Go, Girl! Show those Genes!   Well, finally, a woman has now been officially DNA-sequenced. (Four men have been previously mapped.) The lucky woman is Dr. Marjolein Kriek, who is, handily, a clinical geneticist. Females, it turns out, are less variable, genetically speaking, than their male counterparts. Females have two X-chromosomes, but no Y-chromosome. Since one X-chromosome is present in males—half the population—it has undergone a harsher selection in human evolution.

Super Mappers Strike Again! The race is on. The Wellcome Trust Sanger Institute now produces the amount of DNA sequence in two minutes that it used to take five years to produce. It now has 1,000,000,000,000 letters of genetic code that researchers worldwide can use to uncover fine variations in genes that cause disease.

Baby's Smile Is a Natural High When baby smiles, the reward centers of her mother's brain light up—areas that have also been associated with drug addiction. Perhaps seeing your own baby's smiling face is a natural high!

Temperament, Temper, and the Terrible Twos A new study shows that both the quality of a child's relationship with his mother and the child's temperament shape the "terrible twos." While parents can't necessarily prevent the number of temper tantrums their two-year-old throws, a secure parent-child attachment can make them less intense.

The Least You Need to Know

- We're the product of both nature and nurture; our genes give us our biological potential; our environment, including our culture, determines how we express it.

- Every human being inherits certain behavioral tendencies that helped our human ancestors survive and thrive, but what triggers these tendencies and how often they are expressed varies across cultures and individuals.

- The Human Genome Project gave us a map of all the human genes, and future work may lead to genetic treatments for illnesses and raise some challenging ethical dilemmas.

- Genes never directly control behavior; none of us is born a killer or a saint.

- Some genes are only expressed or "turned on" in response to stimuli from the outside world—environmental influences.

- Because emotional and physical development are inseparable, children need emotional security to grow physically, and one source of that security is a healthy attachment to their parents.

Chapter 4

It's Only a Stage

In This Chapter

- From boredom to brain scans in baby research
- Learning the lingo
- Natural-born psychologists
- Exploring the mind of a child
- Lurching from crisis to crisis

Historically, human beings have had some pretty strange ideas about children. Maybe that's why the field of developmental psychology is still a baby; it wasn't born until the first half of the twentieth century. Since then, we've learned that children are pretty impressive. Research in this area has exploded in the past few years, as new techniques have evolved for finding out what's happening in the minds of even the smallest infants.

In this chapter, we explain how children's thoughts and language develop. As children go through different stages, each stage prepares them to deal more effectively with the world around them.

Understanding how children learn to talk will not only teach you some healthy respect for children's built-in desires to communicate, but it will also give you valuable insight into yourself. As you'll see, children seem to intuitively seek out experiences and create adventures that help them make the most of their biological potential. Do you?

The Development of Child Development

The field of child development was born in the first half of the twentieth century. Because Sigmund Freud had begun talking about the influence of childhood on adult mental health, scientists suddenly became curious about the life and experiences of children. Before that, people had some pretty strange ideas about child development; in the 1500's, for example, children over six years of age were thought to be (and expected to act like) little adults. In England laws protected animals from abuse, but not children!

Studying Bored Babes

Studying child development means studying babies. After all, the most rapid part of child development is in the first 18 to 24 months of life. But how do we do it? Babies aren't exactly giving speeches during these first few years. So how do we know what babies know and how they know it? We used to rely primarily on human nature's built-in tendency to become easily bored. Researchers call this habituation, and babies do it as much as grownups do.

Hundreds of experiments have shown that babies look longer at new things than at familiar ones. When shown a pattern, for example, babies show a lot of interest at first and then, over the course of a few minutes, look at it less and less. They become habituated to it. This aspect of baby nature is so reliable that developmental psychologists use it to assess infants' abilities to perceive and remember.

> **Psychobabble**
>
> Viva la technology! Functional magnetic resonance images (fMRIs) and other visual images of how the brain works look like they will be the "picture" of the future in baby research. In addition, brain wave studies and laser eye tracking let us look at the tiniest responses babies make.

And one of the things we've discovered is that babies are constantly studying things that provide them the most efficient opportunity to learn. For example, not only do babies waste little energy restudying objects they've already seen, but they also prefer objects in their environment that they can control. For example, two-month-old infants show much more interest in a mobile that moves when they touch it as compared to a motor-driven one.

Fast Learners and Good Teachers

Babies learn faster and earlier than we thought. Perhaps they're such good learners because they have some pretty good study habits. Infants across cultures engage in a sophisticated exploration called examining. When they encounter an interesting object, they hold it up in front of their eyes, turn it from side to side, pass it from one hand to the other, squeeze it, mouth it, and generally do whatever they can to figure it out. And they pay attention to detail; they look more at colorful objects, feel objects with different textures, and shake, rattle, and roll objects that make sounds.

Teenagers may not respect their elders, but babies do. They recognize the value of experience and start cashing in on the wisdom of their parents. Six-month-olds will look at their parents' eyes, follow their gaze, and then look at what the adult is viewing. The baby will then check back and forth periodically to see if the parent is still looking. Babies, it seems, are born students, and their best teachers are Mom and Dad.

I Second That Emotion

We used to believe that babies younger than six months didn't recognize emotions. Newer research, though, indicates that infants just a few months old can recognize and react to other people's happiness, anger, and sadness. Some studies suggest babies feel empathy even sooner—perhaps when they are only days or weeks old. By age two, most children will label themselves as sad, mad, or glad depending upon the circumstances they are reporting.

Why is this important? From an early age, babies use emotions to gather information and make decisions; by watching others, they gain important clues about what's important and what's not, what they should avoid and what to seek out. A baby who does not reach certain key "emotional milestones" may have trouble learning to speak, read, or do well in school later.

Learning Baby Talk

I've spent seven years trying to learn Spanish and have failed, so it depresses me to think I could have spoken any one (or more) of 3,000 languages if only I'd started early enough. No matter what their native language, children have pretty much mastered it by the time they are three or four years old.

Babies begin practicing cooing sounds at about two months and progress to babbling at about four to six months. These early sounds appear to be wired in; deaf infants coo and babble at the same age and manner as hearing infants, and early babblers are as likely to contain foreign language sounds as native-language sounds. By 10 months, though, children start babbling in sounds that imitate their parents. A deaf infant exposed to sign language will start babbling with her hands.

Children learn language in three initial stages—one word, two words, and telegraphic speech. They start out by naming things and then begin asking for things. In their early two- and three-word sentences, children's speech is telegraphic, mainly consisting of nouns and verbs that get the message across. "Zachary eat" wouldn't make Zachary's third-grade grammar teacher very happy, but it's pretty effective at getting his mommy to head for the refrigerator.

By 18 months, a naming explosion occurs, and children begin to learn words at an astonishing rate. In fact, between 18 months and 6 years of age, the average child learns about one word per waking hour!

Parents can certainly boost their children's linguistic skills by constantly talking to them. New studies conducted with nine-month-olds suggest there may be no lower limit to the age at which children can learn new words when they are linked to a special context. Parents who make a practice of naming and pointing out objects in their environment can help their kids learn a number of words—even before they say them!

LADS and LASSes

Are we born linguists? Many language theorists believe we have an innate, biologically based mental program for language acquisition. These theorists believe we don't just repeat what we hear but follow a preprogrammed set of instructions to acquire language and vocabulary. Noam Chomsky, a pioneer in this area of linguistics, called these speech-enabling structures _language acquisition devices_ or _LADs_.

Other researchers agree that human beings have a genetic predisposition for language but argue that this built-in capacity is more like a set of lessons and "listening rules" that help us perceive and learn language. For example, babies pay attention to the sounds and rhythm of the sounds they hear others speak, especially the beginnings, endings, and stressed syllables.

In addition, children seem to be born using certain grammar rules. They come into the world with some natural biases in how to use and apply new words. For example, children have natural tendencies to assume all nouns are common nouns (calling all men "Daddy") and overextending common nouns to things that are similar (calling all round objects "balls").

Sure, these assumptions lead to some pretty funny talk, but think how efficient they are. If you're learning a new language, it's much easier to group similar objects together and give them similar names than to assume every new item is a world unto itself.

The jury is still out for LADs but not for *LASS*es, *language acquisition support systems*. In order for our language potential to blossom, we must grow up in a responsive environment with plenty of opportunity to practice. Without it, we miss the opportunity to fully express ourselves.

Remember Victor, the wolf boy from Aveyron (Chapter 3)? Undoubtedly, one of the reasons his language skills never caught up is the fact that he was deprived of a language acquisition support system in childhood; he missed the critical period for language development. In every known case in which children are deprived of early language opportunities, their language skills are permanently impaired. When it comes to LASSes, we either use them or lose them.

def•i•ni•tion

Language acquisition devices (LADs) are the preprogrammed instructions for learning a language that some linguists believe all infants are born with. **Language acquisition support systems (LASSes)** are the circumstances that facilitate the efficient acquisition of language.

Brain Buster

Immigrant children still learning English can be misdiagnosed as speech impaired (and shuffled into special education) because the normal errors made while acquiring a new language often resemble those made by language-impaired, monolingual children. Speech assessment test scores of non-native English-speaking students should be compared to other youngsters who are learning a second language, not monolingual English-speaking children.

But what happens when our LASS changes in midstream? Internationally adopted preschoolers who learn one language and then move to a home where a different language is spoken lose their birth language rapidly. Their learning process is similar to that of infants learning a first language, but they have one advantage over infants: they're older, thus more cognitively mature. Studies show they progress through the same stages—nouns, verbs, one-word utterances, then telegraphic sentences ("Zachery eat"). But they progress through the stages more rapidly than infants and eventually catch up with their peers.

Listen and Learn

Of course, there's another big influence that helps children talk faster: parents. If you're a parent, you're bilingual. You speak your native tongue and also "parentese," a lingo that involves speaking in an exaggerated, high-pitched tone of voice, emphasizing and repeating important words, and using short, staccato bursts ("uh-oh") to signal taboos. Most of us call this "baby talk," and it just happens to be the language babies learn best.

Babies come programmed for speech and are given parents who are natural language teachers. Not only do we speak in parentese, but we also engage our infants in training dialogues. From birth, we talk to our newborns and then wait for a reply. Early on, we'll accept just about anything as a valid reply before continuing the conversation—a burp, a sneeze, a yawn. No wonder children have such a hard time being quiet; it's against their nature! Like any good teacher, though, we make more demands as our children grow, matching our expectations to their abilities.

> **Psychobabble**
>
> Studies show that, in families with two working parents, fathers have a greater impact than mothers on a two- to three-year-old's language development.

The Child Psychologist

Children may start out exploring the outer world, but they pretty quickly show a fascination with their inner world as well. They also begin to use words like *dream*, *forget*, *pretend*, *believe*, and *hope* as they talk about internal states, and not just their own.

As early as 15 months of age, children can understand the concept of false beliefs and how actions can follow them. Between ages two and a half and three and a half, they routinely begin to attribute thoughts, feelings, and motives to the things people do. A four-year-old soap opera fan will assure you the heroine of *As the World Turns* is crying because she's sad or that Daddy is getting a beer because he's thirsty. Luckily for parents, understanding some of the ulterior motives that drive human behavior comes later!

Children also know early on when mommy and daddy are fighting. How parents handle everyday marital conflicts significantly affects a child's emotional security and ultimately his ability to build positive relationships with others. Constructive marital conflict (physical affection, problem solving, compromise), in fact, can actually increase a child's emotional security and provide him with a model for conflict resolution that will serve him well in adulthood.

Even two-year-olds know the difference between make-believe and reality. This early distinction may be a necessary survival tool—a child who understands the difference has the foundation for understanding that beliefs can differ from reality and that people can fool others by manipulating their beliefs. By age four, children become pretty skilled at detecting deception in others—and using it to their own advantage as well. And by age seven, children are able to recognize and discount statements that are clearly aligned with the self-interests of the speaker.

> **Psychobabble**
>
> When do babies learn to read faces? Research suggests that by seven months of age, babies will pay more attention to a fearful face than a happy or neutral one. Apparently, we learn to recognize threats early!

> **Insight**
>
> Read *Life Behind Glass*, a personal account of autism. Oblivious to the minds of others, the author talks of feeling as if she were living among aliens; she could study others and copy them but never truly felt at home.

Psych School for Kids

Some kids are better natural "psychologists" than others. But almost all children can be taught better self-control and greater self-awareness. And new research suggests that helping preschool children develop their emotional intelligence pays off in terms of classroom behavior and mental health.

For example, a group of children were taught a curriculum that focused on self-control and emotional awareness for 20–30 minutes per day, three times per week, over a six-month period. Teachers used "feeling faces" cards to help their students identify what they—and their classmates—were feeling. A year later, they had lower rates of aggression, anxiety, and sadness, greater social competence, and fewer behavioral and emotional problems compared to other students who had not received the curriculum.

The Curious Child

Jean Piaget, the child-mind pioneer, was also fascinated by the minds of children. Watching his three children develop sparked an interest in children's minds that lasted more than 50 years. What he concluded was that children are scientists who begin to experiment and explore their world from the moment they're born. Mental development, he believed, naturally arises out of this exploration.

Of course, infants start with what they can see, taste, touch, hear, and smell. Before long, children start putting two and two together and realizing that certain actions go best with certain objects. Sucking goes best with nipples. Banging goes best with rattles. Smiling goes best with Mommy's face. Piaget called this ability to develop mental blueprints linking actions and objects the development of schemes.

As soon as a baby develops a sucking scheme for nipples, he wastes no more effort in trying to squeeze milk out of a rattle or a teddy bear. Not only do these schemes save time, they are the foundation upon which babies learn more sophisticated lessons, through what Piaget called assimilations and accommodations.

Coping with Curveballs

One thing we learn early is that life is constantly throwing us curveballs and we have to find ways to hit them. Sometimes we can hit that curveball with just a minor tweak (assimilation), and sometimes we have to adjust our way of thinking (accommodation). A baby who's a champion nipple sucker might easily be able to incorporate cups or bottles into her sucking scheme. Eating from a spoon, however, is a whole new challenge.

Piaget considered the assimilation of new experiences similar to the digestion of food. Two people might eat the same food, but each body will assimilate the food differently depending upon the person's digestive system, metabolism, and so forth. Moreover, just as wolfing down crayons or dirt won't help our bodies grow, new experiences that are too different from existing schemes can't be mentally digested and will not result in growth. If you give a toddler your hand calculator, you might get a stellar display of his banging scheme, but you won't teach him arithmetic.

Performing on Stage

Piaget was interested in more than how children think. He was also interested in *what* and *why* they think. Over and over, he watched children solve problems and asked them to explain their reasoning behind their solutions.

He concluded that most children develop their thinking in stages, going from a concrete, here-and-now focus to a more abstract, future-oriented approach. He proposed four stages of cognitive development, each of which roughly correlated to a child's chronological age:

- Sensorimotor stage (birth to 2 years old)

- Preoperational stage (2 to 7 years old)

- Concrete operations (7 to 11 years old)

- Formal operations (12 years old and up)

Sensorimotor Stage

In the sensorimotor stage, thoughts and behaviors are pretty much one and the same. Infants spend their time examining their environment and placing objects into schemes for sucking, shaking, banging, twisting, dropping, and other categories that cause general mayhem for their parents.

Babies take a giant leap forward when they begin to understand the concept of object permanence—that objects still exist even though they're out of baby's sight.

Piaget and other early researchers thought babies didn't grasp object permanence until about nine months. Newer research done by psychologist Su-hua Wang shows that babies may understand the concept as early as 10 weeks. Of course, they still want the concept confirmed by endless games of peek-a-boo.

> **Psychobabble**
>
> Children as young as four years of age will modify their speech to two-year-old siblings to take into account their younger brother's or sister's language abilities, suggesting that preoperational kids may not be as completely self-centered as we once thought.

General theme: monkey see, monkey do.

Preoperational Stage

To you and me, a skillet is a cooking utensil. The only creative energy we spend on a skillet is in deciding what to cook in it. Give a preschooler a skillet and, alakazaam, you have the lead guitar from the newest band or the only Star Wars gun that will kill Darth Vader. Children in this stage have a well-developed ability to magically transform everyday items into symbols and to re-create events they have seen. However, while their thinking is no longer bound by the here and now, it is very much bound by appearances—witness my son's insistence that the taller cup had more water, no matter how often I proved otherwise.

This is also an age of profound self-centeredness. If a child falls off a chair, the chair is "bad" and needs to be punished—after all, *something* made him fall, and it certainly wasn't *his* fault. Ask a four-year-old to tell you another person's point of view, and she'll tell you her own thoughts and feelings because she hasn't developed the cognitive ability to do otherwise.

General theme: it's all about me!

Concrete Operations

By the age of seven, children start to realize that appearances can be deceiving. They have, for instance, developed the concept of *conservation:* they realize that no matter how much outward appearances change, physical properties don't change unless something is added or taken away.

Much of the problem solving children do in this age group consists of what Piaget called operations, mentally reversing the consequences of an action to figure out cause and effect. If you ask a 10-year-old bicyclist whether the chain or the fender is crucial to his cycling, he won't have to take apart his bicycle to tell you. By mentally removing each part, he'll know that the chain is connected to the pedals and the pedals move the wheels and therefore, the chain is critical, but the fender is not.

General theme: take things literally.

Formal Operations

Remember the game "20 Questions," where the winner is the person who guesses the right answer by asking the fewest yes/no questions? Children have trouble playing this game until they reach the formal operations stage, around the age of 12.

Children still in the concrete operations stage tend to limit their questions to specifics. If the correct answer is some kind of animal, a child might ask questions like, "Is it a dog?" or "Is it a monkey?" A formal thinker, on the other hand, might ask questions like, "Does it fly?" or "Does it have hair?" before moving to more specific questions. Formal operations enable us to see the "big picture"; in this stage, we develop general principles we can apply to hypothetical situations.

General theme: think ahead.

Psychobabble

Teenagers are often accused of "not thinking ahead." In their defense, an awful lot of neurological turbulence is going on inside their enormously plastic brains. Parts of the teen brain are literally being overdeveloped and discarded as the brain's structure becomes more refined. The good news is that this overproduction-selective elimination process is highly adaptive and ultimately helps teens mature, think ahead, and make better decisions.

Recent research suggests that Piaget might have been behind the curve in realizing the true learning potential of children. Researchers have found, for example, that as early as three years, some children exhibit nonverbal math skills, comprehending quantity and performing simple addition and subtraction using groups of objects. Because a preschoolers' verbal understanding of conventional math terms is limited, their ability to comprehend quantitative concepts is often overlooked.

From a practical standpoint, parents can tap into this ability by giving children the language to express it. Playing counting games can help children begin to label quantity. Setting the table together can include counting out the number of forks—one ... two ... three— and teach a child an even harder concept: responsibility!

Psychobabble

Most professional magicians hate performing in front of small children unless they have developed special routines for kids. Why? Because magicians generally work on the principle of misdirection, distracting you from something they don't want you to notice. Children before the formal operational stage can be tough to fool because they think differently and aren't easily misdirected.

Speak Before You Think—or Vice Versa

You still might not want to sit next to one on an airplane, but by now you've got to have a healthy respect for children. After all, what adult do you know who can learn any one of 3,000 languages, turn any household device into a lethal weapon, and train grownups to be at his or her beck and call?

Children are linguists; they're psychologists; they're scientists. And according to a psychologist by the name of Lev Vygotsky, they're apprentices as well. In fact, Vygotsky thought children learn much more through their relationships than through their solo adventures in the world. According to this view, we speak first and think second.

Piaget considered language a side effect of children's development of thought. Vygotsky argued that language is the foundation for the development of higher thought. He believed that words not only provide the building blocks for advanced thinking, but they also actually direct our thinking in ways that reflect the activities and values of our culture. Thus, children who grow up in cultures where counting is important develop an efficient set of number words. Some Eskimo cultures have several different words for *snow* because differentiating between different types of snow is critical to their survival.

According to Vygotsky, children first learn words to communicate with others, but then they begin to use those same words as symbols for thinking. In fact, he thought that much of our cognitive development is a matter of internalizing the symbols, ideas, and modes of reasoning that have evolved over the course of history and make up the culture into which we are born. A Vygotskyan would say that all human beings share the same brain, but our individual minds are a reflection of our culture!

The Moral of the Story

"Those are bad thoughts." "I think it's the right thing to do." "She made the wrong decision." From an early age, we do much more than think our thoughts. We evaluate them. In fact, by the time we're adults, rarely a thought goes by without our attaching some moral weight to it. But how do we learn to make these value judgments?

Lawrence Kohlberg was intrigued with how people develop their sense of morality: concepts of what is right and what is wrong. His curiosity eventually led him to develop the best-known psychological explanation for moral development. Similar to Piaget's thoughts on cognitive growth, Kohlberg believed people acquired their morals in stages and that individuals in all cultures went through these stages in the same order. Kohlberg thought our moral development went from a self-centered focus to a higher level that focused on the good of society. Here's how he thought human moral development plays out for most of us:

The Morality Play

The Stage	The Plot	The Motive
Stage 1	Seek pleasure; avoid pain	Avoid pain or getting caught
Stage 2	Weigh the costs and benefits	Achieve the most rewards

The Stage	The Plot	The Motive
Stage 3	Be a good kid	Be popular and avoid disapproval
Stage 4	Be a law-abiding citizen	Stay out of jail; avoid penalties
Stage 5	Make win-win deals	Do what's good for society
Stage 6	Live by your ethics	Be just; don't disappoint yourself
Stage 7	Be in tune with the cosmos	Think about what's best for the universe

As you look at Kohlberg's stages, you may recognize that when it comes to developing morals, many people you know seem to be developmentally delayed. Well, it's true. In reality, many adults never reach stage 5 and few go beyond it. I, personally, still wonder what the heck stage 7 really means!

> ### Psychobabble
>
> Growing up in a war zone amid violence, lawlessness, and deprivation affects a child's moral development. In one study, Colombian children living in war zones all said that stealing or hurting others is wrong; most even said it's wrong to steal or hurt others to survive. But when asked if revenge was a legitimate motive for stealing or hurting others, many said yes.

Empathetically Yours

In addition, there is a big difference between moral beliefs and moral acts. If you want to predict whether someone will behave morally, skip right over these stages and measure his ability to empathize with others. Empathy, the ability to feel another person's feelings, is what motivates a child to behave morally. By age 13 to 15 months, a baby will try to comfort a crying playmate. She may even enlist Mom's help by grabbing her hand and pulling her in the direction of the bawling baby. A baby like this is well on her way to making good moral decisions.

Midlife Isn't the First Crisis

If your life is one crisis after the next, welcome to the club. Psychologist Erik Erikson's life was like that, too. As a middle-age immigrant to America, he faced many conflicts as he adjusted to his new life. He believed we all have conflicts and challenges at different stages in our lives and that our emotional and social development depends upon how well we deal with these crises.

Erickson coined the term *psychosocial crises* to describe successive turning points or choices that influence personality growth across the life span. Each crisis requires a new level of social interaction; if we turn in the right direction, we build a sense of trust, security, and confidence in ourselves. If we don't, life keeps getting harder and harder. Personal crises aside, we all go through these eight developmental crises:

Eight Human Crises and How They Turn Out

Age	Crisis	Good Ending	Bad Ending
0–1½	Trust vs. mistrust	I can rely on others	Insecurity, anxiety
1½–3	Autonomy vs. self-doubt, lack of control, feelings of inadequacy	I am my own person	Helpless to change things
3–6 years	Initiative vs. guilt	I can make things happen	Lack of self-worth
6 years–puberty	Competence vs. inferiority	I can lead	Lack of self-confidence
Adolescence	Identity vs. role confusion	I know who I am	Unclear sense of self

Age	Crisis	Good Ending	Bad Ending
Early adulthood	Intimacy vs. isolation	I can be close to others	Feeling alone, denial of need for closeness
Middle adulthood	Generativity vs. stagnation	I can see beyond myself	Self-indulgent concerns
Late adulthood	Ego-integrity vs. despair	I have contributed	Disappointment

Child development has been the theme of this chapter. As you've seen, however, the way children grow teaches us much about human nature in general. First of all, we come into the world with a lot of neat equipment, and our environment helps us learn how to use it. Second, there is a time and place for everything; our language, our thought, our sense of morality, and our emotional development all take place in stages that can be influenced by our environment but not necessarily altered by it. And finally, there are few shortcuts in life; not resolving one of Erickson's stages is likely to come back to haunt us.

Straight from the Lab

Video Games Groom Good Surgeons and Scientists   Video games improve dexterity and problem-solving skills—critical skills for surgeons and scientists. A study of laparoscopic surgeons found that those who played video games were 27 percent faster at advanced surgical procedures and made 37 percent fewer errors than nongamers.

Let Your Teenager Sleep In!   Test results of eighth-grade students who were allowed to start classes one hour later than the regular start time (7:30) are higher than those for students who have to crawl out at the regular time.

Kids Do Better When They Talk to Themselves   Preschoolers often chat with themselves as they go about their daily activities. Let them! It's perfectly normal, and it improves their communication skills with the outside world. Studies show that 78 percent of five-year-olds perform better on motor tasks when they talk out loud to themselves.

Work Harder, Process Faster   A new study on auditory processing problems in language development suggests that the choice of intervention may matter less than the intensity and format of the intervention. Children receiving 500 minutes of therapy per week—compared to the 30-minutes, twice-weekly services typically offered by public school systems—showed much greater gains than those typical of public school settings (regardless of whether the therapy involved computer programs, speech-language tutoring, or nonlanguage academic enrichment).

The Least You Need to Know

- Babies come into this world with a natural interest in novel experiences and a low tolerance for boredom. And from birth, they're just as busy learning about the internal world of emotion as they are absorbing information about the outside world.

- With the help of a responsive environment and plenty of opportunities to practice, children have a pretty good understanding of grammar by the time they are six years old.

- By the time they're two, children understand that people have reasons for what they do; by the time they're four, they know people's motives aren't always honorable; and by the time they're seven, they have a healthy dose of cynicism.

- Psychologist Jean Piaget discovered that children mentally grow in stages, moving from a clumsy exploration of the immediate environment to the ability to hypothesize and think ahead.

- Morally speaking, children's understanding of what is right and wrong evolves as they get older, but their moral actions are more likely to be guided by their ability to feel empathy for others.

- Life is a series of turning points, and how we handle them will either move us forward or hold us back.

Part 2

Wake Up and Smell the Coffee

Humans have some pretty miraculous senses—and an even more impressive data-processing center, better known as the brain. In this part, you'll learn all about how you take information in from the world around you, and how your mind makes sense of all that data. From learning to memory, from remembering to organizing, your mind is a marvelous tool—here's where you'll learn all about its inner workings.

5

Come to Your Senses

In This Chapter

- ◆ Making sense out of things
- ◆ When the pain is "all in your head"
- ◆ Coming to attention
- ◆ Discovering why you're more organized than you think
- ◆ Life is but a dream

"Seeing is believing" and "Life is but an illusion" are equally considered commonsense descriptions of how the world works. Well, our senses *do* provide us with reasonably reliable information. But the representations they give us of the world aren't as literally accurate as we tend to believe.

Without much conscious effort, we are constantly taking in information about the world and sending it to our brains to make sense of it. In this chapter, we explore sensation and perception: how our senses process information and how our first perceptions set the stage for how we think, feel, and interact with our world. In short, perception is the foreplay to the rest of psychology.

Creating a Sensation

We use our senses to guide us through life. Sometimes, they signal danger: a friend of mine recently commented that a blind date "made the hairs on the back of my neck stand up." She "sensed" he wasn't trustworthy, and if she's smart, she'll trust herself and steer clear of him.

Our senses also give us pleasure—the feel of our boyfriend's lips, the sight of Van Gogh's paintings, or the taste of tiramisu.

But for all the good they do us, our senses never get the credit. Human nature holds fast to the belief that the joys of life are "out there"; we rarely recognize that without our taste buds, we couldn't appreciate a good meal!

Your perception of things is even more complicated. You'll smell the same perfume but perceive it differently depending on the circumstances; the same scent that had you drooling with lust can become nauseating after you've fallen out of love.

The discovery that our perceptions of the world differ from physical reality led scientists to ponder the relationship between our mental world and the physical world in which we live. And this journey led them to another discovery.

On the Threshold of Discovery

The relationship between physical stimuli and the behavior or mental experiences they evoked fascinated early psychologists. In fact, *psychophysics*, the study of psychological reactions to physical stimuli, is the oldest field of psychology.

def•i•ni•tion

Psychophysics is the study of psychological reactions to physical stimuli.

At what point, they wondered, does physical reality become human reality? To answer this question, pioneers began tracking the point at which physical differences in sound or light became mental distinctions. How bright does a light have to be for us to see it glowing? What's the softest sound we can still hear? It depends, they discovered, on the individual. People have different sensitivities to environmental stimuli.

Star Light, Star Bright

Let's say you and a friend are stargazing and you point out a faint star. Your friend says he can't see it. Thinking it's because he's not looking in the right place, you spend several frustrating minutes giving him the exact location of the star and pointing out brighter stars nearby. If he still can't see it, it may be because his absolute threshold for light is lower than yours. An absolute threshold is the smallest, weakest amount of a stimulus a person can detect.

Psychophysicists are also interested in our difference threshold, the smallest physical difference between two stimuli that we can recognize. Let's say you do your best studying with Nirvana blasting in the background. Your roommate, on the other hand, prefers a study atmosphere similar to a funeral parlor. Your earphones are broken, and it's the night before a major exam. Your roommate asks you to turn down the radio; you don't. The least amount you can lower the volume to prove your good intentions while still keeping the volume audible would be the just-noticeable difference.

Crossing the Threshold

We use absolute and difference thresholds to guide safety regulations. For example, when warning lights are built into cars, safety engineers must make sure they're bright enough to take your attention away from other dashboard lights. Without psychology, there'd be a lot more car accidents!

We may not be faster than the speed of sound or able to stop a speeding bullet, but our senses are pretty good at tuning in to our environment. The average person can …

◆ See a candle flame at 30 miles on a dark, clear night.

◆ Hear the tick of a watch under quiet conditions at 20 feet.

◆ Taste 1 teaspoon sugar in 2 gallons of water.

◆ Smell one drop of perfume diffused into a three-bedroom apartment.

◆ Feel the movement of a wing of a bee near his cheek at a distance of 1 centimeter.

Get Your Signals Straight

The work of psychophysicists would be easier if perceptual differences between people were always due to better hearing, sight, touch, smell, or taste. However, early psychophysicists failed to realize that differences in thresholds could be due to psychological reasons. Our responses to environmental stimuli are biased by our past experiences as well as our expectations of the current situation.

Insight

Certain situations obviously pull for one bias over another. A new mother may think she hears her sleeping baby crying because she's so emotionally invested in her child.

That's where signal detection theory comes in. This theory recognizes that psychological as well as physical factors influence our ability to perceive stimuli in the environment. Perceiving sensory stimulation requires more than just responding to it; it requires making a judgment about its presence or absence as well. Just as jurors can be predisposed to vote innocent or guilty, our experience and expectations might lead us to be too ready to say we heard something or we didn't.

Common Senses

Signal detection theory helps us understand all the things that influence our ability to make sense of our environment. But what are the "signals" that we detect? How do things "out there" (light waves) become things "in here" (the perception of a beautiful painting)? It happens through energy. Whether it's sound waves or light waves, physical energy from a stimulus in the environment stimulates our sensory neurons, which, in turn, convert this energy into electrochemical signals the nervous system carries to the brain. This process is known as transduction.

These neural messages are the language through which all our sense organs communicate sensory input to the brain. Your sense organs also tune out stimulation that does not change in intensity or some other quality, a process known as sensory adaptation.

Psychobabble

Viva la aromatherapy? Maybe. Researchers have recently found that certain smells can actually stimulate the other senses, making them either more or less vigilant. Bad smells, for example, may trigger our brain's threat center, signaling our other senses to be on the lookout for possible danger.

When you first put on your shoes, you are aware of how they feel on your feet. But unless they're pinching your toes or rubbing your heels, you quickly forget about them.

Sensory adaptation enables our senses to focus on novelty. From a survival standpoint, it was critical for our ancestors to be able to focus on sudden changes in their environment as they most often signaled danger. If for example, they had been too busy focusing on the constant sense of discomfort that came from sitting on rocks, they might have missed a large predatory animal emerging from the bushes.

What Stimulates You?

Life is a stimulating experience. What stimulates us at any given moment depends upon the part of the body we're talking about. Take a look at what really stimulates us—and what really gets stimulated.

Sense	What Stimulates Us	What Gets Stimulated
Hearing	Sound waves	Pressure-sensitive hair cells in cochlea of inner ear
Vision	Light waves	Light-sensitive rods and cones in retina of eye
Touch	Pressure on skin	Sensitive ends of touch neurons in skin
Pain	Potentially harmful stimuli	Sensitive ends of pain neurons in skin and other tissue
Taste	Molecules dissolved in fluid	Taste cells in taste buds on the tongue
Smell	Molecules dissolved in fluid	Sensitive ends of olfactory neurons in the mucous membranes

The Big Five

We've talked about some of the things our senses have in common. On a daily basis, though, we're much more aware of their differences. Seeing is different from hearing. We use our sense of sight to feast our eyes upon our loved ones and our sense of touch to enjoy the pleasure of human contact. So let's look at the unique contribution each of our senses makes to understanding our world—starting with the "big five": vision, hearing, smell, taste, and touch.

Vision

Most people say they would rather lose their hearing than their sight. Certainly, from an evolutionary perspective, vision has been our most important sense.

To start with, photoreceptors in our eyes gather light, convert its physical energy into neural messages, and send it to the occipital lobe in the brain for decoding and analyzing. Transduction happens in the retina, which is composed of light-sensitive layers of cells at the back of the eyes.

> **Insight**
>
> All of us have a blind spot, a small part of the retina that is not coated with photoreceptors, which creates a small gap in our visual field. We aren't aware of our blind spot because our eyes compensate for each other, and our brains "fill in" the spot with information that matches the background.

Those cells in the retina are called rods and cones. Rods are receptor cells that permit vision in dim light; they are highly sensitive to the perception of light but can't distinguish colors or details. Cones, on the other hand, operate best in bright light, where they permit sharply focused color vision. With their help, we can visually discriminate among five million different colors—but we only have the language to identify 150 to 200 of them.

Hearing

"If a tree falls in the forest and no one's there, does it make a sound?" This Zen riddle plays upon the fact that "sound" refers both to the physical stimulus we hear and to the sensation the stimulus produces. If we were using the term *sound* to refer to the physical stimulus, our answer would be yes. If we were referring to the sensation and no one was around to experience it, the right answer would be no.

Sounds are created when actions, like banging, cause objects, like drums, to vibrate. These vibrating objects push air molecules back and forth and, as a result, change the air pressure. These changes in air pressure travel in sine waves. Picture ocean waves breaking on the shoreline. How fast the waves crash determines the frequency we hear. High frequencies produce high sounds, and low frequencies produce low sounds. How high the waves are at the crest dictates their amplitude. Sound waves with large amplitudes are loud, and those with small amplitudes are soft.

A simple example of a sine wave.

Amplitude

Sound waves travel into the ear, transfer from tissue to bones in the middle ear, and are transformed into fluid waves in the inner ear. The vibrations of these fluid waves stimulate tiny hair cells to generate nerve impulses to the auditory part of the brain. And of course, our brain analyzes these sounds and responds appropriately, such as telling us to cover our ears when we hear fingernails scratching on a chalkboard!

Insight

A cochlear implant is an electronic device that is surgically implanted in the inner ear to restore partial hearing to deaf individuals. Studies show that cochlear implants can be a tremendous boost to self-esteem, social interaction, and overall mental health.

Smell

Smell is our most primitive sense, which may be why we take it for granted. It's a real bummer, though, when we lose it; not only does the world seem bland, but it tastes bland, too. Our sense of smell probably developed as a system for finding food, and anyone with a cold can tell you that our taste buds get a lot of the credit that our nose really deserves.

Odors are chemical molecules. When they hit the membranes of tiny hairs in our noses, the receptors there translate them into nerve impulses, which are relayed to the olfactory bulb, the part of the brain that decodes and interprets smells.

Our sense of smell may also be the one most linked to memory. To this day, the smell of peanuts reminds me of my childhood home in Alabama; a certain men's cologne takes me back to the frat house of a hot-n-heavy college romance.

But smell, as we are all acutely aware, is a two-sided coin. There are good smells, and … well, bad ones. And the bad ones can really stress us out.

Insight

New mothers who wear the same perfume every day are likely to create a strong olfactory memory bond with their baby; in fact, sharing that scent with a babysitter may also help keep the baby calm while Mom's away.

In a recent study, subjects chronicled the odors and sounds of their daily environments for eight days, as well as their stress levels and physical symptoms. Commonly reported odors included hot food, paint, smoke or fire, coffee, and chemicals. Physical symptoms and stress levels worsened when unpleasant odors were stronger. One explanation might be that people come to associate particular odors with symptoms, and experiencing the odor triggers the symptoms.

Taste

A taste bud is no galloping gourmet. It can tell whether foods are sweet, sour, bitter, or salty, and that's about it. Food critics rely on their sense of smell to distinguish between subtle food flavors more than on their ability to taste them.

Your taste receptors, located on the upper side of your tongue, transduct chemical molecules dissolved in saliva to the taste center of your brain. If you've burned your tongue on hot soup, you may have noticed that your sense of taste was temporarily disrupted. But never fear! Those buds are amazingly resilient; they are replaced every few days. In fact, your sense of taste is the most resistant to damage of all your senses.

Insight

An infinitesimal scent can determine whether or not we like someone. Subjects were asked to sniff scents (lemon, good; sweat, bad; or neutral) in varying concentrations, then view a face with a neutral expression and rank the likeability of the face. If they were conscious of the scent, they discounted it in their evaluations, but if the scent was barely perceptible, their judgments about likeability were unconsciously biased.

Touch

Food lovers aside, touch is the most pleasurable of all the senses. Not only is it the main avenue to sexual arousal, but it is also critical for healthy development. Children who are deprived of touch can develop psychosocial dwarfism, a condition whereby their physical development is stunted.

Your skin contains nerve endings that, when stimulated by physical contact with outside objects, produce sensations of pressure, warmth, and cold. These sensations are the skin senses, and you could not survive without them. Not surprisingly, your sensitivity to touch is greatest where you need it the most: on your face, tongue, and hands.

The Sixth Sense?

While we've discussed that there really are more than five senses, when most people talk about "the sixth sense," they are talking about one of two things: either ESP (extrasensory perception) or a really good movie with Bruce Willis.

ESP is the term collectively used for such things as telepathy (reading another person's mind), precognition (predicting the future), and other abilities considered outside the norm of physical senses ("I see dead people"). But does it exist?

The answer is an absolute, resounding "Maybe." Do many people report such experiences? Yes. Can these experiences be reliably, scientifically reproduced under the strict experimental conditions we discussed in Chapter 1? No. ESP studies are often criticized either for the way they're conducted or the way the results are interpreted. And oddly, the same studies yield different results when conducted by different people.

But a surprising new study shows that we're capable of perceiving some pretty strange things. Undergrads at UC Riverside were shown three shapes (a triangle, a disc, and a square cut from sound-insulating foam board covered with black tape); they were then blindfolded and asked to identify which shape was positioned in front of loudspeakers playing a white-noise sound. Some listeners had near-perfect guessing records, demonstrating that humans can hear "silence."

Subjects could also distinguish various rooms on campus by their ambient sounds and echoes (e.g., a men's bathroom, the old gym, a walk-in closet). Other experiments demonstrate that we can "read" unheard speech, not only by lip-reading but also by the simple movements of dots placed on the lips, teeth, and tongue.

Pain in the What?

Although not included in the favored five, pain is a body sense that warns us of potential harm and helps us cope with sickness and injury. It's one of our best defenses but also one of our most puzzling senses because psychological and social factors can influence our experience of pain.

Sometimes pain really is "all in your head." The way we experience our pain, the way we communicate it to others, and even the way we respond to pain-relieving treatment may reveal more about our psychological state than the actual intensity of the pain stimulus. Stomachaches hurt; however, someone who's unhappy at work may find the discomfort unbearable, while someone energized at work may find it merely annoying.

Think of pain as your emotional experience of a physically distressing sensation. Things that intensify your emotions, like upsetting thoughts or events, can magnify your experience of pain. Cultural attitudes and gender roles also play a role in our relationship with pain. For instance, early studies reported that women had a 20 percent lower pain tolerance than men. These findings were initially attributed to biologically different pain thresholds, but recent research suggests that the gender difference in pain tolerance may be in the *expression* of pain, not the *perception* of it.

> **Insight**
>
> We all have a built-in mechanism that temporarily prevents us from feeling pain when, for survival purposes, it is best to ignore our injuries. This phenomenon, stress-induced analgesia, has helped hundreds of firefighters and police officers perform heroic deeds in the face of extreme trauma and in spite of personal injury.

In the lab, men tended to endure temporary discomfort rather than risk losing face by showing vulnerability to the researcher. Women, on the other hand, may be more accurate reporters because they feel less social pressure to endure unnecessary pain and are likely to speak up when something hurts.

The Placebo Effect

The fact that pain is as much about what we perceive as it is about actual physical experience has both advantages and disadvantages. On the down side, researchers just about pull their hair out when one of their control groups—a group that gets no real treatment and is supposed to stay the same—actually gets better. That's because the control group is supposed to be the yardstick; by comparing the treatment group to the control group, we can hypothetically see if our treatment or manipulation actually worked. And yet some people who participate in research studies and take placebos do get better; people in control groups have experienced reduced pain, healed ulcers, eased nausea, and even had warts disappear.

The placebo effect may also provide emotional analgesia as well. Researchers administered an antianxiety drug to reduce subjects' distress while viewing unpleasant pictures (such as mutilated bodies); they then administered an antidote to the drug, telling subjects that it would restore the unpleasant perception. In tests the next day, subjects were told they would receive the same antianxiety drug while viewing the pictures but, instead, received a placebo.

The placebo reduced the subjects' ratings of the unpleasant pictures by about 29 percent—a rate that was commensurate with brain scans showing a reduction in activity in the brain's emotional centers. And interestingly, the placebo increased brain activity in the same "modulatory network" as the one used to relieve physical pain. Expectation of pain relief—whether physical or emotional—bolsters a placebo's effectiveness.

Solving the mystery behind the placebo effect may yield new clues about the mind-body link, whether it's having positive expectations about our medical treatment, receiving support, or developing a supportive and positive relationship with a physician.

> **Psychobabble**
>
> Phantom pain is pain, itching, or pressure in a limb or body part that is no longer there, such as a leg that has been surgically removed. While the arm or leg is gone, the feelings are just as real to the person as any other physical feelings. If someone has phantom pain, trying to "talk him out of it" won't work; he'll need help from a specialist for relief.

Starting from the Top Down and the Bottom Up

If you think your senses are complicated, "you ain't seen nothin' yet." After your senses take in all that stimulation, your brain still has to make sense out of it. What is that round thing? Have we ever seen it—or anything like it—before? Is it a ball, an orange, or the moon? And once we figure out what it is, we have to figure out what to do with it. It's the frontal cortex's job to collect data from all the senses and assemble it into coherent thoughts.

If you've never been particularly proud of your organizational skills, your self-esteem is about to get a boost. Your brain has an amazing ability to automatically sort objects by size, distance, proportion, color, and many other categories. It solves mysteries hundreds of times a day by taking clues (sensory information from the environment) and using them to solve the puzzle by identifying the object. The "detective skills" you use are of two types—top-down processing and bottom-up processing.

Bottoms Up

Bottom-up processing is data driven—it starts with independent information from the outside and works its way inward to an interpretation of that information. When we process this way, we start with the environment; our eyes, for example, pick up colors or other visual cues as they look around. Using this data, our brain instantly tries to put together a visual image.

Interestingly, you are more likely to notice the "big picture" before you see details because your brain is so attuned to figuring out the whole landscape. For instance, you'll know that the shape coming toward you is a human being before you'll detect the color of her hair or eyes or even her gender.

Of course, your brain doesn't just rely on information from your immediate environment to make sense of the world. It also makes use of your past experiences, knowledge, cultural background, motivations, expectations, and memories. This part of perceptual processing is known as top-down processing because your brain is comparing what you're currently seeing, hearing, or touching with your ideas, expectations, and memories of similar objects.

Watch Out! Reality Under Construction

The interaction of top-down and bottom-up processing means that our perceptions of reality are never truly objective. We are constantly constructing reality to fit in with our assumptions. Because of our unique backgrounds, it really is true that no two people ever "see" the same thing.

Not only are we "topping down" and "bottoming up" at the same time, but, ideally, these processes are also constantly balancing each other out. If we relied exclusively on the current sensory stimuli of bottom-up processing to make sense of our world, we'd register experiences, but we wouldn't be able to learn from them.

If we relied too much on top-down processing, we might be caught up in a fantasy world of hopes and expectations and overlook the reality staring us in the face. If you've ever stayed in a bad relationship because you kept pretending it was better than it was, maybe your perceptual processing was top heavy!

Life Is an Illusion

Do you ever wear dark clothes or vertical stripes to make yourself look thinner? If so, you're making use of illusion through your choice of clothing. By taking advantage of perceptual distortions, like dark colors appearing smaller than bright ones, we can artfully steer others into seeing us in a certain light.

Deceptive Appearances

We experience a perceptual illusion when our senses deceive us into perceiving an event or an object in a manner that is demonstrably incorrect. Illusions take advantage of our natural tendency to perceive objects in certain ways; in effect, they trick our senses. For example, from an early age, we learn cues that tell us about the relationship between size and distance. We learn that most objects that we see near the earth's horizon are farther away than objects we see near the zenith (straight up)—so birds or clouds seen near the horizon are usually farther away than those that are directly overhead.

Typically, illusions are more common when the sensory stimulus is ambiguous. When information is missing, elements are combined in unusual ways, or if familiar patterns are not apparent, our senses are much more vulnerable to deception.

Psychobabble

How do ventriloquists trick us into believing the dummy is doing the talking? A new study shows that the inferior colliculus, a tiny round brain structure, actually processes and combines both auditory *and* visual input before it's ever sent to the cortex—the thinking part of the brain. So we make the association between the ventriloquist's voice and the dummy's moving mouth before the cortex even notices—before we even consciously realize it.

Meet Ponzo the Western Illusion

In the following figure, which line is longer, the one on top or the one on bottom? People from the United States often say that the top line is longer, but not everybody sees it that way. The Ponzo illusion is an example of our cultural background influencing our perception of ambiguous information and, alas, leading us astray.

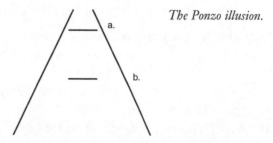

The Ponzo illusion.

If you grew up in the United States, you are used to seeing long, flat highways or train tracks winding off in the distance. You've probably noticed that, if you look at them, the lines seem to come closer together off in the distance. People who grow up with these experiences learn to interpret perspective and distance involving lines and edges; in this case, they use converging lines as a cue for distance.

In the drawing, the top line appears to be longer because its higher position implies it is farther along the converging tracks. On the other hand, people who live in countries that provide little exposure to wide open spaces or, for that matter, tall, right-angled buildings have fewer opportunities to learn the perceptual cue that converging lines imply distance. People in Guam, for example, are much less likely to fall for this illusion and will report that the lines are the same length.

Pay Attention When I'm Talking to You

Great illusionists have the gift of commanding our *attention*. Through their smoke and mirrors, they focus our attention on one thing while they're doing something else. Great illusionists know that attention is the first step in sensation and perception.

def•i•ni•tion

Attention is a state of focused awareness coupled with a readiness to respond.

As we go about our daily activities, hundreds of things compete for our attention. Most of the time, we have a lot of conscious control over what we attend to. In fact, when our elementary school teacher told us to quit goofing off and "pay attention," she was relying on us to exert voluntary control over ourselves and tune in to our schoolwork.

When we "pay attention," we are selectively attending to one source of information and blocking out others. Attention basically does three jobs:

- It helps us screen out irrelevant stimuli and focus on relevant information.

- It helps us consider the most appropriate response.

- It chooses the information that will enter in, and stay in, our awareness. If you don't pay attention to something, it can't be stored in your memory.

Here's an example of how attention works. Have you ever been at a party and suddenly heard your name from across the room? You might have not have heard a word of the buzz of conversation going on around you, but the minute someone says your name, you whip around and tune in to find out what *else* they're saying about you! It may seem that your name was spoken loudly, even though you know it wasn't. It only seems louder. Your name rings an internal bell. Personally interesting or perceptually meaningful information can grab your attention and cause you to suddenly tune in to a new channel.

Working Smarter, Not Harder

Not only is your brain organized, but it's also efficient. It looks for organizational strategies that require the least amount of effort. This brain trait is often referred to as the law of Pragnanz. The simplest organization requiring the least amount of effort will always emerge.

For example, your brain automatically assumes that objects having something in common go together. Objects that look alike are lumped together, and objects moving in the same direction and at the same speed are assumed to share a common goal.

So at a minimum, your brain saves time and conserves energy by processing things in groups. Another natural organizational strategy is your brain's tendency to create maps. Using changes in color and texture as cues, your brain divides the world into meaningful regions. The fact that my shirt is blue and my pants are yellow helps you know that I'm not wearing a one-piece jumpsuit. Hair has a different texture than skin does and our brain instantly recognizes it as a different feature.

Two other perceptual strategies for organizing information have interesting parallels in human behavior. First, we have a tendency to fill in the gaps—our need for perceptual closure is so strong that our brain will often fill in the missing edges, making us see incomplete figures as complete. The fact that we aren't aware of our visual blind spot is one example of our brain's automatic ability to fill in the gaps. Our psyches tend to fill in the gaps, too. How many of us spend hours trying to fill in the gaps left by someone's inexplicable or hurtful behavior?

A second perceptual strategy, our tendency to see a figure against a background, has similarly profound effects. Our brains naturally look for ways to categorize information into foreground (the primary object of interest) and background (the backdrop against which the figure stands out). Colors and textures create regions, and our brains naturally place some in front of others. And of course, we do this psychologically as well; when we go to a party,

Insight

Do you believe that washing your car is a surefire way to make it rain? Scientists think that much of our superstitious behavior may be our brain's tendency to look for patterns—even when they're not there!

Psychobabble

Research suggests that repetition of inaccurate news stories tends to create false memories and that corrected information does not change Americans' beliefs unless they were skeptical of the information to begin with.

a striking member of the opposite sex may quickly become the foreground and everyone else becomes the backdrop.

In everyday life, our tendency to try to lump things into groups can lead to stereotyping. "Well, you know women drivers …"; "All black people have rhythm"; "He's a blond, what do you expect?" In stereotyping people, we do two things: we learn to regard people as either "us or them," and we miss out on treating people as true individuals who have something unique to offer. Sometimes we have to use those frontal lobes to avoid overly organizing the world.

> ### Psychobabble
>
> What letters would you replace the asterisk with in the following two word series?
>
> Sheep, goat, horse, cow, b*ll
>
> Nickel, dime, quarter, dollar b*ll
>
> The four words before the one with the fill-in-the-blank letter create a certain perceptual set, encouraging you to see stimuli in a certain way. In this case, you were perceptually set to read "bull" for the first group of words and "bill" for the second.

Don't Take It Out of Context

The last stage of perception is identification and recognition—how the brain adds meaning to the facts it perceives. It takes all that sensory data and finds the appropriate context in which it belongs. Identification and recognition relies on our memory, expectations, motivation, personality, and social experience to help us understand what we are perceiving.

We rely on context in our environment to help us make sense of things—so much so that if we encounter people or things that are out of their usual context, it can throw us for a perceptual loop. If you always see a business associate in business meetings, you expect to see him in that context. When you see him at the beach, you may not recognize him right away—he's out of his usual context, so it takes you longer to adjust.

Context? Which Context?

Each of us works from different perceptual sets, conditions that determine one's readiness to detect a particular stimulus in a given context. The specific conditions that make up one person's perceptual sets can be very different from the conditions that make up somebody else's.

In fact, a famous saying in psychology is "Don't confuse the map with the territory," meaning that our view of the world—our map—is just one of many possible interpretations of our environment. In the next chapter, we take a look at how we become aware of our map—through consciousness.

Straight from the Lab

Keep Your Hands Where You Can See Them   Humans reflexively (unconsciously) evaluate objects more quickly when their hands are near the object. The research implies an evolutionary brain mechanism that makes us reluctant to shift our attention away from the object in our hands or closest to us because it's the most likely candidate for possible harm, protection, or manipulation.

Comedy: The Great Distracter   Watching funny TV shows helps children tolerate painful medical procedures longer, suggesting that TV comedies may be useful in clinical settings, such as cancer treatment centers.

Sound Speeds Up Vision   A new study of monkeys reveals that perception of one sense might enhance the perception of another without the higher brain areas ever being involved. Once monkeys learned to associate auditory and visual stimuli, their visual cortices integrated the auditory data. Since we may hear faster than we see, when the two occur together, sound may speed up our ability to process visual stimuli.

With Placebos, You Get What You Pay For   A 10-cent pill doesn't kill pain as well as a $2.50 pill—even if the two pills are the same placebo! Eighty-five percent of participants who read a brochure describing the pill as a "newly approved painkiller" for $2.50 experienced a reduction in pain; only 61 percent of the participants who read a brochure describing the pill as "marked down to 10 cents" did.

The Least You Need to Know

- Sensation makes us aware of conditions inside or outside our body; perception makes sense of them.

- Our senses convert physical energy from our environment into neurochemical signals, which they send to the brain to be analyzed and interpreted.

- Our experience of pain is as much a product of our mind as it is of our body; in some circumstances, we can use our minds to overcome pain.

◆ While our ability to pay attention is often under voluntary control, we're programmed to tune in to information that is personally meaningful or relevant.

◆ Our ability to make sense of our world requires the matching of information from our current environment with our prior experiences, memories, and expectations.

Chapter 6

It's Consciousness-Raising Time!

In This Chapter

- ◆ Getting the scoop on sleep
- ◆ We're all dreamers at heart
- ◆ Four paths to an altered consciousness
- ◆ The pharmaceutical problem

Imagine how you'd feel if, in the middle of a breast exam, your doctor blurted out: "Oh, my God, I feel a lump in your breast! It could be cancerous!" The fear this unprofessional remark would cause would be traumatic even if he was wrong. That's why doctors are trained to keep unfounded suspicions to themselves.

Doctors who would never do this in an exam room have unintentionally terrorized patients with similar remarks in the operating room. Because the patient is under anesthesia, doctors assume the patient is unaware of what's being said. But that's not necessarily true. Surgery patients under anesthesia may still hear what is going on around them. Even casual remarks in the operating room can be hazardous to our health!

How can we remember things that happen while we're unconscious? In this chapter, we explain how the line between consciousness and unconsciousness is blurrier than you might think. We take a look at how our brains produce consciousness, how our behavior interacts with our various states of mind, and why there appears to be a human need to alter our own consciousness.

Are You Self-Conscious?

The word *consciousness* gets a bad rap these days, probably because it was overused in the 1960s. Unless you're in California, you're likely to view anyone who talks about of a "higher consciousness" with some degree of suspicion. However, to the extent that a "higher consciousness" is greater self-awareness, it is the ultimate goal of most psychologists.

def•i•ni•tion

Consciousness refers to our awareness of ourselves and all things we think, feel, and do.

As you learned in Chapter 5, we sense much more than we pay attention to. If you think of your consciousness as the front page of your mental newspaper, attention is the lead story you can't resist reading. And your senses tell you the story is in the newspaper to begin with.

On the Wings of Fantasy

On a basic level, you're conscious that you are constantly perceiving and reacting to information in your environment. While you're gazing out your office window at the beautiful grass below, you can imagine yourself lying on the grass and taking a nap. You can wonder why the grass is so green outside and wonder what kind of fertilizer the groundskeeper uses. And on a higher level, you are aware that you're sitting at your office desk daydreaming about being outside and feeling guilty that you aren't getting your work done.

Consciousness is pretty complicated, and as a result, you aren't always aware of what's going on in your head. By the time you're grown up, you're so used to certain thoughts that entire conversations can be going on in your head without your even noticing them. But they're still having an impact.

You Are What You Think

Have you ever felt sad or angry but didn't know why? If you traced the origin of these feelings, chances are you'd discover they were caused by self-defeating or negative thoughts. "I must be a loser going to another get-together by myself" is a surefire bummer of a thought even if you're headed to the shindig of the year. If you let those thoughts stir around in the background of your consciousness long enough, you might decide to skip the party and go home and drown yourself in chocolate ice cream.

Being aware of your consciousness, on the other hand, gives you the power to understand your thoughts and feelings, evaluate their usefulness, and decide how much you'll let them influence your behavior. And the first step in raising your consciousness is to understand how your consciousness works.

Unconscious, Higher Conscious, and Everything in Between

For Freud, consciousness was just the tip of the iceberg. The stuff that crosses your mind lies on the surface, but underneath lurks a whole lot of murky activity completely outside of your awareness. In reality, consciousness functions more like an elevator in a building. It has different levels, and information travels back and forth between them. Let's take a brief look at the four other levels of consciousness:

◆ Nonconscious

◆ Preconscious

◆ Subconscious

◆ Unconscious

Automatic Pilot

Your nonconscious handles information that never makes it into consciousness or memory but is critical to bodily and mental activity; we don't have to remind our hearts to beat or our lungs to exchange air. It just happens.

Insight

With considerable practice, through methods like biofeedback or meditation, some people can even learn to partially control these automatic processes.

The File Cabinet

Your preconscious stores all the information you don't need right now but that you can readily access if something calls your attention to it. If I ask you what you had for dinner last night, your preconscious opens that file and transfers it to your conscious. You aren't aware of that information until it is asked for.

The Secret Service

Subconscious awareness involves information that's not currently in your conscious but can be retrieved by special recall or attention-getting devices. Information stored in your preconscious, such as what you had for dinner last night, was once conscious; however, you may be completely unaware of information stored in your subconscious. For example, under hypnosis, former surgery patients have recalled detailed operating room conversations they were completely unaware of overhearing.

The Clearinghouse

According to Freud, your unconscious handles memories, ideas, and emotions that are just too darned scary to face. While little evidence supports his theory, research does suggest that our unconscious may act as a clearinghouse for sorting through and storing all the data we encounter but don't attend to. London researchers recently discovered that invisible subliminal images do indeed register with us on a subconscious level. Functional MRI (fMRI) scans showed that our occipital lobes respond to subliminal images that reach the retina even if we have no impression of having seen anything.

Subliminal messages are least likely to register when our brain is concentrating on another task. Cramming for an exam is not the time to try out subliminal message diet tapes!

The various levels of consciousness work together to run a pretty organized outfit. While your conscious mind is busy focusing on day-to-day operations, other parts are in the background making sure the office is running smoothly. Of course, even the hardest workers need a break to recharge their batteries. Let's take a look at a "vacation" your consciousness gets every day: sleep.

Alpha, Beta, Delta—the Sleep Fraternity

Evolutionary psychologists believe that sleep evolved to restore your body from the wear and tear of the day and to help keep you out of trouble. Animals that eat low-calorie foods and thus need to spend a lot of time eating don't snooze much; animals that eat high-calorie foods sleep longer. Sleep is nature's way of keeping idle animals from going astray!

In human terms, the sleep club is definitely one in which you want to be an active participant. Sadly, few of us are stellar members; our great-great-grandparents were sleeping about an hour and a half more per night than we are now. Of all groups in Western culture, teens may be most likely to go for long periods of time without enough sleep, mostly due to early class schedules. Even kids under 5 aren't getting enough sleep; on average, they sleep 8.7 hours a night, far below the recommended 10–12.

New research suggests that poor sleep habits are as influential as poor nutrition and lack of physical activity in the development of chronic illness. The potential danger arising from sleep deprivation is obviously greater in some occupations than in others; according to NASA, one in seven pilots nods off at the cockpit, and pilot fatigue contributes to one-third of all aviation accidents. And if that isn't bad enough, preliminary studies indicate that, as counterintuitive as it seems, if you lose enough sleep, the disruption in your hormonal system may actually cause you to gain weight!

In particular, if you're getting six and a half hours of sleep a night or less on a regular basis, your body is more likely to undergo potentially harmful metabolic, hormonal, and immune system changes. You can't cheat and still get the benefit of regular sleep, either, by engaging in "sleep bulimia," a slang term used to describe weekday under-sleepers who try to catch up by sleeping late on the weekend. On a positive note, it might be easier to burn the candle at both ends as you get older; by age 80, six hours or less of sleep per night is normal.

All the World's a Stage

Until the electroencephalograph (EEG) came along, scientists thought sleep was a mindless activity. The EEG enables us to record the electrical activity of the brain at any stage of alertness and quickly put this assumption to rest. The EEG made it clear that when you fall asleep, your brain goes through four predictable stages of sleep.

Stage one is the brief transition stage that occurs when you're falling asleep. On an EEG, your brain waves slow down and become large and regular alpha waves. Stages two through four are successively deeper stages of true sleep. They show up on the EEG as an increasingly large number of slow, irregular, high-amplitude waves called delta waves.

def•i•ni•tion

REM sleep is characterized by rapid eye movement, brain activity close to that of wakefulness, and a complete absence of muscle tone. Most dreaming takes place during REM sleep; research now shows that REM sleep activates the limbic system, the most ancient part of the brain, which controls our emotions.

Insight

Are you working too hard? Learning a new sport? Take a nap. Recent research shows that a midday snooze can prevent burnout and that late-stage (early morning) sleep boosts motor skill performance by 20 percent.

To move through one full sleep cycle takes about 90 minutes. After that, you move through the entire sleep cycle four to five more times during the night. After the first full cycle, however, you start going backward through stages three and two. And instead of repeating stage one, you enter the most exciting period of the night: rapid eye movement (*REM*) *sleep*.

A lot goes on during REM sleep; in fact, if you couldn't see the person snoozing in front of you, the EEG would convince you he was wide awake. The EEG would show beta waves, the same irregular waves your brain makes when you're solving problems in the middle of the day. During your first sleep cycle, you spend about 10 minutes in REM sleep; in your last, you may spend up to an hour.

Trust me; we need our REM sleep. If we are deprived of REM sleep one night, our brain waves play catch-up the next. It may be that REM sleep plays a role in stabilizing our emotions and cataloging and storing memories. One product of REM has captured the imaginations of amateur and professional psychologists all over the world: dreams.

Doc, I Just Can't Sleep

If there's one thing worse than not having time to get enough sleep, it's not being able to sleep once you go to bed. Insomnia is a condition in which you have a normal desire for sleep, put in your seven or eight hours in bed, but for some reason, you can't sleep.

A variety of psychological, environmental, and biological factors, including the following, can cause insomnia:

- ◆ Anxiety or depression
- ◆ Environmental disturbances, such as noisy next-door neighbors, trains, planes, or automobiles

◆ Exercise too close to bedtime

◆ The use of stimulants (such as caffeine and chocolate) prior to bedtime

◆ Changes in work shifts

◆ Physical illness or discomfort

An estimated 20 percent of Americans have occasional sleep problems; one in 10 suffer from chronic insomnia. Insomnia can take different forms. You can have trouble falling asleep, wake up off and on during the night, or crash immediately and wake up at 3 A.M., staring at the wall until it's time to get up. The "cure" for insomnia can be as simple as earplugs or as complex as psychiatric medication or surgery.

Insight

While insomnia has long been recognized as a symptom of depression, recent research suggests that a lack of sleep can actually trigger it. A person who experiences insomnia for longer than five days should call a physician to see if a short-term treatment is warranted.

Brain Buster

Don't make decisions when you're sleep-deprived. Studies show that sleep deprivation can impair our ability to integrate emotion and cognition into decision making, especially when the decision calls for a moral judgment. Sleep-deprived participants, asked to judge "appropriateness" in personal moral dilemmas, had difficulty choosing a course of action and were prone to making choices they wouldn't have made in a rested state.

This Is Your Brain on No Sleep

Sleep deprivation can wreak havoc with our emotions, rendering us unable to put emotional experiences into the proper perspective and respond appropriately. Losing a night's sleep can transform us from rational humans into "emotional JELL-O."

fMRI studies suggest that if you're sleep-deprived, the amygdala—which processes emotions and alerts the body to protect itself in times of danger—kicks into overdrive. It shuts down the prefrontal cortex—which commands logical reasoning—and thwarts the release of chemicals that calm your fight-or-flight reflex. What happens? You overreact.

If for instance, your amygdala reacts strongly to a violent movie, the prefrontal cortex would normally remind your brain, *Hey, it's make-believe—settle down!* But if you're sleep-deprived, instead of connecting to the prefrontal cortex, your brain would connect to the locus coeruleus, an archaic part of the brain that releases noradrenalin to ward off imminent threats. The result is a combustible chemical reaction.

In experiments where subjects were shown gory images (e.g., mutilated bodies, children with tumors), the emotional centers of sleep-deprived brains were over 60 percent more reactive than those of subjects who had a normal night of sleep. In fact, clinical evidence has shown that some form of sleep disruption is present in almost all psychiatric disorders.

Psychobabble

Many primary care physicians are reluctant to prescribe sleep aids for individuals who are suffering from anxiety or mood disorders, believing that they may be more easily abused. Psychiatrists, however, are twice as likely to prescribe sleep medication, believing that the presence of anxiety or depression should not keep a patient from receiving appropriate treatment for their insomnia and recognizing that insomnia can actually exacerbate depression and anxiety symptoms, setting up a vicious cycle.

Another sleep disorder is excessive daytime sleepiness. This circadian rhythm disorder, which afflicts about 4 to 5 percent of the population, might sound hokey; after all, most of us would say we have sleepy spells during the day. But persistent daytime sleepiness can actually prevent you from functioning normally. Of course, before a doctor makes this diagnosis, he has to rule out a number of medical problems, because chronic fatigue is a symptom of a number of serious medical conditions.

Insight

If you're sleep-deprived, forget the sheep-counting. Recent research suggests that listening to soothing music for 45 minutes while lying quietly in bed may be the most effective sleep strategy. Also try to go to bed and get up at the same time every day (yes, even on the weekends) and get regular physical exercise (but not within three hours of bedtime).

Last and most life-threatening of the sleep disorders is sleep apnea, a condition most commonly found in overweight, older men. Sleep apnea is an upper-respiratory sleep disorder that causes a person to quit breathing while asleep. When the blood's oxygen level drops low enough, emergency hormones are secreted and wake the person up. He starts breathing again and falls back asleep. This cycle can literally happen hundreds of times each night. Not only is this exhausting, but without treatment, the sufferer runs the risk of literally dying in his sleep.

I Must Be Dreaming

What do your dreams mean? The answer to that question depends on whom you're talking to. According to Native American tradition, dreams are messengers from the spirit world. Dreamcatchers, wooden hoops filled with a web made from nettle-stalk cord, were hung over the baby's cradle to bestow pleasant dreams and harmony. The good spirit dreams found their way through the tiny center hole and floated down the sacred feathers to the baby. The bad spirit dreams got caught in the web and disappeared in the morning light.

Freudian psychologists think dreams serve two purposes. One, they turn disruptive thoughts into symbols. And two, they provide harmless ways for people to fulfill their darkest desires without suffering the social consequences.

Hard-core scientists suggest that a dream's major job is to provide group exercise for the brain's neurons. According to this somewhat skeptical view, dreams are simply an accidental by-product of random electrical discharges and the only reason they have any meaning is because the brain scrambles to add meaning after these discharges happen.

We don't really know although there is some scientific evidence that your psyche and your dreams are connected. People in stressful situations tend to spend more time in REM sleep; it's as if our psyches need more time to work things out. People who are going through similar life transitions often have similarly themed dreams (pregnant women commonly dream of having deformed children or problems with birth) and people who have survived a traumatic event often relive the experience in dreams.

Psychobabble

Have you ever had a dream in which you were falling off a cliff or showed up at an important event wearing only your birthday suit? Join the universal dream club. A majority of dreamers in 175 countries report similar dreams at least once. However, while universal dream themes exist, our culture fills in the details. While being chased seems to be a universal dream theme, in India you are more likely to dream of being chased by vultures. In Canada, bears are more likely to be your fantasy pursuers.

The Ticking of Your Biological Clock

All of us have biological clocks that affect our arousal and energy levels throughout the day. While biological clocks vary from person to person, they are amazingly consistent within the individual. So if your energy peaks at midnight, your clock is set for you to be a night person; you'll always have trouble jumping up at six A.M.

Your *circadian rhythm* is pretty sophisticated; it's a set of physiological activities that coordinate your hormones, metabolism, body temperature, heart rate, and, of course, level of arousal. Human biology is amazingly precise. Studies suggest that our internal body-clock is regulated by a pair of genes: the gene (appropriately named) CLOCK and its partner BMAL1. And researchers have now identified the chemical switch that triggers this genetic mechanism—a single amino acid (amino acids are the building blocks of proteins).

CLOCK acts as an enzyme and modifies the BMAL1 protein in a cell's DNA, tripping the switch on a genetic chain of events. In fact, around 10 to 15 percent of our genes are regulated by our circadian rhythms. But if this amino-acid modification doesn't go off as designed, your switch is thrown off, and that can lead to a host of disorders, such as insomnia, depression, heart disease, cancer, and neurodegenerative disorders.

Ticking clocks aside, human snoozers have more in common than you might think. Whether we're night owls or early birds, we're all tuned in to circadian rhythms, bodily patterns that repeat approximately every 24 hours. We all spend about one-third of our lives sleeping. But few things knock our consciousness for a loop like a lack of sleep!

def•i•ni•tion

Circadian rhythm means about a day—it's the clock that regulates your sleep-wake cycle. When it's disrupted by flying across several time zones, you get jet lag, which can involve fatigue, sleepiness, and subsequent unusual sleep and wake schedules.

Insight

Try to work out a school or work schedule that matches your natural biorhythms as closely as possible. And you can certainly cut down on relationship quarrels if your partner's clock ticks in sync with yours; it can be pretty frustrating if the time you most feel like snuggling is the time your partner feels like snoozing.

Altered Consciousness

Sleep (and dreaming) is one form of altered consciousness. Human beings have invented thousands of others. Roller coasters, meditation and yoga, and drugs and alcohol are all ways of expanding or altering our state of mind, and they seem to be a universal part of human nature. One benefit of altering our consciousness is that it shifts us out of our normal way of looking at things. By changing our focus, we can get a different perspective on ourselves and our problems.

People also alter their consciousness to avoid their problems or escape from reality. When it comes to mind-altering drugs, there can be a fine line between using them for relaxation, for fun, or as an escape. Let's take a look at four primary ways we can alter our consciousness and the pros and cons of each:

◆ Hypnosis

◆ Meditation

◆ Hallucinations

◆ Drugs

Look Deeply into My Eyes

It is truly amusing to see old movies that include hypnosis as part of the plot. Inevitably, a Svengali look-alike waves a gold watch in front of an innocent and naïve young woman, chanting, "Keep your eyes on the watch as it moves back and forth … back and forth …." His voice gets deeper, and we see her eyelids droop lower. She falls completely under his spell, and the audience spends the rest of the movie watching her try to get out of the spell.

Hypnosis doesn't really work that way. If you've ever been hypnotized, you deserve much more credit than your hypnotist. The single most important factor in hypnosis is the degree to which a participant has a "talent" for becoming hypnotized. Clinical hypnotists call this talent hypnotizability.

You're Getting Very, Very Sleepy

Your hypnotizability is the degree to which you respond to hypnotic suggestions. In a general sense, hypnosis is an induced state of awareness characterized by deep relaxation and increased suggestibility. A hypnotizable person is one who is able to truly immerse himself in the imagination and feeling of life experiences.

Since its inception more than 200 years ago, hypnosis has been cloaked in mystery and confusion—even professionals can't quite agree on what it is. It is *not* the result of gullibility or a deep-seated need to conform to social pressure. A subject under hypnosis is highly responsive to the hypnotist's suggestion; however, it is not a form of mind control. No one under hypnosis can be made to do something against his will, and you can't get stuck in a hypnotic state.

> ### Psychobabble
>
> Researchers have recovered a hypnotically induced, suppressed memory. A new hypnosis study has revealed the brain's "amnesia centers" as hypnotized subjects were told to forget, and then remember, a movie they had watched. Through brain scans, the researchers detected brain activity changes in the subjects' occipital, temporal, and prefrontal regions. The posthypnotic suggestion to forget induced a sort of amnesia, suppressing the memory in the early stages of the retrieval process, but when subjects were given the reversibility cue, MRI scans showed recovery of activity in the suppressed regions.

Hypnotize Your Way to Health

Researchers may disagree about the psychological mechanisms involved in hypnosis, but they do agree about the therapeutic benefit hypnosis can have in reducing the psychological component of pain. Children undergoing cancer treatment, for example, have successfully been taught to use their imagination to distract themselves from painful procedures. Watching a parent and child take a hypnosis-induced trip to Disneyland in the middle of an oncology ward is not only a powerful testament to the science of psychology, but it's also a testament to the human spirit.

A new study reveals that hypnosis may also slow the impact of dementia and improve quality of life. People living with dementia who received hypnosis therapy showed an improvement in concentration, memory, socialization, and overall motivation. It makes sense. You can see how hypnosis—which is a relaxation tool—might be effective for those who are aware of the onset of their dementia and become depressed and anxious over their gradual loss of cognitive ability.

For people who are hypnotizable, research supports the use of hypnosis in the treatment of headache pain, asthma, and a variety of dermatological symptoms. Unfortunately, for most people, hypnosis doesn't seem to help with smoking cessation, weight loss, or alcohol abuse. So if you were counting on a hypnotherapist to help you shed a few extra pounds, you'll be a lot better off investing your money in a good book on motivation techniques—or a gym!

Don't Bother Me, I'm Meditating

Meditation is another way of altering consciousness and one of the fastest-growing ways to alter our state—and with good reason. Anyone can learn it.

Transcendental Meditation, the form of meditation that has received the most scientific investigation, basically involves sitting comfortably with your eyes closed and focusing on a word or phrase you repeat silently to yourself. Practiced 15 to 20 minutes twice daily, it has tremendous health benefits. Over a five-year study, practitioners of Transcendental Meditation got sick less often (doctor visits decreased by more than 50 percent), drank less alcohol, felt less anxious, and felt more resilient and emotionally mature.

Insight

Mindfulness meditation, a practice which involves observing thoughts and feelings as they occur and gently refocusing on the present, is an effective adjunct therapy in progressive hospitals and has been found to help medical patients deal with pain, depression, and anxiety.

I Must Be Hallucinating

If you like having friends, hallucinations might not be the best way to alter your consciousness. Western culture has little tolerance for unusual perceptual experiences, and we tend to be afraid of people who have them. This attitude is not universal; in some cultures, people who hallucinate are viewed as spiritual leaders with a direct connection to the spirit world.

We're Not Talking Beads and Lava Lamps Here

It's easy to confuse hallucinations with illusions—we *all* see illusions. However, an illusion is a distortion of something that's there; a hallucination is seeing something that isn't there.

When you look at the flashing lights on a movie marquee, you see the illusion of a single light zooming around the edge of the sign. The appearance of movement in s tationary lights is common; they look that way to most of us. Most of us don't, however, "see" lights around the heads of the people selling tickets in the box office. If you do, then you're having a hallucination.

In general, hallucinations occur when your brain metabolism is altered from its normal level. They can be a symptom of many different diseases or conditions: high fever, an adverse reaction or side effect from a drug, ingestion of a hallucinogen, renal failure, migraines, or epilepsy.

In addition, under certain conditions, we might all see reality differently. Trauma can cause just about anyone to hallucinate; some Vietnam vets, for example, were bombarded with flashbacks, visual and auditory replays of traumatic combat scenes. And a significant number of ordinary people actually "see" or "hear" a deceased loved one within six weeks of his or her death.

Operating Under the Influence

And now, ladies and gentlemen, for the winner in the Most Popular Way to Alter Your Consciousness Contest: drugs and alcohol. Given the risks involved in this particular form of consciousness altering, it makes you wonder about the judges. Regular use of drugs and alcohol is so darned bad for you that it's hard for me to talk about it without sounding like the poster child for the "Just say no" campaign.

However, drug use does not always lead to drug addiction. Most teenagers try drugs and alcohol and the vast majority of them never become serious users. And yes, there are studies that suggest that one to two drinks a week can be good for your physical health, although if you have a strong family history of substance abuse, it's probably not worth the risk.

Some Pills Make You Larger

Psychoactive drugs—the ones that work on your brain and change your mood—are the ones most likely to become addictive. They attach themselves to synaptic receptors in the brain and block or stimulate certain chemical reactions. It is these chemical reactions that you experience as increased relaxation, lowered inhibition, or greater self-confidence. Psychoactive drugs affect your mental processes and behavior by changing your conscious awareness. Let's take a look at the five classes of major mood changers:

- Hallucinogens
- Marijuana
- Opiates

◆ Depressants

◆ Stimulants

Hallucinogens, also known as psychedelics, distort your senses and alter your perceptions. They can also temporarily blur the boundaries between you and the things around you. Someone on an acid trip, for example, may feel as if she is a physical part of the guitar she is playing, or she can "see" the musical notes floating around her.

Marijuana is often classified as a hallucinogen although it has some distinct properties of its own. The experience depends on the dose; small doses create mild, pleasurable highs, and larger doses result in long, hallucinogenic reactions. The positive effects include a sense of euphoria and well-being and distortions of time and space; the negatives include fear, anxiety, and confusion. Marijuana also impairs motor coordination, making it risky to smoke and drive.

Opiates are highly addictive drugs that suppress one's ability to feel and respond to sensations. Prescription versions are routinely used as painkillers. The most popular street version is heroin—users typically report a rush of euphoria when they first use it, followed by a trancelike state of relaxation, known as a "nod".

Depressants and stimulants are the most widely abused substances, although they tend to have opposite effects. Depressants, including alcohol, slow down the mental and physical activities of the body. They can temporarily relieve anxiety and stress but also quickly impair physical coordination and judgment.

On the other hand, stimulants like cocaine are uppers. They speed up mental and physical activity. Cocaine and amphetamine users report increased confidence and higher energy when they first start out. An overdose of amphetamines can cause frightening hallucinations, dramatic mood swings, and paranoid delusions.

Do you drink coffee? Smoke cigarettes? Have a few beers now and then? If any of the above apply to you, you're a psychoactive drug user. Of course, just because you rely on caffeine to get those peepers open or have an occasional drink at happy hour doesn't mean you're a psychoactive drug *abuser*. That determination depends upon many different factors, including the genetic die you were cast.

 Brain Buster

Self-medicating bad feelings with alcohol or drugs is trading off one problem for another. Don't believe me? Try volunteering a few hours at the local detox center.

Risking Addiction

Your risk for addiction depends many things—your personality, your genetic makeup, your coping skills, and your family history of drug and alcohol abuse. It also depends on your drug of choice.

Mood Alterer	Most Popular Drug	Risk of Dependence
Hallucinogens	LSD	No psychological, unknown physical
Cannabis	Marijuana	Unknown psychological, moderate physical
Opiates	Heroin	High psychological and physical
Depressants	Alcohol, Valium	Moderate to high psychological and physical
Stimulants	Cocaine, speed	High psychological and physical

Lethal Weapons

Another way of looking at the dangers of a psychoactive drug is to compare the amount of the drug it takes to get the desired results (the effective dose or ED) to the dose that will kill you (the lethal dose or LD). For example, many people don't realize they can literally die from a single drinking binge. Fifteen drinks in an hour can usually do it, as the families of some college students have unfortunately found out. That's because, during a hard-drinking party, the usual social dose and the lethal dose can be too close for comfort.

On the other hand, it is almost impossible to die of a lethal dose of marijuana; the ED and LD are very far apart. You might die of smoke inhalation first!

That doesn't make marijuana a great idea. New research shows that learning and memory problems caused by marijuana smoking persist for at least a week after you've smoked. And while the brain seems to physically recover from heavy use after a month of abstinence, heavy marijuana users consistently have significantly lower income and educational levels than nonusers. And, of course, if the authorities find a bale of marijuana in the garage, you can find yourself in the local lockup.

The Monkey on Your Back

Being addicted to drugs has been called "having a monkey on your back." And for good reason! The harder you try to shake it off, the harder it clings to you. It demands to be fed at all hours of the day and night. It screams louder when you try to ignore it. No matter where you go, it's always there.

Psychobabble
Teens may get hooked on cocaine (and relapse more easily) than adults because developing brains are more powerfully motivated by drug-related stimuli. During adolescence, dopamine (a neurotransmitter that signals "reward") may trigger strong messages between frontal cortex learning area to an area involved with reward and addiction. This biochemical express lane forges stronger memories for rewarding stimuli, including the people, places, and events associated with the drug.

It All Sneaks Up on You

Continued use of certain psychoactive drugs lessens their desired effect over time, so more of the drug is needed to achieve the same effect. The body develops a tolerance to the substance. To make matters worse, physiological dependence often goes hand in hand with tolerance. So at the same time that a user needs more of the drug to get the desired mental effects, he needs more of the drug for physical reasons, too.

After a while, addicts only feel "normal" when using. When they try to cut back or quit, they go through a process called withdrawal. Unpleasant physical and mental symptoms occur when a physically addicted substance abuser discontinues the drug.

The Addictive Mind

Psychological dependence can take place with or without physical dependence. When cocaine use became popular in the early 1980s, common wisdom held that it was not physically addictive but was highly addictive psychologically. It was easy for people to become emotionally dependent on the "pseudo-confidence" that cocaine generated.

The psychology of drug use is amazingly complex. Even the immediate effects of drugs on your consciousness may be influenced more by your state of mind than by the physical properties of the drug. The mood that you're in before taking the drug, your expectations of what will happen, and your history of prior drug use all play a crucial role. If you've ever had a few drinks when you were down in the dumps and then wound up feeling more depressed, you know what I mean.

Straight from the Lab

Bad Dreams: A Warning Sign   Young children who have chronic nightmares tend to have other problems as well. Since nightmares usually begin before age 6, and peak by age 10, treatments of early anxiety symptoms in preschoolers and their concerned parents may help prevent more serious problems in later years.

Meditate Your Way to Relationship Harmony   In a compassion meditation study where Tibetan monks were asked to generate feelings of compassion and loving kindness for others, fMRI scans showed significant activity in the insula—a brain area that detects emotions, maps bodily responses to emotion (e.g., heart rate and blood pressure), and distributes that information to other parts of the brain.

Weekend Jet Lag   Teens who stay up late on school nights and sleep in over the weekends are more likely to perform poorly in the classroom. A study that examined circadian rhythms, sleep quality, and morning vigilance showed that forcing the internal body-clock to reset itself, then reset itself again on Monday mornings, leads to poor academic performance at week's start.

The Least You Need to Know

- Consciousness is the awareness of who we are and all the things we think, feel, and do.

- Sleep is a form of altered consciousness that probably evolved to restore our bodies after all the wear and tear of the day and to keep our ancestors from having too much idle time on their hands.

- REM sleep, the most important of the four sleep stages, is the time we dream, and it seems to help stabilize our mood and store our memories.

- A complex combination of psychological and physical factors cause sleep disorders, including insomnia, excessive daytime sleepiness, and sleep apnea.

- Four ways that people have purposefully altered their consciousness are meditation, hypnosis, hallucinations, and psychoactive drugs.

- The use of any psychoactive drugs requires close attention as the line between desire and dependence can be hard to recognize.

Get That Through Your Thick Skull!

In This Chapter

- Learning which associations we're all members of
- Thorndike's cats and Pavlov's dogs
- Facing irrational fears
- Discover the mind-body learning connection
- Meet the operant conditioning gene
- Banishing bad habits

This chapter is all about learning: *how* we learn, *what* we learn, and *when* we learn. We introduce you to some interesting psychologists who, through their work with animals, pioneered our understanding of learning. You'll learn about the power of association and how our interpretation of the consequences of our actions influences our learning curve. And we tell how to apply the magical principles of learning to get rid of irrational fears, alter bad habits, and maybe even improve your love life!

Helpless

"I can't do it," four-year-old Sabrina whines as she hands you the magazine and scissors. "You do it for me." "But Sabrina," you argue. "You haven't even tried. I know you can cut out that picture yourself." Inwardly, you sigh, frustrated and confused by Sabrina's constant clinging and refusal to attempt new things.

What's going on with Sabrina? Why is she constantly demanding assistance from you while other children her age are eager to do things for themselves? Doesn't she want to learn to do things for herself?

We all need a little help now and then, but if we need it all the time, then we may have learned helplessness. Children as young as age four can develop the belief that nothing they do makes any difference, and, as a result, they give up and stop attempting new tasks. Not only does learned helplessness interfere with our ability to take charge of our lives, but many psychologists believe it causes depression. *Learning* obviously isn't just about developing new skills; it's also about believing that we can.

def•i•ni•tion

The term **learning** refers to any process through which experience at one time can change our behavior at another.

Learning About Learning

We've all heard the saying "Experience is the best teacher." And learning theorists would say it's the *only* teacher. By definition, learning involves changing our behavior in response to experience. And, since much of psychology deals with the effects of experiences on our behavior, learning about learning is important.

Learning is one of those psychological concepts that's easy to understand but hard to see. Since learning is something that happens inside us, it can never be observed directly. Teachers give tests because they are looking for evidence, or lack thereof, that we are learning the material in their class. Similarly, learning researchers have to depend on measurable improvements in performance when they're studying learning. Whether it's a grade on a calculus test or the number of trials it takes a rat to find food in a maze, behavior is the ultimate evidence of learning.

But the benefit we get from learning is not confined to behavioral change. Learning also expands our options. For example, even if you decide not to quit smoking right now, by learning effective smoking-cessation strategies, you can increase your ability to quit in the future. Similarly, an inspiring book (perhaps like the one you're reading?)

can increase your appreciation for its subject, motivate you to learn more, and affect your attitudes and choices for years to come.

Insight

Early predictors of reading and writing difficulties include a delay in perceiving and processing the subtleties of a person's voice, sluggishness in naming familiar objects, and difficulty remembering names. The good news is that training and practice, especially in the late preschool years, can significantly reduce learning difficulties. Visit www.lukimat.fi for free exercises and learning disability detection tools.

Does the Name Pavlov Ring a Bell?

Association is the key to learning. A man by the name of Ivan Pavlov first discovered this fact and used it to teach old dogs new tricks. As a scientist, he spent many years studying the digestive processes in dogs. To speed along his studies, he frequently asked his assistants to put powdered meat into the dogs' mouths so they would salivate. One day, he noticed a strange thing: his dogs were drooling before the meat powder even touched their tongues. The sight of the food or the sound of food being poured into the dish sent these dogs into a frenzy of anticipation.

So Pavlov began deliberately controlling the signals that preceded the food. In one famous experiment, he sounded a bell just before placing the food in the dog's mouth. After several pairings of a bell with food, the dogs would drool in response to the bell sound alone. Pavlov was so fascinated with these events that he abandoned his original work on digestion, discovered *classical conditioning*, and changed the course of psychology forever.

If you're a pet owner, you're probably wondering what all the fuss was about. After all, within a week after getting your pet, you probably observed your little darling drooling at the sound of an electric can opener or the sound of food being poured into a dish. At the time, however, Pavlov's discovery was revolutionary.

For the first time, scientists could systematically study human learning by varying the associations between two stimuli and charting out what affect this had on a subject's

def•i•ni•tion

In **classical conditioning**, two stimuli become so closely associated that one of them can elicit the same reactive behavior as the other.

response. Not only did Pavlov's research help us understand and use the power of positive association, but it ultimately paved the way for understanding the role that negative associations can play in the development of irrational fears and phobias.

On a gloomier note, classical conditioning has also given advertisers a lot of effective ammo. Every time they pair sex with their products, they're betting that the association between the two will have you drooling just like Pavlov's dog!

Learning the Classics

You, my friend, have been conditioned—and I'm not talking about your hair. Maybe you formed an association between a certain piece of music and a relationship breakup, and now you feel sad every time you hear that song. Maybe you came down with a stomach virus after eating poached salmon, and now every time you even smell fish, you feel nauseated. Maybe you've been in a recent car accident; now, even though you know it wasn't your fault, you're a little nervous about getting behind the wheel. Whether you know it or not, you have thousands of associations living in your head and many of them were instilled by classical conditioning.

Coming In on Cue

Here's how these associations happen: human beings are biologically programmed to respond in certain ways to certain things in the environment. We salivate when we eat food; we jump if we hear a sudden, loud noise; we jerk our hand away if we touch something hot. These natural reactions are unconditioned responses; we don't have to learn them.

Over time, though, we start noticing that certain cues might help us predict when an environmental stimulus (food, noises, burning) is about to appear. From an evolutionary standpoint, such cues signaling danger or benefits would be highly adaptive. Learning that a grizzly bear makes a certain noise in the bushes would be pretty useful information, especially if it keeps you from having to wait for physical confirmation of his presence! Similarly, the smell of something burning is a pretty good clue that fire is near and gives you the chance to respond to the smell in the same way you would to a fire—take it seriously and investigate immediately before you get burned.

Where There's Smoke

In the fire example, the smell of smoke is the conditioned stimulus, and fire is the unconditioned stimulus. You'll naturally avoid fire—it's your unconditioned response to the unconditioned stimulus signaling danger. But over time, you'll associate that smoke smell with danger and respond to it as if the smell were an actual fire. What separates unconditioned responses from conditioned ones is learning—you have to *learn* conditioned responses. The urge to avoid or escape is an unconditioned response to fire, but it's a conditioned response to the burning smell because you had to learn it.

Here's another example:

Unconditioned Stimulus	Intimate body contact (heavy petting)
Unconditioned Response	Physiological arousal (getting "turned on")
Environmental Cue	Chanel No. 5

At first you get this sequence of behaviors:

Unconditioned Stimulus (petting)

+Environmental Cue (the scent of Chanel)

Unconditioned Response (getting turned on)

After several repetitions, you can cut directly to the chase, so to speak:

the scent of Chanel = getting turned on

In this example, intimate bodily contact is a natural stimulus for physiological arousal. On the other hand, contrary to what advertisers may say, you have not been biologically programmed to respond to the perfume Chanel No. 5. But if you've had enough pairings of this perfume and sexual arousal in, say, the back seat of your car on Friday nights, you can bet that even a whiff of Chanel will send those hormones flying!

Learning Isn't Always Fun

It would be great if all our classical conditioning were built on positive associations. Unfortunately, life doesn't work that way; negative stimuli also conditions us. Sometimes, in fact, learning can be downright aversive.

If the door to your office has a lot of static electricity and you get a jolt every time you touch it, the shock is an example of painful unconditioned stimuli. Your unconditioned response is avoidance. Over time, you may start approaching this innocent door with dread and devise all kinds of quirky strategies for avoiding the shock—using a handkerchief to open the door, always going in after someone else, or rubbing your feet on the floor to ground yourself. This kind of learning is called aversive conditioning: learning an aversion to something that was previously perceived as harmless.

Aversive conditioning can be very powerful because of the fear associated with it. Not only do you want to avoid the object of your aversion, but you also become afraid of it. Fear is a hard emotion to unlearn—in fact, when strong fear is involved, conditioning can take place after only a single pairing between a neutral stimulus and an unconditioned stimulus. And it can last a lifetime.

> **Psychobabble**
>
> Agoraphobia is an example of classically conditioned fear. People who have panic attacks often associate their physical symptoms with the environment in which they occur. In an attempt to ward off future attacks, they'll restrict their activities until they're literally unable to venture out of the house.

During World War II, the signal used to call sailors to battle stations aboard United States Navy ships was a gong. To personnel on board, this sound was quickly associated with danger. Researchers found that even 15 years later, the sound of the old "call to battle stations" struck fear in the hearts of the navy veterans who had been aboard those ships.

If you find yourself having an irrational reaction to something, chances are you're the victim of negative classical conditioning. For this to happen, though, certain conditions must be met.

Learning About Meaningful Relationships

Timing is as critical in classical conditioning as it is in good joke telling. During your lifetime, you'll form thousands of associations among the situations and events in your life. Not all of these become classically conditioned. For example, that song might give you the blues because it was playing on your car radio during a relationship breakup, but you probably aren't heartbroken every time you drive your car.

That's because not all associations are created equal. In a child's early years, just about anything resembling the conditioned stimuli will prompt a similar response. A child who has been bitten by a large dog will initially regard all dogs with suspicion. This is called stimulus generalization. It seems evolution first teaches us that it's better to be safe than sorry.

Developing Discrimination

Over time, though, we become more discriminating. We learn to distinguish between the conditioned stimuli and its relatives. The child begins to realize that one bad dog does not spoil the whole bunch and that she doesn't have to spend the rest of her life fearful of *all* dogs. When Little Albert realizes the rat causes the gong to ring, while Santa Claus brings toys, he is engaging in stimulus discrimination.

Classical conditioning is a lot like dating; it's a balancing act between discriminating too much and responding the same way to too many stimuli! To find the proper balance, we rely on certain clues to help us figure out which associations are worth learning and which ones are not. Three stimulating qualities are most likely to result in classical conditioning:

> **Psychobabble**
>
> Some apparently meaningful associations are just the result of an accidental pairing between two stimuli. These accidents can cause superstitious behavior, like the athletes who believe their "lucky" socks will help them win the championship!

 ◆ Contrast

 ◆ Contingency

 ◆ Information

Contrast

The smell of your mother's favorite perfume is more likely to stir up fond memories of her if you smell it in the middle of a business meeting than if you get your whiff of it at a perfume counter. You are more likely to notice stimuli that stand out from others around them. At the perfume counter, her perfume may get swamped by competing fragrances and lose its power over your associations.

Contingency

The most powerful associations occur when the conditioned stimulus *reliably* predicts the unconditioned stimuli. If you wear a certain perfume every time you and your boyfriend are together, he'll be more likely to associate that fragrance with you.

Information

Conditioned stimuli are most likely to be conditioned if they provide *unique* information about the unconditioned stimulus. Where there's smoke, there isn't always fire, but the smell of something burning generally means there is. That's why you're likely to immediately investigate the smell of something burning; the smell provides important, generally reliable information about danger.

Think of the Consequences

Classical conditioning is a powerful form of learning. From an early age, we learn to associate good feelings with certain things in our environment and bad things with others. These feelings affect what we do. But the environment shapes our behavior in a much more direct way, and parents rely on it every day when they interact with their child. It's the fact that every act has consequences, and the method of teaching which uses this principle is called *operant conditioning*.

Parents know the power of rewarding a child for good behavior and punishing him for bad. Children do, too. They quickly learn that, no matter how good it might feel to punch a brother's lights out, the consequences can be pretty painful. They also learn to do things which have negative associations, like homework, if there's a big enough reward at the end.

> **def•i•ni•tion**
>
> **Operant conditioning** encourages us to behave in ways that exert influence or control over our environment. When a rat learns that pressing a lever gets more food, it has been operant conditioned to push the lever. When a child screams and gets her way, she's been conditioned the same way.

Kitty in a Box

Psychologist Edward Thorndike was the first to get us thinking along these lines. While Pavlov was preoccupied with drooling dogs, Edward Thorndike was studying cats as he watched them try to escape from puzzle boxes. At first the cats tried a number of things that didn't work. Sooner or later, though, they would accidentally do something that enabled them to escape.

Escape was the reward for their efforts—and when Thorndike put them back into the box, they usually found the escape route a little sooner than the last time. After several trips to the box, the cats would immediately trip the lever or push the button that let them out.

Thorndike coined the term *law of effect* to explain his observation that consistently rewarded responses are strengthened and those that aren't are gradually weakened or stamped out. Just as natural selection favored the evolution of characteristics that enabled the human species to survive, the law of effect says that behavior that results in good consequences will be selected again in the future.

Teaching Old Dogs New Tricks

What about behaviors that would never occur if animals were left to their own devices? In Thorndike's box, even the dumbest cat could eventually figure out the right answer. On the other hand, consider assistance animals for people with disabilities. These dogs are trained to act as the arms and legs for their disabled partners. These dogs are taught to open doors, pull wheelchairs, and dial 911 in case of an emergency. We'd be hard-pressed to find an animal that spontaneously turns the light off and on. This form of training is called shaping.

Shaping is a process of reinforcing the small steps that lead in the direction of the desired behavior. Here's how it works: let's say the trainers want Spot to learn to dial 911 in an emergency. First, they look for a natural behavior. For example, Spot wanders over by the telephone on his own, so the trainers reward him with a treat. Every time he walks a little closer to the phone, Spot gets a treat so he starts wandering over there more often.

> **Psychobabble**
>
> Shaping has been successfully used to help mentally impaired adults learn complex behaviors like getting dressed by themselves. Every small step in the right direction, such as pulling a shirt over the top of the person's head, is rewarded by a token the person can exchange for food or another treat.

Eventually Spot only gets the treat if he actually touches the phone. This training progresses until Spot actually learns how and when to pick up the receiver and dial the number. It's a long, difficult process, and not every animal can learn to do it, but it may mean the difference between life and death for Spot's owner.

There's More Than One Way to Skinner a Cat

Thorndike may have gotten the operant conditioning ball rolling, but B. F. Skinner really invented the game. Not only did he invent much of the lingo we use to talk about the process, but his views also dominated psychology for almost 50 years. According to Skinner, understanding another person was simply a matter of understanding the consequences he experienced during a lifetime. To Skinner, operant conditioning and psychology were one and the same.

Insight

If you speak softly, you don't have to carry a big stick: soft reprimands spoken only to the misbehaver are more effective than loud scoldings in front of others. And physical punishment must be immediate and consistent to be effective. However, keep in mind that even when physical punishment works, it sends the message that physical aggression is okay if you're big enough to get away with it.

If you're trying to understand why your boss does the things she does, Skinner would tell you to evaluate the consequences of her actions. For example, what do other employees do when the boss yells at them? Do they snap to attention or get their work done more quickly? And don't forget to take a look at the boss's reinforcement history; maybe that habit of yelling was begun because yelling was the only way she could get attention at home. One thing is certain—somewhere along the line, your boss was rewarded for yelling and, as a result, you suffer the consequences.

Calling in Reinforcements

Skinner called this phenomenon reinforcement—any consequence that increases a particular behavior over time. A smile, a pat on the back, and a gold star are all examples of positive reinforcers (as we get older, we might prefer a raise or a vacation). Reinforcers can also be negative: if you take out the garbage so your mom won't nag you, then her nagging is a negative reinforcer for your garbage duty. As moms know all too well, if those potential consequences weren't there, kids might be tempted to slack off.

Oddly enough, constantly rewarding someone is less effective than rewarding him only occasionally. Say that Tommy, age three, begs for a toy once in a while when you're at the grocery store. You always say no, but once, tired and not in the mood for whining, you get Tommy the toy. Bad idea! Tommy got reinforced for the wrong behavior. Now *every* time you're at the store, he'll whine for a toy—just in case. Chances are it will take months of "no" before he'll go back to just asking occasionally.

The Terminators

Reinforcers explain how we learn new behaviors and why we keep doing them. But if you want to unlearn a behavior, you have only two choices: extinguish it or punish it.

"Just ignore it." Children are given this advice by parents and teachers alike. If you withhold the reinforcers, the behavior is likely to stop over time. But if you're a child, the time it takes to extinguish your classmate's torture can feel like a lifetime, which is why kids routinely reject this advice.

Nipping Bad Behaviors in the Bud

And kids aren't fools—trying to extinguish behaviors rarely works outside of a laboratory because it's difficult to remove all the reinforcers for a particular behavior. He may give his classmate the silent treatment for a year, but if other classmates are giggling every time his teaser calls him "four-eyes," he is still getting *plenty* of reinforcement. In the real world, extinction is much more likely to work if it is paired with *positive* reinforcement of the desired behavior.

"Spare the rod and spoil the child" refers to correcting bad behavior with punishment. Like extinction, punishing a behavior (e.g., spanking, grounding) reduces its frequency over time. The purpose of punishment is to reduce pleasure, either by taking away something the person likes (dessert, attention, TV privileges) or by giving the person something he doesn't like (a swat on the behind, a parking ticket).

Of Carrots and Sticks

But punishment works best in conjunction with positive reinforcement. All companies have disciplinary procedures for unacceptable behavior, but in recent years, one of the most popular recommendations to managers seeking to build employee morale has been to "catch them doing something *right*." If managers see exemplary employee behavior (like getting to work on time, meeting deadlines, or working well with their team), they're encouraged to single out that employee and praise, praise, praise.

The theory is this: a manager can move employees in the right direction with praise, while the disciplinary policies are the "big stick" for behavior that gets out of line.

> **Psychobabble**
>
> New research suggests that learning actually modifies neurons on a synapse-by-synapse basis.

Drosophila and the Operant Conditioning Gene

Thanks to the fruit fly Drosophila, we've discovered an operant conditioning enzyme: the protein kinase C. Researchers blocked this enzyme in a batch of fruit flies, then monitored their learning performance in a cylindrical drum flight simulator (if you can picture that!).

> ### Psychobabble
>
> The enzyme protein kinase C has also been linked to habit formation (e.g., a drug habit), suggesting that compulsive drug-taking might be reduced or even prevented by medication that interferes with the protein kinase C pathway.

The flies-in-training had no trouble learning to avoid an unpleasant heat blast as long as they were given a warning. So for example, if a flashing blue light was paired with a heat blast every time Drosophila headed right, she learned to quickly stay to the left. However, when the signal (blue light) was removed, she couldn't figure out what to do; she flew randomly even though the heat still blasted when she made a right turn. The Pavlovian learning (classical conditioning) somehow suppressed her operant potential when this enzyme was deactivated.

The Mind-Body Learning Connection

Our thoughts and our actions are deeply intertwined, so perhaps it's no surprise that one can help the other. In one study, researchers hooked up a Nintendo Wii to a computer and tracked subjects' arm movements as they sorted unfamiliar symbols into pairs. As they gained mastery over the task, their bodies also seemed to gain confidence; their movements got quicker, and they pressed the Wiimote more firmly.

The reverse is also true. Using gestures while learning may actually help us retain information. For example, in one study, kids who gestured at math problems were nearly three times more likely to remember what they'd learned than nongesturers. Ninety percent of the algebra students who learned algebraic concepts using gestures remembered the concepts three weeks later, whereas only 33 percent of speech-only students did. Even more interesting, 90 percent of students who learned by gesture alone—no speech at all—retained what they learned three weeks later.

How to explain this phenomenon? Gestures may enhance learning because they tap into our normal daily "acting" experience—we learn by interacting with our environment.

Oh, Those Thumb-Sucking, Nose-Picking Kids!

My name is Joni, and I'm a recovering nail biter. From the time I was about four years old, I chewed my nails in spite of icky potions, stern admonishments, and dire threats. No matter what my parents tried, I gnawed my nails down to the quick for years. Gradually, this habit disappeared, seemingly on its own.

Childhood habits seem to start out as coping strategies. Children may resort to these behaviors when they are stressed, bored, tired, frustrated, unhappy, insecure, or falling asleep. The habit may be calming and soothing to the child. Most of the time, behaviors like thumb sucking, hair twirling, and nail biting are just part of a phase that the child will outgrow, not a serious medical problem.

> **Psychobabble**
>
> The hormone ghrelin, which is produced in the stomach, has a direct, rapid, and powerful influence on our hippocampus—a higher brain area critical to learning and memory. Turns out we may actually learn best on an empty stomach, since ghrelin is in highest circulation during the day and when the stomach is empty.

No matter how annoying the behavior, yelling, calling attention to the habit, and punishment do not usually stop the behavior (and may even increase it!); but praise, positive rewards, and patience are likely to help. Instead of beating your head against a stubborn wall, try the following strategies:

- ◆ Try ignoring the behavior. Giving it a lot of attention (even though it's negative) may actually encourage the behavior. Many kids prefer negative attention to no attention at all.

- ◆ Praise your child for good behavior. When you catch her being good, tell her you noticed. For example, tell her you noticed she wasn't chewing her nails, and mention how nice she looks.

- ◆ Be realistic. It is nearly impossible for a parent to stop a child's behavior until the child becomes interested in stopping.

- ◆ Don't try to make too many changes all at once. Start by focusing on one or two of the most bothersome or dangerous ones.

- ◆ Try to figure out what may be stressing your child. Give him chances to talk to you about things that might be worrying him—and make eye contact and listen.

- Let your child make decisions by giving him acceptable choices. For example, "Would you rather have toast or cereal for breakfast?" This will help him feel in control of some aspects of his life and reduce stress and frustration.

- Present natural and logical consequences for problem behavior. The purpose here is to get kids to make the right decision, not to bend them to your will.

- Be patient, firm, and kind. Follow through every time on the natural and logical consequences.

- State rules positively, and explain the reasons behind them. Make sure your child understands the consequences for breaking the rule.

- And follow the golden rule of parenting: be in agreement about the same rules and how to enforce them. If Mom says "No" but Dad says "Who cares?", it's a losing battle.

The Behavior Police

It's easy to confuse negative reinforcement with punishment. However, they actually have opposite effects on our behavior; punishment decreases behavior while reinforcers increase it.

If you treat your significant other well to avoid getting jilted, the possibility of getting dumped is a negative reinforcer. However, if, in spite of your good behavior, your significant other is dumb enough to dump you, you might feel punished for all your good deeds. And as you know if you've been the rebound in a rebound relationship, you might not be so inclined to make such an effort in the next one!

Terminators and Reinforcers

Kind of Stimulus That Follows Response	Do More of the Same (Reinforcer)	Cease and Desist (Punisher)
Positive	Reward, food, prize, praise, thanks	Criticism, disapproval, pain
Negative	Easing pain or discomfort	Privileges, ignoring, grounding

Psychobabble

Reading Learning Disorder (LD) gets the lion's share of attention, but new research shows that school-age children are as likely to have Math LD as Reading LD. In fact, the cumulative incidence of Math LD through age 19 ranges from 6 percent to 14 percent. And boys are more likely to have Math LD than girls.

The Cognitivist View

Cognitive psychologists were uncomfortable with Skinner's strict emphasis on behavior. They concluded that the thoughts and feelings we have about the consequences of our behavior play a key role in the way we learn. They realized, for example, that we don't all feel the same way about what happens to us; a reward for one person might feel like punishment to another. In fact, cognitive psychologists believe that the meaning you assign to the things that happen to you might be more important than the actual events themselves.

Attitudes and Expectations

Cognitive psychologists believe that classical conditioning occurs because the conditioned stimulus creates an expectation that the unconditioned stimulus is about to appear. When your cat hears the clanging of his food dish, he has come to expect dinner, and he'll run to his dining spot.

Cognitive psychologists also think operant conditioning is much more complicated than a simple history of rewards and punishments. They believe learning involves understanding the means to the end, in addition to any thoughts and feelings we have about those means and ends. Whether we eat depends much more on how hungry we are than it does on our knowledge that opening the refrigerator will give us access to food. That knowledge gives us options; it doesn't force us to use them.

Experience and Interpretation

One factor that influences our present "take" on things is our past experience—we're likely to compare current consequences with past ones and be either happy or sad about the results.

Psychobabble
A side effect of television violence is psychic numbing, a reduction in emotional arousal while witnessing violence. In situations where people are getting hurt, reducing the emotional distress of witnesses is a risky social outcome.

My mom's savvy dating advice clearly took this into account: "Don't ever start out doing things for a man that you don't plan on continuing." Mom was warning me of the negative contrast effect, the well-documented tendency for people to compare rewards and be highly dissatisfied with any drop in reinforcement. We're much better off capitalizing on the positive contrast effect in our love lives, starting out slowly and then being kinder and more generous as time goes by.

Attention, Please!

We also learn by what we choose to pay attention to, and people tend to pay more attention to emotionally charged events. For instance, you may spend weeks trying to teach baby to say "ball," only to have her ignore you. But then, when she's in the car and someone cuts you off in traffic, she may happily parrot your yelling "*&@*#!!" in a heartbeat! On the positive side, we can use our emotions to motivate us, such as when we put the swimsuit picture on the refrigerator to help us stick to a diet or when we list all the payoffs for getting out of debt.

Modeling Behavior

Thank goodness we don't always have to learn from our own mistakes. We learn a lot about getting along in the world by observing those around us. We can climb the corporate ladder by imitating our boss; we can learn from our parents' mistakes; and we can set a good example for our children. All these are examples of observational learning.

The positive version of this is known as modeling. Children really do model what their parents do much more than what their parents say. Not only do they imitate their parents' behavior, but they also learn general rules about what is acceptable and what is not by watching others. Grownups also use modeling—if you're going to a party and aren't sure of the protocol, you may spend a few minutes watching the people around you to get the lay of the land.

Unfortunately, modeling doesn't always influence us in a positive direction. Albert Bandura found that children who first watched adults beat up a large inflated Bobo doll were much more aggressive in their play with the doll than children who had watched a gentle adult or no adult at all. Not only did the children imitate the adults' behaviors, but they were also amazingly creative at devising torture strategies of their own. Obviously, they were learning more than certain punches and kicks: they were getting the message that aggressive behavior in general is okay.

Don't Be Scared

Fear is easy to learn and hard to unlearn. Classical conditioning helps us understand irrational fears as links between our emotions and certain stimuli in the environment. We might fear heights, for example, because we have associated them with falling, or we might fear public speaking because we associate it with rejection or humiliation.

One powerful way of unlearning fear is a therapeutic technique called systematic desensitization. You don't have to have a full-blown phobia to benefit from systematic desensitization. Let's say you've been wanting to ask your next-door neighbor out for a date but just haven't gotten up the nerve to do it. Learning the three steps of systematic desensitization will help in any situation, including asking someone on a date. Try these steps:

1. **Write down several situations related to your fear, ranging from least scary to most scary.** Before you declare your undying love to your neighbor or die from the fear that the thought of this evokes, list several baby steps that would get you where you want to go—on a date. Ask a friend's advice about approaching your beloved. Ask a friend to role-play your date request, and then start making small talk with your neighbor. The key is to break down your fear into 10 to 15 small, progressive steps. No matter what your fear is or how strong it is, there's always a first step that's acceptable to you.

2. **Relax.** Relaxation is a powerful weapon against fear because the two feelings are incompatible (see Appendix B for relaxation resources). Assertiveness can also help. As a last resort, try running a couple of miles before you knock on your neighbor's door: it's hard to get all worked up about anything when you're tired!

3. **Just do it—gradually.** Sooner or later, you've got to enter the lion's den. Start with a mildly stressful event, and work your way up. If you've listed your 15 scenarios and role-played with your friend through the first 14, the toughest one isn't going to be all that tough.

> **Psychobabble**
>
> Children with obsessive compulsive disorder develop irrational fears (fear of germs or dirt, getting sick, and so on) and develop obsessive behaviors (repetitive handwashing, avoiding doorknobs, etc.) to cope with those fears. New research shows that cognitive behavior therapy that helps these children practice gradually confronting those fears (for example, practicing touching a doorknob) is twice as effective as medication.

Getting Rid of Bad Habits

Bad habits are often a combination of classical and operant conditioning. Take smoking, for example. There's the classical conditioning component—over time, you associate smoking with many other things you do. You reach for a cigarette after a good meal; you smoke in the morning when you're drinking coffee; and you light up when you're angry or stressed. These activities and conditions become deeply ingrained triggers for smoking.

Then there are the reinforcements. Inhaling smoke causes a temporary relaxation response, so smoking "feels good." If you're physically addicted, your body is rewarded by the nicotine entering your bloodstream. If you use smoking to handle strong feelings or stress, smoking gives you a time-out to regroup and think through the situation. You're caught in a conundrum—you have all these cues and triggers that remind you to smoke and the reinforcements that encourage you to keep smoking.

That's why bad habits can be so persistent—in the short term, they're so gratifying. I might know that eating a chocolate cake will probably add a few pounds, but man, does that chocolate taste good!

Getting rid of bad habits is more than a matter of willpower; you must systematically disarm your triggers, get rid of your reinforcers, and gradually replace your behavior with healthier alternatives. Here are a few tips for starters:

- ◆ **Avoid the triggering situation.** If you smoke with your coffee, then switch to tea. If you can't go to the mall without buying a new outfit, don't go window shopping. If you scarf down potato chips whenever they're around, don't keep them in the house.

- ◆ **Change the situation.** Sit in the nonsmoking section of the restaurant. Put your clothes purchases on hold for a few hours, and then decide whether you will go back and buy them. Don't eat with the television on or standing at the kitchen counter.

◆ **Substitute.** Keep a journal of your thoughts and feelings that lead to your habit and find other ways to fill these needs. If you shop in response to stress, take a bubble bath instead. If you eat when you're emotionally hungry, get a massage or talk on the phone to a friend. The next time you get angry and feel the urge to light up, try a short power walk first.

Chances are, you came into this chapter with some bad habits; whether it's overeating, smoking, or overspending, most of us have at least a few. And in spite of the negative consequences, we keep doing them over and over. I hope, however, this chapter has given you some insight into breaking them. If you've decided to move from insight to action, be patient with yourself; expect some slip-ups; and remind yourself it takes time. In the next chapter, we shed some more light on why we keep doing things that aren't in our best interest.

Straight from the Lab

Why Your Kid Can't Learn from His Mistakes   New fMRI research shows that 8- and 9-year-olds react strongly to positive feedback but barely respond at all to negative feedback. But the opposite is true in 12- and 13-year-olds (and adults, for that matter). For them, the cognitive control center (cerebral cortex) is more strongly activated by negative feedback. They're more capable of processing punishment and using it to learn from their mistakes.

Is Online Learning for You?   Only 30 percent of online course enrollees actually complete their courses. Distance learning is a good learning style match for quiet, introverted personalities who enjoy a degree of anonymity but also works for determined, responsible types who excelled in traditional educational settings if they put their minds to it.

Overlearning Doesn't Last   Continuing to study material immediately after you've mastered it is a waste of time. That extra drilling pays off for a week or so, but by four weeks, completely disappears. Massing all your studying on a single topic into a single session also reduces long-term retention. It's better to walk away for a while and return later.

Get Smart—Take Art!   Performance and appreciation of the arts enlarges cognitive capacities, according to a new study. Arts-motivated children develop attention skills and strategies for memory retrieval that apply to other subject areas. And the bonus is, the arts create a more enjoyable planet to live on.

The Least You Need to Know

- Learning is the ability to profit from experience.

- Much of what we learn is the result of either classical or operant conditioning.

- Classical conditioning occurs when we realize that a previously neutral stimulus predicts an unconditioned stimulus; if this happens often enough, we start responding to the neutral stimulus alone.

- If a child is rewarded for a temper tantrum, chances are he'll do it again; if he doesn't get what he wants, he'll eventually stop—this is called operant conditioning.

- It's not just the consequences that influence our behavior, it's also how we interpret the consequences—a reward for one person can be perceived as a punishment for another.

- Understanding how we learn can help us unlearn fear or get rid of bad habits.

Chapter 8

Coming to Terms with Your Memory

In This Chapter

- ◆ The court jester of the brain
- ◆ Understanding how memories are made
- ◆ How to remember what you learn about memory
- ◆ Sleep, memory's silent partner
- ◆ The truth about false memories
- ◆ Exploring the mystery of repressed memory

For a while stories about recovering repressed memories were all over the news. Then came stories about how those recovered memories were false. How is it possible to remember something that never happened? And how does a repressed memory happen, anyway? Memory distortion research has clearly shown that information that happens after the event, such as stories other people tell us about what happened, can actually be incorporated into our memory. And studies have given us lots of insights into the process by which the mind buries memories we find difficult or painful.

In this chapter, we take a look at the myths and realities of memory: how memory normally works and when and why it doesn't. We'll look at some ways to improve memory and how research into false memory and repressed memory has improved our understanding of both these phenomena. As you read this chapter, remember one thing about memory: it's a lot trickier than you might think!

Kidnapped!

Until he was 15, child psychologist Jean Piaget believed his earliest memory was of nearly being kidnapped at the age of two. He remembered vivid details of the event, such as sitting in his baby carriage and watching his nurse defend herself against the kidnapper. He remembered the scratches on his nurse's face and the short cloak and white baton the police officer was wearing as he chased the kidnapper away.

However, the kidnapping never happened. When Piaget was in his midteens, his parents received a remorseful letter from his former nurse, confessing she had made the whole story up and returning the watch she had been given as a reward. Piaget's memories were false.

But the nurse's confession raised a whole new mystery: how did Piaget remember something that never happened? Obviously, Piaget heard many accounts of this story as a child, imagined what he thought had actually happened, and projected this information into the past in the form of a visual memory.

The Court Jester

Your brain can store 100 trillion bits of information, so why can't you remember the name of the person you sat next to in homeroom during high school? If your brain is a kingdom, surely your memory is the court jester. It's always playing tricks. You can, for example, instantly recall things you never tried to learn (like popular song lyrics), and you can easily forget things you spent hours memorizing (like material you studied for an exam). Often we remember the things we want to forget and forget the things we want to remember.

Whether you want it to or not, your brain stores all kinds of information. *Implicit memory* holds all those trivial facts, song lyrics, and general nonsense your brain files away while you're concentrating on

def·i·ni·tion

Implicit memory is your ability to remember information you haven't deliberately tried to learn. **Explicit memory** is your ability to retain information you've put real effort into learning.

something else. Most of the time, however, researchers are more interested in studying *explicit memory*, which contains the information you consciously process.

Learning About Remembering from Forgetting

When it comes to memory, the proverbial elephant is way ahead of human beings—members of our species constantly forget, misremember, and make mistakes. These mistakes offer valuable clues about how memory normally works. For example, researchers have found that people forget for one of three reasons:

1. They don't get it to begin with.

2. They had it, but they lost it.

3. They have it, but they can't find it.

These mistakes reflect a failure in one of the three mental operations necessary for memory: encoding, storage, and retrieval.

For instance, I simply can't seem to remember my high school classmate's name, even though I sat next to her for years. Chances are, my memory failure is due to a retrieval problem—I have her name filed someplace but can't seem to open the right filing cabinet. If someone gave me a hint, I could probably come up with it. This hint would be a retrieval cue—information that will help me find and open the right cabinet.

On the other hand, if I was so self-absorbed in high school that I never learned my classmate's name in the first place, my inability to come up with it now would be an encoding problem. One clue that a memory failure is due to encoding is the ineffectiveness of hints or clues to prompt memory.

If I never knew that my classmate's name was Denise Johnson, she could tell me her nickname, her initials, and her astrological sign—and I still wouldn't have a clue.

Alternatively, maybe during my high school years I was a conniving social climber, and Denise didn't fit my idea of the popular crowd. Maybe I learned Denise's name long enough to ask her for a favor a few times but then didn't think it was important to remember on a regular basis. In this case, my failure to remember her name would be due to a storage problem.

Psychobabble

Amnesia is the partial or complete loss of memory and can be caused by physical or psychological factors. A traumatic event can trigger psychologically based amnesia; memory almost always returns after a few days. Soap operas aside, very rarely does a person lose her memory for large portions of her life.

Memory Tests

When teachers give us tests, they aren't just measuring our capacity for learning. They're also measuring our ability to remember what we've learned. The way we're tested can have a lot of influence over the results because different types of tests engage our retrieval system differently.

Encoding, storage, and retrieval are the three mental operations required for memory. If you can't recall the items on your grocery list but could recognize the items among a list of foods, your recognition is better than your recall. Recall questions give fewer cues than recognition questions and thus seem harder.

The Long and Short of It

Think of memory in terms of threes. The three mental processes of memory—encoding, storage, and retrieval—happen at least three times as the information makes its way through the three memory systems: sensory memory, working memory, and long-term memory.

Photographer at Work

Have you ever noticed how you can still hear the sound of the television right after you turn it off? That's your sensory memory. Sensory memory holds an impression a split second longer than it's actually present, to ensure you have time to register it. Its goal is to hold information long enough to give you a sense of continuity but short enough that it doesn't interfere with new information coming in.

Sensory memories capture impressions from all our senses. If the impression is a sound, the memory is called an echo, while a visual sensory memory is called an icon. At the most, our sensory memory works for only a second or two, but what it lacks in stamina, it makes up for in volume. If I showed you a picture with a bunch of words on it for only a fraction of a second, you could only say about four of the words before you started forgetting the rest. However, you'd be able to pick out as many as nine because we can remember words faster than we can say them!

Psychobabble
Meet Jill Price, a woman who remembers everything that ever happened to her and whose memories keep playing back in random order. Held hostage by her memory, she has described her life as a series of videotapes of her life, randomly playing back different events. She has been diagnosed with an extremely rare disorder, hyperthymestic syndrome, a day-to-day life invaded by her past.

The Organic Data Processor

Working memory has more stamina than sensory memory, but it's no marathon runner; it only lasts for about 20 seconds. It works through and sorts information transferred from either long-term or sensory memory. When information enters our working memory, it has already been reorganized into meaningful and familiar patterns. For example, when subjects are asked to recall lists of letters they have just seen, they are much more likely to confuse letters that sound similar—like B and T—than letters that look familiar. And this is yet another example of how misremembering teaches us about remembering!

Working memory preserves recent experiences or events. Because it is short term, its capacity is limited. When the items are unrelated, like the digits of a telephone number, we can hold between five and nine bits of information in our working memory. There are, however, strategies that expand our working memory—like rehearsing. When you look up a phone number and repeat it before you dial, you're using a rehearsal strategy to enhance your working memory.

> **Insight**
>
> Use it or lose it? New research suggests that five minutes of math a day can help ward off the negative mental effects of aging. Don't like math? Okay, try some crossword puzzles, or read a few pages out loud.

The Curious Curator

Just as a museum curator takes care of historical artifacts, our long-term memory collects and stores all the experiences, events, facts, emotions, skills, and so forth that have been transferred from our sensory and short-term memory. The information ranges from your mom's birthday to calculus equations. Essentially, the information in long-term memory is our library of knowledge of the world; without it, we'd be lost.

Long-term memory stores words and concepts according to their meaning and files them next to similar words and concepts already in our memory. The smallest unit of meaning we can store is a proposition: an idea that expresses the relationship between ideas, objects, or events. "Men are from Mars; women are from Venus" is a proposition about men and women. "Trees have green leaves" is another proposition. Some psychologists believe these propositions are the building blocks of long-term memory, while others believe we store verbal information in propositions and visual information in images.

Brain Buster _____

> Coffee jump-starts short-term working memory. After being dosed with 100mg of caffeine (approximately two cups of coffee), participants showed improved short-term memory skills and reaction times. But be careful as there can be too much of a good thing; drinking coffee to excess can cause anxiety, the jitters, and lower concentration.

Visiting the Museum

We all have different "artifacts" in our mental museum, but the structure of our "buildings" looks remarkably similar. Think of your memory museum as having two wings, with each holding different kinds of information. These wings are actually two types of long-term memory—procedural and declarative.

I Was Only Following Procedure

The procedural "wing" of your memory museum stores "how-to" information. Remembering how to ride a bicycle, tie your shoelaces, and put on your makeup are all stored in your procedural memory. All the skills you learn consist of small action sequences, and it is these skill memories that get implanted in your long-term memory.

Skill memories are amazingly hardy. Even if you haven't ridden a bike in 30 years, the memory comes back amazingly fast once you have your behind on the seat and your feet on the pedals. The frustrating thing about skill memories, though, is that they are difficult to communicate to others. Ask a gold-medal gymnast to tell you exactly how she does her stuff on the balance beam, and she can't. And if she tries to consciously think it through while she's doing it, chances are her performance won't be as good.

Well, I Declare!

Declarative memory, on the other hand, deals with _what_—the facts. It's the part of our memory that enables us to survive school, succeed at Trivial Pursuit, and win friends and influence people. Unlike procedural memory, declarative memory requires conscious effort, as evidenced by all the eye rolling and facial grimaces we see on the faces of people taking their SATs. Remembering the directions to the dance studio is an example of declarative memory; remembering how to dance is procedural.

The declarative wing of your memory museum has two rooms, one for episodic memory and the other for semantic memory. Episodic memory stores autobiographical information, such as thoughts, feelings, and things that happen to us. Semantic memory is more like an encyclopedia; it stores the basic meaning of words and concepts.

When autobiographical information enters long-term memory, it is tagged with a time stamp and the context in which it took place—a kind of marking that doesn't appear to happen with information stored in procedural memory. On the other hand, you probably can't remember exactly when or where you learned your multiplication tables. When you do remember when or where you learned factual information, it is often because an emotional experience was attached to it. My brother remembers when and where he learned his multiplication tables because he was rapped on the knuckles several times for not practicing them as part of his third-grade homework. Sometimes episodic memory can greatly assist semantic recall!

> **Psychobabble**
>
> Research indicates that all of us have some degree of amnesia. Most of us can accurately recall what has happened in the last half of our lives. If you're 20 years old, you can remember the past 10 years. If you're 60, your memory's good for the last 30. Your 10-year-old child can recall the last 5. For most of us, the rest is a blur.

You've Got Rhythm

Some researchers have suggested that memories occur when different regions of the brain unite. For example, the memory of a dog might unite smell, sound, appearance, and name.

By measuring the electrical rhythms that parts of the brain use to communicate with each other, a team of researchers at the University of Arkansas for Medical Sciences and Johns Hopkins University showed that when someone has a memory of a dog, the thalamus, an important region of the brain that connects areas together, actually regulates the rhythms that connect brain regions. Now that's a pretty sweet move!

Now, Where Did I Put That Thought?

It happens to most of us about once a week. We see someone we've known for years, yet his name suddenly eludes us. We remember other things about this person, like where we met or past conversations we've had. But, temporarily, his name escapes us. Frustrated, we exclaim, "But it's right on the tip of my tongue!"

The tip-of-the-tongue experience has intrigued psychologists since the 1800s. Long-term memory preserves information for retrieval at any later time; a tip-of-the-tongue experience appears to be a breakdown in this retrieval process. Putting information into memory is only half the battle. We still have to find it when we need it. Retrieval failure demonstrates an important concept in long-term memory—the difference between accessibility and availability. Long-term memories may be available somewhere in our mental filing cabinet, but we can't always access them.

> **Insight**
>
> Bad at names? Use the person's name out loud three times in the first few minutes after meeting, and you are much more likely to remember it later.

Generally, when you're trying to retrieve a memory, you'll simply use retrieval cues—mental or environmental prompts that help you retrieve information from long-term memory. For example, the options presented in a multiple-choice question help you recognize learned material. Retracing your steps is another useful retrieval aid—especially when you lose something (like your car keys!).

Retrieval cues work because they capitalize on your memory's natural tendency to organize and store related concepts and experiences together. Of course, if you'd just put the keys in the same place every time, you wouldn't lose them! And, as you're about to see, you wouldn't have so many retrieval failures if you encoded memories right in the first place.

Will You Gain Wisdom or Grow Senile?

Contrary to popular belief, forgetfulness is not an inevitable part of growing old. However, many elderly people consistently list memory loss as one of the most critical problems they face. Are their complaints accurate? That depends on what kind of memory they're talking about. For example, aging has relatively little effect on short-term memory. Young adults and seniors differ, on average, by less than one digit in the number of numbers they can hold in short-term memory.

Coming to (Memory) Terms

Some information in short-term memory is transferred and stored in long-term memory, and it is this kind of memory elderly adults have in mind when they complain about forgetfulness. Their most prominent complaint is remembering the names of people they met recently. Laboratory tests (using lists of words to be remembered) reveal that a moderate decline in memory for recent events accompanies normal aging. Some elderly adults remember as well as many young adults, indicating that this decline is a general pattern and not the inevitable fate for every person over 60.

Long-term memory for remote events (things that happened years ago) is pretty consistent over time. All of us forget personal information at some point during the first five to six years after it's been acquired. What's left after that usually sticks around. In general, elderly adults do have more trouble remembering some things—like when they last took pain medication (temporal memory) and where they left their umbrella (spatial memory)—but if they use cues as reminders of things they need to do, they are no more absent-minded than the rest of us. However, if an elderly person seems to show true memory problems, it is important to get an evaluation by a physician. Many medical conditions can mimic Alzheimer's: vitamin deficiency, small strokes, even depression. And many of these conditions are treatable.

> **Psychobabble**
>
> Alzheimer's disease causes brain deterioration in middle or later life, usually after age 65. Family history plays a role in about 40 percent of people with early-onset Alzheimer's. While we still haven't solved all the mysteries of Alzheimer's, new studies suggest that quinolinic acid, a neurotoxin, may play a key role in speeding the onset and progression of the disease.

Get It Right in the First Place

The way we put information in has a lot to do with how easily we can get it out. Have you ever studied for a multiple-choice test and then been ambushed by an essay exam? It's not a good feeling. No matter how prepared you were for multiple choice, chances are you didn't do as well with the essays. If you're smart, the way you prepare for an essay test is by memorizing the "big picture"—general information about the topic, broad concepts, and an overall analysis of the material. On the other hand, concrete facts and specific distinctions are most easily translated into multiple-choice tests.

Since long-term memory stores information logically and meaningfully, it makes sense to organize information when you first encode it in memory. Let's say you're really interested in the psychology of memory and want to maximize the chances that you'll remember the information in this chapter. One of the best encoding strategies was developed by Francis Robinson in 1970. It's the SQ3R method: Survey, Question, and Read, Recite, and Review.

How does it work? Let's use this book chapter as an example. First, *survey* the chapter—take a quick look and get an idea of how it is organized. Second, develop some *questions* about each subheading.

Insight _____

Think getting older is a bummer? Nip that attitude in the bud. Studies show that keeping a positive attitude about aging can extend a person's life by seven and a half years, which is longer than gains made by exercising regularly and not smoking. And the more you believe you can control your memory, the more likely you are to employ adaptive memory strategies (e.g., mnemonic devices, written reminders, and retrieval cues) and the less you worry about forgetting.

Then _read_ the chapter, and write down the answers to the questions you had. After that, without looking, _recite_ out loud those answers you wrote down. Now, _review_ all the material again, and keep reciting information aloud.

The SQ3R method makes the most of your long-term memory's natural organizer. Surveying helps your brain get organized. Questioning assists in breaking the information down into manageable chunks and also makes it more meaningful to you. Reading, reciting, and rehearsing all work to store the information. And, of course, taking the time to use these encoding strategies helps you overcome one of the critical personality traits that leads to forgetfulness—plain, old-fashioned laziness!

Hooked on Mnemonics

"Use i before e except after c." "Thirty days hath September, April, June, and November." "In 1492, Columbus sailed the ocean blue." No, I haven't regressed to the third grade. I'm giving you examples of mnemonics: short, verbal devices that encode a long series of facts by associating them with familiar and previously encoded information.

Mnemonics help us encode information in a creative and distinctive way, which makes it much easier to recall. Acronyms and jingles are commonly used mnemonics. AT&T is easier to remember than American Telephone and Telegraph. Marketers devise clever jingles and rhymes to build product recognition and keep that annoying commercial playing in your head long after you've changed the channel.

Psychological research has studied three types of mnemonic strategies: natural language mediators, the method of loci, and visual imagery.

Using natural language mediators involves associating new information with already stored meanings or spellings of words. Creating a story to link items together is an example of using natural language mediators. For instance, to remember the three stages of memory, you might say, "It doesn't make sense (sensory memory) that she's working (working memory) so long (long-term memory)."

The method of loci could help you remember a grocery list. Imagine a familiar place, like your office or bedroom, and mentally place the items on various objects around the room. When you need to recall them, take a trip around the room and retrieve them.

Visual imagery is a third mnemonic device. In this method, you just create vivid mental pictures of your grocery items. Mentally picturing a cat mixing shampoo and eggs to make cat food would certainly create a lasting impression on your memory.

Insight

Getting ready for a high-school reunion? Get out that yearbook, and you're sure to be "Most Popular." Forty-eight years after graduation, students were only able to recall 20 percent of their schoolmates' names. But after looking at old photos, they could name them 90 percent of the time.

Mnemonics Boosters

All mnemonic images are not created equal. Our brains prefer some cues over others; positive over negative images, vivid/colorful over bland/dull, and funny/peculiar over normal. Using all your senses and giving your images movement are added memory-enhancers.

Insight

Are you having trouble remembering difficult information? Don't say it, sing it! Many medical schools teach their students songs with familiar tunes but new words to help them memorize anatomy, diseases, and so on. Don't believe me? Ask your doctor to sing the "Supercallifragalistic" song—it probably won't be the words you learned!

Warning: Under Construction

Your memories are often under construction. They can change with time, and your past history, current values, and future expectations influence them. In addition, they can be strengthened, or even built, by social influence.

How accurate and reliable is memory? It's a hard worker, but it gets easily confused. Memory studies show that we often construct our memories after the fact and that we are susceptible to suggestions from others to fill in any gaps. A police officer can screw up a victim's identification of an assailant just by showing a photograph of the suspect in advance of the lineup; the lineup is contaminated by the photograph and makes it harder for the identifier to know whether the victim recognizes the suspect from the crime scene or the photograph.

And don't rely on your gut instincts to improve your memory. Research clearly shows that the fact that we feel certain about a memory doesn't necessarily mean it's accurate.

Sleep: The Silent Partner

Sleep improves the brain's ability to remember information. But sleep does not simply passively protect memories; rather, sleep plays an active role in memory consolidation.

Most sleep researchers agree that sleep strengthens procedural or "how-to" memories. There's still some debate about the degree to which sleep benefits declarative or "what" memory, but some new studies suggest that people who sleep between learning and testing are able to recall more of what they learned (for example, word pairs) than those who don't sleep after learning.

Here's how new memories are created …

Daily events become short-term memories in the hippocampus and are then transferred to a long-term storage area in the neocortex or new bark, which is the gray matter covering the hippocampus. And all this happens while we snooze.

The 90-Minute Power Snooze

And here's good news! You don't have to wait till bedtime to consolidate your memory. A 90-minute nap helps speed up learning by consolidating long-term memory faster. You can not only grab an extra forty winks without guilt, but you can also make yourself smarter, faster.

When subjects performed a motor task they had practiced repeatedly earlier in the day, those who had a 90-minute nap after learning showed a distinct performance improvement by that evening, while those who were napless showed none. After a night's sleep, the two groups performed at the same level, though the nappers improved much faster than the napless.

A snooze can also prevent interference. When subjects learned a new task two hours after practicing the first task, the second task interfered with the memory consolidation process. The learners showed no performance improvement, either that night or the following morning—unless they had taken a 90-minute nap in between the two learning sessions. Interestingly, the snooze-induced improved performance didn't show up until the next morning; both nappers and nonnappers showed the same amount of learning interference the evening in which the two tasks were introduced. Apparently, daytime sleep between learning activities shortens the amount of time it takes for procedural memories to become immune to interference and forgetting.

Use It or Lose It

Brain stimulation—building your brain reserve over your lifetime and staying mentally active during old age—may reduce the risk of Alzheimer's and other dementias by as much as 46 percent! Learning appears to slow the development of two brain lesions that are the hallmarks of Alzheimer's, suggesting that seniors who keep their minds active may actually be able to delay the onset of the disease. Even mild learning (e.g., reading, crossword puzzles) may reduce both the pathology and cognitive decline of Alzheimer's.

Physical exercise helps our brains, too. Studies show that older people who exercise three or more times per week have a 30 to 40 percent lower risk of developing dementia. Even light activity, such as walking for half an hour three times a week, may boost mental skills such as abstract reasoning by 15 percent. One study shows that just 20 minutes of activity each day can prevent memory deterioration and lead to a lasting improvement in overall memory function. And exercise has the important emotional side effect of boosting overall mood and well-being.

Insight

Brain Training for Adults, a Nintendo package of cerebral workouts aimed at grey gamers, is said to improve mental agility and even slow the onset of dementia and Alzheimer's disease. If you prefer something a little more social, take an acting class. One study shows that older adults who participated in a four-week acting course showed significantly improved word-recall and problem-solving abilities—gains which persisted four months later.

The Truth About False Memories

In 1990, teenager Donna Smith began therapy with Cathy M., a private social worker who specialized in child abuse. Although Donna had entered treatment reporting she had been sexually abused by a neighbor at age three, Cathy M. repeatedly interrogated

Donna about her father. After several months of pressured questioning by her therapist, Donna lied and said her father had touched her. When her therapist reported her father to the authorities, Donna tried to set the record straight, only to be told by her therapist that all abuse victims tried to recant their stories.

Donna was confused but continued to work with Cathy M., who continued to make suggestions and reinforce any suggestion of incest. Over the course of several months, Donna came to believe that her father had been a chronic sexual abuser. She began "remembering" him practicing ritual satanic abuse on her younger brothers. Only after she was placed in foster care away from her therapist did Donna regain her perspective and the courage to tell the truth. By this time, her family was emotionally and financially devastated.

Psychobabble

Were you watching television the morning of September 11, 2001? If so, do you remember seeing images of the first plane, and then the second plane, hitting the towers? If you do, you are one of the majority of Americans who has a false memory about this! Only the video of the second plane hitting a tower was shown on that day. The video of the first plane striking the other tower was not shown until the following day—September 12. But almost three out of four of us remember it incorrectly.

Sorting the True from the False

Unfortunately, Donna's experience is not an isolated incident. There are similar stories of adults who enter therapy to resolve some conflict or gain happiness and, with the therapist's "support," suddenly start remembering traumatic abuse or incest. As these *repressed memories* are unleashed, the person may take long-delayed action such as criminal prosecution or public denouncement.

def•i•ni•tion

A **repressed memory** is the memory of a traumatic event retained in the unconscious mind, where it is said to affect conscious thoughts, feelings, and behaviors even though there is no conscious memory of the alleged trauma.

But while false memories do occur, by no means are most memories of child sexual abuse false. Given that studies estimate that one out of every four girls will be sexually exploited before the age of 18, odds are that anyone who remembers child sexual abuse is telling the truth. The rare occurrence of false memory is likely to happen when a vulnerable person hooks up with a therapist who, intentionally or not, implants false memories through hypnotic suggestion, by asking leading questions, or by defining abuse and incest so broadly that, in retrospect, innocent actions suddenly take on menacing meaning.

One recent large-scale study sought to corroborate memories of childhood sexual abuse through outside sources. Subjects were sorted into three categories:

- Spontaneously recovered: Victim had forgotten but spontaneously recalled the abuse outside of therapy with no prompting

- Recovered in therapy: Victim recovered the abuse during therapy, prompted by suggestion

- Continuous: Victim had always been able to recall the abuse

Overall, spontaneously recovered memories were corroborated about as often (37 percent of the time) as continuous memories (45 percent). Interestingly, memories recovered in therapy could not be corroborated at all. While the absence of corroboration doesn't imply that a memory is false, this study suggests that memories recovered in therapy should be viewed cautiously. There is a very real fear that a few misguided therapists and their clients could undermine the true stories of thousands of others.

We also know that false memories about childhood events can have long-term effects on our attitudes and behavior. Researchers falsely suggested to subjects that egg salad made them ill as a child; then they offered them various sandwiches—including egg salad. When the experiment was repeated four months later, subjects gave the egg salad lower evaluations than the other sandwiches and lower evaluations than those of subjects who hadn't developed false memories.

From the Mouth of Babes

When courts instruct a witness to tell the whole truth and nothing but the truth, they're telling him not to lie. But they're not allowing for a third possibility: a poor (or false) memory. And they generally assume the memory of adults is more reliable than that of children.

But maybe not.

Studies conducted by Cornell University's Valerie Reyna and Chuck Brainerd suggest that children may be more reliable court witnesses because they depend more heavily on a part of the mind which records *what actually happened*, while adults depend more on another part which records the *meaning of what happened*. Meaning-based memories are largely responsible for false memories—especially in adults, who have far more meaning-based experience than children.

Apparently, people store two types of experience records or memories: verbatim traces and gist traces. Verbatim traces are memories of what actually happened. Gist traces are records of a person's understanding of what happened or what the event meant to him or her. You can see how gist traces could stimulate phantom recollections or vivid illusions of things that never happened; for example, misremembering that the object in a person's hand was a gun when it wasn't. Since witness testimony is the primary evidence in many criminal prosecutions, false memories are a primary reason for convictions of innocent people.

> ### Psychobabble
>
> Studies show that emotionally negative events stimulate higher levels of false memory than neutral or positive events; in fact, the likelihood of false memory increases with the degree of aversion a person feels.

Exploring Repressed Memories

I vividly remember the exact moment the Columbia space shuttle exploded on February 1, 2003. My mom could vividly remember where she was and what she was doing when she heard that John F. Kennedy had been assassinated. Nineteenth-century researchers discovered the same phenomenon when they asked people what they were doing when they heard that Abraham Lincoln had been shot.

These memories are called flashbulb memories, long-lasting and deep memories that occur in response to traumatic events. Not everyone has flashbulb memories, and not every tragic situation causes them. Recent research, in fact, has questioned the validity of the flashbulb effect, but what it does support is our tendency to remember upsetting or traumatic events, particularly the emotions we felt.

Memory research shows that, during times of extreme stress or trauma, we can store the emotional experience separately from the personal facts of what actually happened. Studies show that under conditions of extreme stress, the hippocampus (the part of our brain that records personal facts) may dysfunction, causing the details of the traumatic event to be poorly stored. On the other hand, the amygdala, that part of our cortex that stores emotional memories, often becomes overactive when under stress, enhancing the emotional memory of a trauma. As a result, a 25-year-old might be terrified of flying because of a traumatic plane ride as a child and yet not remember the childhood experience that triggered the fear.

Real-life traumas in children and adults—such as school ground shootings or natural disasters—are generally well remembered. Complete amnesia for these terrifying episodes is virtually nonexistent. People who have experienced war traumas, even children, generally remember their experiences. In fact, many of them report having great difficulty getting the events out of their dreams or minds; they can't repress them even though they want to.

We know people forget things. We know people later remember things they had forgotten earlier. And psychologists generally agree it is quite common to consciously repress unpleasant experiences, even sexual abuse, and to spontaneously remember such events long afterward.

Intuitively, the ability to block out repeated childhood trauma seems like a pretty good survival strategy; if you can't get away from it physically, at least you can in your mind. I've had therapy clients who were victims of documented incest (the perpetrator had confessed and been sent to prison), and yet siblings who were also victims claimed to have no memory at all that abuse had ever occurred.

Straight from the Lab

Extinguishing the Trauma Response   Researchers have identified a small brain protein that switches off the bad feelings associated with trauma memories: Neuropeptide S. This discovery may help researchers develop new drugs to treat conditions such as posttraumatic stress disorder and other panic disorders.

Women Win Most Memory Games!   Episodic memory significantly favors women, a new study shows. Women excel at remembering words, objects, pictures, or everyday events, but men outperform women in remembering symbolic, nonlinguistic (visuospatial) information, such as remembering the way out of the forest. Women are better at remembering where they put the car keys, which requires both verbal and visuospatial processing, and remembering faces, especially female faces.

The Fear Factor Glue   How do fearful memories get stuck in the brain? The glue may be a protein called beta-catenin. While a "fear factor" gene controls how neurons fire in the brain during imminent danger, beta-catenin may be a hub for synaptic changes that occur during memory formation. This finding suggests that medications that inhibit beta-catenin may help prevent post-traumatic stress disorder by interfering with memory formation after trauma.

The Least You Need to Know

- Our memory doesn't mind very well—it often misremembers, forgets, and makes mistakes.

- The three mental operations required for memory are encoding (putting information in), storage (filing it away), and retrieval (finding it); forgetting is a failure in one of these areas.

- Mnemonics are very effective memory aids that help us store information in a way that enables us to easily recall it later on. And the use of written reminders and other memory strategies can be especially useful for the elderly, who have more problems remembering recent events.

- Sleep is believed to be actively involved in consolidating memory, especially procedural memories.

- Mental and physical exercise can slow the impact of degenerative neurological diseases, such as Alzheimer's.

- False memories can fool us and professionals as well; although not likely, it is possible to remember serious childhood trauma that never happened. As far as forgetting traumatic things that *did* happen, the truth is still up in the air. However, the vast majority of people remember ongoing traumatic events.

Part 3

The Forces Are with You

What's the most important thing that a detective looks for when solving a crime? Elementary, my dear Watson: it's motivation. Almost all of human behavior is driven by motives, whether or not we're conscious of them at the time. Here's where you'll get the scoop on all the forces that cause us to do the things we do—our feelings, our drives, our thoughts and, during tough times, our stress level.

9

What's Your Motive?

In This Chapter

- ◆ The body's balancing act
- ◆ The dieter's dilemma
- ◆ Sex, a state of mind
- ◆ The roots of sexual orientation
- ◆ The thirst for power and the drive to achievement

As a child, Michael Phelps couldn't sit still, couldn't focus, couldn't buckle down. His third-grade teacher wondered if he'd ever be motivated to focus on anything. But on August 18, 2008, he set seven world records and won his eighth Olympic gold medal for swimming the butterfly leg on the United States 4x100-meter medley relay. His third-grade teacher wrote Phelps' mother, remarking that perhaps Michael had never lacked focus but, rather, a goal worthy of his focus.

Today, his coach, who calls him "the motivation machine," says Michael can turn just about anything into motivation: failure, success, money, feedback from others. Michael is a shining example of how the impossible can become possible.

Motivation is what makes us do what we do. But where does motivation come from? How do we stick to our diet, study when we feel like sleeping, and keep going when life tries to knock us down?

In this chapter, we explore the drives that power human behavior and the juicy motives, like hunger and sex; you'll see why you need them and what you'll do to get them. We explore the mind-motive connection and the pluses and minuses of having a brain that can influence our base instincts. And we visit some of the "higher" motives, such as the need for achievement, and give you a chance to find out what motives drive you to work every day.

It's a Jungle in Here

How are you feeling right now? Hungry? Sleepy? Angry? Your mental state will cause you to pay attention to some things over others; if you're hungry, the fantasies of home cooking might get sandwiched in between these appetizing paragraphs. If you're feeling down, you might have begun this book by reading the chapter on mood disorders. Clearly, your mental state affects your thoughts and your actions.

But what makes you hungry or sleepy or angry? What causes you to behave in a certain way at a particular time? When we look at the complexity of human motivation, one thing becomes clear: it isn't just a jungle out *there*. It's a jungle in *here*, too.

Let's Get Motivatin'

When psychologists use the term *motivation*, they're talking about all the factors, inside us and in the world around us, that cause us to behave in a particular way at a particular time. Many things, like our genes, our learning histories, our personalities, and our social experiences, all contribute to motivation. Internal conditions that push us toward a goal are called drives. External motivations we call incentives.

Motivated behavior is always directed toward an incentive—the sought-after object or result that will satisfy a drive. My hunger drive sends me heading toward the refrigerator, and the mint chocolate-chip ice cream in the freezer is an incentive for me to walk a little faster.

Hungry Like a Wolf

Drives and incentives always complement each other. If one is weak, the other must be strong enough to motivate the goal-directed behavior. If the only thing in the fridge is cottage cheese, I've got to be pretty darned hungry to traipse to the refrigerator. Of course, if I'm hungry enough, even cottage cheese can look pretty tasty. So not only can drives and incentives influence one another, but they can also influence each other's strength; hypothetically, at least, I could be full enough that even mint chocolate-chip ice cream wouldn't be very appealing.

Professors wonder whether students who fail exams aren't motivated enough. Coaches speculate that winning teams were "hungrier" and more motivated than their opponents. Detectives seek to establish the motive for crimes. Clients come to therapy looking for the motivation to quit bingeing. Not only is motivation one of the most commonly used psychological terms, but it's also something we never seem to have enough of!

What Drives Your Body?

Homeostasis is the equilibrium our bodies must maintain to keep us alive. For example, body temperature, oxygen, minerals, and water must be kept within a certain range, going neither too high nor too low. When our equilibrium is off, our bodies encourage us to take action to regain our balance. When you chug a quart of water after running a few miles, your motivation to drink is an upset in homeostatic balance, and your behavior is designed to correct it. You can even blame your high air-conditioning bills on homeostasis; when you're too hot, your body signals you to find cooler temperatures!

Homeostasis is helpful in understanding thirst, hunger, and our need for oxygen, salt, and temperature control. But many things which motivate us aren't necessary for our immediate survival. Take sex, for example. Most of us are pretty motivated by it, but despite what an overly amorous paramour may have told you, nobody can die from lack of sex.

Psychologists have puzzled over this glitch in the homeostasis theory until their puzzlers were sore. To solve this dilemma, they distinguished between *regulatory* drives that are necessary for physiological equilibrium, and *nonregulatory* drives, like sex, which serve some other purpose. However, as you're about to see, even regulatory drives like hunger can have hidden motives.

Investigating Motives

Psychologists must always infer motives from behaviors—after all, we can't *observe* motives directly. If you're drinking (water, at least), you must be thirsty. Psychologists are constantly looking for links between the stimuli (including conditions and situations) that lead to motivation, and the responses (behaviors) produced by motivational states.

Psychologists also look for the "whodunit" in your brain. In the early 1950s, scientists began poking around in the brains of animals to see which parts controlled what drives. They'd either create lesions to remove any stimulation from reaching that part of the brain, or they'd plant electrodes that would provide more stimulation. Then they'd watch to see what happened. What they observed formed the basis of much of what we know today about human drives, particularly hunger.

The Brain's Motivation Station

Researchers have identified the brain circuitry responsible for reward-motivated learning, a mechanism that appears to allow events to interact with expectations and motivation to influence what we learn.

In one study, for instance, subjects were shown "value" symbols that signified whether the image of the scene that followed would yield $5 or 10 cents if they remembered it the next day. Not surprisingly, subjects were far more likely to remember five-dollar scenes than dime scenes. Anticipating a reward activated the subjects' reward areas of the brain's emotion-processing mesolimbic region, then alerted the learning- and memory-related hippocampus in the medial temporal lobe (MTL).

This suggests that our brain actually prepares in advance to selectively filter rather than simply react to the world. Subjects with greater MTL activation showed better memory performance, suggesting that anticipatory activation of this mesolimbic circuit may help motivate our memory.

The Mystery of Hunger

In the 1950s, scientists discovered the hunger-hypothalamus connection. They found that animals with lesions to the lateral area of the hypothalamus were completely disinterested in food. These animals would literally starve to death if they weren't force-fed through a tube. On the other hand, if the lateral part of the hypothalamus was stimulated, the animals would gorge themselves. Excited, these researchers quickly proclaimed the lateral hypothalamus as the "hunger center" of the brain.

If you're looking for a scapegoat to blame those few extra pounds on, don't jump the gun. Later experiments showed that the hypothalamus was interested in a lot more than food. When researchers presented these same overly stimulated animals with other incentives, like sexual partners, access to water, or nest-building materials, the animals engaged in a frenzy of behavior that matched whatever incentive was provided. If sexual partners were available, they had an orgy. If water was handy, they drank it until they were about to explode!

While stimulation to the lateral part of the hypothalamus causes bingeing, manipulating another part of the hypothalamus, the ventromedial part, has the opposite effect. Stimulation here can cause an animal to stop eating altogether.

Is Your Hunger in Your Head?

We've come a long way in understanding the roots of the hunger drive. We now believe that a tract of neurons running through the hypothalamus was responsible for the initial research findings. This bunch of neurons isn't actually part of the hypothalamus; they just travel through it on their journey from the brain stem to the basal ganglia. Also as previously noted by the frenzy of activity, this tract seems to be part of a general activation system—stimulation seems to give the message, "You've got to do something." What that "something" is depends upon the available incentives.

We're All Picky Eaters

When it comes to hunger, the hypothalamus isn't completely innocent. It has neurons that, at the very least, can modify our appetite. When researchers destroy parts of the lateral hypothalamus, lab animals cut back on their eating but don't completely quit. They eat enough to survive but remain at a lower-than-normal weight, and most of their other drives are normal. No, this procedure isn't available in humans!

To see whether the lateral hypothalamus did indeed play a role in hunger and wasn't just a thoroughfare for that tract of hungry neurons, researchers implanted tiny electrodes in this part of a monkey's brain. What they found is that the hypothalamus is a picky eater.

First of all, the monkey would only become excited by food if it was hungry and food was available. The cells would become active when the hungry monkey saw or smelled food but

Psychobabble
Apparently, the beginning of a new year is not enough motivation for most of us to shed extra pounds. At the stroke of midnight every New Year's Eve, more than 130 million Americans resolve to lose weight but only 14 percent will keep those resolutions.

not when the monkey was exposed to stimuli never associated with food. In addition, the hypothalamus would get "tired" of certain foods; if the monkey had eaten several bananas, the cells would stop responding to bananas but would continue to respond to peanuts and oranges!

What all this means to us, then, is that the hunger motive involves a part of the brain that is programmed to respond to food cues when we're hungry. When we're not hungry, those same food cues would leave us cold, at least from a physiological perspective. If you've ever been on a diet and found yourself drooling over every food commercial, your response is literally all in your head! It's in your brain.

The Dieter's Dilemma

Now let's get a few things straight. A person's weight has little to do with willpower. Studies show that thin people have no more willpower than fat people do. Skinny people are not more conscientious or less anxious. They are not morally superior. In fact, fat people and thin people do not differ on any personality characteristics.

But don't obese people eat more than people of normal weight? Maybe. Research indicates that while most people of normal weight generally eat only when hungry, most overweight people frequently eat for emotional, rather than physical, reasons. And the same neurochemical imbalance that leads to depression can also tempt us to consume excessive amounts of carbohydrate-rich foods, raising the possibility that some people who chronically overeat may, in fact, be depressed.

Of course, the relationship between food and feelings is complex for many of us. All dieters, regardless of their weight, are more likely to eat in response to stress; the weight difference between stress eaters and nonstress eaters may be that overweight people are more likely to be on a diet. Stress can make all of us vulnerable to the munchies, but if we've been fighting hunger cues already, we're more likely to give in to temptation.

> **Insight**
>
> Want to lose weight? Strike the word *diet* from your vocabulary forever. Instead, exercise five times a week (for at least 30 minutes); don't dip below 1,200 calories per day or try to cut fat out completely; quit depriving yourself of favorite foods; and get reacquainted with your body's hunger and fullness cues.

> **Psychobabble**
>
> The average American consumes 3,800 calories a day, more than twice the daily requirement for most adults.

Mmmmmm, It's So Appetizing!

Another challenge for dieters is our culture's appetizer effect, which tricks our bodies' normal methods of food-regulation. Here's how it works: all of us have built-in bodily signals for hunger and fullness. When we're hungry, our stomachs growl; when we're full, our stomachs send signals to the brain, telling us to stop eating. The amount of sugar (glucose) in the blood also cues our bodies to start or stop eating; high blood sugar says stop, and low blood sugar says go. And our fat cells secrete a hormone, leptin, at a rate proportional to the amount of fat being stored in our cells. The greater the amount of leptin, the less our hunger drive is stimulated.

The problem is that our hunger isn't just dictated by the amount of food in the stomach, blood, or fat cells. Our environment can have a powerful influence. Any stimulus in our environment that reminds us of good food can increase our hunger drive—and that's where the appetizer effect kicks in.

Anyone who's ever had a second slice of pecan pie can attest to the fact that the appetizer effect, plus the availability of yummy foods, can easily overwhelm the body's fullness signals. In addition, the appetizer effect can actually stimulate physical hunger. Just the smell of McDonald's french fries can make our insulin drop and cause us to head to the drive-through.

I'll Take Just One!

Humans have a tendency to eat a single unit of food, regardless of the unit's size or caloric value. We have, it seems, a unit bias.

In a fascinating experiment, researchers placed a mixing bowl of M&Ms in a lobby and experimented with various spoon sizes. Indulgers tended to take only a single spoonful of M&Ms, regardless of spoon size or M&M quantity. Since some munchers weren't aware they were being observed, we can't attribute this unit bias solely to participants' concerns that they'd be perceived as gluttonous. It appears that we may have a culturally enforced consumption norm that tells us a single unit is the proper amount to eat.

Unit bias may provide insight into how portion and package size affects consumption, and perhaps, ultimately, obesity. It also argues for eating on smaller plates!

My Genes Made Me Do It!

Just in case you aren't completely bummed out by now, there's yet another reason why dieting is so hard. We each inherit a certain weight range, and it is difficult, without a major life change, to get below it. If your genetic weight range is between 120 and 140, you can comfortably maintain a weight of 120 through a healthy diet and regular exercise. If, however, you wouldn't be caught dead in a bathing suit until you're below 110 and are constantly dieting to reach this goal, you're setting yourself up for failure.

Insight

Obesity sleuths have found clues to at least 20 of the most chronic and deadly medical disorders (breast cancer, cardiovascular disease, Type II diabetes, and so on) in the conflict between our sedentary lifestyle and our built-in genome for physical activity. Apparently, we inherited our need for exercise from our Paleolithic ancestors; when we don't engage in regular physical exercise, it can lead to an altered protein expression of this genome that leads to chronic illness.

Even if you starve yourself down to this weight, you'll have a lot of trouble maintaining it. And losing and regaining weight, known as yo-yo dieting, tends to make you fatter over time. In fact, while dieting is often promoted as a solution for weight loss, it is often what causes average-size people to gain weight in the first place!

Come On, Baby, Light My Fire

But that's enough about food. Let's talk about sex. First of all, how interested are you in it? How much do you know about it? Interest and knowledge are not the same thing, and interest without knowledge can cause serious problems. Here's a little quiz to assess your knowledge about male and female sexuality.

Answer true or false to the following questions:

1. Men and women go through the same sequences and phases of sexual response. ____True ____False

2. Many women can have multiple orgasms, while men rarely do in a comparable time frame. ____True ____False

3. Penis size is generally unrelated to any aspect of sexual performance. ____True ____False

4. Women tend to get aroused more slowly, but often remain aroused much longer. ____True ____False

If you answered true for all of them, go to the head of the class. Masters and Johnson shocked the nation when, in the 1960s, they began studying human sexuality by observing and recording what people actually did when they had sex. Surveys about American sexual behavior had been done before, but Masters and Johnson were well aware that people aren't always honest about what does or doesn't happen in the bedroom. Perhaps they had overheard one too many locker-room bragging sessions and decided to see the truth with their own eyes.

What they saw were men and women exhibiting remarkably similar patterns of sexual arousal and response. Differences that did exist had to do with timing and stamina. Women were slower on the uptake, but once they got going, they could last longer than the Energizer Bunny. Men, on the other hand, got off to a faster start but fizzled out sooner.

Penis size had nothing to do with any aspect of sexual performance, with one exception. Men who thought it mattered were less secure about their sexual prowess, leading the researchers to conclude that a man's attitude about his penis size could have a big impact on his sexuality even when his actual penis size doesn't. On the other hand, a big attitude can quickly make up for a small penis.

As it turns out, the same is true for a woman's feelings about her body. You don't have to be built like Angelina Jolie to enjoy a roll in the hay. And if you believe it, your sexual confidence alone will turn a few heads!

> **Psychobabble**
>
> New United States Centers for Disease Control and Prevention studies show that teens who've had formal sex education are far more likely to put off having sex. Boys were 71 percent less likely to have intercourse before age 15; girls 59 percent less likely. And boys were three times more likely to use birth control the first time they did have intercourse.

Ready, Set, Blast Off

Physically, both men and women go through four stages of sexual response. Hopefully you've experienced them for yourself. Just in case you haven't, or you want to see if your experience matches everybody else's, they are:

1. **Excitement.** This is the beginning of arousal. Everything heats up; blood rushes to the pelvis, and sex organs enlarge.

2. **Plateau.** This is the peak of arousal. You breathe faster, your heartbeat speeds up, and you get ready for the climax.

3. **Orgasm.** This is the release of sexual tension. Men ejaculate and women experience genital contractions.

4. **Resolution.** This is the letdown as the body gradually returns to normal.

> **Insight**
>
> If you're getting ready for a hot date, don't skimp on the fragrance. A recent study found that a few whiffs of men's cologne actually increased physiological arousal in women. And another study found that men guessed a woman's weight as being lower when she wore perfume than when she didn't!

Driving the Sex Machine

I hate to burst your bubble, but calling someone "an animal" in bed is not a compliment. When it comes to sex, we humans are much wilder and have a lot more fun. A lot of female animals, for example, only have intercourse at certain times of the month, whereas women are liberated from the control of their menstrual cycle. We can, and do, get turned on at any time during the month. Among animals, intercourse occurs in a stereotyped way. Among humans, sexual positions are limited only by our imagination. It'd be much more flattering for a rat to playfully paw her sexual partner and call him "a sexual human."

Those Sexy Hormones!

We do have some things in common with our less sexually evolved friends, however, and one of those things is hormones. In all mammals, including humans, the production of sex hormones speeds up at the onset of puberty. Men get jolted with testosterone, and women get an estrogen charge. However, these famous hormones have a silent partner that gives us a head start in the sex department. This less-known helper, produced by our adrenal glands, is called *droepiandrosterone* or DHEA.

Before we enter that tumultuous time called puberty, DHEA is already behind the scenes stirring things up. Boys and girls begin to secrete DHEA at about age six, and the amount rises until the midteens, when it stabilizes at adult levels. Most men and women recall their earliest clear feelings of sexual attraction as occurring at about 10 years of age, well before the physical changes brought on by estrogen or testosterone. Research suggests that DHEA brings on these feelings.

Tanking Up on Testosterone

Once things get stirred up, though, testosterone keeps us stirred up—and yes, that includes women. Testosterone maintains a man's sexual drive during adulthood by stimulating his desire; this hormone has little to do with sexual performance. Men castrated in accidents almost always experience a decline in their sex drive and behavior, and testosterone injections bring it back. Similarly, men with unusually low levels of testosterone show a dramatic increase in sex after a few booster shots. However, a couple of extra testosterone doses won't turn a man into a sex maniac; if his testosterone is within normal limits, any additional amount doesn't seem to have any effect. In fact, taking unneeded testosterone can affect a man's body's ability to produce it naturally.

In women, ovarian hormones, like estrogen, play a role in our sex drive. Our adrenal glands also play a role; they produce DHEA and, believe it or not, testosterone. Women who've had a hysterectomy and women whose adrenal glands have been removed often report a plummeting libido. Like with men, testosterone treatment can give a low libido a much-needed jolt; while it hasn't yet received FDA approval, a testosterone patch has been developed to reverse sexual apathy. However, let's not forget that, for women, much of our sexual desire is based on interpersonal and contextual—not physical—factors. If we're trying to restore our sexual flames, improving the intimacy in our romantic relationships, having plenty of time and energy to give and eliminating stressors like the fear of getting pregnant may be much more effective (and less expensive) than a trip to the doctor's office.

Sex in Low Gear

Fabulous orgasms aside, sex is mainly in your head. Unlike other animals, what turns humans on has less to do with physiological need than with cognitive desires. We fantasize; we interpret sexual experiences; and we have sexual beliefs and values. Even the subjective experience of an orgasm can depend on interpersonal factors (feeling safe or liking a person) as well as physical stimulation. For humans, the real sex organ is the brain.

I Love You for Your Mind

The complexity of human sexuality is wonderful, but the rewards have their risks. Because human sexuality is as influenced by the mind as it is by the body, physical and psychological factors can throw one's sex drive out of gear. Traumatic sexual experiences, fears of pregnancy or disease, relationship conflict, performance pressure, and

Insight

While the most common sexual dysfunction in men is premature ejaculation, half of all men experience occasional impotence, and, for one out of every eight men, it's a chronic problem that tends to increase with age. While drugs for erectile dysfunction (like Viagra and others) can be helpful if the cause is purely physical or related to confidence alone, the drugs can't heal relationship problems or underlying psychological issues.

shameful messages about sexuality can reduce sexual desire and can even prevent your body from functioning normally. Physical causes include various drugs, medications, and chronic medical conditions. The causes of sexual difficulties are as varied and unique as the problems that result from them.

When a person has ongoing difficulties, he or she may have a sexual dysfunction—a frequently occurring impairment during any stage of the sexual response cycle that prevents satisfaction from sexual activity. These disorders generally fall into four categories: sexual desire disorders, sexual arousal disorders, orgasm disorders, and sexual pain disorders. The two most widely publicized disorders have been sexual arousal disorder in women and impotence (erectile dysfunction) in men.

Dealing with Dysfunction

The most effective treatment, of course, depends upon the nature of the sexual dysfunction. Some sexual dysfunctions, like a chronic lack of desire, tend to be psychological in nature, while others, like sexual pain disorder and erective dysfunction, can have numerous causes. In many situations, a combination of physical and psychological treatments is most effective.

The Fragile Sex

Sexual dysfunction is not an inevitable part of aging. It can, however, result from many factors, including demographics, culture, lifetime experiences, and changing mental and physical health.

For instance, a history of sexually transmitted disease can affect sexual health later in life. According to a National Institutes of Health study of people ages 57 to 85, having had an STD quadruples a woman's odds of reporting sexual pain and triples her lubrication problems. Men who have had an STD are more than five times as likely to report sex as nonpleasurable.

Women may be more likely than men to experience sexual dysfunction due to physical health issues. In older women, physical problems such as urinary tract syndrome or pain from lack of lubrication, commonly decrease sexual interest. Among men, mental health issues and relationship problems contribute both to a lack of sexual interest and the inability to achieve orgasm, while urinary tract problems can cause erectile dysfunction.

> **Psychobabble**
>
> Moderate, daily alcohol consumption may actually increase a woman's sexual interest and pleasure and doesn't usually impact a man's sexual health.

Oriented Toward Sex

Clearly, human sexuality is pretty complicated. Even your most primitive sexual urges are often at the whim of your thoughts and feelings. And while these thoughts and feelings can certainly add spark to your sex life, they can also dampen your ardor. Your sex drive can go up or down depending on a lot of physical and psychological factors.

Sexual orientation, however, is not a matter of "getting up" or "lying down." It's a different ballpark altogether, and its causes have been a matter of political debate and scientific inquiry. In fact, so many theories have been thrown around, so many political agendas mixed in with science, and so much misinformation distributed that it's hard to tease out truth from fiction. Psychologists haven't exactly been at the forefront of the tolerance movement; in the 1980s, homosexuality was still classified as a mental disorder.

Insight

Our sexual orientation is an *enduring* emotional, romantic, sexual, or affectional attraction toward a certain gender (or genders). Having fantasies about, or even one or two sexual encounters with, your same gender does not necessarily mean a person is homosexual. In 2005, the Centers for Disease Control released a survey showing that 11.5 percent of "straight" women and 6 percent of "straight" men had experimented in gay sex at least once.

Birds Do It, Bees Do It; Fruit Flies, Too?

In the past, most psychologists argued that sexual orientation was learned. Some still do. However, there are a few problems with this explanation.

First, if sexual orientation is learned, why is it that the vast number of children raised by two homosexual parents are heterosexual? Why does homosexuality exist in other species—are they learning it from the dog next door or the monkey in the next tree?

Between 1 and 5 percent of men and women are homosexual in every culture, in countries where homosexuality is accepted and in countries where it's outlawed. Further support has come from an unexpected source—the nose. Scientists trying to sniff out biological differences between gay and straight men have found that sniffing a chemical from testosterone, the male sex hormone, causes a response in the sexual area of both gay men's and straight women's brains—not, however, in the brains of straight men. And finally, scientists have located a gene in fruit flies that, when altered, completely changes the sexual orientation of the insect. While all the evidence isn't in, the pendulum seems to be swinging toward a biological basis for sexual orientation.

It's Just the Way It Is

We know genetic differences play some role in determining sexual orientation. Roughly 50 percent of identical twins share the same sexual orientation. In contrast, if you have a gay sibling, your chances of also being gay are about 15 percent, compared to the 1 to 5 percent of the general population.

Recent studies suggest that sexual orientation is something we discover about ourselves, not something we choose. Think about your own sexual orientation. When did you first know you were attracted to men or women? Homosexuals and heterosexuals alike say their sexual orientation was present in their childhood thoughts and fantasies, typically by age 10 or 11.

> **Psychobabble**
>
> It seems our politics are catching up with our research. As of 2008, 20 states and the District of Columbia have laws that prohibit discrimination because of a person's sexual orientation, and bills to add this demographic to the national civil rights laws are regularly cropping up in our nation's capital.

Did you consider all the alternatives and then consciously choose the one that felt right to you? Did you ever think you made a mistake or that you should give a different sexual orientation a chance? Odds are, at some point you just knew your sexual orientation, probably long before you understood it. Whatever its cause or causes, sexual orientation is a deeply rooted and early emerging aspect of our self.

Psychobabble

A 10-year APA study suggests that bisexuality in women appears to be a distinctive sexual orientation, not an experimental or transitional stage on the way to lesbianism. The study also debunks the stereotype that bisexual women can't commit to long-term relationships (1+ years). By year 10, a large majority were involved in long-term, monogamous relationships.

In Search of Higher Ground

Sex is a lot of fun, but we can't spend all our time doing it. In fact, in the late 1960s, Abraham Maslow proposed the revolutionary idea that people are ultimately motivated to grow and reach their potential. At a time when most psychologists thought motivation was driven by a need to make up for some physical or psychological deficit, Maslow's optimistic view of human motivation was a breath of fresh air.

Beginning with Basics

Maslow would certainly agree that we have to put first things first—basic needs have to be met before we search for higher ground. If we're starving, worries about our self-esteem take a back seat. That fight you had with your best friend pales in comparison to the rumbles in your tummy. If you're hungry enough, even concern over whether you reset the house alarm might be forgotten in your race to the refrigerator. In wartime and other times of starvation, people have been known to kill family members or sell children for food.

It's hard to even think about anything else when our basic hunger drive is not being met. Missionaries around the world often feed and clothe people before they try to convert them. They understand that the need for knowledge and understanding is not a priority until we're fed and clothed.

Brain Buster

Believe it or not, it's possible to be too motivated. While motivation energizes us on simple tasks, it can quickly disrupt our performance on difficult or more complex ones because the high need to achieve gets consumed by pressure-induced anxiety. A highly motivated (and, of course, prepared) student may be better off exercising for an hour before a test than cramming up to the last minute.

Moving on Up

Maslow believed that our basic needs naturally form a hierarchy, from primitive to more advanced goals. At the very bottom are our most basic biological needs, like hunger and thirst. The next rung up the ladder is our need for safety and security. In the middle are our needs for knowledge and a sense of belonging, and at the very top are the spiritual needs that enable us to identify with all humankind.

Of course, not all of us get to the top of the ladder before our time on Earth runs out. If you were raised in the ambitious United States, chances are you got far enough up to reach a need for achievement. Let's take a look at a motive which, for better or worse, has made our country what it is today.

The Need to Achieve

If you had to predict who would be a success in life, would you pick the person with the highest I.Q. score, the best grades, or the strongest need to achieve? Personally, I'd pick the person motivated to do well. We all know bright people who chronically underachieve. And we also know some high school graduates who tanked the SATs and could now afford to buy the company that publishes them. In the long run, desire and perseverance exceeds talent or brains.

> **Brain Buster**
>
> Children who enjoyed reading were given gold stars as an added incentive, and the experiment backfired! Being handed external rewards for doing something we genuinely like shifts the motivation outside of ourselves; instead, reinforce the internal rewards by asking the child to tell you about the stories he or she reads, read together, or join a parent/child book club.

The "need for achievement," first identified by Harvard psychologist David Murray, refers to differences between individuals in their drive to meet a variety of goals. When your need for achievement is high, you're energized and focused toward success and motivated to continually evaluate and improve your performance. When channeled properly, this can be an organizing force in linking your thoughts, feelings, and actions. Taken to an extreme, it can be a monkey on your back. Perfectionism is a need for achievement that has gone haywire.

One of the most interesting ways your need for achievement influences you is in the way you approach a challenge. For high achievers, knowing a task is difficult can be a motivator to keep on going. Low-need achievers, however, tend to persist only when they believe the task is easy. Low-need achievers who were told a task was difficult either didn't think it was worth the effort or weren't willing to spend it.

Insight

Visualizing yourself performing successfully can be a great motivator. Studies show that imagining yourself performing well through the eyes of others (third-person perspective) seems to add more meaning to the task. So next time you're rehearsing for that play, ball game, or killer exam, see yourself through your audience's eyes.

What Motive Works for You?

All of us work better when our jobs match our personal motivation. Psychologists David McClellan and John Atkinson studied motives that drive people in work situations and found that all people have three motivational characteristics and a person's behavior is likely determined by the degree to which each is present. These three motives are a need to achieve, a need for power, and a need for affiliation.

Will your motives steer you into politics, business, or nonprofit work? Let's look at each of these three needs in action.

- **Achievement.** At work, you appreciate a supervisor who gets down to business and lets you work independently. You hate for people to waste your time and prefer to focus on the "bottom line" of what you need to do. When you daydream, you are most likely to think about how to do a better job, how to advance your career, or how you can overcome the obstacles you are facing. You can motivate yourself well and like to succeed in situations that require outstanding performance.

- **Power.** You have a thirst for power and want a supervisor who's a mover and shaker and can serve as a role model. You are good at office politics and know that the best way to get to the top is by who you know and who they know. You have strong feelings about status and prestige and are

Insight

Not sure what your work motives are? Check out this website to discover your work personality and land the job of your dreams: www.allthetests.com/personality.php3?katb=0470.

good at influencing others and getting them to change their minds or behavior. When you daydream, you are most likely to think about how you can use your influence to win arguments or improve your status or authority. You like public speaking and negotiating.

◆ **Affiliation.** You're a team player, a people person. You want a supervisor who is also your friend and who values who you are and what you do. You are excellent at establishing rapport with others and enjoy assignments that allow you to work within a group. You are very loyal and get many of your social needs met in your job. You are well-liked, great at planning company social functions, and people come to you with their problems and value your advice.

Human motives are fascinating, ranging from basic, universal needs for shelter, food, and clothing to complex, unique drives for self-esteem and achievement. Richard Nixon and Mother Theresa may have both needed to eat, but their "higher" motives led them down vastly different career paths. Whether you're a born Richard Nixon or Mother Theresa, though, one motivator lights a fire under all of us. In the next chapter, we take a look at the motivational power of emotions.

Work That Culture!

Culture affects our motivation, too, as international managers have learned the hard way. They quickly learn that what motivates a United States employee might not matter to one in Dubai.

In the United States, managers seem to believe that work itself is not and cannot be intrinsically motivating and so tend to motivate their workers through incentives (bonuses, paid time off, etc.). Other factors, however, motivate employees in Eastern cultures.

In China, for example, the focus of motivating individuals in the workplace is on moralistic duty. Beginning in adolescence, young learners are instilled with a consciousness of moral obligation and familial role. Individuals are encouraged to recognize their moral duties to perform, whether in the workplace, the classroom, or at home. In this culture, all people work together for the good of the many versus the Western approach of working primarily for the self.

The anchor of the Japanese motivational approach is trust. Even when they hate their job, many Japanese workers will remain highly motivated and committed to their jobs and their company in spite of low work satisfaction. The workers seem to experience a devotion to their company because of the belief in a future reward for all as a result of their commitment. An employer is seen as an extension of family, and it is logical to support that family for the benefit of all included.

Straight from the Lab

She's Just Not That Into You … Is She?   Scientists have long known that college-age men are more likely than women to confuse friendly nonverbal cues with sexual interest. The popular theory has been that young men tend to over-sexualize their social environment. But new research suggests that women may simply have the advantage when it comes to interpreting facial expressions and body language and that young men may simply be less skilled at accurately identifying nonverbal cues.

On a Diet? Hide the Credit Cards!   Don't shop if you're starting a new diet or giving up cigarettes. Research shows that people who are working hard to exercise self-control in some way are more vulnerable to impulse buying.

Programmed to Love Boxing   Studies show that the human brain processes aggression as a reward—not unlike sex, food, or drugs—which helps explain our love of violent sports such as boxing. The reward pathway in the brain activates in response to aggression, and that well-known motivation reinforcer dopamine kicks in.

Beware the Bidding Frenzy   If you've ever experienced the adrenalin rush of winning an intense eBay bidding war in the last 57 seconds, you may have fallen prey to bidding frenzy, a first cousin to gambling addiction. Under intense pressure, logic loses out to excitement, competitiveness, and a burning desire to win. We're most vulnerable to bidding frenzy when competing directly with other human bidders, so silent auctions may be safest!

The Least You Need to Know

- Our bodies seek to maintain homeostasis or balance—if our equilibrium is off, our body signals us to take action to fix it.

- The hunger drive is a strong part of our body's balancing act, but not all hunger is based on bodily needs—strong food cues from the environment can cause physical hunger even if we don't need food.

- Human beings are the sexiest creatures on the planet, with a wider sexual repertoire and an ability to respond to a number of physical and psychological stimuli. However, our sexuality can be disrupted by a number of factors, including our culture, lifetime experiences, and changing mental and physical health.

- Sexual orientation is much more a discovery about oneself than a conscious choice; determined early, it is very rarely changed.

- Until we meet our basic survival needs, it's hard to be concerned with love, self-improvement, or spirituality.

- At work, people may be motivated by a need for power, achievement, or affiliation, or a combination of the three.

10

Emotions in Motion

In This Chapter

- ◆ Finding the source of your feelings
- ◆ Tuning in to your body
- ◆ Who's in charge here?
- ◆ What's your emotional I.Q.?
- ◆ Managing everyday moods

The powerful love between Romeo and Juliet, the bitter rivalry between Caesar and Mark Anthony, the passion of Martin Luther King Jr.—when it comes to human beings, emotions move us.

How do couples maintain their love in the face of constant danger? How do the spouses of firefighters and police officers kiss them good-bye every day, knowing each time that this could be the last time they see them alive? In the face of stress, do we learn to ration our emotions? Do we gradually lose our ability to feel? This chapter explores the psychology of emotions: how we feel and express them, how our culture influences them, what purpose they serve, and how we can handle our own moods more effectively.

Hooked on a Feeling

Whether we admit it or not, our emotions guide much of what we do; they focus our attention, help us record experiences more strongly in our memory, and arouse us.

Most of us equate emotions with feelings. We feel angry, sad, afraid, or happy. But, in reality, emotions are much more complicated. When we feel an emotion, we experience a complex pattern of physical arousal, feelings, and thoughts in response to a personally significant situation. Imagine your boss humiliating you in front of your co-workers. Not only would you feel angry, but you would also think angry thoughts. You might find yourself plotting revenge or obsessing over why he did what he did. And although your blood wouldn't literally boil, your heart would beat faster and your blood pressure would rise.

Your emotions would stimulate you to take action. You might yell or cry in the privacy of your office, or you might spit in his coffee cup when he wasn't looking. If it happened often enough, you might quit your job. Or you might decide to reframe your boss's rude behavior as his problem and not take it so personally. No matter what you do, you are responding to your emotions; they have signaled danger and geared you for action.

> **Brain Buster**
>
> So you think you can hide your feelings from your children? Think again. By age five, children can recognize surprise, disgust, happiness, sadness, anger, and fear about as well as most college students.

> **Psychobabble**
>
> Romantic love is much more than lust. In fact, brain images of newly-in-love young men and women showed neurons firing in the areas of the brain associated with motivation and reward, which may be why we feel "driven" to win the affection of our loved one. Sex and love involve quite different brain systems.

Situations that are perceived as highly threatening or highly rewarding will be highly emotional. So how angry you get about your boss's rude behavior will depend on how personally significant the situation is to you. If your boss's opinion is important to you or if his comments challenge your sense of self-worth, you'll feel much angrier than if you discount what he says or refuse to take it personally. Similarly, if you had a great time on a first date, you're going to be more disappointed if she never calls you again. You've had a taste of the rewards, and now they've been taken away!

For better or worse, deadlines, transitions, and approaching endings also add fuel to our feelings. In one study, participants were asked to picture themselves having a disastrous dinner at a close colleague's home; she burns the meal and nothing goes as planned. Half the participants were told to imagine that the colleague was retiring and moving to another city the next week, while the other half were advised that it was "dinner as usual." Even though both groups imagined the same event, the relocating, time-limited participants said they would feel more closeness, more patience, more respect, more sadness, and less irritation for their well-intentioned but culinary-challenged colleague.

Adjust Your Attitude and Improve Your Love Life!

For many of us, one of the easiest mistakes to make in our relationships with other people is to assume that there's a "right" amount of emotional intensity for any situation (which, of course, is usually the amount *we* are feeling). Someone who feels more strongly than we do is overreacting. And of course, when we try to "help" him by pointing this out, he blows a fuse!

Certainly, some people are hotheads, and some people are unusually sensitive. However, most of the time, people have emotional reactions that are consistent with the importance of the topic to them. You might not mind being called "Baldy," but to someone who invests a lot of self-esteem in his physical appearance, that teasing comment can be highly threatening and provoke strong feelings. So the next time someone "overreacts," don't waste your energy trying to change his feelings. Try changing your *own* attitude!

Where Did These Feelings Come From?

Let's face it. Love may not make the world go 'round, but it sure helps people put up with each other. It gives us rose-colored glasses in the beginning of a relationship. It gets us through the hassles of meeting someone, courting him, getting married, and fighting over the remote control. Could parents put up with all the sleepless nights, poopy diapers, and Barney videos without that incredible emotional bond with their child? Evolution thought not.

Psychobabble
Researchers have found that 70 percent of the outcomes of recent political races could be predicted based on the candidates' babyfacedness! Apparently, the same facial features that endear us to newborns cause us to question the competency and maturity of babyfaced adults.

Do you notice how cute babies are, whether they're baby humans, baby kittens, or baby chimps? Of course you do—you're genetically programmed to respond to "neonatal (baby) features"—especially those big eyes. As children grow up, their features become more proportionate and adult, and you stop feeling quite as protective toward them unless they're your own.

Our emotional capacity may also have been naturally selected. Ancestors with the strongest feelings may have been more motivated to defend their turf, protect their young, and impress their mate than those who were less passionate. Emotions aren't just feelings; they are feelings that drive us to behave in certain ways. They are inherited, specialized mental states designed to deal with recurring situations in the world.

> **Insight**
>
> Are you furious at a loved one? Before approaching her, do something physical (jog, exercise) to blow off steam and reduce physical arousal and then think about it. Don't let yourself plot revenge strategies or relive what's happened; instead, set a goal that will help you maintain self-control (for example, "I want to get this resolved before our party tonight").

Don't Be So Jealous!

From an evolutionary perspective, sexual jealousy can be viewed as a special switch that is turned on to deal with an unfaithful mate. It energizes us for possible conflict. It also may have motivated our ancestors to either eliminate the rival or punish or leave the mate. Luckily for all of us, evolution also gave us some control buttons which prevent us from acting impulsively on our feelings!

Seen this way, emotions evolved to push us to deal with a given situation. They may also help us use our energy most effectively. For example, happiness and sadness are moods that regulate our energy in opposite directions. When we're "on a roll" and things are going well, we feel happy. When we're happy, we're more optimistic, active, and energetic, which of course, helps *keep* us on that roll.

In-the-Body Experiences

Your emotions aren't all in your head—they're whole-body experiences. People who are anxious say their heart is racing, they can't breathe, they feel jittery, and they can't sit still. People suffering from depression lose their appetite and can't sleep. Your body and your mind are constantly interacting with each other, and the messages your body sends can either magnify or inhibit your emotions.

This emotional connection between your mind and your body is formed in your brain. While certain parts of your body respond to different emotions, your brain is the matchmaker that coordinates these bodily changes and emotional feelings. Specifically, the amygdala in the limbic system and the frontal lobes in the cerebral cortex act as your emotional regulators (see Chapter 12).

Animals get pretty whacked out when their amygdalas are removed. For example, monkeys who have no amygdalas demonstrate a fascinating phenomenon known as psychic blindness. They can still see objects, but they seem to be completely indifferent to the psychological significance of them. Nothing scares them. Nothing angers them. And they become pretty indiscriminate in their search for pleasure; some of them attempted to eat or have sex with just about anything—alive or not!

> **Insight**
>
> When it comes to interpreting facial expressions, our brains are speed-readers; they can process them at 40 milliseconds or less! Studies show that our brains detect fearful expressions more rapidly than happy or neutral expressions. Perhaps it's no mystery that we perceive happy faces the slowest. Happy faces, after all, signal safety. If something is safe, we don't need to pay attention to it.

Humans aren't quite that indiscriminate, even without their amygdalas. People who have suffered damage to the amygdala experience a subtle version of psychic blindness in which they lose the ability to detect fear or anger in the voices or faces of others.

What We Think About Feelings

You can't blame (or credit) *all* your emotions on your amygdala, however. Your frontal lobes are also critical in your conscious experience of feelings, and they help you get a grip on the way you express them. Your frontal lobes help you plan, and initiate, your responses to your feelings. We probably don't have fewer emotions than our most primitive ancestors; we've just developed the brakes—our frontal lobes—to help control them. Without our frontal lobes, we'd still be bopping each other over the head with clubs!

> **Insight**
>
> If you're about to fall on your head, you might want to turn to your right. Damage to the left frontal lobe typically lowers positive emotions (like happiness), while damage to your right frontal lobe produces a decline in negative ones (like anger).

In Chapter 3, we talked about the nature-versus-nurture debate in child development. Here's another chicken-or-egg argument, and this is an emotional one: does your body react to your feelings or are your feelings an interpretation of your bodily sensations?

Common sense argues for the first explanation. First we get angry, and then our body gets all fired up. However, William James, the father of American psychology, thought the reverse was true. In his view, we don't cry because we're sad; we're sad because we cry. (James's beliefs, it bears noting, arose from a single research subject: himself!)

The essence of James's theory is that our first "take" of a situation (e.g., that a snake is poisonous) and the subsequent physical arousal occurs quickly, automatically, and without conscious thought. James believed that emotions came later, as a result of the physical sensations. The sequence went like this:

1. You get punched.

2. Your body responds to the punch automatically.

3. Your mind registers your bodily response and interprets it to mean you're angry.

Cognitive psychologist Stanley Schachter recognized that emotions are dependent on more than feedback from the body. In his view, our perceptions and thoughts about what's happening influence which emotion we feel (anger, fear, joy), and sensory feedback from the body influences how intensely we feel it (very joyful or mildly happy). If we see a snake, for instance, our belief that snakes are dangerous will cause us to feel fear. And if our body gets all fired up (we start sweating, our heart starts pounding), our fear might turn to terror.

Our perception of the world isn't always right, especially if it's clouded by painful past experiences. For example, children who have been physically abused are much more likely to think that others are angry—even when they're not. When shown pictures of faces, these children were able to accurately recognize the pictures but interpreted the expressions differently; they were much more sensitive to anger.

Psychobabble

When are emotions real? In one study that measured brain waves, the auditory hallucinations of schizophrenics actually stimulated the parts of the brain that involve motivation and emotion. In addition, there was no corresponding activity in the part of the brain that checks out reality. This brain pattern suggested there would be no way of knowing whether these voices were real or whether an emotional response to them was reasonable.

Perhaps physically abused children develop a broader category of anger because it's adaptive for them to notice when adults are angry. But while this sensitivity could be protective in a threatening environment, it could be disadvantageous in others. An abused child might overinterpret a social cue, such as an accidental ball toss during recess, to be hostile. As a result, the child might try to protect herself by lashing out, calling names, or exhibiting other inappropriate behaviors.

Our emotions can also be manipulated. Research subjects were injected with adrenaline and then exposed to emotion-eliciting stimuli such as a sad movie or an angry story. Adrenaline itself did not produce any particular emotion; the subjects might have felt jittery or jazzed up, but they didn't associate it with a feeling. However, when the drug was combined with an emotional situation, their emotions were stronger. They felt angrier in response to the angry story and sadder over the tear-jerking movie.

Brain Buster

Because of the strong link between physical and emotional arousal, it's easy to misinterpret bodily sensations as emotions. Being overheated can be interpreted as feeling anxious, while being tired can feel like depression. This means that taking care of our bodies is one of the best paths to good mental health—being tired or hungry, for example, makes us much more vulnerable to mood swings.

Touchy-Feely Psychology

Adrenaline isn't the only thing that can jumble up our feelings. Apparently, so can wishful thinking. A few years ago, a friend of mine told me he was attracted to a new co-worker, Linda, and was convinced she felt the same way. "She's so cute. Whenever I go into her office, she seems so nervous. She gets so distracted when I talk to her; she stumbles over her words, and yesterday, she dropped her pencil. I know she likes me."

Recently, at a dinner celebrating their wedding anniversary, Linda was talking about their early courtship. "I don't know why Rob was attracted to me. I was a nervous wreck over having my first job. I was so preoccupied with doing well, I barely even noticed Rob's existence until he asked me out." What Rob had optimistically interpreted as a sign of Linda's interest in him was a bad case of first-job jitters!

Unfortunately, these kinds of emotional misinterpretations can lead to tragedy. In some date-rape situations, the male may be thinking, "Well, if she really wanted me to stop, she'd scream or hit me or run away" while the female freezes, thinking, "If I scream or hit him or try to run, he might hurt me even worse. Maybe if I just don't respond, he'll realize how scared I am and stop."

Human emotions are tricky little devils that don't always follow common psychological sense. For instance, one of motivational psychology's core assumptions is that humans pursue pleasure and avoid pain, right? So how do we explain our seemingly perverse love of horror flicks, which we know—even as we're buying the tickets—will provoke in us feelings of fear and perhaps disgust?

New research may suggest that horror movie fans are happy to be unhappy and may actually even *enjoy* being scared. When we feel protected (say, inside a safe, comfy movie theatre), we may be able to disengage or detach psychologically and experience positive feelings at the same time we're scared out of our wits!

> ### Psychobabble
>
> In one fascinating study, a female experimenter showed two groups of men a picture of a woman and asked them to tell a story about her. Half of the men had just crossed a rickety, wobbly bridge, and half had just crossed a safe bridge. The rickety-bridge crossers were much more likely to use sexual themes than the men who had just crossed a safe bridge. They were also four times more likely to call the researcher later!

Are Your Feelings Cultured?

All human beings are remarkably similar with regard to the kinds of emotions we feel. We also speak and understand the same emotional language; the facial expression of a sad New Guinean is similar to our sad face. But if you've ever traveled in another country, you've noticed that culture sets the standard for when to show certain emotions and for the social appropriateness of various emotional displays and that those standards vary from one place to the next.

I've worked quite a bit with a Finnish-owned company that has a huge headquarters in the United States. One of the biggest cultural differences between Americans and Finns is in the expression of emotion. In fact, early on, I was given a cartoon titled "The Finnish Expression of Emotions." Underneath it was a list of numerous emotions—sad, happy, afraid, surprised, angry—and above each emotion was a picture of the exact same stone face!

From an American perspective, the Finnish culture seems to breed a bunch of Mr. Spock clones. From a Finnish perspective, Americans probably seem like a bunch of impulsive, irrational children! While Americans and Finns feel the same feelings, their culture sends very different messages about what a person can do and say about them.

Psychobabble
According to a new brain imaging study, men and women's brains use different strategies to remember highly emotional images, a finding that helps explain how women manage to remember emotional events better than men. This still doesn't excuse your hubby from forgetting your wedding anniversary, but you might let him off the hook if he can't remember the songs that were played when you tied the knot.

Guilt Trippin'

If someone has ever laid a guilt trip on you, you know what a powerful social influence it can be; when I miss a lunch date with my son, the guilt he can induce suddenly gives my grammar schooler a tremendous amount of power!

Some psychologists believe guilt is designed to keep us from repeating bad behaviors in the future (withdrawal motivation). Others see guilt as a form of social control that motivates us to keep our behavior in line with the moral standards of our community (approach motivation). But a new study suggests that guilt may be punitive initially but can transform into more positive behavior when we have a chance to make amends.

Study participants, who viewed pictures of white, black, and Asian faces and were told their EEG results revealed a negative response to black faces, reported significantly increased anxiety, sadness, and guilt—especially guilt. But after reading a cluster of magazine headlines which included prejudice-reducing headlines (e.g., "Ways to Eliminate Your Own Racism"), their feelings of guilt triggered a desire to engage in more positive, prejudice-reducing behavior.

Coding and Decoding

I once watched a *60 Minutes* episode featuring a woman who was conned out of thousands of dollars by a man pretending to love her. This brave woman went public with a humiliating tale of a con artist who not only manipulated her feelings but also did a remarkable job of disguising his own.

Apparently, evolution thought human beings would benefit more from the ability to hide our emotions than from the ability to detect a lying salesperson or a con artist. Most people I know, though, think they can have it both ways. Most of us think we are good judges of character, and we're sure we'd never have been as gullible or naïve as that woman on *60 Minutes*. If that's what you think, it's time to be honest with yourself.

> **Psychobabble**
>
> Evolution programmed us to respond emotionally to threats in our environment, and we're still doing it. The percentage of airline travelers who felt nervous about flying jumped from 60 percent to 81 percent in the six months following the 9/11 hijackings.

Most of us are also poor lie detectors. The key to detecting deception rests in perceiving patterns of the liar's behavior and facial expressions over time. Once you've established a baseline of how a person normally behaves, you're more likely to smell a rat. Without the chance to observe that person in different situations over time, you're unlikely to accurately judge her honesty.

Smart Feelings

Eleanor Roosevelt was known as "First Lady of the World" decades after her husband, President Franklin D. Roosevelt, died. Biographers, who spent years interviewing her closest friends and family, discovered that Eleanor possessed an uncanny understanding of people, an endless compassion for the underdog, and an incredible ability to motivate and channel her emotions into purposeful goals. In pop-psychology terms, Eleanor Roosevelt was a genius of emotional intelligence.

Emotional intelligence teaches us that, in the contest of life, we're much better off being Miss Congeniality than Miss America. Positive interpersonal relationships, we're finding, are the key to the best of what life has to offer, and our ability to understand ourselves and others gets us that key. In his groundbreaking book *Emotional Intelligence*, psychologist Daniel Goleman outlines interpersonal skills that he believes greatly enhance or hurt our quality of life:

◆ **Self-awareness**—knowing what we're feeling when we feel it

◆ **Managing our emotions**—knowing what to do with our feelings

◆ **Motivating ourselves**—channeling our feelings in the right direction without acting impulsively

◆ **Empathy**—feeling for others and accepting their feelings, too

◆ **Handling relationships**—having good interpersonal skills so others feel good about us

The phrase *emotional intelligence* was first coined by Yale psychologist Peter Salovey and the University of New Hampshire's John Mayer to describe qualities such as understanding one's own feelings, empathy for the feelings of others, and the ability to use one's emotions in a productive way. An emotional quotient (E.Q.) is not the opposite of I.Q.; some of us are blessed with lots of both, while some with little of either. Researchers are now trying to understand how the two complement each other—how our smarts about our feelings help us put our intelligence to better use.

Why are some people more emotionally intelligent than others? Emotions might be built-in, but they can also be shaped by experience. Even very young children develop a repertoire of sensitive responses when they see others acting compassionately.

If, on the other hand, the feelings a child expresses are not recognized and reinforced by the adults in her life, the child will gradually become less able to recognize them in herself or in others. Not only will this cause problems in her relationships, but she will also have lifelong trouble with something we all struggle with now and then—managing her everyday moods.

> **Insight**
>
> A recent study of former NFL football players showed that a low E.Q. is highly predictive of addiction, depression, relationship problems, financial woes, and a tendency toward violence. Athletes with a high E.Q. enjoy a greater overall quality of life, both in the glare of the spotlight and after the spotlight fades. Perhaps if teams invested in a little emotional intelligence training, they'd create winners for life.

Managing Your Everyday Moods

Do you ever wake up on the wrong side of the bed? Do you sometimes get in a bad mood for no reason? Do you have a temper that's hotter than a jalapeño? If you answered yes to all three questions, here's your diagnosis: you're moody!

Your health, sleep, food, amount of recent exercise, and even the time of day are contributors to your mood, too. In fact, moods are crucial indicators of your physiological functioning and your psychological experience at any given moment. Your mood is like a clinical thermometer, reflecting all the inner and outer events that affect you.

Meet the Mood Managers

What are *your* mood shifters? Do you listen to music? Exercise? Watch T.V.? Have sex? Eat? Call someone? Or do you try to avoid people or what's upsetting you?

If you use physical exercise as one of your mood-management strategies, go to the head of the class. Studies show that regular physical exercise is one of the most effective mood regulators we have. Even a 10-minute walk can beat the blues and raise our energy level.

Other effective mood managers are listening to music, using relaxation techniques, challenging negative thoughts, enjoying humor, and getting lost in a hobby or productive activity. Expressing your feelings through writing (such as keeping a diary or journaling) may actually not only help your emotional health but also your physical health as well! And as any psychologist will tell you, focusing on others can be amazingly effective at taking the focus off yourself and gaining some emotional perspective!

On the other hand, avoidance, isolating yourself from others, and behaviors such as eating, smoking, and drinking reduce tension in the short run but may increase tension over time. Yes, eating chocolate can boost your serotonin levels temporarily and make you feel happier for a little while—probably until the next time you see your backside in the mirror.

Talking things over with a friend is a good strategy as long as you end your conversation with an action plan and don't get stuck wallowing in your emotions! Co-rumination, excessively rehashing problems with another person and dwelling on the negative feelings associated with those problems, tends to build high-quality friendships. That's the good news.

But studies show that friendships based on a pattern of co-rumination can lead to increased depressive and anxiety symptoms, which in turn perpetuates a vicious cycle of more co-rumination. Teenage girls are believed to be especially susceptible to the co-rumination factor, perhaps because—some psychologists suggest—they're more likely than boys to take personal responsibility for failures. High anxiety, coupled with a high-quality friend to talk to, may actually provide a uniquely reinforcing context for co-rumination.

> **Psychobabble**
>
> The clinical concept of rumination is a nod to the mammal suborder Ruminantia (you know them as cows, sheep, goats, deer, and giraffes), who are prone to perpetually chewing a cud of regurgitated, partially digested food. Does that sound like any human Ruminants you know?

Drugs and Emotions

It's no coincidence that most cases of sexual assault and domestic violence occur when the perpetrator is under the influence of a drug—usually alcohol. Drugs can heighten our emotions and make us care less about the other person's feelings or lead us to feel the other person "deserves" punishment. Then we can find ourselves sobering up later in a jail cell, not believing what we've done.

The use of some drugs, such as PCP or ketamine, "Special K", has been associated with some especially horrific episodes of violence. Despite the old Reefer Madness–type movies, though, this is not an effect of marijuana.

Does all this mean we can't even have a glass of wine with dinner? Of course not. But keep away from all drugs—including alcohol—when you're already angry. Remember, alcohol can *feel* like a stimulant at times, but in reality, it's a depressant.

Some evidence even shows that years of heavy drug or alcohol abuse can stunt emotional growth. Have you ever met a 30-year-old alcoholic who still seems like a teenager emotionally? If he spent 15 years drinking every time he was upset instead of learning to cope with his emotions, he may still react like he's 15 instead of 30.

Ground to Trauma Control: Do You Read Me?

Rape, a devastating earthquake, the murder of a child—these are experiences that, thankfully, most of us will never encounter. And not surprising, our emotional reaction to extreme trauma can feel like an out-of-body experience when, in reality, it's our body's amazing way of helping us cope at a pace we can handle.

Physiologically, many people report initially feeling numb, disoriented, or shocked. Unfortunately, this kind of response can easily be misinterpreted by loved ones as either an inappropriate lack of feeling (why isn't she crying about what happened?) or a lack of emotional impact (she's such a strong person; maybe she just didn't let it get to her). This physical and emotional numbing is often short-lived, however, and can be followed by a flood of emotions including terror, rage, grief, and physiological arousal.

def•i•ni•tion

Posttraumatic stress disorder, PTSD, is a psychiatric disorder that can occur following the experience or witnessing of life-threatening events such as military combat, natural disasters, serious accidents, or violent personal assaults like rape. People who suffer from PTSD often relive the experience through nightmares and flashbacks, have difficulty sleeping, and feel detached or estranged; these symptoms can be severe and impair the person's daily life.

People with *posttraumatic stress disorder*, PTSD, are often completely unable to control emotional intrusion into their thoughts. They get caught up in a physiological loop between the amygdala, where we process emotions, and the hippocampus, the main memory-processing center. The emotion triggers the memory; the memory triggers the feelings again more intensely; and we're trapped in a painful cycle from which we can't seem to escape.

New research reveals that the brain actually has a built-in mechanism for preventing emotional distractors from interfering with mental functioning. The anterior cingulate cortex (ACC), the executive processing region of the cortex, has the ability to inhibit activity in the emotion-processing cortex, bringing hope for eventual treatment of intrusive thoughts.

Don't Do Me Any Favors

In the wake of cataclysmic disasters such as terrorist attacks, hurricanes, or school shootings, debriefings—counseling sessions which allow survivors to discuss their feelings and reactions—are often provided for survivors immediately following the traumatic event.

But a new study exploring the aftermath of the 9/11 terrorist attacks suggests that the theory that one must express his distress in order to recover may not only be false, but, for some people, also downright harmful. Study participants who chose *not* to express thoughts and emotions about the attacks through an anonymous Web-based survey appeared to cope more successfully and actually reported fewer diagnosed physical and mental disorders over a two-year period than people who did express their thoughts and feelings.

Psychobabble

The number-one cause of PTSD is motor-vehicle accidents. Accident survivors most at risk for PTSD are those who suffered a serious physical injury, witnessed the death or serious injury of a loved one, had reason to fear that they might die during the accident, and have limited social support during the recovery process.

Not everyone copes in the same way. The normal recovery time from a trauma varies from person to person and can take up to two years. A one-size-fits-all approach to trauma counseling can result in diverting resources away from people who are truly at risk and may interfere with an individual's natural coping process of seeking support from family and friends, a process that some studies have shown to be equally effective in facilitating long-term recovery.

Families of victims and first responders such as law enforcement officers and firefighters, who are at higher risk for long-term problems, may also require special attention. For these individuals, intensive treatments such as cognitive behavioral therapy (CBT) may be effective in reducing long-term trauma. CBT can help trauma survivors neutralize trauma and learn to re-experience the traumatic event without *reliving* it.

Straight from the Lab

Is Anxiety Eating You?   A recent National Institute of Mental Health study found that nearly one in four cases of obesity is associated with a mood or anxiety disorder. Does obesity cause mood and anxiety disorders? We don't know which one comes first, but we do know that each likely contributes to the other.

Wait Before You Buy   Do you ever suffer buyer's remorse? Studies show that, before we hand over the cash, most of us tend to overestimate how happy we'll be and underestimate how much we'll regret an impulse buy.

No PDA (Public Display of Anger), Ladies!   Here's a new twist on workplace gender bias. According to a study of Hillary Clinton's 2008 presidential campaign, people accept—and even reward—men who get angry but view women who lose their cool as less competent. (Women only get a pass when angry about treatment of a family member.) What is the solution? Stay emotionally neutral, and if you can't be, at least explain what ticked you off!

Drugs Compete with Kids   Drugs such as cocaine and heroin affect brain pathways associated with behavior initiation, hedonic reward, and motivation—all pathways thought to be involved in caring for a child. Continued drug abuse sets up a competition between caring for children and using drugs. New therapies for substance-abusing mothers may focus on resetting the mother's reward system.

The Least You Need to Know

- Evolution apparently gave us emotions to motivate us to take care of ourselves and to stick with the people we love.

- Emotions are whole-body experiences, combining feelings, thoughts, and bodily sensations.

- Emotional intelligence is the ability to be aware of and effectively use our own feelings and the emotions of those around us.

- Our moods are like clinical thermometers that tell us how we're doing physically and psychologically; physical exercise is perhaps the best way to regulate them.

- Drugs, including alcohol, can intensify emotions—often in a negative or dangerous way.

- We all handle posttraumatic stress differently, and talking it out immediately after a traumatic event is not always necessary—or even beneficial—for long-term emotional and physical health.

Think Before You Speak

In This Chapter

- ◆ Meeting the mind detectives
- ◆ Putting together prototypes
- ◆ Seeing how culture changes one's mind
- ◆ Examining the evidence
- ◆ Investigating the Sherlock Holmes in your head

Long before serial killer Wayne Williams was caught, psychologist John Douglas described him as a 20-something black male and a police buff. He described another serial killer, known as the Trailside Murderer, as a stutterer. And he pegged the Unabomber as a highly intelligent white male with an obsessive-compulsive personality and a previous university affiliation. In all three cases, Douglas' profiles were right on the mark.

Now John Douglas isn't psychic; he just understands the criminal mind. Douglas spent 25 years working as a behavioral profiler with the FBI, spending hundreds of hours in prisons, crawling inside the minds of convicted serial killers. And what he learned helped him build accurate behavior profiles of criminal offenders.

How did he build accurate profiles of murderers he'd never even met? You're about to find out as we explore how thoughts form and how we use mental scripts and schemata to solve the mysteries of daily life. You'll also learn problem-solving strategies and mental shortcuts that can help you find solutions more efficiently (but can, sometimes, lead you astray).

Mind Detectives

When I was 16, my high school vocational test suggested I should become a private investigator. I laughed at the time—this was hardly the advice I had expected! But in a way, the joke was on me. Years later I realized I *had* become a private investigator after all: a mind investigator. During therapy sessions, my clients and I work to solve the mysteries that brought them to my office. Psychologists are, in essence, mind detectives who are constantly looking for clues about human nature by examining thoughts, feelings, and behaviors.

The human mind is uniquely suited to solving mysteries and going beyond the evidence to find a solution that seizes new insights, opportunities, and interpretations. Sometimes the results are as impressive as Douglas's profiles of killers who were total strangers. Other times the mysteries the mind solves are more mundane. In every case, the tools the mind uses in problem solving are called *cognitive processes.*

def•i•ni•tion

Cognitive processes are the mental abilities that enable us to know and understand the things around us. They include attending, thinking, remembering, and reasoning.

Solving problems is what we all do, every day. Our ability to go beyond the surface of things—to make sense of clues and solve mysteries—is the gift of our cognitive processes. Our minds enable us to carry around mental representations of our physical and social worlds wherever we go. They enable us to look back and investigate why we behaved in a certain way and to look ahead to predict what might happen. Our cognitive processes are our detective tools; we use them to explore and improve the world around us.

Models of the Mind

Cognitive psychology is the science of the mind. It all started in 1945, when a mathematician named John von Neumann compared the electronic circuits of a new digital computer to the brain's neurons and the computer program to the brain's memory, introducing the human computer analogy for the first time. Psychological researchers Herbert Simon and Allen Newell continued von Neumann's research and developed computer programs that mimicked human problem solving, thereby giving us new ways to study mental processes.

Cognitive models caught on. Today, researchers build conceptual models to help them understand how to processes information. These cognitive models are metaphors that explain how information is detected, stored, and used; the most popular model for years has been the information-processing model.

def•i•ni•tion

A **cognitive model** is a hypothetical representation of how thought processes work. Just as a model airplane is a small replica of a real one, cognitive psychologists build cognitive models to explain how the human mind takes in and uses information.

Information Overload!

The information-processing model hypothesizes that we can break thinking into component parts that work together to create a system of information flow. According to this model, the key to understanding cognition is to examine these parts and determine how they work together. In this model, thoughts are either "on" or "off" and are in a static (still) state until moving on.

But there's a new model in town: the dynamical-systems approach. A Cornell University study suggests that our thoughts may behave less like a computer and more like a living organism, flowing back and forth in a continuous stream.

According to this model, your mind may be able to hover between two or more thoughts. For example, let's say you're in a study where you're asked to click on the computer image that matches the experimenter's spoken word. If you're asked to click on a "candle," and the two images are of a jacket and a candle, the mouse would immediately move to the candle. However, if the images are of candy and candle, your mouse is likely to move in a curve, as if your brain starts processing the "can" part first and, as a result, hovers between the two (keeping both options open) until it hears the rest of the word.

Brain Buster

No matter how impressive our cognitive abilities are, we just aren't programmed for multi-tasking—at least when it comes to sights and sounds. New research indicates that both talking and listening while driving impair our ability to navigate safely. Turn off those cell phones when on the road and keep heated driver-to-passenger conversations to a minimum.

Investigating Thoughts

Cognition is an active process: you aren't just taking information in; you're also simultaneously sorting it, making sense of it, and transforming it. This transformation of basic input into news you can use involves a number of sophisticated tasks—judging, problem solving, planning, reasoning, imagining, and, sometimes, creating.

As complex as it is, though, thinking is also practical. Thinking is *always* some form of problem solving. Just about everything you think is directed toward making things clearer, better, or different. Think of thinking as your built-in, automatic self-improvement program!

You might be wondering how we know so much about thoughts since we can't directly observe them. Well, cognitive psychologists have developed some pretty clever investigative tools to measure the mind. Some of the most popular mind measures are …

- Introspection
- Behavioral observation
- Error analysis
- Brain scanning

Introspection

In the late 1800s, psychologist Wilhelm Wundt taught people to study their own minds. Using a self-report method called introspection, he encouraged them to write down their sensations, images, and feelings *as they were having them.* By getting people to record their mental processes as they were occurring, Wundt hoped to break them down into their smallest unit.

> **Psychobabble**
>
> Cognitive psychotherapy, the fastest-growing talk therapy in the world, focuses on helping clients change negative thinking patterns that lead to depression, anxiety, and other mental problems.

Wundt thought that through this process, we should begin to see patterns of sensations, images, and feelings emerge and, over time, be able to present various individuals with certain stimuli and generate the same images, thoughts, and feelings in all of them, just as in classically conditioned behavior. Wundt optimistically believed that if we could understand human thought, we could predict it, and when our thoughts weren't working properly, we could change them.

Alas, he was dead wrong. People are much more complicated than Wundt thought, which makes them much more interesting, unpredictable, and, bummer, much harder to study. Even within the same person, insight doesn't necessarily translate into behavior change. Introspection, as it turns out, is a great psychological parlor game but a poor research tool.

Behavioral Observations

Have you ever noticed how your thoughts and actions don't always match up? You can be thinking about strangling your boss at the same time you're smiling and nodding in response to her inane comments. Nevertheless, observing what a person is doing, and the situation in which it occurs, can help us figure out the thoughts, feelings, and motivations guiding them. If we see someone crying, we know to interpret it differently if we see it at a funeral (probably grief) versus a wedding (happiness—we hope!).

Although Wundt's thoughts were off the mark in terms of how thoughts develop, he did solve a few research problems. One useful contribution was his observation that reaction time is a useful measure of the complexity of thinking required for any given task; the longer it takes to perform a task, the more complex its solution is likely to be. Today, cognitive psychologists often use reaction-time tests to gauge mental flexibility and quickness.

Analyzing Errors

Do you make the same mistake over and over? Well, we all do, and cognitive psychologists are pretty darned happy about it because it helps them get to know us better. In fact, cognitive psychologists study errors in thinking about as much as they do anything else. Every cognitivist knows that people don't just jump to the wrong conclusion, they often jump to the same wrong conclusion over and over.

Brain Scanning

When Benjamin Franklin discovered electricity, he unwittingly illuminated the path for researchers to see the different brain waves we produce when we sleep (see Chapter 5) and to measure changes in activity related to a particular mental event—a pattern known as an event-related potential (ERP).

In fact, with electrical measurements, researchers can even tell which light bulbs are going off in what part of the brain. For example, while you're reading these pages, lights are going off in the part of your brain that perceives the words, the part that compares them to other words you've read, and the part that organizes their individual meanings into coherent thoughts. Even the sentences themselves can cause different ERPs; the part of the brain that gets excited over an unfamiliar word is different than the part of the brain that tries to untangle a confusing sentence structure.

Mind detectives use a variety of tools in their exploration of the mysterious human mind. Let's take a look at how we structure thoughts.

Jeopardy of the Mind

If your brain were a game show, it would be *Jeopardy*. It loves categories—creating categories, putting information into categories, and fitting new stuff into old categories. But it's also lazy. It would rather stuff information into existing categories than build new ones. As a result, your brain looks for similarities among individual experiences—it prefers to treat new information as instances of familiar, remembered categories. "Been there, done that" seems to be the brain's motto.

> **Psychobabble**
>
> The thought process associated with a single object is not isolated to a single area of the brain; it's distributed across multiple locations in the brain. Thinking about a saw, for instance, activates one area for the shape of the saw, one area for the use of a saw, and a motor area for how to use the saw.

It's not that the brain isn't capable of drawing distinctions between similar objects because it is. In fact, new Carnegie Mellon research shows it's possible for our brain to easily distinguish between items with very similar meanings, such as two closely related tools. With the help of an MRI, researchers can pinpoint where thoughts and perceptions of familiar objects originate in the brain and observe the specific brain activity patterns associated with each object. They could even identify one participant's thoughts from the patterns extracted from *other* participants!

I'll Take "Building Blocks" for $200, Alex

The categories are the building blocks of thinking—we call them concepts. *Animal*, for example, is a concept that conjures up many related creatures we've grouped together into a single category. *Dog* is another concept, although the category is a smaller one. Concepts can also represent activities (your idea of exercise may differ from mine), relationships (apples and bananas are both fruit), and abstract ideas (truth, justice).

In relationships, concepts can cause trouble. Here's an example. If, on our first date, I asked you if you thought honesty in a relationship is important, you'd probably say yes. Social pressure aside (who would go out with someone who said no?), you'd probably mean it. However, your understanding of the concept of *honesty* might be entirely different from mine, and the concepts *important* and *relationship* can muddy the waters even further. Your definition of honesty might mean that outright lying is off limits, but it's okay to leave out a few things. Or I might agree that honesty is important but not as important as staying out of trouble!

The best way to understand a person's concept of a complex term like honesty is to see whether he acts in ways that are trustworthy. If there's a discrepancy between someone's words and actions, believe what he does, not what he says. Actions do speak louder than words!

Building the Building Blocks

Just as a good relationship involves finding someone with whom you have a lot in common, a basic task of thinking is concept formation—identifying what objects or ideas have in common and grouping them accordingly. "How are they the same?" is a fundamental question that your mind is always asking. Psychologists still aren't exactly sure, though, what features the mind considers when answering this question.

In other words, when your mind asks this question, what does "the same" mean? Do the objects need to look similar, do similar things, or what? Let's take a look at two schools of thought that attempt to solve this riddle—the critical features theory and the prototype hypothesis.

> **Insight**
>
> To understand the difference between *necessary* and *sufficient* features, think of the birds and the bees. Both have wings—a necessary feature to define either one. But wings alone are not sufficient to tell the two apart.

You're Just My Prototype

According to critical features theory, our brain stores mental lists of important characteristics that define concepts. If the concept is *bird*, then *feathers* and *beaks* would be critical features. These critical features are qualities or characteristics that are both necessary and sufficient for a concept to be included in a category. A concept is a member of the category if (and only if) it has every feature on the list.

The second school of thought, the prototype hypothesis, proposes that we build a mental model of our conceptual category—an ideal or representative example that all other members of the category must resemble. This ideal is called a prototype. Teenagers are notorious for modeling their behavior on a "what I think is the coolest kid in the world" prototype.

We all process decision-making information in one of two ways: a reasoned path that leads to intention to engage in a behavior or an intuitive path that leads to an openness to engage in a behavior. But a particular situation may aim an adolescent toward one path or the other, and he may not choose the most prudent path!

Often teenagers' decisions are not premeditated; they simply react to risk-conducive circumstances which usually involve friends or peers. In the reasoned, thoughtful mode, they'll weigh the risks of the behavior. But in the impulsive mode, image is everything. They often hold a favorable prototype in their minds of the kind of person who engages in a particular risky behavior, an image that's usually formed by age seven or eight. Conversely, if they're not willing to engage in a risky behavior, it may be because they don't have a favorable prototype of someone who engages in that behavior.

Lists or Likeness?

Here's how the two schools of thought differ. Let's say you're trying to define the concept "potential marriage candidate." According to critical-features theory, you'd make a list of characteristics: handsome, funny, intelligent, ambitious, generous, and empathic. Then you'd look only for those individuals who meet all these criteria.

The prototype hypothesis, however, suggests that you would be more likely to build a mental model of your ideal mate. If you worship the ground your mom or dad walks on, you're likely to use him or her as the prototype of the perfect wife or husband and date only those individuals who are similar to that parent in significant ways.

The critical-features approach is rigid. If a person doesn't live up to all the features on the list, he simply doesn't count as a member of the category. The prototype approach is a little more flexible; if a person does not exactly match the ideal model, he can still be classified as belonging to the same category. No one will ever be *exactly* like Mom or Dad, so you can settle for someone who is close enough.

One from Column A, One from Column B

Recent research suggests that these two schools of thought are both right—sometimes. When it comes to concepts such as mammals, the critical-features approach works well; all mammals are warm-blooded, have vertebrae, and nurse their young.

Other concepts—like birds—are harder to peg. *Wings*, *feathers*, and *ability to fly* seem like pretty safe critical features, but what about penguins and ostriches? They're birds, but they don't fit neatly into our critical-features category. "Bird" is a blurry category; it has no clear boundaries between members of its class who fly and do not fly. To correct this fuzziness, we probably define our concept of bird not only by critical features (feathers) but also in relation to our ideas about typical members of the category— our prototype.

> **Psychobabble**
>
> Police use prototypes all the time when they help witnesses identify criminal suspects. They prepare a prototype face made of plastic overlays of different facial features taken from a commercially prepared Identi-Kit and then ask the witness to modify the prototype model until it is most similar to the suspect's face.

Great Expectations

Quick! Name 10 things you associate with picnics. Here are the 10 that come to my mind: sunshine, a blanket, a picnic basket, fried chicken, hard-boiled eggs, potato salad, salt, relaxation, sand, and ants. That's my schema for picnic; it's what I expect.

Schemas are packets of information that help us anticipate what we'll find when we encounter a certain concept, category, person, or situation. These expectations come from our understanding of, and experience with, this person, place, or thing. For example, I've certainly had my picnic rained out, but that doesn't usually happen— so rain is not part of my picnic schema. On the other hand, I've never been able to prevent a certain number of ants from sharing my lunch.

New information is easier to handle when we can relate it to existing knowledge. If you invite me to a picnic, I can quickly review my picnic schema and compare the costs (ants, sand) to the rewards (fried chicken!). But schemas do more than help us make quick decisions. They also help us fill in the gaps when something is missing.

Unfortunately, schemas can also help us fill in the blanks incorrectly. If we assign a preconceived set of characteristics to a group, we then jump to conclusions about individual members

> **Psychobabble**
>
> We may be especially susceptible to racial bias when forced to make fast life-or-death decisions. Although not a consistent finding, some studies show that police officers are more likely to wrongfully shoot Black suspects than White suspects when making a split-second decision as to whether the suspect is brandishing a gun.

of that group, even ignoring evidence to the contrary. Unconscious biases leak into our judgments, especially under time pressure.

Do You Mind?

We value our minds so much that many of our legal and moral decisions revolve around our ideas of who has one and who doesn't. The death penalty, abortion, and pulling the plug all revolve around what it means to "have a mind." New findings suggest that we evaluate the right to life based on whether or not we think the person in question has the capacity for self-control, morality and planning (agency), and the capacity to feel sensations such as fear and pain (experience).

Our position on animal rights is also guided by the extent to which we believe they feel and think. Entities who we believe have the capacity for experience are also believed to have moral worth (and hence, the right to life). And to the extent that we think our pet knows right from wrong, we hold it accountable for its actions.

The Big Fish or the Whole Ocean?

Our culture, not surprisingly, greatly influences our mental schemas. We all use the same attention machinery for cognitive tasks, but culture trains us to use that machinery differently. Ask a Japanese student to describe an underwater scene, and she is likely to start with the background and describe the scene as a whole. We Americans start with the biggest, brightest, fastest fish!

Cultural differences also influence how we interpret social events. Explanations for mother-daughter conflict, from the Japanese perspective, center on a lack of understanding between the two. From this cultural perspective, it's easy to see both sides and preferred compromise, while Americans tend to side with one or the other—we Americans tend to think "win-lose"! American culture values the individual, emphasizing the independence of objects from their contexts. East Asian societies emphasize the collective, mutual dependence between context and objects.

Different mental schemas can foster radically different behaviors. Not understanding others' schemas (or being unaware of our own!) can lead us to assign personality labels to people or stereotypes to groups rather than try to understand the cultural assumptions guiding the behavior.

Psychobabble

When students in a college intro biology class were given freedom to think through their own approach to a lab experiment instead of following the usual step-by-step "cookbook method" instructions, the result was a four-fold increase in test scores. But the real success, perhaps, was that students emerged from that class as confident, independent, objective thinkers who could intelligently discuss bigger issues such as stem cell biology and evolution.

Danger, Danger, Danger

Our minds are constantly drawing on old information to make sense out of new data. If we find a discrepancy between new input and already-stored schemata, we adjust by either updating old information or ignoring the new input.

Unfortunately, if we approach new information with an already-formed idea of how it's supposed to fit into our grand conceptual schema, we are likely to tune in to information that confirms our expectations and tune out the information that doesn't fit. For example, people who are told that they are about to meet someone with schizophrenia often "see" these characteristics in their new acquaintance, even when the information is completely false. Our schemata may make it easier for us to understand information but, if we're not careful, our schemata can also distort it.

Insight

Improve your problem-solving skills by thinking outside the box. Don't get trapped by the rules of a game; after you've whipped your friend at backgammon, make up another game with the backgammon board and pieces. Engage in an activity that uses skills you don't normally use. If you have a left-brain job that involves a lot of reading and writing, play chess or create a 3-D puzzle. And if you're having trouble finding a solution to a specific problem, shift your perspective by asking yourself what someone you admire would do in your situation.

We're All Actors Following Scripts

Reese Witherspoon may get $18 million a movie, but we're all pretty good actors. After all, we've been reading scripts since we were small. From a psychological standpoint, a script is a special name for a schema about how things are supposed to happen. And as long as everyone knows (and plays) his or her part, everything is fine.

We have scripts for marriage proposals (bended knee, romance, diamond ring) and birthday celebrations (cake, jokes, gifts). We have expectations (scripts again) about how our boss should behave. These scripts help us know what actions and events are appropriate for a particular setting; they help us decide what to expect or how people should behave under certain circumstances.

When you and I are following similar scripts, we understand the meaning of that situation in the same way and have the same expectations of each other. This script may not always be good for our relationship; after all, if your script for romantic involvement includes violence and so does mine, our script may be familiar to both of us, but it's not healthy. We would both benefit from a script rewrite!

Also it can be pretty uncomfortable when people follow different scripts. If your script for a first date includes being wined and dined by someone eagerly picking up the tab, you aren't going to be happy when your date asks you to split the check.

At the same time, while it might be more comfortable for people to stick with what's familiar, it's also limiting. If we aren't exposed to new ways of being, we have less opportunity to reexamine old schemata or scripts to see if they're still relevant. And we have virtually no opportunity to learn new ones.

Many of us gripe about our parents' occasional tendency to forget we've reached voting age; we complain that they're "stuck in the past" or "trying to keep us from growing up." However, as always, there's more than one side to this story. It may be that we haven't reexamined our own scripts for our parents, so we're still relating to *them* in ways that were more appropriate to our more youthful selves. And dare I mention how easy it is, after a few days of this treatment, to start acting like a teenager again?

Be Reasonable

Now that we've examined the basics of thinking, let's take a look at the really fascinating, creative stuff our minds do with all these concepts, schemata, and scripts. We use our mental building blocks to solve problems and glean new insights. This creative process begins with *reasoning*. We are reasonable *before* we're creative.

def•i•ni•tion

Reasoning is a process of realistic, goal-directed thinking in which conclusions are drawn from a set of facts.

There are two types of reasoning: inductive and deductive. Deductive reasoning starts from your ideas about the "big picture" and tries to apply it to the current situation. Let's say your theory is "all bosses are out to get their employees." If you are using deductive reasoning, you might generate several hypotheses that, once tested, should confirm or discount your cynical theory about bosses—and figure out whether or not she's out to get *you*.

Hypothesis 1: Conniving bosses take credit for their employee's work. (Uh-oh! Just last week, your boss got a pat on the back for the filing system *you* devised!) Hypothesis 2: Conniving bosses say one thing and do another. (You just remembered your boss promised you a raise a week ago, but your paycheck isn't any bigger!) And so on. In this case, perhaps there's enough evidence to apply your general "conniving-boss theory" to your current boss.

But what if you not only got credit for that filing system, but you also received a bonus in your paycheck and a rave review at evaluation time? This is hardly the behavior of a con-niver! At first, you might decide your boss is that one-in-a-million exception to the still-true general rule. However, over time, especially if you encounter several benevolent bosses, you will hopefully begin to reexamine your general theory. But there's no guarantee! We hold fast to existing beliefs and are most likely to judge as true the conclusions with which we already agree!

> **Psychobabble**
>
> Police interrogators are using a new technique to make it easier to spot deception: ask the suspect to tell his story in reverse order. Lying is strenuous and requires tremendous mental effort, so raising the suspect's cognitive load provokes additional nonverbal cues that tattle on liars.

Inductive reasoning, on the other hand, starts with *specific* observations and clues. For example, let's say your boss "forgets" to give you credit for an idea at a staff meeting. Being the generous person you are, you shrug it off as a mere oversight. Then it happens again. Later, your boss encourages you to apply for a higher position in another department, and then you learn he sabotaged your candidacy. With inductive reasoning, once you begin to detect patterns and regularities among those observations, you formulate some tentative hypotheses to explore and end up developing some general conclusions or theories. In the conniving-boss scenario, you don't have to be psychic to see a pattern of deception emerging. If you're smart, you'll watch your back.

Problem Solving

What's the fastest way to get to work in the morning traffic? How are we going to get a 24-hour project done in 8 hours? And how can we get that cute guy in cubicle number 27 to acknowledge our existence? Problem solving is the space between what we know and what we need to know. Any time our thinking is directed toward solving specific challenges, we're doing it.

Insight

Are you going to Vegas? Don't gamble without a good night's sleep! Research suggests that sleep deprivation screws up our ability to accurately assess the risks and rewards of high-rolling; we're more likely to overestimate the odds of winning and underestimate the likelihood we'll lose.

Defining Your Puzzles

Sometimes it's hard to know what the problem really is. For example, an unhappily married friend of mine wanted to try to "fix" her relationship by going to therapy. However, her husband repeatedly said he was happy, nothing was wrong, and they didn't need any professional help. When her communication strategy didn't work, she began to rethink the problem. Maybe her unhappiness was her problem alone and she ought to find a way to be happy herself.

Once she reframed her problem in this way, she quit trying to wrangle her husband into couples' therapy; she made an appointment to get her own life back on track. Within a few months, her husband was sitting on the couch right beside her. He later said he had been terrified to go to therapy, but seeing the changes his wife was making, he didn't want to get left behind! Sometimes, if we just can't come up with the right solution, it pays to take a second look at the problem.

Desperately Seeking Solutions

Of course, even when we know what the problem is, we still have to solve it. Algorithms and heuristics are two strategies that may help us find our way through life's maze.

An algorithmic approach to solving problems involves systematically thinking through every possible solution. A heuristic approach, on the other hand, adopts a "rule of thumb" that serves as a shortcut to solving complex problems. This rule of thumb is based on general strategies that have worked in similar situations in the past. Heuristic advice like "never go to bed when you're mad" has helped thousands of newlyweds.

Psychobabble
A 2002 poll found that 48 percent of Americans believe UFOs have visited Earth over the years. More than one-third believe that humans have already interacted with some form of extraterrestrial life. Strange beliefs might not be reasonable, but they sure are common.

Guilty Until Proven Innocent

Algorithms can be terrifically time-consuming, so it's no wonder that people often use heuristics to solve problems. Sometimes they're useful; it's probably hard to go wrong with the "never go to bed when you're mad" heuristic. However, our use of mental shortcuts can also result in cognitive bias, leading to thinking errors that affect our judgment and impede our decision-making ability. In fact, we humans seem to have a number of built-in biases.

Remember that one of our natural biases seems to be our mind's need to find connections between events and concepts. Our minds will look for connections between even random events and see events that occur together as somehow causing each other. Many medical professionals will tell you that a full moon "makes people crazy" and will give you erroneous anecdote after anecdote about ER statistics on full-moon weekends.

Another cognitive bias is our tendency to believe that we control our own fate. While this is generally a healthy belief, this bias can also lead us to make faulty *judgments*.

But faulty judgments, such as blaming the victim, can be not only unfair but also dangerous. The "she asked for it" attitude toward rape victims is an extreme example of out-of-control human logic.

def•i•ni•tion

A **judgment** is the process of using available information to form opinions, draw conclusions, and evaluate people and situations. Judgments have a lot of influence over what we decide to do.

Strangely enough, though, faulty assessments can work in our favor if they promote a more favorable opinion of ourselves. A recent study shows that those of us who think we look younger than our age are more satisfied with life than those of us who think we look our age or older. And this seems to hold true regardless of whether other people (or the mirror) agree with us!

Insight

Beef up your immunity to faulty logic by looking for these kinds of fallacies: the "slippery slope" (once someone drinks a beer, she's doomed to alcoholism), the "hasty generalization" (I know that women are inferior to men; my former co-worker, Jane, always held our team back), and the "false alternative" (what doesn't kill you makes you stronger).

Another cognitive bias, the availability heuristic, encourages us to estimate probabilities based on our personal knowledge; if we've experienced it, we're likely to overestimate the frequency of its occurrence. The representativeness heuristic, based on the idea that people and events can be grouped into categories, can also do some social damage. Once you've been categorized, the assumption is that you share all the features of other members in that category—and they share all your features, too. How would you like others to judge you as the official representative of your race or gender? Fortunately, people, places, and things do not neatly fit into categories simply because we lazily assign them to certain groups.

Comparing Apples to Oranges

Turns out we *can* compare apples to oranges. We do it all the time when we're evaluating facts in the context of memories and past experiences. We make choices by assigning values to different options. The law of transitivity holds that, if you consistently prefer A (lasagna) to B (last night's leftovers) and B (leftovers) to C (liver and onions), then you should predictably prefer A (lasagna) to C (liver and onions). If we perceive values as constant, our preferences will be transitive.

Researchers believe that the rational concept of economic value may actually be encoded at the level of individual neurons in the frontal lobe and that the stability of these frontal lobe neurons may help explain why we make consistent decisions over the short term. Researchers are just beginning to investigate decision-making at the level of individual neurons, a new research terrain called neuroeconomics. Such research might eventually shed more light on disorders that involve chronically poor choices, such as compulsive gambling and other addictions.

Psychobabble

Monkeys also recognize value when they see it! In a study where monkeys were required to choose between grape juice or apple juice and move towards their chosen target, they tended to choose the target associated with the highest reward. Even though they consistently liked grape juice over apple juice, they'd go for apple half the time if it was offered in larger quantities.

Decisions: Older and Wiser?

No doubt you've heard stories about elderly people getting bilked out of their life savings. But are they really more vulnerable to fraud than younger adults? New research suggests that some of them are and that vulnerability may be caused by a breakdown in the ventromedial prefrontal cortex, a brain region critical to good decision-making.

Healthy adults were given the Iowa Gambling Task (IGT), a computerized decision-making test. IGT is a game where participants win by drawing cards from advantageous decks and avoiding high-risk decks. Thirty-five to forty of the neurologically normal seniors made poor decisions. These findings also generalized to the real world; the same people who scored badly on the IGT were also more likely to fall prey to deceptive advertising. They were far less likely to spot deceptive statements and inconsistencies than good decision-makers, and worse, more likely to buy.

Insight

Memory comes in two forms. When you recall facts and concepts, such as a phone number or something that someone said to you, you are retrieving a declarative memory. When you remember how to employ your wicked backhand in a tennis match, you're retrieving a procedural memory, which includes skill sets and instruction sets.

Psychobabble

Psychologists have now mapped the evolution of a decision. Brain scans show that we use different parts of our brain during the evaluation process than we do during the "eureka" moment a decision is made.

Seven Strategies for Improving Your Decision-Making Batting Average

In many ways, we're a result of all of the decisions we've made in our lives to date. Recognizing this, use these tips to enhance your decision-making batting average.

♦ Write down the pros and cons of a line of action. It clarifies your thinking and makes for a better decision.

♦ Consider who your decision will affect. Whenever feasible, get them involved to increase their commitment.

♦ Determine alternative courses of action before gathering data.

> **Psychobabble**
>
> Multi-tasking is highly overrated, at least when we're trying to learn something that requires focus. A recent study found that multi-tasking (such as listening to music while we're studying) requires us to juggle multiple brain systems—not a good thing when we're trying to learn calculus or absorb Chaucer.

◆ Before implementing what appears to be the best choice, assess the risk by asking, "What can I think of that might go wrong with this alternative?"

◆ Mentally rehearse implementation of your choice, and reflect in your imagination what outcomes will result.

◆ As part of your decision-making process, always consider how you will implement your decision.

◆ Once you've made the decision and begun what you're going to do, put the "what ifs" aside and commit yourself to your plan of action.

Our cognitive processes have an impact upon every single aspect of our lives. Not only do they enable us to solve life's mysteries, but they also strongly influence how we feel about them. "I think, therefore I am" may be somewhat of an overstatement, but not by much!

Straight from the Lab

Bikinis and Sex Scramble Men's Brains   In experiments where men were shown images of either landscapes or bikini-clad women and then offered a choice between receiving cash immediately or bargaining for a larger sum they must wait a week or a month for, the bikini-gazers settled for a less lucrative bargain than the landscape-viewers. Sexually aroused men value immediate gratification more and may do things they would not otherwise do.

Nip Temptation in the Bud   If you ask people to predict how often they will succumb to a temptation, a new study shows you may increase the number of times they actually do. "Intention" questions, which we perceive as harmless, may lower our guard and even act as a liberating influence that encourages us to succumb to vices more often than we otherwise would.

Think Fast   Fast thinking actually elevates our mood and makes us feel happier. In one study, participants asked to read a series of statements at twice the normal reading speed felt more energetic, creative, powerful, and self-assured afterward, regardless of whether the statements were depressing (e.g., "I want to go to sleep and never wake up") or exhilarating (e.g., "Wow! I feel great!"). In other words, thought speed may have a more powerful impact on mood than the actual thought content.

Don't Think Why, Think How   In a recent study, students who listed the reasons why they should exercise failed to improve their performance. However, those who listed the actions they could take to up their exercise followed through.

The Least You Need to Know

- ◆ Psychologists are detectives of the mind—by observing human behavior, analyzing errors, and scanning our brains, they gather clues about the way our minds work.

- ◆ Thinking is like a highly sophisticated assembly line made up of concepts, schemata, and scripts, and our past experience and culture partly determine what these conceptual parts look like.

- ◆ There are two types of reasoning: inductive (which moves from general principles to specific cases) and deductive (which moves from specific clues to general conclusions).

- ◆ All thinking is geared toward solving problems and uses either algorithmic (considering all solutions) or heuristic (shortcuts based on prior information) strategies.

- ◆ Heuristics save time but can lead to cognitive errors.

Don't Blow a Fuse!

In This Chapter

◆ The many ways you can be stressed

◆ Stress is just a *GAS!*

◆ The difference between coping and moping

◆ Meeting at the mind-body immunity connection

◆ Write to reduce your stress

"Stress is when you wake up screaming and realize you haven't fallen asleep yet." "Hand over the chocolate, and no one gets hurt." "If stress burned calories, I'd be a size 5." Even our t-shirts seem to admit that stress is a constant factor in our lives!

This chapter focuses on one of the greatest mental-health challenges facing Americans today: stress. Find out what stress is and what causes it. We also take a look at the psychological effects of physical illness, ways psychological illnesses can cause physical symptoms, and the complex interaction between our brain, body, emotions, and immune system. But don't get stressed by all this; we have a whole chapter later on about positive psychology and coping!

Defining Stress

Public speaking, the GREs, getting laid off—these words may fill some of us with delight (at last, I don't have to go through that daily grind anymore!) and some of us with terror (I'll die if I have to get up in front of that group). While some life events are stressful for all of us, the fact that we feel differently about the same events confirms an important part of stress—to some extent, stress is in the eyes of the beholder.

In fact, for something to be stressful, we must consider it threatening to us in some way—either physically or emotionally. And for stress to occur, we have to have some doubt or question about our ability to deal effectively with the stressor. Getting married or starting a new job is often stressful because we're treading on new ground and haven't yet proven to ourselves that we can handle it.

How Can I Be Stressed? Let Me Count the Ways ...

Psychologists Suzanne Segerstrom, Ph.D. and Gregory Miller, Ph.D. analyzed the results of nearly 300 studies and sorted *stress* into five different categories:

- **Acute time-limited stressors**—lab challenges such as public speaking or mental math.

- **Brief naturalistic stressors**—real-world challenges such as academic tests or job interviews.

- **Stressful event sequences**—a focal event such as loss of a spouse or a major natural disaster, such as Hurricane Katrina in September 2005. These events give rise to a series of related challenges (rebuilding a home, recovering from the fear) that at some point will end.

- **Chronic stressors**—pervasive demands that force people to restructure their identity or social roles, without any clear end point, such as injury resulting in permanent disability, caring for a spouse with severe dementia, or being a refugee forced from one's native country by war.

- **Distant stressors**—traumatic experiences that occurred in the distant past yet can have long-lasting effects, such as child abuse, combat trauma, or having been a prisoner of war.

A sixth class of *stressor* we shouldn't overlook is the background stressors, also known as daily hassles: the neighbor's car alarm that went off at 3 A.M., the ATM that was out of cash, the kitty that missed the litterbox again. As minor as these may seem, they do add up. If your life is filled with hassles, take care of them or, at the least, change your attitude toward them.

def•i•ni•tion

Stress is a general term that includes all the physical, behavioral, emotional, and cognitive responses we make to a disruptive internal or external event. **Stressors** are the events that trigger a stress response.

Stress Is All Around

Have you ever heard anyone say he needed *more* stress in his life? I haven't. Literally hundreds of stress-management tapes, books, and courses are on the market, and not one of them offers strategies for increasing it. In the high-powered era in which we live, stress reduction has become a part of the American dream.

Given that we're constantly trying to get rid of stress, wouldn't we all be better off without any? Not really. Without stress, we would have no problems to overcome, goals to reach, or inventions to create. Pretty soon, we'd wind up as lazy couch potatoes with dull wits and no motivation. Life would be pretty boring, which can be pretty stressful itself!

Stress and the Individual

Stress is a part of being alive. Being stressed out, however, isn't. Stress becomes a problem for us when we have too much of it and not enough resources to cope with what we have. Yet what is too much stress?

We've all known people who bounce back from even the toughest challenges, while others seem to have trouble coping with life's daily hassles. People also respond differently to the same stressor; the next time you're stuck in traffic, take a look around. You'll see some people calmly beebopping to the radio while others are frantically pulling onto the shoulder and craning their necks looking for a break in the traffic.

The difference between the beeboppers and the neckcraners is how they interpret the stressor and the coping resources they rely on to deal with it.

Stress Up-Close and Personal

Stress is uniquely personal. Our response to stress is a combination of bodily reactions, thoughts, feelings, and behaviors. And one person's pleasure is another person's poison.

Factors Affecting Your Personal Stress Level

Internal Factors	External Factors
Physical health	Medical care
Genetic vulnerabilities	Finances
Mental health	Skills and training
Self-esteem	Support systems
Temperament	Counseling
Self-confidence	Predictability of stressor
Cultural expectations	Frequency of stressor's occurrence
Cultural definitions	Intensity of stressor's occurrence

Your unique combination of personal factors, available resources, and certain attributes of the stressor itself are what determine just how much stress (if any) you feel in response to a given stressor.

Your ability to cope with small to medium stressors right now is also affected by major stressful events in the past, especially if they're in the recent past; for example, you'll be much more upset if you get into a fender-bender on the way home from your father's funeral than on the way back from the 7-11.

Making Change

Historically, changes in food supply, weather, or safety were the stressors our human ancestors faced. While today's challenges are more likely to involve our self-esteem than our physical safety, they still require coping with change.

Change is the culprit behind much of our stress. Whether it's the loss of a loved one or the birth of a baby, adjustment to a new situation requires a lot of energy and, sometimes, different coping strategies. A good change can be especially difficult because our expectations don't match reality.

For example, society tells expectant parents that the birth of a child is an utterly joyful event. When a new parent feels less than thrilled with existing on two hours of sleep and changing diapers every 10 minutes, she can easily interpret the resulting stress as a sign of bad or incompetent parenting. This, of course, only adds more stress. If new parents can see their stress as a normal reaction to this dramatic lifestyle change, they might applaud themselves for surviving rather than berate themselves for feeling grouchy and tired!

Sometimes, stress appears before change even takes place. The cold feet many people get before their marriage is an example of the anticipatory stress of getting hitched.

 Brain Buster

Too much change can be hazardous to your health. Recent widows and widowers are much more vulnerable to all types of disease in the six months following the death of a spouse. Losing someone close to you is a red flag to take extra good care of your mental and physical health.

Brain Buster

If possible, avoid major decisions when you're stressed out; stress distorts and clouds your thinking. In addition, since stress impairs your ability to hold your tongue, avoid people or situations in which it might not be in your best interest to blurt out the truth!

How Do You Know If You're Stressed Out?

"I'm stressed out," you tell your best friend. But how do you know you are? Since people experience stress differently, it's important to know what being stressed out feels like to you. When you're stressed, it can help to write down what you do, how you feel, and what you're thinking—and use your responses to conduct regular stress checkups. To get you started, here are some of the most common symptoms of stress:

- ◆ Feeling on edge, frustrated, easily annoyed
- ◆ Having trouble concentrating or making decisions
- ◆ Finding even simple things burdensome or difficult
- ◆ Eating more or less than usual
- ◆ Experiencing mood swings
- ◆ Feeling distracted—having a hard time keeping track of little things
- ◆ Being irritable or impatient

◆ Overreacting with strong feelings to minor events

◆ Not getting as much pleasure out of things that you usually enjoy

◆ Drinking more to relax or feel less tense

Burning Out

I once read that the average career life of a therapist was seven years. After seven years, most psychotherapists who are on the "front lines" dealing with clients every day go AWOL. They quit. They change careers. They burn out.

Burnout is a combination of emotional exhaustion, personal detachment, and a reduced sense of accomplishment that most often plagues professionals in the service industries—doctors, lawyers, mental health professionals, and teachers. Anyone who has high-intensity contact with others on a daily basis is at risk for job burnout. Unfortunately, not only does the professional suffer, but inadequate or impersonal care may also shortchange the person on the receiving end.

The Fires of Burnout Build over Time

Burnout is the end result of chronic, interpersonal stress. And it can happen in our personal lives, too. Do you have a friend whose life is one crisis after another? With the first crisis, you probably mobilized all your resources to help your buddy out. With the second, you also responded to the "fire alarm." By the tenth or eleventh, however, your attitude may be a little more cynical and your offer to help a lot slower. Your friend has cried wolf one too many times and burned your caring right out of you!

Buffering Against Burnout!

Chronic stress can cause serious physical and mental problems, most of which can be prevented, and burnout is one of them. Health-care professionals who regulate the amount of face-to-face patient contact, take regular vacations and mental health days, schedule in leisure activities, and get support from work colleagues and family members are much less likely to burn out.

But what kind of support do we need? While the old adage "Misery loves company" is well and good, new research suggests that equally stressed partners or friends aren't the best social buffers when we're trying to get a grip. We may be better off talking to someone who's in a better frame of reference. In other words, when you've gone over the side, it's best not to expect reinforcement from someone who's also struggling to stay afloat.

Insight

Stressed workers under 50 have a 68 percent higher risk of developing coronary heart disease than their work-fulfilled counterparts. In the workplace, pressure, monotony, or danger don't cause the most stress. The greatest stressors are feeling we don't have control over our jobs or the resources to do the job well and having no sense of how the job we do will benefit others.

I Feel Like Fighting or Flying Away

Are you a quick judge of character? Can you leap tall buildings at the first sign of danger? Thank your amygdala—your own personal crisis manager. It does a quick survival check by assessing the emotional significance of a situation and generating some of your immediate responses. Through connections to the hypothalamus, your amygdala gears your body for action by stimulating the hormones that produce the physical responses (like increasing heart rate and blood pressure) that accompany strong emotions.

Remember the endocrine system from Chapter 2? This communication system helps regulate things like blood pressure, metabolism, and heart rate. When you experience the fight-or-flight syndrome, a sequence of internal processes are triggered by your endocrine system as it prepares for a threatening situation. This syndrome is not to be taken lightly; at least 15 bodily changes are triggered at once.

Psychobabble

Men and women returning from combat in the Iraq war showed similar levels of—and reactions to—stress. Gender differences in coping, when present, are limited to the events considered most stressful on a daily basis; women typically say that relationship hassles top the stress list, and men complain most about work-related problems.

But I Feel Like Tending and Befriending

A stress response that may manifest as fight-or-flight in men may often manifest as tend-and-befriend in women. Evolutionarily, males may have tended to stressors either by overcoming or fleeing them, whereas women may have responded by nurturing offspring and affiliating with social groups.

Research shows that the neural response to stress differs between men and women. When pressured to perform a challenging math task, men showed increased activity in the right prefrontal cortex, whereas women showed increased activity in the limbic system—the area of the brain involved with emotion. And the brain changes lasted longer in women. Perhaps this helps explain why the rate of depression and anxiety disorders is twice as high in women.

> ### Psychobabble
>
> Preliminary research findings suggest that stress and aggression may be intertwined at the biological level; stress lowers our brain's ability to inhibit aggression, and acting aggressively triggers more stress hormones (making it harder to stop). This stress-violence cycle may partially explain why a bad day at the office could lead to more fights at home.

It's a GAS, GAS, GAS

Of course, the long term isn't necessarily our strong suit. In some respects, human beings are better equipped for the short run. We get tired of the same foods; we get bored with the same activities; we get burned out on our jobs; and, yes, sometimes we do punch out our friends—even if only verbally. Even our stress responses work better in the short term; if we have to fight or flee too much, our emergency response system breaks down.

Hans Selye was a man with great endurance and a psychologist's interest in the effects of chronic, severe stress on the body. He started wondering what would happen if the body were in a constant state of alarm. He found his answer—nothing good. Over time, chronic stress can tear us down and wear us out.

GASsing Up

According to Selye, one of the reasons that life stressors have a cumulative effect is that our bodies can't distinguish between them. Instead of generating different physical reactions to different life events, our bodies have a general physical response to any stress. Selye called the pattern of bodily reactions to an ongoing, serious threat the *general adaptation syndrome (GAS)*, and identified three stages:

1. Alarm

2. Resistance

3. Exhaustion

def•i•ni•tion

The **general adaptation syndrome (GAS)** is a pattern of general physical responses triggered by any stressors, no matter what kind.

All Stations on Alert!

The alarm stage is the fight-or-flight response in action. The body mobilizes energy to deal with a specific stressor, such as nearly having a car accident, making a public speech, or getting married. Adrenaline is released into the bloodstream, commonly causing sweaty palms, a pounding heart, rapid breathing, increased blood pressure, and slowed digestion. Although these symptoms can be uncomfortable, your body returns to normal fairly quickly once you alleviate the stressor. No harm is done.

Fighting Harder

If the stressor continues, however, the body tries to compensate by kicking into overdrive. Temporarily, it works harder to resist the stress; hormones continue to pump adrenaline, physical arousal remains high, and the immune system works harder. Of course, you might not feel any of these things. What you may feel, though, is anxiety and a sense of being pressured or driven. You may begin having problems remembering details, and you may start to feel fatigued. If you find yourself drinking more coffee, smoking more cigarettes, or boozing more than normal, your body may be trying to cope with too much stress.

Ending in Exhaustion

Over time, chronic stress consumes more energy resources than your body can produce. Stress directly affects your neuroendocrine stress pathways. Your hormones burn out, leaving you with less resistance to emotional stress and physical illness. The emotional burnout that chronic stress produces is often known by another name: depression.

You'd save your body a lot of wear and tear if you could just switch your stress response on and off as needed or if you could teach it the difference between a life-threatening event and a stressful, but happy, occasion. Unfortunately, you can't. What you *can* do is work with your stress response by building up your emotional "muscles" to handle stress more effectively.

Coping or Moping

I once had a client who was a young, single mother of two special needs children. This woman received no financial or emotional support from her ex-spouse, who had left her for a younger woman and quit his job. Week after week, she worked full time, juggled her bills, and did a pretty darned good job of single parenting. Yet she often came into my office in tears, berating herself for occasionally losing her temper or feeling stressed out; in her mind, she was not coping. In my professional opinion, the fact that she got through each day was a miracle and worthy of an Olympic gold medal in the coping department.

We all know exercising regularly, eating healthy food, and getting plenty of sleep can build up our stress tolerance. But a good lifestyle can't keep bad things from happening. When they do, the way we cope with them can mean the difference between bouncing back and getting knocked on our behind.

Not All Coping Is Created Equal

Coping is any strategy you can use to deal with a situation that strains or overwhelms your emotional or physical resources. For example, if you get laid off from your job, you might feel angry and hurt, fantasize about revenge, and then polish your resumé and hit the pavement. Different stressors require different coping strategies; grieving the loss of a child would require different coping strategies than putting up with a chronically nagging spouse.

Let's say you applied for your dream job three months ago. You believe you were qualified for the job and were sure you'd get it. However, six weeks ago, harsh reality knocked on your door—you found out they hired someone else. Now all you can think about is how it should have been. Even though you know you should pick yourself up and start job-hunting again, you find yourself daydreaming about what would've happened if you'd been hired. You spend hours plotting revenge on the company official whom you're sure gave you the thumbs down. Are you coping?

Therapists would say no. Instead, they'd say you're defending against the pain of rejection by escaping into fantasies. Coping, on the other hand, involves identifying and eliminating the source of your problem—your lack of a job and your disappointment over not getting the job of your dreams.

The difference between coping and moping can be tricky to understand and even harder to detect in our own lives. As a rule of thumb, defending ourselves merely lessens the symptoms of the problems, often only temporarily. Coping, on the other hand, gets to the root of the problem and focuses on changing what we can change and making peace with what we can't.

Insight

The next time you find yourself worrying, channel your stress into anticipatory coping. Mentally review similar past experiences; these will reacquaint you with what mistakes to avoid repeating, what reactions to expect, how you will feel, and what resources can help. Plan what you will do to cope with this stressor more effectively than you have in the past. Whereas worrying can increase stress, anticipatory coping can help you prepare for a stressful event.

Categories of Coping

Life would be a lot easier if the perfect solution to every argument was to look your opponents in the eye and tell them your honest thoughts and feelings. This coping strategy might work well with your spouse, but not many job supervisors want to hear that you think they're incompetent boobs. Psychologists would agree that facing up to a stressful situation is always a pretty good idea, but finding the best way to face up to it depends on the situation.

Insight

Avoidance coping strategies ultimately cause more stress. Common avoidance tactics include denial (hey, there's no problem), distraction (having an affair instead of dealing with marital problems), venting (yelling or worrying without taking any action), and sedation (numbing through drugs, alcohol, overeating, and so on).

In general, coping strategies fall into two categories—problem-focused and emotion-focused. Each has its strengths and weaknesses, and each is better suited to certain categories of stressors.

Focusing on the Problem

With problem-focused coping, you deal directly with the stressor to change or eliminate it. You confront your teenager about running up your long-distance phone bill or, more realistically, you put on a block so she can't dial out. You take a self-defense class to cope with your fear of being victimized. Problem-focused coping works best when the stressor is controllable—when you can actually do something to change it.

Gaining the Emotional Edge

With emotion-focused coping, the goal is to change the way you feel and think about whatever is stressing you. For example, unless you can afford to quit your job, you might not want to confront a critical or controlling boss. You can, however, get emotional support from co-workers in the same boat. You can also use self-talk that lessens your boss's impact on you; the next time he criticizes you, mentally remind yourself that it's your boss's problem and he's the one who should be embarrassed by such behavior, not you.

Psychobabble
As our economy suffers, more people point to their empty wallet as a sign of stress. A recent survey of people trapped in the debt-stress crunch showed that 44 percent suffered migraine headaches, 29 percent had severe anxiety, 23 percent suffered severe depression, and 50 percent had some form of muscle tension or back pain.

Emotion-focused coping works best for stressors that you can't control. It doesn't eliminate the source of the stress, but it can change what the stressor means to you. It's a lot more stressful to think of divorce as a personal failure than to think of it as a painful learning experience.

In reality, of course, many stressors in our lives have both uncontrollable *and* controllable parts. A person who has cancer can seek the best medical care and take control of her illness. At the same time, however, that person can't change the diagnosis and will have to find ways to cope with the fear, anger, and sadness that accompany such a scary illness.

Identifying Your Stressors

If you frequently feel victimized by life's events, you may be using emotion-focused coping to deal with situations you can change. One of the complicated parts of coping is identifying which events are controllable and which are not. How many times have you heard a friend complain about her boyfriend over and over, yet she never tells him what is bothering or hurting her? It's fine that she's dealing with her emotions by complaining to her friends, but she should have an action plan in place before she hangs up the phone!

Stressful Thoughts

Oh, no, I have only seven more weeks to finish this book! That's not enough time! What if I miss my deadline? I'll be finished in the publishing world! They may not even publish this one …

Do those thoughts sound like a good coping strategy to you? Probably not; in fact, you may have started getting nervous about my deadline, too. The way we think about the stressors in our lives influences both the emotions we have about them and the solutions we come up with. To some extent, they're the key to both emotion-focused *and* problem-focused coping.

For example, before you can decide what to do about whatever event is stressing you out, you have to identify it and evaluate its severity. This is called cognitive appraisal, a highly subjective and amazingly powerful process. As you can see from my frantic thoughts about my deadline, the time pressure (the stressor) of writing this book sometimes became much greater because of the catastrophic thoughts (the cognitive appraisal) that went with it. Even psychologists have trouble coping sometimes!

Brain Buster

People who procrastinate over school or work tasks are more likely to have health problems. Although procrastination itself is linked to stress, procrastinators are also more likely to behave in an unhealthy way (put off sleep, grab something to eat on the run) or delay medical treatment (canceling a doctor's appointment).

Psychobabble

In 1974, bank employees in Stockholm, Sweden, were imprisoned in a bank vault for five days during a robbery. Upon their release, the employees expressed warmth—and even attraction—for the men who had taken them hostage. This bizarre emotional response became known as the Stockholm Syndrome, a coping pattern in which hostages and prisoners identify and sympathize with their captors. Sometimes, extreme situations trigger extreme forms of coping.

I Think I Can, I Think I Can, I Think I Can

And it helps to believe you can cope with your stressors. People often underestimate their ability to cope with life's curveballs. One of the most powerful stress-busting strategies is to keep track of your coping history. Reviewing your impressive track record helps you keep at bay any untrue negative self-statements like, "I'll never get this right" or "I just can't stand this." And it may ultimately keep you healthier.

The Mind-Body Immunity Connection

The boundary between our mind and our body is so thin it's practically nonexistent. Psychological stress jolts our bodies. Depression compromises our immune systems. But thinking more positively about a stressful event can actually help our bodies relax; after all, our brain is responsible for our thoughts and feelings as well as the regulation of many of our bodily functions. No wonder experiences that affect our thoughts and feelings can also affect our physical functioning.

In fact, sometimes the body expresses what the mind can't. For example, a person may continually experience symptoms of physical illness but have no medical disease that could cause the symptoms. Psychologists call this *somatoform disorder*. The most dramatic of these disorders is conversion disorder, in which the person temporarily loses some bodily function in ways that cannot be explained by physical illness.

def•i•ni•tion

Somatoform disorders are mental disorders in which the person experiences symptoms of physical illness but has no medical disease that could cause them.

A less dramatic version of this phenomenon is somatization disorder, which is characterized by a long history of vague and unverifiable medical complaints. Most typically, the person complains of symptoms of several disorders, for example, headaches, dizziness, heart palpitations, and nausea. While a certain percentage of people with these diagnoses turn out to have underlying medical conditions, a significant number have an underlying psychological condition—depression.

Culture and Stress

In many cultures, it's not acceptable to seek help for a psychological or emotional problem, but it *is* okay to go to the doctor for a physical issue. Physicians dealing with people from different cultures have to learn when a stomachache is probably an ulcer and when it's probably a mother-in-law!

If you notice your headaches only seem to flair up at work or your stomach only cramps when your spouse walks in the door, your emotional stress may be talking to you through your body.

You're Wearing Me Down

The field of psychoneuroimmunology is the study of the interactions between the brain, the body, the emotions, and the immune system. Research confirms that mental stress puts us at risk for physical illness; it increasingly shows that emotional distress shuts down some of the body's defenses, making us more vulnerable to disease.

While stress doesn't guarantee we'll get sick, we know it plays a major role in triggering and worsening depression, cardiovascular disease, and some (e.g., viral) cancers and infectious diseases. For example, stress causes changes in the autonomic nervous system that influence the replication of the HIV virus. Research with mice shows that stress even increases a susceptibility to skin infections.

The stress hormone cortisol seems to be the culprit. Every cell contains a tiny clock called a telomere, which shortens each time the cell divides. The telomerase enzyme within each cell keeps immune cells young by preserving their telomere length—that is, their ability to keep dividing.

Research shows that the stress hormone cortisol suppresses immune cells' ability to activate telomerase, which may explain why the cells of chronically stressed people have shorter telomeres. Under stress, increased cortisol supports the flight-or-flight response but wears down the immune system.

> **Psychobabble**
>
> Short-term stress actually revs up the immune system, an adaptive response preparing for injury or infection; it's long-term or chronic stress that causes too much wear and tear.

Seeking Immunity Through Killer Ts

The good news is that we can significantly impact our body's response to stress. For example, we can manufacture natural killer cells called T-cells. These amazing fighting units have the ability to recognize and selectively kill both cancer cells and virus-infected cells. Researchers have actually measured variations in T-cell activity based on interactions between stress and attitude.

For example, Dr. Steven Locke at Harvard Medical School questioned subjects about stressful events in their lives and also about their psychiatric symptoms of distress. He then took blood samples and measured their natural killer cell activity. He found that the T-cell activity level of the group with high stress and low symptoms was *three times higher* than the group with high stress and high symptoms. People under stress who know how to deal with it emotionally appear to have more immune activity than even unstressed people with poor mental habits.

Writing with a Capital T

Writing is one way to up those T cells. Scientists at Southern Methodist University and Ohio State University College of Medicine have proven that writing positively affects your mental and physical health. Subjects who wrote thoughtfully and emotionally about traumatic experiences achieved increased T-cell production, a drop in physician visits, fewer absentee days, and generally improved physical health.

Try these writing therapies:

◆ **Reflective writing.** Shift your perspective by writing about events in your life as if you were an outside observer. This strategy is especially effective for life changes—new job, relationship changes, etc. Begin with the phrase, "It was a time when she …" and then describe the event in detail, using your senses— sounds, smells, sights, and feelings.

◆ **Cathartic writing.** Write about your feelings, all of them. Pour out your pain, fear, anger, frustrations, and grief. But don't just write when you're feeling upset or sad—write when you're feeling joyful and grateful, too. Begin with: "Right now I feel …" And don't edit. Don't censor. If you get stuck, reread what you wrote and then just add the next thing that comes to mind.

◆ **Unsent letters.** Unsent letters allow you to express your true feelings when you're not comfortable expressing them face-to-face. This technique is especially helpful in dealing with death or divorce—situations where you may not be able to speak to the person directly. Begin with a salutation, such as "Dear …" Then just let your pen guide you. You may be surprised at the power and clarity you gain from this exercise; in fact, this may launch a whole new level of communication with others.

Playing Catch-Up

We began this chapter looking at the evolution of our fight-or-flight response to emergencies. In some respects, our bodies have not caught up with the times; they're still using the same old emergency system our ancestors used to fight off bears and defend their territory. We have the capacity to develop some nifty coping strategies to handle the stress in our lives. If we use them, we can help the evolution of our own bodies—that is, the aging process—go more smoothly.

Straight from the Lab

Pregnant and Stressed? Listen to Music   Music therapy studies show that pregnant women can significantly reduce stress, anxiety, and depression in two weeks simply by inserting 30 minutes of relaxing music into their daily routine. Faves were lullabies, such as "Brahms' Lullaby" and "Twinkle, Twinkle Little Star," and nature and crystal sounds.

The Teenage Catch-22   Adolescents who experience family stressors have more problems with attendance and learning at school the next day. And those who had attendance and learning problems experienced more family stress the following day. This bi-directional spillover lasted for two days after the initial stressor occurred. As for the long-term, those with higher levels of family stress and school problems in ninth grade saw declining academic performance until the end of twelfth grade.

Kids Feel Combat Stress, Too   War significantly elevates stress not only in soldiers but also in the families they leave behind. Children with military parents have higher blood pressure, heart rates, and general stress levels than their peers.

Float Your Stress Away   A new Swedish study shows that floating in large, sound-proof, light-proof tanks of warm high-saltwater can be effective in alleviating long-term stress-related pain. This "float therapy" activates the body's own healing system and decreases stress hormones and blood pressure. People with long-term fibromyalgia, depression, anxiety, and long-term stress-related pain felt substantially better after only twelve treatments.

The Least You Need to Know

- We feel stressed when we consider an event to be threatening and we aren't sure we have the resources to cope with it; this is a normal response to overwhelming internal or external events.

- Common symptoms of stress include feeling irritable and on edge, overreacting to minor events, mood swings, and difficulty concentrating.

- While stress initially energizes the body to take action, over time it is physically exhausting and weakens our immune system.

◆ Stress plays a major role in triggering and worsening depression, cardiovascular disease, and some (e.g., viral) cancers and infectious diseases.

◆ We handle threatening situations by coping—either through changing the situation or by altering the ways we think and feel about it.

◆ Psychological difficulties can get channeled into physical symptoms; psychologists call these somatization disorders.

Part 4

All for One and One for All

Who are you and how do you know who "you" are? How did you develop your unique mix of personality traits, values, behavioral styles, and beliefs? You're about to find out as we explore identity formation and personality types. Not only will we look at how our "selves" are made, we'll look at how our relationships with others can either drive us over the edge or send us to the moon.

Chapter 3

Me, Myself, and I

In This Chapter

- ◆ Bending gender
- ◆ Results of disturbed identities
- ◆ Understanding hidden motives and urges
- ◆ The personalities behind the personality theories
- ◆ Strategies for psychic self-defenses

Who are you? *What* are you? *How* are you? These are all aspects of a larger question: how is your identity formed?

In this chapter, we explore ways we develop our self-concepts: how our backgrounds and beliefs influence our everyday lives and how our conflicts and needs shape who we are. We straighten out that overused but frequently misunderstood thing called self-esteem, explore various theories of personality development, and examine how we defend and protect our psyches.

Know Thyself

Self-awareness starts early. By about 15 months of age, babies stop reacting to their image in a mirror as if it were a stranger and begin to see it as their own reflection. If a researcher places a bright red spot of rouge on an infant's nose while she's watching in a mirror, the 15-month-old responds by touching her own nose to feel or rub off the rouge.

But Who Is Thyself?

If psychologist William James had known Madonna, he would have said she was right on when she sang about being a "material girl." James believed we're all partly material girls or guys. In his view, the material self is an essential part of who we are; the social self and the spiritual self are the other two parts. Each of these is essential to the way we experience ourselves.

James thought just about everything we routinely come into contact with becomes part of our identity. The material me, James believed, is the part of the self that is concerned with the body and with material possessions. A second part of James's self, the "social me," revolves around our interactions and reputation with others. James believed our relationships with other people comprised a strong part of our identity. The "spiritual me" is the part that holds our private thoughts and feelings. You don't have to go to church to get in touch with your spiritual side, but you do have to get to know yourself.

Psychobabble

Self-concept is like a spider web: some self-perceived traits are attached to specific roles (the knots in the web), whereas others are attached to several roles. These strands tie our identities together. Ask me what kind of mother I am, and I will say "playful, loving, and a student in the art of patience." As a writer, I define myself as "committed, passionate, and outspoken."

Mirror, Mirror on the Wall

Many years ago, sociologist Charles Cooley coined the phrase *looking-glass self* to describe the influence others have on our self-concept, especially when we're young. He believed that we define ourselves, in part, by what others "reflect" back to us about who we are and what we do. A child who is treated lovingly comes to believe she is lovable. And if you want a child to develop a certain quality, treating her as if she has it can actually shape the child in the right direction.

Of course, most adults aren't that easily manipulated, though we can be amazingly vulnerable to the whims and feedback of others if we haven't developed a strong sense of identity. If you don't know who you are, you may change your self-perception every time someone misperceives you; if your sense of self is strong, however, you're more likely to correct the misperceptions of others than to change your self-concept to fit them.

> **Psychobabble**
>
> Parents tend to interpret the same behavior differently for a child, depending on the sex of the child. A traditional-thinking parent is much more likely to believe that a bawling six-month-old boy is angry but a squalling six-month-old daughter is sad or afraid.

Gender and Selfhood

Our gender is the most defining characteristic of who we are. From birth, a boy and a girl will have a dramatically different experience—just because they are of different sexes.

Our gender identity, our personal sense of maleness or femaleness, isn't fully established until we're about three years old. Until that age, gender reassignments have some flexibility; after that, children think of themselves as either permanently male or permanently female. Although our genes determine our sex, our gender identity may be like language—easily acquired but only in a critical "window" during early childhood.

Our gender identity is much more complicated than our sexual identity—it's our total pattern of traits, tastes, and interests. In the past, masculinity and femininity were thought to be polar opposites (pink or blue, passive or aggressive). Men were thought to have instrumental qualities (to take action), and women were believed to have expressive qualities (nurturing, gentleness). Often dire consequences occurred for failing to conform to these gender norms.

Luckily, gender roles are becoming much more blurred, and we all have more choices in terms of how we express our gender. In fact, new research suggests that the happiest people are those who take on the best of both worlds!

> **Psychobabble**
>
> The issue of political correctness may have some merit, after all. Research suggests that referring to doctors, college professors, bankers, and executives by the generic "he" may contribute to the gender stereotyping of these professions as appropriate for men, but not for women. That's peer pressure at its worst!

Gender, Worth, and Self-Worth

In many cultures families have a great celebration at the arrival of a new son, while plans for the daughter include selling her off in marriage for a good price. Already in China, the "one-child" policy has resulted in many Chinese couples giving girls up for adoption in order to be able to have (and keep) a boy. Imagine what these practices do to a girl's self-esteem from day one.

Psychobabble

Research shows that women who identify themselves as very "feminine" and associate math abilities and professions with "male" perform worse in an intro calculus course. Some women might distance themselves from stereotypically male math-related fields to prevent losing their feminine identity.

Gender Bending

Not so long ago, many people (including a fair number of psychologists) assumed that the "proper" personality for a man did not include nurturing or child care and that women should be compliant and nurturing and essentially passive. In fact, if you asked a man if he was in touch with his feminine side, he might have punched your lights out!

Insight

Your definition of what is "masculine" and "feminine" depends largely on the culture you are reared in. While North American men are taught to shake hands or playfully "knock each other around" to show affection, in Thailand it is considered "masculine" for men to walk down the street holding hands; in Russia, men often kiss each other in greeting.

We now know that women who get in touch with their masculine side and men who discover the "woman" within are better off for doing so. Men and women with androgynous personalities are far more successful (and happier) than are people with stereotypically masculine and feminine personalities.

The androgynous personality incorporates the positive feminine or expressive qualities of nurturing, kindness, and an ability to listen to others, with the positive qualities stereotypically associated with masculinity—such as self-assurance, decisiveness, and leadership ability. In other words, anyone can have the tastes, abilities, and temperaments of both a male and a female.

Big-Time Gender Blues

Transsexuals have a condition known as gender identity disorder (commonly called gender dysphoria). While we don't know the exact prevalence of this disorder, the National Center for Transgender Equality estimates that between 750,000 and 3 million Americans have the biological makeup of one sex and the psychological makeup of the other.

A boy with gender dysphoria may prefer dressing in girls' or women's clothing, show a strong attraction for the stereotypical games and pastimes of girls, express a strong wish to be a girl, and, when young, express the belief that he will grow up to be a woman. Girls with gender dysphoria display intensely negative reactions to parental expectations or attempts to have them wear dresses or other feminine attire, have powerful male figures as fantasy heroes, and may dress and act like boys.

> **Psychobabble**
>
> Forget Mars and Venus—we're all from Earth! A review of 46 studies found that gender differences portrayed in the media are vastly overestimated and that men and women are more similar in personality, communication, cognitive ability, and leadership than we've ever realized.

Children do not "grow out of" their belief that they are one gender trapped in the body of another and often spend years trying to come to terms with their gender and confusion. Treatment for gender dysphoria helps people become content with their gender identity. For some people, this means dressing and living as their preferred gender. For others, it may involve taking hormones that change their physical appearance. For most transsexuals, it means having surgery to permanently alter their anatomical gender.

Sex-change surgery is a gradual and strict process. The individual must live as the other gender for one to two years before surgery, endure a rigorous battery of psychological tests, and undergo hormone replacement treatment before the final decision is made. Although only a handful of patients qualify for sex-reassignment surgery each year, most transsexuals are much happier with their new lives.

It's Like, You Know, a Teen Thing

Although our self-concept begins at birth, between ages 12 and 18 our identity really takes shape. In fact, Eric Ericson believed that the first identity crisis happens in adolescence as a teen struggles to find his or her true identity among the many different roles she or he plays for different audiences: parents, teachers, friends. In fact, much of adolescents' "rebellion" against parents and other authority figures is a healthy attempt to get some space and figure out the lay of the land for themselves.

As teens spend less time at home and more time with peers, they try out different social behaviors, experimenting with different norms, such as clothing or hairstyle, within the security of a peer group, a clique, or a romantic partner. Finding themselves without losing the comfort of belonging with friends and family members can be a tough balance to achieve; 15 to 25 percent of adolescents report feeling very lonely as they search for the real "me" inside. However, teens who successfully develop an identity that remains stable regardless of the setting or the social group in which they find themselves have a clearer sense of who they are and they're better able to make independent decisions and choices about their career, relationships, and life in general.

Insight _____

Do you want to see if your self-concept jives with how others see you? Write down the top five adjectives you'd use to describe yourself, and then ask two friends to describe you by doing the same.

Insight _____

Celebrate your ethnic heritage—it's good for you! Studies show that black children from home environments rich in African American culture had greater factual knowledge and better problem-solving skills—a finding that held true even when the researchers took family income into account. Also, racial pride was associated with fewer behavioral problems.

In Defense of the Midlife Identity Crisis

After adolescence, most of us have a couple of peaceful decades before the next identity crisis hits. This one you've surely heard about: your friend turns 40, ditches her vice-presidency and six-figure salary, and buys a cabin in the backwoods of Montana. Or the stable family man buys a red Porsche and finds a girlfriend half his age.

In truth, only 1 in 10 midlifers goes through a true crisis, where his world suddenly turns upside down and he considers radically changing his lifestyle. However, many are likely to experience a midlife review of their accomplishments and make some adjustments to their expectations and goals.

Getting Older and Better?

For years, we assumed our personalities were pretty much formed by early adulthood. But more recent research suggests otherwise. And on the whole, the changes our personalities go through are good ones.

In our 20s, we're likely to become more conscientious, which helps us be more organized and committed at work. In our 30s, our relationships may blossom as we become more agreeable. We females, in particular, age as well as the finest wine; as we get older, we worry less and our moods level out. Sorry, guys; research suggests that unless you take some active steps to change, a worrier at age 20 will be a worrier at age 40.

Brain Buster

There's a difference between healthy self-esteem and narcissism. If your new beau tends to consistently think he's more attractive, smarter, and more unique than others, consider this a red flag. Research shows that he is more likely to avoid intimacy, play emotional games, and cheat on you.

Hello, Your High Esteemness!

The number-one most popular psychology buzzword today is *self-esteem*. Low self-esteem has been used to explain everything from a car that won't run to a boyfriend who won't commit. This malady, it seems, is either a worldwide epidemic or a popular excuse for bratty behavior—maybe both!

While we most frequently think of it as a feeling ("I don't feel good about myself"), self-esteem is really a way of *being*. Self-esteem is the degree to which you experience yourself as being capable of coping with life's challenges (your self-confidence) and of being worthy of happiness and love (your self-respect). New research, however, shows that not all high-esteemers are created equally. Some people tend to have "fragile" high self-esteem. When the beliefs or values of these people are threatened,

Insight

If you're female, get out there and play ball! Numerous studies show that girls who participate in competitive sports have higher self-esteem, score better on achievement tests, are more likely to attend college, and are less likely to get involved in drugs and alcohol.

they tend to compensate for their self-doubts by aggressively defending and enhancing their feelings of self-worth. Those with secure high self-esteem are able to view differences of opinion with curiosity and openness.

Safeguarding Self-Esteem

You consider yourself a principled, loyal person who would never cheat on your spouse or loved one. Yet at a recent work conference, you gave in to temptation and hit the sack with a colleague. Now what do you do?

Chances are, the first thing you'd do is try to get rid of the emotional turmoil your actions have created. We're uncomfortable when our actions don't match our self-perceptions, beliefs, and values. According to cognitive theorist Leon Festinger, we experience an internal tension he calls cognitive dissonance.

Festinger's theory of cognitive dissonance says that we all have a strong need to perceive a consistency between our thoughts, words, actions, and values. When we do something we think we shouldn't have, we try to rationalize our contradictory behaviors so that they seem to follow naturally from personal beliefs and attitudes. For your conference fling, you might try denial ("It wasn't really sex"), or you might revise your attitudes to make them fit your actions ("As long as my spouse doesn't find out, no harm was done" or "I'll make it up to him in some way"). You then might internalize your attitude to make acceptable what otherwise appears to be unacceptable.

> **Psychobabble**
>
> Research shows that Mexican American men have more traditional "macho man" views of masculinity than European American or black men. Be tough; suck it up; don't complain. The problem is, the emotional pressure of living up to these ideals puts them at greater risk for depression, substance abuse, violence—and unfortunately—a reluctance to seek therapy, if necessary.

Psychic Self-Defense

We all defend and protect our psyches against emotional pain—although some defenses are less dramatic than others.

While some of Sigmund Freud's ideas are under attack today, there's no question that he was the personality pioneer. As a young physician in the late nineteenth century, Freud came to believe that many of his patients' complaints were not due to physical illnesses but to mental conflicts of which they were unaware. He ultimately developed an elaborate model of the mind that he believed explained why and how people cope with the psychological stresses of their daily lives.

Freud's theory was the first of the psychodynamic personality theories—theories that emphasize the interplay of mental forces (the word *dynamic* refers to energy or force). While each of these theories emphasizes different influences on personality development, they share two beliefs:

- We are often clueless about our real motives

- Our minds develop self-protective strategies called defenses, which keep unacceptable or distressing motives, thoughts, and feelings out of our awareness

Freud believed that the main causes of behavior lie buried in the unconscious mind, a part of the mind that affects our conscious thought and action but is not itself open to conscious inspection. Freud's unconscious is a kind of psychic storehouse of primitive and repressed impulses that allows us to function as law-abiding citizens. The differences between my personality and yours, Freud thought, were variations in our unconscious motives, in how these motives pop up in our daily lives, and in the ways you and I protect ourselves from emotional pain or anxiety.

Brain Buster

Freud thought that physical and behavioral symptoms were meaningfully related to significant life events. If you are constantly late for a date or always miss your appointment with your therapist because you "forgot," Freud would say these represent unconscious conflicts that are playing with your conscious life.

Sex in Overdrive

There's no doubt that Freud thought about sex a lot, wrote a lot about sex, and believed that the sex drive had a powerful influence on the personality. But before you start wondering if Freud had a few skeletons in his sexual closet, it's important to realize that he believed the sex drive was much more than the simple desire to have sex. He saw it as the human drive toward pleasure-seeking and life-creating activities. And since the most direct ways to express this drive were often unacceptable to the prudish Viennese society of his day, people had to channel their energy into something less dangerous.

> ### Psychobabble
>
> Freud may have been on to something with his preoccupation with sex. Modern studies show that, in many cases, an animal even on the verge of starvation will choose a sexually receptive partner over food. As for humans, one psychology professor I know emphasizes that the "Four Fs" are the most basic of human drives. In his words, they are *feeding, fighting, fleeing,* and … reproduction!

Freud believed most of us channel our sex drives into productive activities like work and hobbies. As if constantly reining in our sexual impulses wasn't work enough, Freud also believed human beings were naturally aggressive and that this aggression, like the sex drive, had to be channeled into more acceptable forms of behavior or we'd commit more murders than we already do. In Freud's view, then, people were pretty asocial, forced into society more by necessity than desire, and interacting principally in terms of sex, aggression, and various squashed versions of these drives. And to Freud's way of thinking, this all begins in childhood.

Urges "R" Us

Freud believed a person's personality is shaped most strongly during infancy and early childhood by how well we progress through a series of predictable stages in which we associate pleasure with the stimulation of certain body areas at certain times. The three stages in Freud's personality play are …

- **The oral stage.** In the first year of life, the mouth is the center of pleasure. A baby sucks, drools, and mouths objects like crazy. If the baby gets the right amount of mouth stimulation, he will move on to other pleasure centers; if not, he might grow up to be a needy, dependent adult and develop some bad habits like overeating or smoking.

- **The anal stage.** From ages one to three—prime toilet-training time—babies feel good about the process of elimination, but they also learn that there are pretty strict social rules about bodily functions, self-control, and personal hygiene. Freud would say that people who are stingy and obsessively neat got stuck here.

◆ **The phallic stage.** From the ages of three to six, a child's genitals become the major focus of his pleasure. Freud believed that this was the age when boys wanted to marry their moms and kill their dads (the Oedipus complex) and girls wanted to kill their moms and marry their dads (the Electra complex). The way we resolve this conflict, according to Freud, is by identifying more with the same-sex parent.

On the Mat with Freud

Freud also believed what we *should* do and what we *want* to do were constantly warring with each other. He called these warring parts of our personality the *id*, the *ego*, and the *superego*, whose characteristics are summarized as follows:

◆ **Id:** Primitive, impulsive, immediate gratification, no concern for consequences

◆ **Superego:** Conscience—values, moral attitudes, oughts and shouldn'ts, your ego ideal, seeks perfection

◆ **Ego:** Referee, mediates between id and superego; seeks compromise that satisfies the id, while keeping you out of trouble

Post-Freudian Personalities

Not all psychoanalysts share Freud's grim view of human nature or believe that the inner battle between selfishness and self-control is quite as primordial as Freud would have it. In fact, the neo-Freudians had a few bones to pick with Freud's perspective:

◆ Neo-Freudians did not believe that sexual urges primarily motivated behavior.

◆ Neo-Freudians thought events throughout the lifespan (not just childhood experiences) influenced personality.

◆ Neo-Freudians did not share Freud's pessimistic view of human nature and society.

Three of the most famous neo-Freudians were Carl Jung, Karen Horney, and Alfred Adler. Each brought his or her unique perspective to what shapes our human psyches.

Neo-Freudian	Main Ideas
Carl Jung	According to Jung, the unconscious was not limited to one person's unique life experiences but was filled with universal psychological truths shared by the whole human race. This *collective unconscious*, in Jung's view, is an inherited storehouse of unconscious ideas and forces common to all human beings; he was interested in the creative parts of the personality.
Karen Horney	This inborn human need for security can only be filled by other people, and if it isn't filled when we're little, we'll spend the rest of our lives looking for it.
Alfred Adler	One of the biggest struggles people face throughout their lives is the need to feel competent. We start out dependent and helpless in childhood and the manner in which we learn to cope with or overcome this feeling provides the basis for our lifelong personality.

Psychobabble

Penis envy? Puh-leeze! Karen Horney thought women might be much more envious of the superior status and greater power men held in our society. She suggested that Freud should get over his idea that women long for a penis and take a look at the desperate social circumstances in which many women live.

Sacrificing Identity to Escape Pain

We work hard to build and then protect our identity. If our emotional pain is great enough, however, we might sacrifice parts of who we are to get away from the hurt we feel. This is what happens with dissociative disorders. A dissociative disorder is a psychological disorder characterized by a disturbance in the integration of identity, memory, or consciousness; some aspect of the person's personality seems separated from the rest. Dissociative disorders are involuntary psychic tradeoffs. Let's take a look at four of them:

♦ **Dissociative amnesia** (formerly *psychogenic amnesia*)—a psychological disorder in which a person loses the memory of important (usually stressful or traumatic) personal experiences for no apparent physical reason.

♦ **Dissociative fugue states**—a fascinating and rare phenomenon in which someone suddenly leaves home but doesn't remember how or why, loses his or her identity, and sometimes actually develops a new identity. Contrary to popular soap opera plots, most fugue states involve purposeful travel, are brief, and typically involve only partial construction of a new identity.

♦ **Depersonalization**—an ongoing and persistent sense of feeling detached from yourself. Extreme stress can bring this feeling on for all of us, but for the clinically depersonalized individual, this is an ongoing, distressing part of everyday life.

♦ **Dissociative identity disorder** (formerly known as multiple personality disorder)—is a psychological disorder in which two or more distinct personalities, "alters," coexist in the same person and control her behavior. Many mental-health professionals don't believe *dissociative identity disorder* (DID) actually exists, but those who do believe in it agree that the "alters" develop before age 12 and almost always in response to severe, repetitive physical or sexual abuse.

Any dissociative disorder disrupts the continuity of life—people report missing time. They are unable to account for blocks of time or learn they've done things they don't remember. If you've ever been awakened while sleepwalking, you've had a glimpse of how frightening it is to come to your senses and not know where you are or how you got there—something people suffering from DID have to deal with regularly.

Psychobabble

Sybil, starring Sally Field, was one of the first movies to look at a real-life example of multiple personality disorder; but was it true? Dr. Herbert Spiegel, who also treated "Sybil" (Shirley Ardell Mason), believes that the therapist featured in the film, Cornelia Wilbur, actually suggested the personalities as part of Shirley's therapy and that the patient adopted them with the help of hypnosis and sodium pentothal. Shirley apparently had no DID symptoms before her therapy began.

The Well-Defended Mind

Whew! If you add up Freud's sex and aggression, Jung's creativity, Horney's security, and Adler's competence, one thing becomes quickly apparent—we've all got a lot of needs to meet! And the rest of the world is not cooperating with us as we go about the business of meeting them. Society says that we can't have sex whenever we want to; we're likely to find out the relationship we were counting on wasn't as secure as we thought; and the boss doesn't give us the promotion we think we deserve! How do we keep our personalities from getting beaten down while we're building them?

Defenses, my dear Watson. We all have them. The theory of *defense mechanisms* was most thoroughly developed by Freud's daughter, Anna, who became a psychoanalyst herself. You might think of defense mechanisms as doing for anxiety what endorphins do for physical pain—they reduce its impact.

def•i•ni•tion

A **defense mechanism** is a mental process of self-deception that reduces our awareness of threatening or anxiety-producing thoughts, wishes, or memories.

Our defense mechanisms are a way to reduce the amount of anxiety we feel, and—to the degree that they help us worry less about things not worth worrying about or that we can't do much about anyway—defense mechanisms are helpful. But sometimes they distort reality or keep us from taking action to improve a situation, and that's when they hurt us.

Repression, projection, rationalization, reaction formation, displacement, and sublimation are the most common defense mechanisms.

Summary of Defense Mechanisms	
Repression	Primitive, our first-line of defense—pushing thoughts from the mind, sometimes permanently
Projection	Consciously experiencing an unconscious drive and attributing it to someone else (e.g., you're in a bad mood but accuse someone else of being in a bad mood)
Rationalization	Using conscious reasoning to explain away anxiety-producing thoughts (e.g., a sexual abuser rationalizes that a 4-year-old was "coming on to him")

Reaction Formation	Doing or saying the opposite of how we really feel because our true feelings are unacceptable (e.g., a woman who doesn't want her child becomes overprotective and smothering)
Displacement	Unacceptable unconscious wishes or drives are redirected toward someone or something else (e.g., punching your pillow to vent anger)
Sublimation	Turning unacceptable urges into their opposites that are acceptable to society (e.g., Martin Luther King Jr. channeled his anger into activism)

The Best Defense

Which of these defense mechanisms works best? Well, it generally depends on the situation we're in, although some generally promote more effective coping than others. Don't put your money on projection, for instance, which blocks self-awareness (*you're* the one with the problem) and often interferes with interpersonal relationships (it's always *your* fault).

Repression and reaction formation distort reality less than projection does but they still use up unnecessary amounts of psychic energy. Two of the best defenses are suppression, the conscious avoidance of negative thinking, and humor. Humor relieves anxiety and simultaneously enables you to face fears because you're poking fun at them.

Ultimately, however, the best defense is no defense at all. Many people learn that once they face a painful memory or a fearful situation, the reality is not as bad as it first seemed and they may have power to change their behavior toward it or their feelings about it.

> **Psychobabble**
>
> Robbie Robertson, rock-and-roll songwriter and guitarist with The Band, suffered from stage fright before each performance. He even wrote a song about it, called "Stage Fright." This is one good way to practice sublimation! Robertson's fear never prevented him from being one of the most acclaimed guitarists in rock history.

Psychobabble

In their minds, young children tend to separate their "good" mother who provides food and shelter from the "bad" mother who provides punishment or just a feeling of absence when she's not there. These merge as the child matures. A person with an underdeveloped psyche, however, continues to think in extreme terms; she may see herself as "all good" and others as "all bad" or, in love relationships, switch between idealizing and "hating" her lover. This immature defense mechanism is known as splitting.

Freeing the Psychic Balloons!

While psychodynamic theorists see personality development as a battle, humanists think of it as a natural, free-flowing process that's sometimes weighed down by outside forces. To them, we're not so much driven by unconscious conflicts and defenses against anxiety as we are inspired to adapt, learn, and grow. If we free the psychic balloons, they proclaim, our personalities will fly!

Humanistic personality theorists believe that the motivation for behavior comes from a unique blend of biological and learned tendencies to develop and change and grow positively. Self-actualization is a constant striving to realize our full potential, to fully develop our abilities and talents. This innate quest moves us toward generally positive behaviors.

Problems arise, however, when our drive for self-actualization conflicts with our need for approval—from ourselves and from others—especially when we feel we must meet certain obligations or conditions in order to gain that approval. For example, if you're a natural-born artist, your drive for self-actualization might be sabotaged if you fear disapproval from one of your parents. Or you might take up sports, not because you want to play but because you need approval from your father.

The Personality Habit

According to the social-cognitivists, beliefs and habits of thought acquired through each individual's unique experiences in the social environment shape personalities. Over time, these learned beliefs and habits become so ingrained and automatic that they exert their influence without our even realizing it. The self-talk we engage in every day is a good example of automatic ways of thinking that influence how we feel and what we do; until we stop and listen to ourselves, we might not even know what our self-talk is saying.

If, for instance, I kept telling myself I could not write this book because I had too much else to do, I might have given up before I got started. Instead, I told myself I *could* write it—if I reorganized my life to make room for it. Voilà! The book *did* happen! Two thinking habits, in particular, have a tremendous impact on our lives: our *locus of control* and our self-efficacy.

def•i•ni•tion

A **locus of control** is a person's perception of the usual source of control over rewards. An internal locus of control means we believe our behavior determines our fate; an external locus of control means we think our fate is controlled by external forces (destiny, luck, or the gods).

Who's in the Driver's Seat?

At an early age, you figured out that in some situations you could control what happened, and in others you couldn't. You learned that saying please and thank you usually made people like you better but that no matter *what* you did, your third-grade teacher had it in for you.

However, in some situations, the reason you succeeded or failed might be unclear. If you bombed a test, for example, it could be that you didn't study hard enough, or maybe it was because the test was unfair and biased. Julian Rotter found that in these situations, people responded differently according to their general belief, acquired from their personal experiences, that rewards either are or are not *usually* controlled by their own efforts. He called this disposition the locus of control.

People who believe they can control their own fate are said to have an internal locus of control. People who believe life is essentially a crapshoot have an external locus of control. Not surprisingly, when tested, people who score toward the internal end on locus of control try to control their own fate more often than those who score at the external end.

Albert Bandura's self-efficacy refers to your sense of your ability to perform a particular task. If you *think* you can do it, then you have high self-efficacy. Take singing, for example. You might believe your voice is so fabulous that Barbra Streisand could learn a few things from you. At the same time, you might believe your chances of being discovered as a singing talent are determined by some cosmic roll of the dice. So you'd have high self-efficacy but an external locus of control.

We human beings have amazing ways of expressing our personalities and coping with the curveballs life throws at us. And just as our personalities are always changing and growing, our theories about how personality develops continue to evolve. Freud was certainly right about one thing—we'll probably never uncover all the layers of the human psyche.

Straight from the Lab

Not So Different After All?   East Asians, Japanese in particular, are often described as modest, self-effacing, and having lower self-esteem than Americans. But a new study comparing college students from three countries found that Japanese students scored higher in the self-esteem department than Chinese and American students! Perhaps the explicit Japanese cultural idea that "no one is better than the others" is negated by adoring Japanese parents.

Boost Confidence with Magic   A British study reveals that mastering a few magic tricks can work wonders for building confidence and sociability in kids. The act of performing seemingly impossible illusions builds self-esteem and self-discipline and helps kids develop an understanding of how others think and how to interact with them.

Maybe Men Do Marry Their Mothers   Whether a man's mother earned a college degree and had a successful career strongly influences his vision of the ideal wife many years later, studies show. Many of today's high-achieving men are the sons of women who role-modeled nurturing *and* were successful.

The Least You Need to Know

- We develop our self-concept by relating to the world and internalizing feedback from the people around us. Our self-esteem has to do with how much we value and respect ourselves.

- Our gender has a strong influence on our identity formation; if we can develop both our masculine and our feminine traits, we're likely to be happier.

- Dissociative disorders involve a disturbance in identity, memory, or consciousness, and treatment often centers around integrating these "split" parts of oneself.

♦ Freud, the father of psychoanalysis, believed that personalities developed through a battle between primitive urges and the need to get along with others.

♦ Jung, Horney, and Adler believed that needs for creativity, security, and competence drive humans.

♦ Defense mechanisms, such as repression, projection, rationalization, reaction formation, displacement, and sublimation, help us cope with unbearable thoughts, feelings, and wishes.

Chapter 14

He's Got ... Personality!

In This Chapter

- Unlocking the secrets of personality
- Explore why Minnesota is the personality state
- Discover the state your traits are in
- Smooth out the sharp edges of your personality
- Spotting the "sick" personality

Like many nurses in the early 1900s, Margaret Sanger watched countless women, desperate to avoid having yet another mouth to feed, die from illegal abortions. Unlike other nurses, she decided to find an answer to her patients' pleas for safe contraception no matter what the cost. For 40 years, Sanger challenged the laws that made contraception a criminal act, insisting that women take control of, and responsibility for, their sexuality and childbearing.

She left nursing and put her husband and children in the background—and ultimately changed women's lives forever. She eventually lost her husband and was jailed several times for illegally distributing information about birth control. But she won! In 1960, the United States Food and Drug Administration approved the pill, a contraceptive that Sanger co-sponsored.

What drove Sanger in her crusade? What personality qualities empowered her to endure such personal sacrifice and punishment? In this chapter, you discover what made Sanger the person she was—and what makes you the person you are. We explore all the ingredients that go into personalities and establish how much depends upon genes, hormones, environment, or birth order. You'll learn how psychologists test personalities, how stable our personalities really are, and what the difference is between an offbeat personality and a serious personality disorder.

Finding the Person in Personality

In the study of personality, psychologists try to determine how individuals differ from each other yet are the same within themselves. They tend to focus on two qualities: uniqueness and consistency. Personality is the sum of all the unique psychological qualities that influence an individual's behavior across situations and time. Someone who is shy may blush easily, avoid parties, and wait for other people to take the initiative in conversation. On the other hand, a person who is reticent about public speaking but is the life of the party in other situations wouldn't be classified as having a shy personality.

Understanding personality traits gives us a sense of who we are and helps us (to some degree) predict the behavior of the people around us. And through personality testing, it gives psychologists an x-ray of our psyches.

X-rays of the Psyche

Personality tests don't measure *how much* personality we have but rather *what kind*. There are two kinds of personality tests: objective and projective. Objective personality tests are paper-and-pencil, "self-report" tests with true-or-false questions. You answer questions about your thoughts, feelings, and actions by checking *true* if the statement is generally or mostly true and *false* if it is false most of the time. Projective tests, including the well-known inkblots, are subject to interpretation by the person giving them.

Personality testing scares many people because they misunderstand what it can and can't do. First of all, personality testing is more like taking an x-ray than looking into a crystal ball: the results can suggest what's wrong, but they can't tell us how it got broken or to what extent it's affecting our lives. The same test results that indicate antisocial behavior might show up in a politician *and* in a convicted felon!

Second, personality test results are practically useless unless they take into account the test subject's current life situation. Someone who is usually reticent may become very effusive if she just won the lottery. And a person who's just lost a loved one might look seriously depressed on a personality test when, in fact, he is just experiencing the normal throes of grief.

> ### Psychobabble
>
> People who score as extroverts on personality questionnaires choose to live and work with more people, prefer a wider range of sexual activities, and talk more in group meetings, when compared to introverted personalities.

Minnesota, the Personality State

The most popular objective personality test was developed at the University of Minnesota. The Minnesota Multiphasic Personality Inventory, or MMPI, which first appeared in the 1940s, originally consisted of more than 500 true-and-false questions that asked about a person's mood, physical symptoms, current functioning, and a whole lot more. In the late 1980s, the original version underwent a significant revision (MMPI-2) because some questions were deemed inappropriate, politically insensitive, or outdated.

The MMPI-2 has 10 *clinical* scales, each designed to tell the difference between a special clinical group (like people suffering from major depression) and a normal group. These scales measure problems like paranoia, schizophrenia, depression, and antisocial personality traits. The higher a person scores on a clinical scale, the more likely it is that he or she belongs in the clinical group.

The MMPI-2 also has 15 *content* scales which measure various mental health problems that aren't, in and of themselves, diagnosable psychiatric disorders. Some of these content scales measure low self-esteem, anger, family problems, and workaholism, among other problems. The job of these scales is to pinpoint specific problems that either contribute to, or put someone at risk for, a full-blown psychological disorder.

Can You Pull the Wool over Your Psychologist's Eyes?

Since objective tests like the MMPI-2 are self-reporting, you might think they'd be easy to fake if, for example, you were faced with the choice of either going directly to jail or looking crazy and staying out.

Not really. The MMPI-2 has built-in lie detectors, safeguards that detect lying, carelessness, defensiveness, and evasiveness. So while you're free to answer "true" or "false" however you please, it's almost impossible to convince the test you're answering honestly if you're not.

> ### Psychobabble
>
> Psychologists are getting harder to fool. A new personality inventory in development at the University of Toronto can predict who is most likely to succeed, even when the subject attempts to exaggerate his skills/abilities. Studies conducted in the workplace suggest that using this bias-resistant test instead of current personality assessments could result in a potential productivity gain of 23 percent per employee.

Projecting Your Personality

It'd be even harder to fake a projective test like the Rorschach because there are thousands of possible answers. And even if you tried to second-guess the test, the answers you gave would still provide valuable clues about your true personality.

> ### Insight
>
> Do you want a partner who'll be faithful and stay away from the booze? Rate your mate! Go to www.members.aol.com/HOON4VR/personality.html for a virtual bonanza of personality quizzes. Hint: you've struck gold if he scores high on the conscientious scale.

Projective personality tests are based on the theory that our inner feelings, motives, and conflicts color our perception of the world. The less structured our world, the more likely our psyche will spill over onto what we see. This is what happens when you and a friend look at clouds. You might see a dancing clown while your friend spies a rocket poised for blastoff. Both of you are right—the cloud shapes are ambiguous and open to several interpretations. Psychologists rely on this same process when they give those famous ink blots known as Rorschach cards.

Ink Blots of the Mind

Swiss psychiatrist Hermann Rorschach (pronounced *raw-shock*) developed the Rorschach test. While working with teenagers in a psychiatric hospital, Hermann watched children giving different answers to a popular game called "Blotto." He surmised that these different answers might provide clues into the minds and personalities of the players. Using this premise, he fooled around with a bunch of ink blots and published the Rorschach in 1921.

When you take the Rorschach test, the examiner gives you 10 cards, each with an ink-blot on it, and asks you to describe what you see. There are literally hundreds of *right* answers and a tremendous amount of room for creative responses as well.

However, our personalities also change the brain's wiring; hence, our personalities can change with our experiences. When the noisiest, most rambunctious subjects hit their 20s, they were still more aggressive than their peers, yet they had become considerably more laid back. It appears that negative feedback from peers over the years made them more self-conscious and quiet.

Even if kids start out overcontrolling or undercontrolling, experience and learning can round their sharp edges. Undercontrollers can be taught to rein in their emotions and be more sensitive to others. And overcontrollers can work at being more outwardly sociable, even if they're still introverts on the inside.

Insight

One simple but effective "therapy" for teens is a part-time job. Having a job has been shown to lessen aggressiveness in both overcontrollers and undercontrollers.

Insight

Different personality traits help us at different ages. Openness to new situations predicts intelligence earlier in life, but disagreeableness predicts intelligence later in life (perhaps because we have to work harder to challenge the status quo).

The Theories Behind the Tests

I bet you choose your relationships based on a personal theory about what personalities make good friends and good mates. We also naturally assume that certain personality characteristics (trustworthiness, for example) will lead to certain behaviors (telling the truth), and we try to associate with people who will do things that make us happy. In other words, every single one of us is a personality theorist.

Through observations, interviews, biographical information, and life events, researchers in personality theory have developed beliefs about the structure and functioning of individual personalities. Their goal is to understand the personality and to predict what a person will do based upon what is already known about him. The tricky part is in separating the *traits* from the *states*; in other words, figuring out if a person acts

def•i•ni•tion

A **trait** is a stable characteristic that influences your thoughts, feelings, and behavior. A **state** is a temporary emotional condition.

in a certain way because of who he is or in response to a sticky situation in which he's landed.

What State Are Your Traits In?

A personality trait is a relatively stable tendency to act in a certain way. Generosity, shyness, aggressiveness—these are all examples of traits. Traits are considered ongoing parts of the person, not the environment; they follow us wherever we go.

That's not to say that the situation, for better or worse, doesn't influence our expression of the traits we have. If someone runs into your car in a parking lot, you're more likely to fight or yell if you're a hothead than is someone who's more laid back. For a hot-blooded temperament, then, the environment provides the spark that sets it afire.

Mental states make personality assessment harder. If someone comes to therapy complaining of depression, a psychologist has to figure out whether that person is in a state of sadness or has a depressive personality trait. And, of course, there's some relationship between the two—an aggressive personality trait will lead to more angry states!

Psychologist Walter Mischel thinks there may be a "happy medium" between states and traits, which he calls situation-specific dispositions. These are behaviors that are highly consistent over time in response to the same situation but may not generalize across settings. For example, if you were a cheater on tests in high school, chances are you'll also cheat on tests in graduate school. This doesn't necessarily mean, though, that you'd cheat on your taxes or on your spouse.

Allport's Search for Personality

If you checked the dictionary, you'd find over 18,000 adjectives that could describe personality characteristics! Psychologist Gordon Allport thought personality traits were the building blocks of an individual's overall personality. He also thought some traits were big building blocks, some were medium-size, and some were smaller. These three different-size blocks represented the varying degrees of influence the trait had on a person's life.

According to Allport, a cardinal trait is a single giant-size trait around which someone organizes his life. Martin Luther King Jr. for example, may have organized his life around social consciousness, seeking to improve the quality of life for African Americans. Not everyone has a cardinal trait.

Cardinal Trait   Central Traits   Secondary Traits

The building blocks of personality.

A central trait represents a major characteristic of a person, such as honesty or optimism. Surely Gloria Steinem's outspokenness is a central trait that enables her to withstand criticism and controversy and speak before large audiences about women's rights. A person can have more than one central trait.

A secondary trait is an enduring personality trait, but it doesn't explain general behavioral patterns. Preferences (she has some unusual sexual preferences) and attitudes (he hates when you tickle him) are examples of secondary traits. We all have many secondary traits.

Apparently, patience was a central (if not cardinal) trait in Gordon Allport's personality; he spent his entire career boiling down all of the dictionary's personality-related adjectives into 200 clusters of synonyms (groupings like easygoing, lighthearted, and carefree). He then formed two-ended trait dimensions. For example, on one such dimension, "responsible" might be at one end, and "irresponsible" would be at the other. All of us fall somewhere on the continuum between these two adjectives.

After having countless people rate themselves on these 200 dimensions, Allport found there were only five basic characteristics underlying all the adjectives people used to describe themselves. These became known as the "Big Five" dimensions of human personality—the five categories into which Allport organized all our traits and behaviors. It's easy to remember them by the acronym *OCEAN:*

- ◆ **Openness to experiences.** At one end would be individuals who are creative, intellectual, and open-minded versus, on the other, people who are shallow, simple, and less intelligent.

- ◆ **Conscientiousness.** Here would be organized, responsible, and cautious persons as opposed to those who are irresponsible, careless, and frivolous.

- ◆ **Extroversion.** These people are assertive, outgoing, and energetic rather than quiet, reserved, and shy.

> ### Psychobabble
>
> Personality does count in the love department. People who exhibit positive traits, such as honesty and helpfulness, are perceived as better looking than those who exhibit negative traits, such as unfairness and rudeness. And our perception of someone's physical attractiveness can change over time, depending on whether he is endearing or annoying.

◆ **Agreeableness.** Here individuals who are sympathetic, kind, and affectionate contrast with those who are cold, argumentative, and cruel.

◆ **Neuroticism.** Here we contrast an anxious, unstable, and moody personality with one that is emotionally stable, calm, and content.

The Eysenck Alternative

Another psychologist, Professor Hans Eysenck of the University of London, came to believe there were 21 personality traits that were consistent with three major dimensions of personality. If you take his personality assessment, the Eysenck Personality Profiler, your scores will fit into three categories:

◆ **Extraversion.** Measures traits including activity level, sociability, expressiveness, assertiveness, ambition, dogmatism, and aggressiveness.

◆ **Neuroticism.** Measures traits like inferiority, unhappiness, anxiety, dependence, hypochondria, guilt, and obsessiveness.

◆ **Psychoticism.** Measures traits such as risk-taking, impulsivity, irresponsibility, manipulativeness, sensation-seeking, tough-mindedness, and practicality.

You'll notice some overlap in the two personality theories we've discussed. Each emphasizes the ability to get along with others, general emotional adjustment, and flexibility and open-mindedness as key parts of a person's personality. But how do people become more open-minded or outgoing? Are we born with pizzazz, or do we have to go to charm school to get it?

The Personalities Behind the Theories

Before you buy into someone's analysis of your psyche, it's important to understand the time within history that the theory was developed; each theory of personality was developed in a social and cultural context that influenced the theorist's thinking. In addition, just as your personality theories are based on your life experience, so have the trials and tribulations of the theorist contributed significantly to his theoretical views.

So when you read about the latest or greatest personality theory, pay particularly close attention to the following:

◆ Whether the theory focuses on normal or abnormal behavior, or both

◆ How much scientific method versus clinical intuition has contributed to the theory

◆ Whether the theory explains how personality develops or focuses on the adult personality

In addition, look for the assumptions behind the theory. Does she think our behavior is more influenced by past events or future goals and aspirations? Does the theorist think personalities can grow and change, or does he think we're stuck with the personalities we're born with? Neither side of these questions is necessarily right or wrong, although my personal theory is that some of these sure do give us more options than others. When it comes to my personality development, I want some room to grow!

Those Temperamental Genes

If you were voted "Best Personality" in high school, is your child destined for popularity? This question brings us right back to the "nature-versus-nurture" debate (see Chapter 3).

Well, you can't blame a people-pleasing personality on a "dependency" gene; on the other hand, you can take full credit for developing your conscientiousness and extroversion. While there are biological parts of our personalities, we have some control over how they take shape.

Our genes provide some of the raw material, e.g., temperament that makes it easier for certain personality traits to blossom. A baby with an easy temperament may more easily develop an optimistic outlook, while an irritable infant may grow into an emotionally expressive child. These temperamental genes appear to interact in very complicated ways, though; in fact, any one gene is likely to account for only 1 or 2 percent of the variability in any given personality trait.

> ### Psychobabble
>
> Identical twins share about 50 percent of the same personality traits, the same percentage that they share when it comes to measuring intelligence. And identical twins reared apart are more similar in personality than are siblings or fraternal twins who are raised together. In fact, people raised in the same family are just about as different as any two people picked at random off the street, perhaps because siblings have such different experiences in the same family.

Since the 1950s, researchers have found that newborns and infants vary widely in the following nine temperaments:

- **Activity level.** The amount of physical motion exhibited during the day.

- **Persistence.** The extent of continuation of behavior with or without interruption.

- **Distractibility.** The ease of being interrupted by sound, light, or other unrelated behavior.

- **Initial Reaction.** Response to novel situations, whether approaching or withdrawing.

- **Adaptability.** The ease of changing behavior in a socially desirable direction.

- **Mood.** The quality of emotional expression, positive or negative.

- **Intensity.** The amount of energy exhibited in emotional expression.

- **Sensitivity.** The degree to which a person reacts to light, sound, and so on.

- **Regularity.** The extent to which patterns of eating, sleeping, elimination, and so on, are consistent or inconsistent from day-to-day.

These temperament characteristics have an effect on how we experience our upbringing and may lead us to choose very different friends, activities, and life experiences. With all these variables, maybe no two people ever grow up in the "same" family!

Insight _____

Children with extreme personalities marked by aggressiveness, mood swings, a sense of alienation, and a high need for excitement may be at greater risk for attention deficit hyperactivity disorder and/or conduct disorder, a new study shows. Kids with both disorders (an estimated 15–35 percent) are at much higher risk of academic failure, criminal activity, substance abuse, and depression.

Rounding Out the Sharp Edges

We know our states can change like the wind, but how about our basic personality traits? While the debate still goes on, new research suggests that, despite the fact that we are born with a certain set of predispositions that lead us in specific directions, we also have the capacity for a certain amount of change throughout our lives.

In fact, time itself seems to round out the sharp edges of our personalities. A group of Stanford researchers found that certain aspects of our personality do change—gradually but consistently—as the circumstances in our lives change. What's more, over time many of our less desirable traits seem to fade quite naturally, with more pleasing and social parts of our personality coming forward.

Personality by Birth Order

Numerous studies suggest that we're likely to share some of the same personality traits with people in other families who share the same birth order. For example, because firstborns are older, they're first to receive privileges and the first to be asked to take care of younger siblings. The firstborns' position makes them special and, at times, burdens them—and their personalities are likely to reflect this mixed bag. For example, they tend to be leaders, but they also may be hard to get along with and are most likely to feel insecure and jealous.

Middle children tend to be diplomats, while last-borns are the rebels—with or without a cause. Having been picked on and dominated by firstborns, later children are more likely to be open to new ideas and experiences and support innovative ideas in science and politics. Later-born children are also more agreeable and more sociable—firstborns may be most likely to achieve, but later-borns are clearly most popular.

Insight

Do you think all the birth order stuff is nonsense? Mention it to the next Ph.D. you meet. About 90 percent of people with doctorates—not to mention the vast majority of U.S. presidents—are first-borns or only children!

Personality by Gender

The uniqueness of our own personalities and the diversity of personality traits within each gender far outweigh any personality differences based on gender. The most consistent difference by far is that women are easier to get along with. In every study in every country, women score higher on agreeableness, and lower on antagonism, than men. To be specific, about 84 percent of women score higher on measures of the ability to get along with others than the average man.

But it's not all bad news for men. Men still tend to earn more. Why? Social equality issues aside, men seem to develop personality traits that encourage risk-taking, and in general, risk-taking jobs often pay more. (Think firefighter versus preschool teacher or salesperson on commission versus salesperson receiving an hourly wage.)

Look Out, I'm Culture Bound!

Our culture shapes the development of our personality in many ways—by encouraging differing parenting strategies, communicating certain values, reinforcing certain behaviors, and teaching social rituals. In fact, some researchers think that various cultures have a "national character" that permeates social interactions and results in the tendency for certain personality characteristics to develop in members of that culture.

For example, although no definitive culture traits define Americans, the following general attitudes/traits are often cited by expatriates who've survived the culture shock of living in the United States—and are helping their compadres who are about to do the same:

- **Friendly.** Accepting of strangers.

- **Open.** Share personal information easily, little need for personal privacy.

- **Insular.** Unaware of other cultures (but often curious and interested).

- **Fast-paced and impatient.** In a hurry, place a premium on time.

- **Assertive.** Make little effort to hide thoughts and feelings.

- **Noisy.** Uncomfortable with silence, play music when studying, and so on.

Understanding different cultures can be a great help in avoiding the "labels" that can easily be attributed to a person who behaves in an unexpected way. The Japanese cultural value of respectfully allowing a person to "save face" by communicating bad news indirectly was often misinterpreted as dishonesty or manipulation before cultural-awareness training came into vogue for executives.

Disturbing Personalities

So far, we've spent our time talking about normal personalities and how we get them. But how does an *abnormal* personality develop? And when does an eccentric personality become a personality disorder?

We're All a Little Bit "Off"

Personality disorders are chronic mental disorders that affect a person's ability to function in everyday activities. While most people can live pretty normally with mildly self-defeating personality traits (to some extent, we all do), during times of increased stress the symptoms of a personality disorder will gain strength and begin to seriously interfere with their functioning. Personality disorders are at the extreme end of the continuum.

For example, we all know someone who hogs the limelight or seems to constantly seek approval or recognition. But although we might not like such people or find them pleasant to be around, their self-centered personality traits don't necessarily indicate a narcissistic personality disorder.

def•i•ni•tion

A **personality disorder** is a long-standing, inflexible, and maladaptive pattern of thinking, perceiving, or behaving that usually causes serious problems in the person's social or work environment.

But It's All About Me and My Needs!

A person with narcissistic personality disorder, on the other hand, has a grandiose sense of self-importance, a preoccupation with fantasies of success or power, and a constant need for attention and admiration. He might "overreact" to the mildest criticism, defeat, or rejection. In addition, he's likely to have an unrealistic sense of entitlement and a limited ability to empathize with others. This lack of empathy, tendency to exploit others, and lack of insight almost always results in serious relationship problems. This is not a person who is merely selfish; he genuinely can't relate to others.

Keep in mind that true personality disorders are usually severe enough to interfere with a person's life in some way. A hunger for the limelight can be healthy if it's channeled in the right direction; without it, many of our greatest actors might not have chosen acting as a profession.

What's Your Tonic?

Psychological disorders are often classified as either *ego-dystonic* or *ego-syntonic*. Behaviors, thoughts, or feelings that upset you and make you uncomfortable are ego-dystonic. You don't like them; you don't want them; and you're motivated to get rid of them. But personality disorders are often ego-syntonic. That means you can have what everyone *else* considers a disorder—they don't like it, and you make them uncomfortable—but as far as you're concerned, it's everyone else's problem, not yours.

How Personality Disorders Develop

Mental-health professionals disagree about the prevalence and makeup of personality disorders. But a few things are generally accepted as true on the subject.

For one thing, it's largely accepted that personality disorders are recognizable by the time a person reaches late adolescence or early adulthood—and that there are no personality disorders among children because their personalities are still being shaped. A personality disorder may be a combination of parental upbringing, one's innate personality, and social development, as well as genetic and biological factors.

Table of Personality Disorders

Paranoid PD	OVERLY: suspicious, mistrustful, conspiracy theories. Holds grudges, sensitive to criticism.
Schizoid/Schizotypal PD	Detached, solitary, emotionally cold, eccentric (e.g., superstitious, telepathic), vague speech.
Borderline PD	Poor interpersonal relationships—people seen as either wonderful or terrible. Hates being alone, impulsive and moody. May exhibit self-mutilating behaviors, eating disorders, depression.
Narcissistic PD	Self absorbed, needs to be constantly admired, lack of empathy with others, arrogant. May over-flatter or criticize if total attention not given.
Antisocial PD	History of conduct disorder in adolescents. Disregard for the rights of others. Unlawful, lying, impulsive, aggressive, irresponsible, lack of remorse, reckless with self and others. May be charismatic and manipulative.
Histrionic PD	Attention seeking and over- emotional, dramatic. Over-use of metaphor and flowery language. Easily falls in love.

Obsessive-Compulsive PD	Perfectionist, rigid, in control, no spontaneity. Irritable or angry when his order is threatened. Depressed if he can't meet his own expectations.
Avoidant PD	Distant social relationships (although unlike Schizoid PD, these would like intimate relationships but fear rejection). May be anxious and depressed.
Dependent PD	Relies on others to make decisions and care for him. Requires constant reassurance and rarely disagrees for fear of loss of relationship. Severe depression may accompany relationship disharmony.

Insight

For a detailed description of the personality disorders, check out www.psychcentral.com/personality.

The Borderline Brain

Brain scans now enable us to observe personality disorders in action by linking structural brain differences to dysfunctional behavior. In people with borderline personality disorder (BPD), for example, MRI scans show impairment of an emotion-regulating circuit—not surprising, since people with BPD have notorious difficulty regulating their emotions.

When BPD subjects viewed faces with fearful expressions, their amygdalas—the brain's fear hub—overreacted. Meanwhile, the part of the brain responsible for reining the amygdala in was underactive and deficient in grey matter. In other words, there were no brakes for the borderline's runaway fear response.

In addition, different patterns of brain activity in people with borderline personality disorder were associated with problems in interpersonal relationships. In an experimental game requiring collaboration to succeed, trust and cooperation faltered over time in pairs that included a person with borderline personality disorder. People with the illness tended to behave in ways that caused a breakdown in cooperation with their healthy partners. Moreover, they were half as likely as normal subjects to try to repair the relationship through coaxing. This self-sabotaging behavior correlated to abnormal brain waves in parts of the brain involved in the understanding of social norms and meanings. As a result, researchers concluded that people with borderline personality disorder either have a distorted sense of generally accepted social norms or may not sense these norms at all.

Playing the Best Treatment Odds with Personality Disorders

Personality disorders can be difficult and time-consuming to treat but are not impossible. The treatment of choice is structured psychotherapy actively focused on reducing self-defeating behaviors, improving interpersonal relationships, and teaching the client to handle difficult emotions (for example, by learning to mentally observe one's feelings rather than getting overwhelmed by them). Medications for personality disorders are usually aimed at alleviating symptoms associated with the disorder, such as the impulsivity and unstable moods associated with borderline personality disorder, rather than the disorder itself. Popular antidepressants include the SSRI category (serotonin-specific reuptake inhibitors) like Prozac, Paxil, or Effexor.

Psychobabble
New research suggests that the main benefit of treatment of personality disorders may be to speed up a recovery process that occurs naturally as we age. About 90 percent of clients diagnosed with borderline personality disorder in their 20s no longer meet the criteria by midlife—even without treatment.

Now you know how difficult it can be to predict someone's behavior no matter how well we think we know them. However, personality tests are one tool that can help us understand how traits lead to behavioral patterns. In the next chapter, you'll learn about the methods people use to protect their personalities and defend themselves emotionally.

Straight from the Lab

Physician's Personality Influences Patient Diagnosis   According to a study of primary care physicians, a physician's own personality affects her assessment of his patients' emotional state. Dutiful/conscientious doctors were more likely to explore a patient's psychosocial and life circumstances but asked fewer questions—perhaps due to concerns about time-economy or a reluctance to broach sensitive topics. Highly empathetic doctors with average—as opposed to extremely high—levels of conscientiousness were most likely to be trusted by patients.

Narcissists Emerge as Leaders   Narcissists are perceived as natural leaders by others (and certainly themselves!). But once in power, they tend to be volatile and make risky decisions that can lead to ineffective and destructive leadership.

Tattoos Predict Antisocial Behavior   New research suggests that forensic patients with tattoos are more likely to have Antisocial Personality Disorder (ASPD), histories of suicide attempts, substance abuse, and sexual abuse.

The Least You Need to Know

◆ Your personality is a complex assortment of unique traits that are stable over time and across settings.

◆ Psychologists use both objective and projective personality tests to figure out who we are and sometimes (but not always) predict what we will do.

◆ We all have traits, characteristics of personality that are relatively stable and consistent over time, and we all have states, temporary emotional responses to specific situations.

◆ A number of things, including genetics, environment, culture, birth order, and gender, influence personality development.

◆ Personality disorders are chronic mental disorders that affect a person's ability to function in everyday activities; they are complex, somewhat fuzzy, and difficult but not impossible—to treat.

15

Conform to the Norm!

In This Chapter

◆ Discover what a devilish situation can make you do

◆ Find out just how far we'll follow the leader

◆ The three R's of social psychology

◆ Get help when you need it

◆ Some attributes we all share

◆ Meet the spin-doctor within

Go to jail. Go *directly* to jail. This order may not upset you too much if you're playing Monopoly, but how would you feel if you really had to go to jail? Would being a prisoner change your behavior? Or could you rise above the circumstances? The Stanford Prison Experiment suggests the answer may surprise you.

College students who were law-abiding, emotionally stable, physically healthy, and normal were randomly assigned the role of prisoner or guard and lived in a true-to-life mock prison for several days. In the role of prison guard, "nice guy" students behaved aggressively, sometimes even sadistically. The "prisoners" also behaved pathologically, passively resigning themselves to their new fate. The power of the pretend prison quickly became a real prison in the minds of jailers and captives alike. In fact, the results were so dramatic that some prisoners had to be released early due to their extreme stress reactions, and the researchers ended the two-week experiment after only six days!

We'd all like to believe we'd be good guards and heroic prisoners, but the best way to predict how we would act—in any situation—is to look at the way others actually behave. Welcome to the study of social psychology, which investigates how people are influenced by their interactions and relationships with others. In this chapter, we take a look at how social settings influence how we think, feel, and act, and how we look to others for cues to guide our own behavior, often without realizing it.

Blame It on the Situation

Most of us believe we're the captain of our ship, charting the course of our lives with perhaps minor input from our shipmates. We tend to view situations as strong winds; sure, they may blow our sails around a little, but we can just batten down the hatches and tough it out.

> **Insight**
>
> Keep your eyes peeled for *The Stanford Prison Experiment*, scheduled for release sometime in 2009. The movie, described as both a drama and a thriller, will be based on Zimbardo's famous prison experiments.

Social psychologists don't buy that. They understand that each person has a unique personality, core beliefs, and values. But they also believe that the major influence over our behavior is the social situation in which it occurs, a philosophy known as situationism. They argue that social situations can dominate our personalities, no matter what our values or beliefs. And the mere presence of others can powerfully—even unconsciously—influence our behavior. Let's take a look at three ways a situation wields power over us—roles, rules, and norms.

Learn Your Roles

The roles available to us are determined by where and how we live and work. Being an engineer, for example, reduces the chances that we will become a mercenary, a priest, or a drug pusher. It does increase the odds we'll become a member of some technical association.

Of course, most of us play many different social roles every day—wife, mother, executive, friend. These roles can be refreshing and energizing if they allow us to express complimentary parts of ourselves or confusing and upsetting if they call for conflicting behaviors. Imagine being the top executive at a company where you boss people around all day. At six o'clock, you come home and are immediately expected to be warm and nurturing. This can cause role strain, not to mention a few extra gray hairs.

Play by the Rules

You might be wondering where we learn all the rules for our roles. There is no role school, after all. Yet we obey (or rebel against) social rules everyday, everywhere. Rules are so much a part of our lives that we hardly think about them. "No Shirt, No Shoes, No Service." "No Smoking." "No Gum Chewing During Aerobics Class."

We learn rules through our transactions with others, sometimes the hard way. Pretty quickly, we learn to size up a situation and adjust our behavior accordingly—or pay the consequences. Like good method actors, we have learned to gauge our roles from observation, past experience, and role models. We can't rely on learning the "right" behaviors; the same behavior may be interpreted differently depending upon the role. A tough, no-nonsense approach to business may boost the company's bottom line, but it won't score brownie points with family members.

That's why role models can be so powerful. They provide us with clues about how to function most effectively in various situations. In fact, when we find someone who is successful in a role we cherish, we should latch on and not let go until she promises to show us the ropes!

Conform to the Norms

In the realm of psychology, the term "norm" is not an endearment for Norman—it's short for normal. When social psychologists use it, they're talking about what's "normal" behavior for a particular group. In addition to developing expectations about appropriate role behaviors, groups develop social guidelines for how their members should act. Every time we adjust our behavior to get along with someone, we're adapting to his norms. For example, after working for a particular boss for a while, you might get a sense of what political ideas are appropriate to express and which ones might be best kept to yourself. If your boss is a gun-toting, card-carrying member of the NRA, for example, your performance review might not be the time to argue for gun control.

Insight _____

For women who grow up with abusive parents, a battering relationship can seem normal. A startling one-fourth of United States women suffer domestic violence in their lifetimes, leading to ongoing, long-term health problems that the CDC (Centers for Disease Control and Prevention) likens to "living in a war zone."

Social norms can enforce dress code, lingo, and certain standards of conduct, such as not hanging with the "nerds" if you're part of the "jockcracy." For example, the machismo of high-contact sports such as football and wrestling may actually fuel aggressive and violent behavior among males, both on and off the field or mat. Research shows that the risk of getting involved in fights increases dramatically for football players and wrestlers who hang out primarily with their teammates. In one study, males with all-football friends had a 45 percent probability of getting into a serious fight, more than 8 percent higher than guys with no football friends and almost 20 percent higher than males with all-tennis friends. Wrestlers were 45 percent more likely to get into a fight than non-wrestlers.

Insight _____

What are the five qualities that most clearly define who you are? What are the three skills at which you truly excel? One of the best ways to avoid group pressure is to have a strong self-concept; studies show that people with well-grounded identities are less influenced by even the most pessimistic feedback from others.

Norms aren't all bad. They can provide comfort and a clear sense of knowing what to expect from others in the group: how to dress, what to say and do, and what type of behavior will gain acceptance and approval. Norms provide us with the first steps in identifying with a group and feeling like we belong. The question, of course, is what price are we paying for it?

The Three R's of Social School

What happens when we break the behavior code of our group? When do groups rein rebels in, and when do they decide to cut them off? Of course, it depends on the situation—and the group. Part of establishing a group's norms involves deciding how much leeway members have to stray from them.

Depending on the group, we may get some good-natured teasing, or we could be booted out on our keister. In any group, we know that if we go too far, disagree too much with accepted beliefs or customs, we may no longer be welcome in the group.

And while the degree of deviation that is tolerated varies from group to group, they all rely on the same strategies to keep group members in line: ridicule, re-education, and rejection.

The sorority I joined in college was known as the "brainy good girls." No one ever spelled this out, but I quickly realized that curse words were frowned upon, grades were rewarded, and maintaining a stellar reputation was an unspoken pledge promise. Sure, there were a few partiers on the sorority floor, but they weren't part of the "in" clique, and they certainly didn't brag about their hangovers at sorority meetings. In contrast, my best friend joined a sorority whose reputation was "fun-loving party girls," and she, in a strange way, felt equal pressure to live up to these expectations.

Warning: Check Your References

Cosmopolitan. Glamour. Vogue. By reading these magazines, you're applying for membership in a club—"the beautiful people club," the "sexy women club," or the "women of the millennium." Women's magazines capitalize on both our desire to be members of these groups and our perpetual belief that we don't yet belong.

When we belong or hope to belong to the group, we refer to the group's standards and customs for information, direction, and support. This group becomes our *reference group.* Parents get quite a shock when a teenager's reference group shifts from the family to peers.

Sometimes, we are most influenced by a reference group that is not a real social group but an imaginary set of wished-for friends and colleagues. These aspirational groups can be formal ones like the Junior League or simply social categories we find appealing. For example, in the Learning Annex catalog I get every month, there is a class called "How to Marry the Wealthy" for rich spouse club wannabes.

The more we aspire to belong to a group, the more influenced we may be, although not necessarily by the group itself. We may

def•i•ni•tion

A **reference group** is a group to whom we look to get information about what attitudes and behaviors are acceptable and appropriate. It can be a formal group (church or club) or an informal one (peers or family).

Insight

A reference group can be a powerful force. Women entering Bennington College in the 1930's brought conservative values into a liberal political and social environment. Not only had their conservatism disappeared by their senior year, but 20 years after graduating they were still liberals.

not even know them or they know us. But we direct our energy toward being like the people we hope will accept us. In placing too much emphasis on aspirational reference groups, however, we can get a distorted view of what the group is actually like.

Nonconformists Are Hard to Find

It's easy to understand how we might conform to group norms when the group means a lot to us. Human nature tempts us to do what others are doing in order to be accepted and approved of. And when a situation is unclear, we are likely to rely on others for cues as to the appropriate or right way to do things.

But even if we don't need the strokes, we all want to know the right way to act in any given situation. When we don't, we typically turn to others in the situation for clues to help us understand what is happening. For some reason, when we don't have a clue about how to act, we automatically assume that other people around us do. In fact, we so often look to others for information about how to act that sometimes we go along even when the facts are wrong.

Social psychologist Solomon Asch, a firm believer in the power of social influence, wondered whether the influence of the social context could actually be stronger that the real facts. In his study, college students were told they would be participating in a study of simple visual perception. They were shown cards with three lines of differing lengths and asked which of the three lines was the same length as a separate, standard line. The lines were different enough so that mistakes were rare, and their relative sizes changed on each trial.

On the first three trials, everyone agreed on the right answer. However, on the fourth trial, each member of the study agreed on the wrong line and the subject had to decide whether to go along with the incorrect majority or go out on a limb and stick with the right answer. Asch found that 75 percent of the student subjects conformed to the false judgment of the group one or more times. Only a quarter of them remained completely independent. Through a series of experiments, he also found that people were less inclined to conform if there was someone else in the group who also bucked the status quo, if the size of the unanimous group was smaller, and if there was less discrepancy between the majority's answer and the right answer.

The Asch effect has become the classic illustration of how people conform. Unless we pay close attention to the power of the situation and buffer ourselves from it, we may conform to group pressure without being aware that we're doing so.

Psychobabble

One way to increase conformity is to make the target less than human. During World War I, the "willingness to kill" among soldiers was only 15 percent, despite the fact that most of them were familiar with guns and hunted. To raise willingness, the army uses video games as training tools; the kill ratio is up to 90 percent. (Imagine what happens to children who spend hours at these games.)

In the 1930's, Adolph Hitler managed to transform rational German citizens into mindless masses who were unquestioningly loyal to an evil ideology. Now, we've examined how groups influence individuals, but how does one individual influence a group? How does propaganda and persuasive communication work its magic? And even with the most powerful propaganda, how can people become so blindly obedient to authority?

A social psychologist and renegade researcher, Stanley Milgram, showed that the blind obedience of Nazis was less a product of warped personalities than it was the outcome of situational forces that could engulf anyone—even you and me. In a controversial experiment, Milligram told volunteers they were participating in a study of the effects of punishment on learning and memory. The goal was to improve learning and memory through a proper balance of reward and punishment. Volunteers were assigned roles as teachers or learners; unknown to the volunteers, the "learners" were actually actors who knew what the test was really about.

Before the experiment each "teacher" was given a real shock of about 75 volts to feel the amount of pain it caused. The role of the learner was played by a pleasant, mild-mannered man, about 50 years old, who mentioned having a "heart condition" but was willing to go along with the experiment. Each time this "learner" made an error, the volunteer teacher increased the level of shock by a fixed amount until the learning was error-free. If a teacher argued or hesitated to increase the shock level, the white-coated authority figure restated the rules and ordered the teachers to do their jobs. The true goal of increasing the level of shock was to find out just how much punishment a "teacher" was willing to deliver.

Insight

Flemish artist Pieter Bruegel (The Elder) painted his famous "Parable of the Blind" in 1568, showing men following each other into the abyss. This famous picture is the source of the expression, "the blind leading the blind."

Beforehand, psychiatrists guessed that most "teachers" would not go beyond 150 volts. They predicted less than 4 percent would go to 300 volts and less than .01 of a percent would go all the way to 450 volts; presumably, the 450 volters would be the real "sickies" whose personalities were abnormal in some way.

Guess what? The majority of subjects obeyed the researcher completely. Nearly two-thirds delivered the maximum volts to the learner, and the average teacher did not quit until about 300 volts. No subject who got within five switches of the end ever refused to go all the way. Most were very upset by what they were doing; they complained and argued with the researcher, but nevertheless, they complied. And if you're the one in the electric chair, that's all that matters!

When Authority Rules

Milgram concluded that we are most likely to obey an authority figure when:

- we see a peer blindly complying with an authority figure

- the target of the violence cannot be seen or heard

- the person is being watched or supervised by the authority figure giving the commands

- the authority figure has a higher status or more power

- the person can feel like he is merely assisting someone else who's actually doing the dirty work

These are situational factors, not personality characteristics. In fact, personality tests administered to Milgram's subjects revealed no personality trait differences between the people who obeyed fully and those who ultimately refused to give more shock, nor did they identify any mental illness or abnormality in those who administered the maximum voltage.

Can we make sense of this disturbing news? Could it be that the subjects didn't really believe the "cover story" they were given in the shock experiment? Another investigator decided to find out with a similar shock test, this time making the effects of obedience clear to the people doing the shocks. (Makes you wonder about the personalities of some of the people who come up with these experiments!)

Shock the Puppy

This time, college students were asked to train a puppy by shocking it whenever it made a mistake. They could actually see the puppy jumping around on an electric grid (in reality, the puppy only received enough of a shock to make it squeal but not enough to hurt it). Each time the students shocked the puppy, they got upset. Some of them argued, complained, even cried. But still they shocked the puppy.

Then, as if this wasn't enough torture for the poor students (not to mention the puppy), an undetectable anesthesia was released, putting the puppy to sleep. The subjects, of course, thought they had killed it. The experimenter again reminded the subjects of the rules: failure to respond was a punishable error—give more shock!

In the puppy experiment, the students had no doubt that their compliance had "harmful" consequences, so we can rule out the explanation that the subjects rationalized that no one was being harmed. We can also rule out callousness or meanness on the part of the students; they were clearly distressed by what they were doing. So how do we explain this behavior? Let's take a look at a fascinating facet of human nature—the power of situations to "demand" certain responses.

Demanding Characteristics

We are constantly getting cues about the right thing to do in any given situation. We get these cues, often called demand characteristics, from watching other people, from direct instructions, or by watching the behavior or tone of the leader.

For instance, when we're around a person in a position of authority, there is an underlying demand characteristic for obedience. Being a student often makes us hesitant to question or challenge a professor, even when we believe we have a good reason for doing so. We may leave our doctor's office and realize we were too intimidated to question his diagnosis even if we view ourselves as independent thinkers.

The undertow of demand characteristics can drown even the most educated professional's judgment. In a study assessing

> **Insight**
>
> Most of us have a sense of whether or not we're about to get into a risky situation. One of the best ways to avoid giving in to peer pressure is to be ready for it. Use humor to deflect a request you don't want to comply with and have a ready-made excuse (even if it's exaggerated) that allows you to leave or decline.

demand characteristics of a hospital setting, 20 out of 22 nurses obeyed fake physicians' orders and began to administer twice the clearly labeled maximum dosage of a drug (which was actually a harmless substance). Even when we have good reasons to defy authority, it can be incredibly hard to do so.

Take Responsibility!

When it comes to psychology, as in life, the majority often rules, which is one reason why we have spent several rather grim pages talking about our tendency to obey authority, to give in to social pressure, and to be molded by the situation around us. But perhaps you've overlooked the small but not silent minority who *don't* obey blindly, who wouldn't shock a person or a puppy, or who wouldn't follow the doctor's orders when they are bad ones. Who are these brave individuals? And what makes them different from the majority of us?

Surprisingly, the answer is rather simple. These brave souls are the people who truly feel responsible for the outcome. The two nurses in the group who felt equally responsible for their patient's welfare bucked the trend by refusing to administer the drug.

This may not be as altruistic as it seems. In fact, taking responsibility may simply mean we know there's no one else we can blame! Our willingness to obey an authority increases if that authority can be blamed for any wrongdoing. On the other hand, if we feel like the buck stops here or if we share responsibility with the person giving the order, we're more likely to resist any behavior that can cause someone harm.

How to Be a Rebel

Knowing how to resist is one way to escape the conformity trap. For example, if we don't know how to stick to our guns, we may wind up saying "yes" when a person persists after we've said "no." Many salespeople count on this, and some men refuse to believe a woman means it when she says no to his sexual advances. And finally, we all have an ingrained habit of obeying authority without question; remember the "obey your elders" rule of thumb? One of the best ways to resist unwanted influence is to build in a delay before we make a decision. Whether we're resisting the pressure to do our boss yet another uncompensated favor or being strong-armed into paying more for that car than we want, if we take a "time out" to think things over, we can give ourselves the space to make sure we're swimming in the right direction. Also getting second opinions from a doctor, comparison shopping, or talking things over with a colleague or an expert can get us out of the "total situation" and into a balanced frame of mind.

Psychobabble

A study found that, when a man allegedly in need of assistance was slumped in the doorway to the church, only 10 percent of the seminary students helped when they were late for their sermon! This probably wouldn't happen in France, where Good Samaritan laws require citizens to assist someone in trouble (or face arrest).

Give Me Some Help Here

In March 1964, 38 respectable, law-abiding citizens watched a killer stalk and stab a woman in three separate attacks. For over an hour, witnesses watched a killer leave and return, only to stab her again. Not a single person telephoned the police during the assault. One person eventually did—after the woman was dead. Three decades later, in August of 1995, a young woman named Deletha Word was chased and attacked by a man whose fender she had dented. She eventually jumped from a bridge after threatening to kill herself if her attacker continued to beat her. Two young men, who actually jumped into the water in an attempt to save her, later described the other onlookers as standing around "like they were taking an interest in sports."

The newspaper accounts of these tragedies stunned millions of readers who could not understand how respectable citizens could stand by without doing anything. The public outrage drew national attention to the problem of bystander apathy, an apparent lack of concern from people who had the power to help.

Why didn't someone stop to help Kitty or more people help Deletha? Research shows that the best predictor of whether someone will run to the rescue depends on the size of the group in which it happens. Oddly enough, the more people who see what's going on, the less likely any one of them will try to help. In a group, we tend to assume that someone else will do the dirty work. Someone else will make the phone call or help the driver stranded on the side of the road. The technical term for this "pass the buck" philosophy is *diffusion of responsibility*.

def•i•ni•tion

Diffusion of responsibility is a weakening of each person's sense of personal responsibility and obligation to help. It happens when one person perceives that the responsibility is shared with other group members.

That's the bad news. The good news is that, like heroic Lawrence Walker and Orlando Brown jumping in to help Deletha Word, people do help more often than not. In a staged emergency inside a New York subway train, one or more persons tried to help in 81 out of 103 cases. Certainly, the offers of assistance took a little longer when the situation was grim (the subject was bleeding, for example), but they still came.

Psychobabble

President Harry Truman had a sign on his desk in the oval office that said, "The Buck Stops Here." Truman, who had to take responsibility for some pretty tough decisions, is also credited with saying, "If you can't stand the heat, get out of the kitchen." This expression resulted in his advisors being called "The Kitchen Cabinet."

Sometimes, we can convert apathy into kindness just by asking for it. The next time you could use a helping hand, increase your chances of getting help by doing the following:

Psychobabble

Experiments showed that when bystanders had temporarily agreed to watch someone's belongings and then a "thief" (research accomplice) came along and stole them, every single bystander called for help. In fact, some of them even chased the thief down and tackled him!

- **Ask for it**. You might think a person would have to be in a coma to miss your need for help, but don't assume it. Let them know.

- **Give clear instructions**. Clearly explain the situation, and tell the person what she could do. "My mom just fainted! Call 911 and give them this address!"

- **Don't let them off the hook**. "Hey, you in the red shirt, please call for a tow truck." There's nothing like being volunteered out loud to get people to take responsibility for their actions and help you.

Fields of Prophecies

What we believe and expect from each other has tremendous power in our relationships. Social psychologists use the term *self-fulfilling prophecies* to describe the circular relationship between our expectations and beliefs about some behavior or event and what actually happens. In fact, much research suggests that the very nature of some situations can be changed for better or worse by the beliefs and expectations people have about them. In essence, we often find what we are looking for.

def•i•ni•tion

Self-fulfilling prophecies are predictions about a behavior or event that actually shape its outcome in the expected direction. If, for example, I expect you to behave aggressively, I might react defensively or guardedly to whatever you say, increasing the odds that you will respond in kind. If you do, then because of my original expectations, I get the satisfaction of saying, "Aha, just as I thought!"

Sometimes, we see it even if it isn't there. If you've been in a bad relationship, it might be easy for you to believe the worst of the next few guys you date. If you've been hurt enough, you may start to believe the contents of every date's emotional suitcase looks the same. And you may find what you're looking for—either by picking men with similar challenges or focusing on behaviors that confirm your dour expectations.

As you can see, relationships exist as much in our heads as they do in our actual interactions. Over time, it's natural to form expectations and beliefs about how relationships should work. But negative expectations and beliefs can create a vicious cycle that serves to confirm our worst fears and dour predictions.

Sometimes, though, our expectations and beliefs about people arise less from our personal experiences and more from family legacies and cultural myths—in a word: *prejudice.*

def•i•ni•tion

Prejudice is a learned negative attitude toward a person based on his or her membership in a particular group.

Psychobabble

Do you think it doesn't matter what others think of us? Elementary school teachers were told that certain students were "intellectual bloomers" who would make great academic strides over the next year. By the end of the school year, 30 percent of these randomly assigned children had gained an average of 22 I.Q. points and almost all of them had gained 10.

Prejudice: Social Reality Running Amok

A prejudiced attitude acts as a biased filter through which negative emotions and beliefs cloud the perception of a target group. Once formed, prejudice exerts a powerful force for selectively attending to, organizing, and remembering pertinent information. If you think cat owners are lazy and sneaky, by gosh, you are going to find cat owners who are, and you are going to remember them.

A common question about prejudice is whether there might be a grain of truth in some of the stereotypes and beliefs that support it. After all, why else would there be these negative attitudes and discriminatory actions? Let me tell you a story, and you can answer this question for yourself.

Third-grade teacher Jane Elliott was worried that her pupils from an all-white Iowa farm town were unable to understand how difficult and complex life can be for different groups. So one day she arbitrarily stated that the brown-eyed students were "superior" to the blue-eyed students. The brown-eyed students, whom she categorized as more intelligent, were given special privileges, while the inferior "blue eyes" were stuck with their lowly second-grade status.

By the end of the day, the schoolwork of the blue-eyed students had declined, and they became depressed, pouty, and angry. The brown-eyed geniuses were quick to catch on to a good thing. They refused to play with their former friends and began mistreating them. They got into fights with them and even began worrying that school officials should be notified that the blue-eyed children might steal their belongings.

When teacher Jane reversed the hierarchy on day two, the exact same thing happened in reverse. The blue-eyed children got their revenge, and the brown-eyed children learned what it was like to be at the bottom of the totem pole. You can understand what happens to children who experience genuine prejudice every day.

As we've looked at the good, the bad, and the ugly of human nature, you've seen how people can buckle under group pressure and rise above the toughest problems. After all, if we expect good from someone, he usually delivers. If we let someone know we care, he usually cares back. And if we ask for his help, he almost always grants it. We are still evolving, but let's hope we never lose that special and mysterious complexity that makes us all too human.

Insight

Efforts to talk about race are vulnerable to misunderstandings. College student participants were paired with either a white or black partner, presented with 30 photos of faces of varying races, and told to guess which photo their partner was holding by asking questions. White participants whose black partner asked about race first mentioned race on their own turn 95 percent of the time, but in cases where the black partner didn't set the precedent by mentioning race first, white participants only mentioned it 10 percent of the time. However, when white people—even children as young as 10—avoided mentioning or even noticing race altogether in order to appear unbiased, the black subjects tended to view this "colorblindness" as evidence of prejudice, especially when race is clearly relevant.

Straight from the Lab

Boys are Catty, Too   You know the conventional wisdom: boys are more directly aggressive than girls. They punch and shove, while girls gossip and exclude—known as indirect, relational, or social aggression. But studies show that boys can be socially aggressive, too; in fact, kids who exercise one form of aggression are inclined to exercise the other—especially boys.

Beating Loneliness: Other Humans Not Required   Assigning human qualities to inanimate objects may help fight loneliness. (Think Tom Hanks and "Wilson" in Castaway.) One study shows that lonely people often compensate for their lack of social connections by creating humanlike connections with pets, gadgets, or the supernatural (God, angels, or miracles), even perceiving them as having mental states, such as thoughtfulness, considerateness, or compassion.

Don't Argue on an Empty Stomach   New research suggests that the neurotransmitter serotonin plays a critical role in regulating aggression in social encounters. Since the essential amino acid necessary for the body to create serotonin can be obtained through diet, this may explain why some of us may become combative or aggressive when we haven't eaten.

The Least You Need to Know

- Social psychologists believe that the situation we're in, rather than our personality, is a much better predictor of what we'll do.

- Social situations influence behavior through rules, roles, and norms established by the society or a group to which we belong; when we don't follow the group, we risk being ridiculed, rejected, or re-educated.

- Even the nicest people will follow orders to inflict pain if they believe others will do the same thing or if they fear rebelling against the authority.

- If we take responsibility for what happens and take a time-out when we feel pressure to conform, we, too, can be rebels.

- We're all self-serving in some ways; we tend to take credit for the good things that happen to us and blame others for the bad.

- Our built-in spin-doctors manage the impressions we attempt to make.

Part 5

Just What Is Normal, Anyway?

Get ready for a wild ride! This part deals with the tricky question of what's normal and what's not. How do clinical psychologists identify mental illness? How do they determine the best way to treat it? And on the flip side, how do we get happier if our life is just okay? In these chapters, you'll learn all about psychological diagnoses—how they're made and what they mean. You'll also learn how to build up those mental muscles so that when life's challenges throw you for a loop, you can bounce back and party hardy. In the end, you'll have a good idea of what you can do to take charge of your own life—you'll learn when and how self-improvement techniques can make a positive difference in your life

16

Are You Out of Your *Mind?*

In This Chapter

- ◆ Normal vs. abnormal
- ◆ MUUDI-ing the waters of the mind
- ◆ Labels should come with warnings
- ◆ A "classy" diagnosis
- ◆ The perils of pleading insanity
- ◆ The new kid on the block: the DSM-V

In 1973, psychologist Dr. David Rosenhan and seven other sane individuals faked mental illness to gain admission to a total of 12 different psychiatric hospitals. It wasn't hard; they all complained of hearing voices that said "empty, hollow, thud." Other than this one symptom, they answered every question honestly. Once in the hospital, they behaved normally—just as they would have outside the hospital. When asked about "the voices," they said they no longer heard them.

You'd think the hospital's staff would've soon realized these individuals had never been "crazy" or, if they had been, they weren't any longer. But they didn't. The only people who suspected anything were the other patients, who'd say, "You're not crazy. I bet you're a reporter doing research on the hospital."

Worse still, the staff talked about the patients in front of them as if they couldn't hear or understand what they were saying. And in the hospital notes, normal behavior was often written up as symptoms of emotional instability. For example, each pseudo-patient kept a journal of his experiences. No one on staff asked about it, but they made notes on the patients' charts about "excessive writing."

The material in this chapter explains how psychiatric labels are made—what psychologists define as abnormal, how diagnoses are classified, and the pros and cons of our current classification system. You'll get a sense of the "politics" of mental illness and the implications for anyone trying to overcome mental illness. You'll learn the psychiatric diagnoses currently in use and why you should use them with caution.

Warning! Don't succumb to the "psychology student's disease"—a tendency to discover in yourself the symptoms of every disorder discussed in the book. By the time I'd finished my first abnormal psychology course, the only mental illness I could rule out for sure was anorexia because I weighed too much and loved to eat!.

Meet Abby Normal

In a hilarious scene in the movie *Young Frankenstein*, Igor mistakenly chooses a physically abnormal brain for Dr. Frankenstein's experiments. The resulting "monster" looks physically abnormal, is intellectually impaired, and certainly doesn't know how to win friends and influence people.

The underlying psychological explanation for the movie would be that the monster's abnormal behavior came about as a result of his abnormal brain. This biological perspective of mental illness has dominated research on mental illness the past 15 years.

Brain Buster

A major National Institute of Mental Health study found that, in any given month, about 15 percent of the population is suffering from a diagnosable mental health problem and almost one out of every three people will suffer from one in the course of a lifetime.

But what exactly *is* abnormal? Have you ever worried excessively, felt depressed for no apparent reason, or felt afraid of something you knew couldn't really hurt you? I certainly have—I have been known to mow people down in my frantic need to get away from a harmless cockroach. A few irrational fears and occasional periods of worry or sadness seem to be part of life. The challenge is in knowing how many are too many and how long is too long.

Mental health professionals face a difficult task when they try to come up with a definition of mental illness because it's hard to determine at what point eccentric or free-spirited behavior becomes a marker of mental illness. But when a person begins to behave in a way that causes significant personal distress and disrupts his ability to function effectively at work or at home, it seems obvious that something must be done. So mental-health professionals need to designate some point at which a person's behavior crosses the (sometimes fine) line between health and illness. This cutoff point is called a *psychological diagnosis*.

Psychological diagnoses are interpretations based on a person's behavior. In order for someone to receive a psychological diagnosis, that person must have had the problem for some time—to make certain that it's not just a temporary state. For some diagnoses, like clinical depression, the minimum time period could be as short as two weeks; for personality disorders, the time frame must be at least two years.

def•i•ni•tion

A **psychological diagnosis** is a label used to identify and describe a mental disorder, based on information collected by observation, testing, and analysis. It is also a judgment about a person's current level of functioning.

In addition, the person's behavioral problems must be bad enough to disrupt normal daily activities. Maybe you've been waking up in the middle of the night and can't go back to sleep. Maybe you're calling in sick at work quite often, or maybe you're drinking too much. Whatever the problem is, to warrant a psychological diagnosis, it must be severe enough that you'd function much better without it.

How Psychologists MUUDI the Waters

Clinical psychologists generally evaluate a person's behavior according to five basic criteria: whether it is maladaptive, unpredictable, unconventional, distressing, or irrational. If at least two of these criteria are present, a warning bell alerts the psychologist to look more closely at the person's symptoms. In the world of diagnosis, this is how mental health professionals often MUUDI the waters of the mind.

- **Maladaptive.** The person fails to adapt to the demands of everyday life, either by acting counter to his own well-being or against the goals and needs of society.

- **Unpredictable.** The person loses control or acts erratically from one situation to another. For example, the child who suddenly smashes a toy for no apparent reason is behaving unpredictably.

- **Unconventional.** Behavior psychologists define as unconventional is both rare and undesirable. Geniuses may be eccentric, but a psychologist wouldn't apply the term *unconventional* unless their behavior violates social standards of what is morally acceptable or desirable.

◆ **Distressing.** The person is suffering from severe personal distress or intensely negative emotions. If a person is nervous before an exam, that's normal; if he throws up, can't concentrate, and eventually gets up and walks out, that's abnormal.

◆ **Irrational.** The person acts in ways that are incomprehensible to others. Hearing voices or believing that you're overweight at 95 pounds are examples of irrational behavior.

Of course, there's another factor involved in any psychological diagnosis—the level of discomfort in the person making the judgment! Certainly, what is defined as "abnormal" partly depends on the comfort level of the society in which we live. A person who hears voices in the United States is much more likely to be labeled "mentally ill" than someone who lives in a culture that views hallucinations as a form of spiritual guidance.

Sick Societies

For hundreds of years, most societies have had a "sick" view of mental illness—they saw abnormal behavior as a sign of evil. Throughout the Middle Ages, for example, concepts of mental illness were intertwined with superstition and religion, and the outcome wasn't pretty. How'd you like having holes drilled in your head to let the evil spirits out?

Until the end of the eighteenth century, the mentally ill in Western cultures were viewed as mindless beasts who could only be controlled with chains and physical discipline. "Psychiatric hospitals" were nothing more than jail cells, when they weren't amusement parks—curious visitors could sometimes pay to view the mentally ill like animals in a zoo. (We actually treat our modern zoo animals more kindly.)

Psychobabble
In Salem, Massachusetts, in 1692, several young girls began experiencing convulsions, nausea, and weakness. They reported sensations of being bitten or pinched, and some became temporarily blind or deaf. Believing the girls' symptoms were the work of the devil, villagers became caught up in a witchcraft panic that led to the execution of more than 20 men and women believed to be witches. Theories have ranged from ergot poisoning, a fungus that grows on rye and is a source of LSD, to diagnoses of the principle "witnesses" as having histrionic personality disorder or other disorders.

In the 1700s, however, Phillipe Pinel began preaching that the mentally ill were neither immoral nor demonically possessed—they were simply suffering from a sickness. Believing that disorders of thought, mood, and behavior were similar to physical illnesses, he developed the first system to classify psychological disorders. His classifications were a huge step forward because they made it easier for clinicians to identify and design treatments for common disorders.

It wasn't until 1896, however, that the German psychiatrist Emil Kraeplin created the first truly comprehensive system of classifying psychological disorders. When psychiatrists today speak of "mental illness" and talk of treating "patients," they are borrowing from Kraeplin's medical view of the origins of mental illness. While Kraeplin's medical approach helped reduce the stigma of mental illness, it also slowed down the discovery of the psychological, social, and environmental influences on mental-health problems. Sigmund Freud later swung attention back in that direction.

> **Psychobabble**
>
> Here's good news! A 2004 study found that 76 percent of United States managers believe that an employee's acknowledgment of depression would not prevent him from getting ahead. And the bad news is? Only 41 percent of employees believe this.

Psychology Today

Well, today's psychologists have ruled out evil spirits as the source of mental illness—but that's just about as far as we've come. The search for the causes of mental illness is still alive and well and currently led by teams divided into two camps: the biological team and the psychological team.

Walking the Biological Beat

The biological team follows the medical model in assuming that psychological problems are directly attributable to underlying brain or nervous system disorders. The brain is a complex and delicate organ; subtle alterations in its tissue or its chemical messengers can have a dramatic influence on a person's mental health. For example, tumors in certain areas of the brain can cause extremely violent behavior; an autopsy of Charles Joseph Whitman, the "Texas tower" sniper who gunned down 45 people before being killed by two police officers, revealed one. And having too little or too much of even one neurotransmitter can mean the difference between happiness and despair.

The biological approach to mental illness is responsible for developing the powerful psychiatric medications that are available today, some of which enable people to live normal, satisfying lives. Years ago, these same people would have spent their lives chained to the wall of an insane asylum.

Pulling for the Psychological Team

The psychological team, of course, focuses on the causal role of social or psychological factors in the development of *psychopathology*. They search for the personal experiences, traumas, conflicts, parenting styles, and so forth that lead to psychological disorders. A therapist relying on the psychodynamic perspective, for example, might focus on a person's past actions and relationships and the conflicts in these. Behaviorists would examine problem behaviors and the conditions in the environment that keep them in place, while therapists using the cognitive approach would investigate unhealthy reasoning or poor problem solving and its impact on our lives.

def•i•ni•tion

Psychopathology is the clinical term for an abnormality or disorder in thought, emotion, or behavior.

The biological and psychological camps are beginning to work together. Both are becoming increasingly aware that psychopathology is the product of a complex interaction between biology and psychology. This *diathesis-stress* model of mental illness says that an individual who has a biological predisposition to a certain mental disorder will tend to develop it when under stress.

A person might have a genetic susceptibility for depression (biology) but doesn't get depressed until his divorce (psychology). In fact, many mental illnesses seem to work this way; a person is vulnerable to a mental illness because of faulty hormones or neurotransmitters, but certain stresses or maladaptive coping strategies are necessary for the illness to fully develop.

Of course, it's pretty useless to argue about what *causes* mental illness unless you are in agreement about what it *is*. To create greater consistency among clinicians with various theoretical backgrounds, psychologists and psychiatrists have developed a system of diagnosis and classification that provides precise descriptions of symptoms. At its best, our classification system provides an objective framework for evaluating a person's behavior and picking the most effective treatment. At its worst, it promotes labeling and focuses on the illness rather than on the person who has it.

> **Psychobabble**
>
> The current *DSM-IV-TR* attempts to be more culturally sensitive, with even an appendix of disorders apparently only found in certain cultures (for instance, "ghost sickness," a condition associated with some Native American tribes and characterized by very specific psychological and physical symptoms).

DSM-IV-TR: The Mental Health Catalog

Without an agreed-upon system to identify people whose disorders are similar to each other, the accumulation of knowledge about causes and effective treatments would be impossible. The system that is currently in vogue is the *DSM-IV-TR*. The "DSM" stands for *Diagnostic and Statistical Manual of Mental Disorders*, and the "IV" means that this is the fourth attempt to get it right. The "TR" stands for "text revision," meaning this was a minor revision and that the changes were made to some of the descriptions of the disorders but not to the diagnoses themselves.

As classification systems go, *DSM-IV-TR* isn't too shabby. First of all, it's pretty reliable: the agreement among diagnosticians as to who has or doesn't have a particular disorder is pretty high. And that's an important point—after all, they must be able to agree on the diagnosis before they compare the individuals who have it.

But is the *DSM-IV-TR* clinically meaningful? That's still a matter of debate. Critics argue that two people with the same diagnosis may suffer in very different ways and respond to different treatments.

> **Psychobabble**
>
> The ICD 10 is the European version of our DSM-IV-R. Currently, your diagnosis could shift with a move across the ocean; for instance, schizotypal disorder is viewed as a major mental illness in Europe while it's seen more as a personality disorder here in the United States. The DSM-V task force is working to reconcile the discrepancies between the DSM and Europe's ICD.

Shopping in the *DSM-IV-TR* Catalog

The *DSM-IV-TR* lists more than 200 mental illnesses, grouped under 16 diagnostic categories, summarized as follows.

- ◆ **Anxiety disorders.** In this group of disorders either fear or anxiety is a major symptom. Examples include panic disorder, phobias, obsessive-compulsive disorder, and post-traumatic stress disorder.

◆ **Mood disorders.** These disorders are characterized by depression or mania. Examples include major depression, bipolar disorder (formerly called manic-depression), dysthymia, and cyclothymia.

◆ **Somataform disorders.** In these disorders physical symptoms arise from psychological problems. Examples include somatization disorder and conversion disorder.

◆ **Substance-related disorders.** Disorders are caused by drugs, including alcohol, cocaine, amphetamines, or opiates. Examples include amphetamine withdrawal and alcohol dependence.

◆ **Dissociative disorders.** Disorders occur when a part of one's experience is separated from one's conscious memory or identity. Examples include dissociative identity disorder and psychogenic amnesia.

◆ **Psychotic disorders.** Disorders are characterized by a loss of contact with reality, either through hallucinations, delusions, or inappropriate emotions. Examples include schizophrenia and delusional disorder.

◆ **Sexual and gender identity disorders.** Sexual disorders are disorders of sexual functioning. Examples include fetishism, exhibitionism, and psychosexual dysfunction. Gender identity disorders involve a persistent desire to be, or appear to be, a member of the opposite sex.

◆ **Eating disorders.** Disorders are marked by excessive concern about weight gain accompanied by extreme dieting, overeating, or purging. Examples include anorexia nervosa and bulimia nervosa.

◆ **Sleep disorders.** Disorders involve disrupted sleep, sleepwalking, fear of nightmares, or fear of sleep. Examples include insomnia and sleep-wake disorder.

◆ **Impulse control disorders.** Disorders result in impulsive behaviors that harm the self or others. Examples include intermittent explosive disorder, kleptomania, and pathological gambling.

◆ **Disorders usually first diagnosed in infancy, childhood, or adolescence.** This wide range of disorders appear before adulthood. Examples include mental retardation, learning disorders, and language development disorders.

◆ **Adjustment disorder.** An extreme emotional reaction to a stressor that occurred within the previous month (much greater than most people would experience).

- **Personality disorders.** These long-term disorders are characterized by rigid, maladaptive personality traits. Examples include antisocial personality disorder, histrionic personality disorder, and narcissistic personality disorder.

- **Delirium, dementia, amnestic, and other cognitive disorders.** This diverse group of disorders of memory and cognition is caused by identifiable brain damage. Examples include Alzheimer's disease, intellectual impairment due to stroke or head injury, and delirium (change in consciousness) as a result of a drug overdose.

- **Mental disorders due to a general medical condition.** This group of mental disorders can be directly traced to a medical cause. Examples include personality changes due to frontal lobe injury, psychotic disorder due to epilepsy, and depression secondary to diabetes.

- **Factitious disorders.** Physical or psychological symptoms are faked in order to assume the "sick" role. Examples include making up physical complaints, exaggerating genuine medical symptoms, or self-inflicting wounds and then seeking medical treatment.

In order for a diagnostic decision to be made, classification systems must designate a cutoff point; below that point a person doesn't have a disorder, and above it he does. In real life, though, mental health and emotional challenges exist on a continuum.

Psychobabble

Concerns about conflicts of interest have always swirled around the DSM. Critics point out, for example, that 16 of the 28 members on the DSM-V task force have financial ties to pharmaceutical or medical device companies. And, of course, the careers of some task force experts depend on ensuring that their diagnostic category is not only represented but also expanded. (Imagine if the disorder you've dedicated your life to researching were suddenly downsized or booted out of the DSM altogether!) But the APA argues that conflicts of interest are limited by the fact that the DSM is a diagnostic manual, not a treatment manual.

Get Ready for the New Kid on the Block: DSM-V

Do you ever wonder how (or why) a disorder makes it into the DSM? A crack team of world-wide experts compiles new research, clinical data, and expert testimony and then presents recommendations at American Psychiatric Association symposiums. The

DSM-V, to be published in 2012, will be the product of years of extensive research and collaborative efforts from hundreds of investigators in every subdiscipline of psychiatry.

What changes will the DSM-V bring? While the process is still at the question rather than the answer stage, new disorders may be unveiled. For example, psychopathy continues to be bantered around for possible inclusion, either as a stand-alone diagnosis or as a subtype of antisocial personality disorder. Internet addiction may be added to the impulse disorder category, and anxious-depression is being investigated for possible inclusion.

The DSM-V will also be more culturally sensitive, weighing the effects of stigma, racism, biological gender differences, religion, and violence and trauma unique to certain cultures. Alternative diagnostic methods such as neuroimaging and well-validated psychological tests may be factored into diagnoses. And the personality disorders may be overhauled; many experts believe the current DSM's distinction between normal personality traits and personality disorder is largely arbitrary and that no distinct boundaries exist between personality disorders. (This is ironic, considering that "lack of distinct boundaries" is a symptom of certain personality disorders, such as borderline personality disorder!) As such, there's talk of scrapping the current categorical approach in favor of a more dimensional approach that views personality disorders as maladaptive versions of general personality function.

Warning: Labels Can Be Hazardous to Your Health

Pretend you and I are getting ready to go out with another friend of mine, Jan. You've never met Jan, so you're asking me for a little bit of information about her in preparation for our dinner together. I'm singing her praises. "She's really smart; she's headed up the corporate ladder; she's funny, generous, and attractive. Oh, and by the way, she suffers from depression and is on Prozac." Did your level of enthusiasm drop a little with that last remark?

If so, you're like most of us. Diagnosing and labeling may be essential for the scientific study of mental illness. Insurance companies may require them. However, we should use them with caution.

> **Psychobabble**
>
> A review of all United States newspapers with subscribers of 250,000 or more found that the vast majority (39 percent) of newspaper stories portray mental illness as a dangerous disease. These stories were mainly on the front page, increasing impact— and stigma.

When we meet a person who is labeled as having a mental disorder, we're often blinded to the person's qualities that aren't captured by the label. For example, now that Jan has the label "depressed," you're less likely to notice her sense of humor. And unfortunately, this tunnel vision isn't limited to the layperson—psychotherapists are as susceptible to it as anyone else.

There's a person under that label, and that label can hurt the person who carries it. Former patients in a psychiatric hospital, for example, were found to be much more socially inept if they believed that their psychiatric treatment was known to the person with whom they were interacting.

Both professionals *and* laypersons should work hard to use language that distinguishes the person from his diagnosis. Calling someone "an anorexic" or "a schizophrenic" is dangerous and damaging. Such language implies that the diagnosis sums up the entire person. If I had my way, we'd say, "Joni has received the diagnosis of anorexia nervosa from a mental-health professional." That way, the person is distinct from the illness, *and* we'd be acknowledging that the diagnosis itself is a judgment made by a fallible human being. It's subjective and never completely reliable.

Psychobabble

In the nineteenth century, Samuel Cartwright argued that slaves were suffering from two forms of mental illness: (1) drapetomania, an uncontrollable urge to escape from slavery, and (2) dyasthesia aethiopica, which included symptoms such as being disobedient, talking back, refusing to work, and fighting back when being beaten. I can think of a few labels that might fit Mr. Cartwright; how about you?

The Gender Politics of Mental Illness

Before I step down from my soapbox, I want to tell you a story. In the 1970s, a study asked a number of mental health professionals to describe a mentally healthy man. They used adjectives like *assertive* and *confident*. Then these same people were asked to describe a mentally healthy woman. This time words like *warm, sensitive, nurturing* appeared. Then came the biggest challenge: describe a mentally healthy *person*. Do you want to know what happened? The mentally healthy person had the same traits as the mentally healthy man. So where does that leave those of us of the female persuasion?

Gender differences in mental health diagnoses exist, and their causes have been debated ever since they were noticed. Although little difference is found between men and women in the overall prevalence of mental illness, large gender differences are found for specific disorders. Women are much more likely to be diagnosed with anxiety and mood disorders, and men are more likely than women to be diagnosed with substance-abuse problems and antisocial personality disorder.

It is possible that such differences might directly come from biological differences between the sexes. Most attention, though, has been paid to the sociocultural explanations for these differences, such as self-reporting differences, biased observers, and gender-based differences in life experiences.

Insight

A 2002 NIMH study revealed that the demographic group with the biggest mistrust of the mental health care system and the least likely to seek help from it is white, non-Latino, males. They are also the group most likely to stigmatize mental illness and mental health concerns.

Psychologists are people, too, with their own biases, opinions, and values, which may at times influence their clinical decisions. For example, studies suggest that because some diagnoses occur more frequently in men or women, clinicians may expect to find them and, not surprisingly, find what they are looking for! These preconceptions can also influence treatment decisions; just being female is a pretty good predictor of whether or not your psychiatrist will prescribe medication.

Are You Insane?

On March 30, 1981, John W. Hinckley Jr. shot President Ronald Reagan. His defense attorneys did not dispute that he had planned and committed the act. Instead, they argued he was not guilty by reason of insanity. Specifically, they argued that Hinckley's life was controlled by his pathological obsession with the movie *Taxi Driver*, starring Jodie Foster. In that movie, Foster's character is terrorized by a stalker, who eventually gets into a shootout. The defense attorney argued that Hinckley was schizophrenic and that the movie was the force behind his assassination attempt against the president. The jury believed it.

Mental Illness vs. Insanity

Mental illness is a medical decision. Insanity, on the other hand, is a legal one. To be insane, a person must be unable to control her behavior and be unaware that her behavior is wrong. If Mr. X, on trial for shooting his boss, truly believed he needed to defend himself against a corporate conspiracy that was ruining his life, he might honestly think his actions were justified; in fact, he might believe his actions would protect others from receiving similar treatment. Serial killers like Ted Bundy, on the other hand, do bizarre things but have a clear awareness that their behavior is morally and socially wrong.

The insanity defense is based on the principle that punishment is justified only if the defendant is capable of understanding and controlling his behavior. Because some people suffering from a mental disorder are not capable of knowing or choosing right from wrong, the insanity defense prevents them from going to prison.

> **Psychobabble**
>
> Perhaps you've mused about what it would be like to redo high school. A 33-year-old Wisconsin woman actually did it. She's facing a felony identity theft charge for stealing her 15-year-old daughter's identity in order to attend high school and join the cheerleading team. She pled not guilty by reason of insanity.

The Perils of Pleading Insanity

Despite popular belief, the insanity defense is not the easy way out. Defendants rarely enter pleas of "not guilty by reason of insanity," probably because it works less than 1 percent of the time. Also defendants who are successful may wish they hadn't been. Their "successful" defense gets them confined to a mental institution until their sanity is established. Some of these defendants spend more time in a mental institution than they would have served in prison. There's an excellent movie on the subject, appropriately entitled *Nuts*. (And there's always *One Flew Over the Cuckoo's Nest* as a cautionary tale!)

Stigma Is a Dirty Word

If you missed Tom Cruise railing against psychiatrists and antidepressants in 2005, you were probably either suffering from a power outage or engaging in a media strike. After Brooke Shields publicized her agonizing battle with postpartum depression, Mr. Cruise criticized her "misguided" use of antidepressants and stated that she was irresponsible for promoting the use of psychotropic medication; instead, he stated that vitamins, a proper diet, and exercise should have been her drugs of choice. In reality, while Cruise was correct in that exercise and proper diet can certainly be effective with *mild* depression, trying to treat a suicidal individual with a bowl of Wheaties and a jog around the block is not likely to cut the mustard.

In spite of numerous public education campaigns, you can still find major American newspapers running articles that advise the depressed to "Buck up," "Throw away your antidepressants," or "Go away and sulk until you're ready to be sociable." Such stigmatizing attitudes lead many who would benefit from treatment to avoid getting it and hide their pain from friends and family members.

These attitudes ignore the fact that many mental illnesses have a biological basis. It seems that, so far, psychology has done a better job at diagnosing individual problems than "treating" the society that condemns them.

Five Things You Can Do to Fight Stigma

You might not be a psychologist, but you can do a lot to improve our *society's* mental health. Here are five ideas:

- ◆ Wise up. Mental illness is not a character flaw, a lack of willpower, or a luxury. People with mental illness are much more likely to be victims, not perpetrators of crime. And people who suffer from a mental illness can be just as successful as anyone else. (Do the names Winston Churchill and Abraham Lincoln ring a bell?)

- ◆ Avoid using slang like "crazy," "loony," or "nuts" to describe people or situations, even if you're just kidding around.

- ◆ Be a media watchdog. Fire off letters to editors, writers, and producers who include demeaning expressions or inaccurate descriptions of mental illness in their work.

- ◆ Don't be afraid to tell someone you're concerned about his emotional well-being, especially if you know he's received psychiatric treatment in the past. Asking about someone's mental health problems does not make him worse.

- ◆ Take charge of your own mental health. If you've struggled with depression or anxiety for a while, get some help.

Straight from the Lab

Reducing Stigma Through Stories   A study of children ages 5 to 11 shows that reading stories about friendships between their group and a stigmatized group can make them feel more favorably toward the stigmatized group. When English children read stories about refugees, they were more likely to say they would like to play with the refugees—especially when the story emphasized something the two groups had in common.

Bad Genes Don't Always Let You Off the Hook   While more and more Americans believe mental illness has genetic causes, we're no more tolerant of some mental illnesses than we were 10 years ago, research shows. People who believe there is a genetic link in schizophrenia still view people suffering from this disorder as "damaged" and violence-prone. However, a genetic view of depression does reduce stigma; we see the person as less blameworthy.

The Least You Need to Know

- Many mental illnesses are a complex interaction between a biological predisposition and stressful life events.

- Diagnoses are labels that mental health professionals use to group together people who have the same symptoms and behaviors.

- The most popular classification system in the United States is the *DSM-IV-TR*, *which* lists more than 200 mental diagnoses, grouped into 16 categories.

- While mental illness is a medical decision, insanity—the inability to control one's behavior and distinguish between right and wrong—is strictly a legal determination.

- The stigma of mental illness is one of the greatest barriers people face in finding the courage to get help for mental problems.

Look on the Bright Side

In This Chapter

- ◆ Move from surviving to thriving
- ◆ Join the "hardy" party
- ◆ Raise children who bounce back from tough times
- ◆ Explore why laughter may be the best medicine
- ◆ Discover when self-distancing is an effective coping strategy
- ◆ Go with the flow

In 1998, APA president Martin Seligman was working in his garden when he had an epiphany that "the entire psychology profession was 'half-baked.'" The catalyst for this unsettling revelation was his five-year-old daughter, Nikki, who had joined her weed-pulling father in the garden. While his goal was to leave the garden with fewer weeds than when he arrived, hers was to incorporate each pile of pulled weeds into her spontaneous song-and-dance routine by throwing them into the air.

A self-confessed grouch, Dr. Seligman yelled at his daughter for her unproductive shenanigans. "Daddy," she responded, "do you remember before my fifth birthday? From the time I was three to the time I was five, I was a whiner. I whined every day. When I turned five, I decided not to whine anymore. That was the hardest thing I've ever done. And if I can stop whining, you can stop being such a grouch."

Nikki's proclamation triggered a little self-analysis in her father and ultimately led to some questions about the field of psychology. Dr. Seligman wondered why it was that his psychological training had little to offer Nikki by way of encouraging a positive attitude or strengthening the will she'd already evinced. "What about the positive aspects of human nature that so often make life such a thrilling, rewarding experience?" he wondered. Once psychology got hurting people back into the game of life, how could psychology help them win? And so began the field of positive psychology.

This chapter is about building the human strengths that make a good life better, help us thrive in the face of adversity, and act as buffers against mental illness—strengths like resilience, optimism, and the capacity for flow and insight. You'll discover how exercising our mental muscles can do as much for our psyche as physical exercise can do for our bodies and how we can help our children develop the psyches to deal with life's curveballs.

> **Insight**
>
> Contrary to popular belief, it's not necessarily selfish to pursue happiness. Contented people are more creative, better problem solvers, more compassionate, and more productive than unhappy people, who tend to be self-focused and withdrawn.

Going Back to Square One

By redirecting the focus from illness to strength, Dr. Seligman brought psychology back to its roots. Before World War II, psychology understood itself as having three specific missions: (1) diagnosing and treating mental illness, (2) maximizing the happiness and productivity of all people, and (3) identifying and nurturing extraordinary talents and qualities. Psychological research routinely looked at positive human aspects such as the nature of genius, effective parenting, and marital happiness. For example, the great Carl Jung did a lot of work on our innate human need to discover a true and rewarding meaning to life.

After the war, however, psychology began to concern itself more and more with mental illness. World War II left thousands of soldiers psychologically damaged. In 1946, the Veteran's Administration was founded, and scores of psychologists began treating mental illness through the VA system.

A year later, the National Institute of Mental Health (NIMH) was founded upon the medical model of healing disease. The Institute began rewarding significant grant money to academics and/or psychologists whose research was about pathology.

Suddenly it paid to think less about happiness, productivity, and giftedness and more about disease, dysfunction, and deviation from the norm. However, in real life, positive events and interactions occur much more frequently than negative ones. Studies show that, in the average week, most people experience 3.2 positive events for every 1 negative event.

Indeed, because positive events occur more often, their impact in the long run may be greater than negative ones even though the impact of any single positive experience may be more subtle than that of a solo unpleasant one.

Insight

"Positive" doesn't mean unrealistic. In fact, while it has been well documented that happy adults tend to live longer, make more friends, and achieve more at work, new research suggests that a relentlessly positive outlook may make us less motivated and less conscientious. Mildly negative moods can help us be more analytical, giving us vital feedback about the need to shift directions or change our strategy. And those of us who are constantly happy may not have the internal gauge that tells us when we need to apply more effort or energy to get what we want; in the long run, this may not serve us well.

"Positive" doesn't mean engaging in denial. The very real negative side of life, for virtually all of us, results in a certain degree of emotional pain. People in denial avoid facing facts and resist their feelings. On the other hand, a positive spin on life's crises means the opposite: not distracting oneself by dwelling on what might have happened and confronting problems by focusing on solutions.

Positive psychology research does tell us that we can learn to create more pleasurable life experiences (satisfaction with the past, happiness in the present, and hope for the future) and that certain traits can help us thrive in the face of life's toughest challenges. We can use these traits to create the kind of families and institutions that will foster the best in all of us.

Insight

For chronic worriers, thinking through the worst-case scenario and having a plan in advance can actually work better than trying to see the glass as half full. On the other hand, those of us who aren't anxious do well to set high expectations and then avoid thinking about what might happen.

Don't Just Follow Your Bliss—Create It!

As we've seen, positive psychology is not about denial, boundless optimism, or eternally cheerful emotions. It's a research-based approach to understanding and building emotional well-being and finding meaningful, measurable, and attainable ways to be happy.

Seligman, in fact, talks about three different forms of happiness: the pleasant life, the good life, and the meaningful life. The pleasant life is what most of us think of when we consider whether we are happy or not in any given moment; it's the "feel good" part of happiness. When we don't feel happy, we are more likely to take shortcuts to alter our moods—through drugs, mindless entertainment, food, and so on.

However, there are other paths to happiness: the good life and the meaningful life. We can reach both of these by recognizing and harnessing our strengths. The good life comes through deep engagement in work, family life, or other activities. The meaningful life comes through finding a purpose in our existence, whether it's through spirituality or a cause greater than ourselves. Of course, positive psychologists would also encourage us to avoid the negative while we're pursuing the positive; it's hard to be upbeat when we're watching endless hours of tragedy on the news, living at the hub of a gossip circle, or talking excessively about a political smear campaign.

> **Insight**
>
> Contrary to popular belief, we may actually be happier as we get older. For most of us, happiness is a U-shaped; we start out pretty happy, struggle between 35 and 55, and then get happier again.

> **Psychobabble**
>
> A study of lottery winners showed that within months of their initial elation, they were exactly as happy (or unhappy) as they'd been before they'd won. Research shows that our mood is largely dependent on genes. However, while we may inherit a potential range of good cheer, we can develop ways to make sure we are at the upper end of that range.

From Surviving to Thriving

Trisha Meili, the Central Park jogger, was given last rites after her rape and savage beating in New York. Only the soles of her feet were unbruised. Multiple gashes split Meili's scalp; an eye socket was fractured in 21 places. She could not breathe on her own, lost most of her blood, and had severe brain damage.

But she didn't die. In fact, she thrived. She pushed herself through an accelerated rehabilitation and returned to work despite not feeling 100 percent mentally or physically. She was promoted to vice-president. She gathered the strength to testify at two criminal trials of the five teenagers accused of assaulting her and later coped with the knowledge that she had unwittingly testified against innocent men. Today she's a motivational speaker and volunteer who discusses her healing with medical and mental-health groups, patients, and others recovering from traumatic events.

The "Hardy" Partiers

Meili's mega-recovery came as no surprise to *resilience* researchers, the psychologists who spend their time studying what separates those of us who thrive under adversity from those of us who barely keep our heads above water. Even before that fateful day in Central Park, Meili's personal history suggested that she had developed coping strategies similar to those identified by Dr. Salvatore R. Maddi, the father of the "hardy personality."

It all started with telephone workers. In 1981 Illinois Bell Telephone downsized from 26,000 employees to just over half that many. The remaining employees faced changing job descriptions, company goals, and supervisors. Dr. Maddi and his research team, who were already studying more than 400 supervisors, managers, and executives at IBT before the downsizing, continued following them until 1987. Results revealed that about two-thirds of the employees in the study suffered significant performance, leadership, and health declines as the result of extreme stress. However, the other one-third actually thrived during the upheaval, despite experiencing the same disruption and stressful events as their co-workers. These employees maintained their health, happiness, and performance and felt renewed enthusiasm.

def•i•ni•tion

Resilience is the ability to bounce back—to thrive, mature, and increase competence in the face of risk and adversity.

Two Steps Forward Comes from One Step Back

Processing our painful emotions is supposed to help us cope better, right? Too much of a good thing, though, can backfire and leave us wallowing in our misery. And sure, distracting ourselves helps but only for the short-term. Denial and distraction are not effective solutions for the long-term.

A new University of Michigan study suggests the best way to move ahead emotionally may be to analyze your feelings from a distance, as if you were watching a movie or listening to what happened to a close friend. For example, let's say you still haven't gotten over the loss of an old love. Go back to the time and place of your breakup and try to understand your feelings from the perspective of someone else. Why did "she" hurt so much? What meaning did "she" give to this rejection? And what will help her move forward?

Self-analysis from a distance can help us cope with overwhelming feelings in the short-term as well as work through negative experiences over time. And studies show that self-distancing improves cardiovascular recovery (lower blood pressure) from painful feelings and helps protect us from depression. It just takes a little practice.

Insight

Research indicates that our genes influence how rosy our disposition naturally is. However, we can all learn ways to be resilient, stay in the present, keep things in perspective, and work on the problems at hand.

But what made the two groups so different? Dr. Maddi found that those who thrived maintained three key beliefs or attitudes which helped them turn adversity into an advantage: commitment, control, and challenge. The commitment attitude led them to strive to be involved in ongoing events rather than feeling isolated. The control attitude led them to struggle and try to influence outcomes rather than lapse into passivity and powerlessness. And the challenge attitude led them to view changes, whether positive or negative, as opportunities for learning.

Raising Tiggers Who Bounce Back from Stress

Resilience is a skill we can develop no matter what age we are. Of course, it helps if we get a leg up from the beginning. As parents we can plant the seeds of resilience that will bloom into an ongoing sense of challenge, commitment, and control.

Commitment starts with the right connections. We can help our child develop empathy by having empathy for our child. For example, before you utter parenting words like "try harder" or "speak up," think about how you would feel if someone gave that advice to you. Which is more likely to foster resilience in a shy child: "If you don't start speaking up, your teacher is going to think you don't care" or "Many kids who have trouble speaking in front of a group at the beginning of the year feel more comfortable as they get to know their classmates"? The latter statement is more likely to give the child a sense of hope and understanding—two things she needs to develop a sense of optimism.

A sense of control starts with a balanced perspective between what we can change and what we can't. When your child has a new problem or challenge, ask her to write down all the possible actions she could take to solve—or at least change—the problem. And don't forget to address the self-talk that goes along with the problem; one of the greatest strengths any parent can give a child is helping her learn to recognize—and gain control over—the internal dialogue that takes place as we go through every day.

> **Brain Buster**
>
> Don't sabotage yourself! New research shows that how we view our skills and abilities determines whether we thrive in a particular situation—and whether we're likely to sabotage ourselves. People who view their intelligence as something that doesn't change tend to become anxious when they dramatically exceed their own expectations—and are more likely to do worse in an additional task. On the other hand, those of us who think hard work and effort pays off tend to become unnerved—and do worse—if a couple of tries results in failure.

Challenge starts with self-confidence. Identify and nurture your child's strengths; every kid needs to feel capable and good about himself. And one of the best ways you can grow your kid's confidence is to ask him for help. In fact, when 1,500 adults were asked, "What is your favorite positive memory of school?" the number-one positive memory was being asked to help out. Feeling like they can make a positive difference makes kids more confident, more hopeful, and more resilient.

> **Insight**
>
> Increase your family optimism by having each member keep track of the positive events in his life. For example, for the next month, have each family member keep a daily log of three things that went well and why, and share them with each other once a week.

Going with the Flow at Work

There were times when I was so engrossed in writing this book that I lost track of time and felt slightly disoriented when briefly (but, alas, frequently) interrupted by one of my children. When I found an interesting tidbit to include, I felt pure, unadulterated joy. In fact, I was enjoying this process so much that I felt as if I were going through withdrawal when I had to turn off my computer and direct my attention elsewhere. According to Dr. Mihaly Csikszentmihalyi, a psychology professor at the

def•i•ni•tion

According to Mihaly Csikszentmihalyi, **flow** is the sense of effortless action we feel when we are totally absorbed in a task.

University of Chicago who pioneered research on optimal experiences, I was in a state of effortless concentration and enjoyment called *flow*. And given the right circumstances, we can all create it.

Flow can occur in any experience—from singing and dancing to performing surgery to playing with a baby. Athletes often call it "being in the zone." These exceptional moments provide vibrant intensity against the dull background of everydayness.

When John Coltrane was expanding the boundaries of the well-known song "My Favorite Things" at the Village Vanguard in May 1966, no one could have known what inspired him to take the musical turns he took. But imaging researchers now have a better picture of how the brain was helping to carry him there. Through some creative thinking of their own, these researchers designed a protocol in which jazz musicians could play a keyboard while in the confines of a functional MRI scanner. And in doing so, they were able to pinpoint differences in how the brain functioned when the musicians were improvising as opposed to playing a simple melody from memory.

Scientists have found that when jazz musicians are improvising, a large region of the brain involved in monitoring one's performance is shut down, while a small region involved in organizing self-initiated thoughts and behaviors is highly activated (the same part of the brain that is active when we describe an event or make up a story). Another unusual finding was that there was increased neural activity in each of the sensory areas responsible for touch, hearing, and vision as if the brain ramps up its sensorimotor processing in order to be in a creative state. The systems that regulate emotion were also engaged during improvisation.

Insight

Just as over-thinking a jump shot can cause a basketball player to fall out of the zone and perform poorly, the suppression of self-monitoring brain mechanisms helps to promote the free flow of novel ideas and impulses. While this brain pattern is unusual, it resembles the pattern seen in people when they are dreaming.

We tend to enter flow when the activity provides us with a clear set of goals, clearly outlined responses or actions, and unambiguous and immediate feedback. As a result, it is easier to enter flow in games like tennis or poker or activities like mountain climbing or piano playing than in the muddier day-to-day life of multitasking, ongoing projects, and unclear feedback. Flow also happens when the challenge we are tackling is pretty compatible with our skill level; if it's too easy, we get bored, and if it's too hard, we get frustrated.

Work That Flow!

Believe it or not, people find flow most often at work. Nevertheless, research suggests we aren't obtaining flow at work as often as we could. Short of making a dramatic career switch, we have many ways to make our job produce more flow, and the secret may lie in the way we approach the job.

Try turning a job with repetitive tasks into an efficiency or productivity game. Let's say you're waiting tables while waiting for that big Hollywood director to discover your acting talent. What would make your job more efficient, easier, faster, or more tip-inducing? What additional steps could make your customers happier? Is it possible that you might enjoy working more if you devoted as much attention to accomplishing more on the job as you do daydreaming about your future on the big screen?

Use the secrets of flow to tackle work stress. Successful people often make lists or flowcharts of all the things they have to do and quickly decide which tasks they can delegate or forget and which ones they have to tackle personally and in what order. The next step is to match your skills with whatever challenges you have identified. Some tasks you may feel incompetent to deal with. Can you learn the skills required in time? Can you get help? Can you transform or break the task into simpler parts? Usually the answer to one of these questions will provide a solution which can transform a potentially stressful situation into a flow experience.

Watch Two Simpsons and Call Me in the Morning

In this age of high-tech therapies, the best medicine may be a free one: laughter. After the birth of my oldest son, I went into a serious postpartum funk. Recovering from a C-section with a colicky infant, the joys of motherhood were not readily apparent to me, a fact about which I felt frightened and ashamed.

Luckily for me, one of my mentors, a fellow psychologist, visited me shortly after I returned from the hospital. In talking about how she coped with the stress of sleep deprivation and bawling babies, she casually mentioned she had rented a lot of funny movies. To this day, I can't watch John Candy in *Planes, Trains, and Automobiles* without flashing back to myself 11 years ago—bloodshot eyes, saggy and sore tummy and all—sitting on the couch and howling with laughter.

Escaping into John Candy's world didn't change my challenges of adjusting to motherhood; it just helped me see reality in a different light. From a mental health standpoint, humor helps us get a perspective rather than wallow in the cognitive distortion ("My life is over!") that often accompanies emotional distress. In other words, humor helps us adjust the meaning of an event so it's not so overwhelming.

Here are some additional ways we can use humor to improve our mood, enjoyment of life, and mental health:

◆ Attempt to laugh at situations rather than bemoan them—this helps improve our disposition and the dispositions of those around us. A friend of mine cracked her teenage kids up by getting a mohawk before she started chemotherapy.

◆ Use cathartic laughter to release pent-up feelings of anger and frustration in socially acceptable ways. According to psychologist William James, we don't laugh because we're happy; we're happy because we laugh.

◆ Lower anxiety by visualizing a humorous situation to replace the view of an anxiety-producing situation. Remember the old antidote for speech anxiety, picturing the audience in their underwear?

Laughter also improves our physical well-being. Countless studies show that people who laugh more live longer and feel better throughout the course of their lives. In fact, for Norman Cousins, diagnosed in the mid-1960s with a degenerative disease that causes the breakdown of the tissues that bind together the body's cells, it was a matter of life and death. Cousins, barely able to move and given but a few months to live, checked himself out of the hospital, stopped taking drugs, and self-prescribed a new regime of pain killers: lots of vitamin C and a minimum of one Laurel and Hardy movie per day. He found that 15 minutes of laughing and guffawing could provide him with up to two hours of pain relief. He gradually regained his health and eventually resumed his job as editor of the *Saturday Review*.

The increase of our pain threshold during and after bouts of laughter has since been confirmed in many studies. Besides triggering the release of endorphins (the body's natural pain killer), laughter also removes stress hormones and boosts our immune function by raising T-cell levels, disease-fighting proteins called Gamma-interferon, and B-cells, which produce antibodies that destroy disease. Laughter is also a solid cardiovascular workout: it increases our heart's activity, stimulates our circulation, and, afterward, helps our bodies relax.

Get a Sense of Humor!

Studies show that humor is one common denominator among people with good coping skills and a high degree of life satisfaction. Students also learn more from humorous teachers. And employees who work for a funny boss or one with a good sense of humor enjoy their jobs more.

There are two distinct kinds of laughter: laughter because of something that's happened (e.g., resulting from a joke or funny incident) and laughter that's self-generated and strategic, such as laughing to smooth over a conversational hiccup or build rapport.

Laughter has evolved over the years. In fact, researchers have recently plotted the evolutionary trajectory of laughter over the last seven million years. Laughing, they believe, may have evolved from apes "play-panting" two to four million years ago in response to things that happened around them. Then around two million years ago, our ancestors began using facial expressions to communicate feelings or ideas, such as embarrassment or ridicule. Thanks to them, we can now voluntarily access our humor program whenever we need to.

Now, we've explored positive psychology—the science of investigating what can make an okay life better and what qualities increase the odds we'll bounce back from adversity. And we've examined ways we can increase the amount of pleasure in our lives, be more resilient, find more flow in our work, and use laughter to boost our mental and physical health.

But what if our lives aren't okay? What if we find ourselves staring down into such a black hole of depression we can't get out of bed in the morning? What if we're so anxious we haven't slept for weeks and are starting to wonder if life is worth living? In Chapter 18, we'll take a look at what state-of-the-art weapons psychology has to help us conquer, or at least control, mental illness.

> **Insight**
>
> Studies show that 20 seconds of a good, hard belly laugh is worth 3 minutes on the rowing machine. In laughter Yoga (hasya yoga), students spend about 30 minutes chanting "Ho ho, ha ha ha," giggling self-consciously and belly laughing. Laughter Yoga has been shown to reduce stress, enhance the immune system, strengthen cardiovascular functions, improve circulation, and boost the respiratory system. Oh, and you'll actually tone muscles, too!

Straight from the Lab

Control Your Emotional Climate If you're not as happy as you thought you'd be, perhaps you expected too much. Studies show we pay more attention to disappointments than to experiences that exceed our expectations. When we feel better about an outcome than we anticipated we would, we take it for granted. But when something fails to meet our expectations (such as a promising new relationship that loses its sheen), we take notice. And we feel worse than we thought we would.

Happiness: The Key to Success Most of us think success leads to happiness, but new research suggests that it may be the other way around. Chronically happy people are more likely than their less happy peers to have fulfilling relationships, high incomes, superior work performance, robust health, and a longer life. Happiness breeds confidence, persistence, optimism, and social likeability.

***Do* Touch That Dial** TV takes up more than half of Americans' free time. An analysis of 30,000 adults by researchers from the University of Maryland examined the leisure activities of happy versus dissatisfied adults and found that TV watching may provide momentary pleasure but lead to long-term malaise. In theory, engaging in a highly enjoyable activity like watching television should improve the quality of people's lives. However, the opposite is true; unhappy people watched 20 percent more television than very happy people. Of course, unhappy people were also more likely to have too much time on their hands, making it unclear whether TV watching leads to unhappiness or unhappiness leads to zoning out in front of the telly.

The Gift That Keeps On Giving Most of us believe spending money on ourselves will make us happier. But a new study shows that people who dole out money for gifts for friends or charities receive a bigger happiness boost than the Ebenezer Scrooges—those who spend only on themselves—regardless of income. And the pro-social spending buzz lasts longer—even spending as little as $5 a day on others can produce a surge in happiness. Charitable spending makes our lives feel meaningful and significant, which is why we spend money in the first place.

The Global Mood-Warming Crisis According to a recent study, the number of "very happy" people around the world has increased by 7 percent over the past 17 years. Denmark is the happiest nation, Zimbabwe the unhappiest. The United States ranks sixteenth. The happiness surge is believed to result from economic growth, democratization, and the rise in gender equality and social tolerance of ethnic minorities and gays and lesbians. In other words, the happiest societies are those which give people the freedom to choose how to live their lives.

Self-Service Starts with Serving Others   If you're looking for a satisfying career, consider a profession that focuses on serving others. In a new study of American workers, the three careers that ranked highest in self-fulfillment were clergy (87 percent were very satisfied), firefighters (80 percent), and physical therapists (78 percent). Runners-up included education administrators, painters and sculptors, teachers, authors, psychologists, special education teachers, operating engineers, office supervisors, and security and financial services salespersons.

The Least You Need to Know

- Whereas traditional psychology has focused on understanding and fixing what goes wrong with the human psyche, positive psychology focuses on discovering, and nurturing, what's right with it.

- Just as we can systematically learn to undo negative ways of responding to stress, we can also learn how to become stronger, braver, wiser, more resilient, and ultimately happier, too.

- Dr. Salvatore Maddi discovered the "hardy personality," a cluster of coping attitudes that help individuals bounce back from the toughest adversity, which include an ongoing commitment to others, a sense of control over one's life, and a pattern of viewing adversity as a challenge rather than a crisis.

- Self-analysis from a distance can help an individual cope with intense feelings adaptively in the short-term as well as work through negative experiences over time.

- Dr. Mihaly Csikszentmihalyi coined the term "flow" to describe the pleasant state we all experience when we're so involved in what we're doing that we, in essence, lose ourselves.

- Countless studies show the power of laughter to help us cope and enhance our physical and mental well-being.

Chapter 18

Weapons Against Mental Dysfunction

In This Chapter

- Discovering how psychiatric meds can smooth out moods and lift your spirits
- Finding out the shocking truth about shock therapy
- Learning what all good therapists (and therapies) have in common
- Investigating the latest trends in the psychotherapy business

Irene was an isolated 29-year-old woman with two children, an unemployed and substance-abusing husband, and a severe case of depression. For help she turned to Dr. Aaron Beck, a pioneer in treating depression with psychotherapy.

After six months with Dr. Beck, Irene was a new woman. She joined a tennis club, got a job as a waitress, and enrolled in a college course. She also left her husband when he refused to participate in couples' therapy and continued to treat her badly. Dr. Beck pronounced Irene "depression free," and she proclaimed her therapy was money well spent.

On the other hand, Julie's depression had been unresponsive to antidepressants, lithium, and years of psychotherapy. Desperate at age 32, she tried electroshock therapy. "It's a miracle," she says. "Years ago I would have been locked up in a mental hospital. Today, my depression has lifted, and I'm doing better than a lot of people who never suffered from it."

In this chapter, we explore the two paths people travel when seeking help for emotional problems: biological and psychotherapeutic. The former involves medical treatments, including psychotropic drugs, electroconvulsive (shock) therapy, and psychosurgery. The other consists of the various "talking cures," which may involve one-on-one counseling, couples or family therapy, or group sessions. We explore the myths and realities of psychiatric medications and take a look at some of the more controversial treatments from yesterday and today. We also take a look at the who, what, when, where, and whys of psychotherapy and how new trends can help us get the most bang for our treatment buck.

Better Living Through Chemistry

Psychiatrists use their understanding of the biology of the brain to alter the mind. If you think of the mind as a computer, medical treatments are trying to fix the hardware (the brain) to heal the mind (the software). And one of the most effective ways to bring a misfiring brain back to normal is through psychiatric medication. The right dose of the right medication can dissolve hallucinations, douse depression, level out moods, and soothe anxiety.

Insight

Challenging recent claims linking antidepressant use to suicidal behavior, a February 2005 UCLA study showed that American suicide rates have dropped steadily since the introduction of Prozac and other serotonin reuptake inhibitor (SSRI) drugs and cautions that regulatory actions to limit SSRI prescriptions may actually increase death rates from untreated depression.

It all started in France. In the 1950s, French psychiatrists Jean Delay and Pierre Deniker used chlorpromazine to treat the symptoms of schizophrenia and started a whole new era in the treatment of mental disorders. Today, psychiatric medications are available for just about any disorder ranging from attention deficit disorder to depression. Considering the short time they've been around, psychiatric medications have made dramatic changes in the treatment of mental disorders. People who, years ago, might have spent many years in mental hospitals may now only go in for brief treatment or might receive all their treatment at an outpatient clinic.

Psychotherapeutic medications also may make other kinds of treatment more effective. Someone who is too depressed to talk, for instance, can't get much benefit from psychotherapy or counseling but might be highly receptive to the right medication.

Another benefit from these medications is an increased understanding of the causes of mental illness. Scientists have learned a great deal more about the workings of the brain as a result of their investigations into how psychotherapeutic medications relieve disorders such as psychosis, depression, anxiety, obsessive-compulsive disorder, and panic disorder.

Can't You Get the Dose Right?

On the other hand, medication evaluation is not an exact science, and that can be frustrating. How long someone must take a psychotherapeutic medication depends on the disorder. Many depressed and anxious people may need medication for a single period, perhaps for several months, and then never have to take it again. For some conditions, such as schizophrenia or manic-depressive illness, a person may have to take medication intermittently or, perhaps, for the rest of his or her life.

Psychobabble

Good news may be on the horizon, though. For the first time, researchers at the National Institute of Mental Health have discovered a biomarker that identifies who is likely to benefit from a new antidepressant. Shown a series of flashing, frightful faces, depressed patients showed increased brain activity in a mood-regulating hub while healthy controls showed the opposite response. The more the emotion-regulator fired, the more likely a new, fast-acting antidepressant was to zap the patient's depression—often in a matter of minutes. While the experimental drug's side effects make it an unlikely candidate for future use, this finding suggests that one day we may be able to prescribe the right medication just by looking at a person's brain waves.

Now we need to discover how to convince desperate people to take these medications! The biggest barrier to antidepressant medication is the fear and confusion about what the drug might do. Having a frank conversation with your physician (not to mention doing some personal research on the internet) about side effects, length of time you need to be on it, and so on, is a good way to channel this fear.

Choosing Your Drugs Carefully

Before we move along to other biological treatments of psychological disorders, let's nail down some basic information to help keep all these drugs straight. Medications used to treat psychological disorders are classified according to their clinical class, chemical class, and action:

◆ Clinical class is the drug's purpose, such as antipsychotic, antidepressant, sedative, or antianxiety. Valium is clinically classed as a sedative/hypnotic; Zyprexa and Clozaril are antipsychotics; Xanax is clinically classed as an antianxiety drug; and Prozac is clinically classed as an antidepressant.

◆ Chemical class is what the drug is made of. Xanax and Klonopin are chemically classed as benzodiazepines, for example. (*Benzo* means amphetamine and *diazepine* means relaxant.)

◆ Action refers to what the drug does. For example, Prozac works as a selective serotonin reuptake inhibitor, rather than as a direct stimulant to the nervous system, like Ritalin.

> **Psychobabble**
>
> New depression-busting drugs like ketamine, which targets the brain chemical glutamate, can lift depression in just hours instead of weeks, suggesting that glutamate likely acts closer to the sources of depression than serotonin.

Plenty of information is available about these medications, and one place to look them up quickly is on the Internet. Try www.intelihealth.com and click on its drug-information section. The *Physicians' Desk Reference* at your local library is also a good source. And before you take any meds, ask your doctor these questions:

1. What is the goal of this medication and how does it work?

2. How long will I need to take it?

3. When can I expect to feel better?

4. What are the side effects?

5. What are my treatment alternatives?

6. What happens when I stop taking it?

7. Is this FDA drug approved for the disorder and patient demographics for which I might use it?

> **Brain Buster**
>
> If you're taking psychiatric medication, never go off it "cold turkey" no matter how good you feel. Any medication changes should take place under medical supervision.

Brain Buster

Anyone who talks about suicide should be closely monitored by a mental health professional. And don't count on Prozac to stifle the urge to self-injure; a review of more than 71,000 patients in clinical trials of 52 psychotropic medications found an equal risk of suicide among those given medication and those taking placebos.

Kiddy Cures

About 15 percent of United States children below age 18—about 9 million—have a mental-health problem severe enough to interfere with their ability to function. Mental health treatment—including psychotropic medication—can be a lifesaver for these kids as long as we take the risks as seriously as the rewards.

For instance, in 2004, the United States Food and Drug Administration (FDA) warned that people with heart problems—especially children—should not take the hyperactivity drug Adderall; and in 2005, Cyalert, an attention deficit/hyperactivity disorder (ADHD) medication that has been around for 30 years, was taken off the market completely. That same year, the FDA required all antidepressants to carry "black box" warnings that they "may increase the risk of suicidal thinking and behavior" in children who take them.

New research, however, shows just how tricky it is to strike the proper balance when it comes to giving antidepressants to kids. After a decade-long drop in suicide among kids, suicides spiked sharply in 2004, and the rate remained much higher than expected in 2005 (the last year for which we have data).

Ironically, this upward trend in the pediatric suicide rate may be an unintended side effect of the "black box" warnings on antidepressants required by the FDA. Antidepressant prescriptions for kids have dropped 20 percent since this warning went into effect; as a result, kids who truly need pharmacological help may not be getting it. We have no proven link between the two, but the fact that they've happened at the same time is worrisome.

Psychobabble

When it comes to mental health treatment for children, parents may need to be most vigilant about practitioners using combinations of prescription drugs and unproven, and often unsupported, therapeutic approaches. Many doctors and therapists treat traumatized children with unproven approaches such as art therapy, play therapy, or psychological debriefing in spite of the fact that old-fashioned cognitive behavioral therapy works.

The ABCs of ECT

Does the thought of electric shock therapy give you the heebie-jeebies? Even with the clinical knowledge I have, it's hard for me to stomach the thought of shocking someone. But unfortunately, some people's mental illness grabs them so tightly that neither psychotherapy nor medication loosens its grip. For the 20 percent of schizophrenia sufferers who don't respond to medication or the person with major depression so profound that suicidal thoughts are a constant companion, electroconvulsive therapy (ECT), commonly called shock therapy, can be a viable option.

> **Psychobabble**
>
> About 70 percent of those suffering from major depression who have not responded to other treatments get better with ECT. Sometimes the depression goes away for good; other times it reoccurs after several months.

ECT has split the psychiatric community since it was pioneered more than 50 years ago. Back then, its bad reputation was well deserved. Before modern procedures were invented, the seizure induced by the electric shock was so violent that the muscular contractions would break bones. Today ECT is painless and quite safe. Patients are given drugs to block muscle and nerve activity so that no pain or muscular contractions occur. Doctors may disagree about when, or whether, to use ECT, but all agree the technology has steadily improved.

Still, some patients complain of lifelong memory lapses after ECT. Studies on the brain show no evidence of permanent memory loss, nor do brain scans show any chemical or structural changes after repeated ECT shocks. However, until this discrepancy between science and personal anecdote is resolved, ECT will continue to be seen as a treatment alternative that should come only after medications and therapy have been tried and have failed.

Frances Farmer Doesn't Live Here Anymore

Is there any word scarier than "lobotomy"? When physician Gottlieb Burhardt first performed the operation in 1892 on six schizophrenic patients, a few became calmer afterward—but two died. So it's no small wonder that for the next 40 years doctors weren't eager to duplicate Dr. Burhardt's efforts. That view shifted, however, when several research labs in the United States began making amazing discoveries about the role of the temporal and frontal lobes in controlling emotional behavior and aggressiveness.

From the late 1930s to the early 1950s, thousands of men and women were subjected to a prefrontal lobotomy, in which the front portions of their frontal lobes were surgically separated from the rest of their brain. The operation treated people with severe cases of schizophrenia, bipolar disorder, depression, obsessive-compulsive disorder, and pathological violence. (At the time lobotomies were so highly regarded that in 1949, the Portuguese neurosurgeon who pioneered the new technique, Antonio Egas Moniz, was awarded the Nobel Prize.)

Sadly, while lobotomies did relieve patients of their incapacitating emotions, it also left them with lifelong deficits in their ability to make plans and follow through with them; they became ghosts of their former selves. Sometimes, it seems, the very parts of ourselves that are the most troublesome are also those that make us uniquely human.

Psychosurgery Revised

Although lobotomies are no longer performed, a rare few individuals are helped by a new kind of psychosurgery known as cingulotomy. The cingulum, a small structure in the limbic system involved in emotionality, is partially destroyed with radio-frequency current applied through fine wire electrodes temporarily implanted in the brain. Follow-up studies suggest these operations most often reduce or abolish major depression and obsessive-compulsive disorder and have rarely left the patient worse off than before.

Cingulotomy, like the earlier lobotomy, is still controversial, but to someone who has been seriously depressed for many years has gotten no relief from ECT and every antidepressant medication on the market, it's something to consider. Blessedly, this degree of treatment failure rarely happens. And no matter how you feel about it, cingulotomy does help.

The Biology of Feeling Better

New research confirms what most of us already knew: putting feelings into words produces therapeutic effects in the brain. A new brain imaging study by UCLA researchers reveals why talking our feelings out makes our sadness or anger less intense.

When people see a photograph of an angry or fearful face, they have increased activity in a region of the brain called the amygdala, which serves as an alarm to activate a cascade of biological systems to protect the body in times of danger. However, attaching the word "angry" to this picture, i.e., labeling the emotion, decreases the amygdala's alarm and makes another area, the ventrolateral prefrontal cortex, work harder. This section has been implicated in inhibiting behavior and processing emotions.

Mindfulness is another technique in which one pays attention to present-moment experiences without judging or fighting them. By witnessing, and labeling, emotions as they come and go ("This is what anger feels like"; "I'm feeling angry right now"), our brain signals switch from an alarm state to an ability to process what we're feeling.

Insight _____

Keeping a journal or diary, talking things over with a friend, or meditating on a problem—all are ways we label our thoughts and feelings. Not only does this labeling productively shift our perspective from the "tunnel-vision" trees to the "big picture" forest, but it also gives some much-needed distance from the emotional turmoil that upsetting thoughts and feelings create.

Meet the Media Shrink

Whenever I used to travel on business, the person sitting next to me on the plane or train would inevitably ask, "What do you do for a living?" and like an idiot, I always said "psychologist." Before I could blink an eye, my seatmate would be deep into a discussion of his latest problems. Now I'm tempted to tell my travel mates I'm a funeral director; I'm sure my travels would be more peaceful.

While travelers are often willing to unload their inner feelings to a total stranger on a train, bus, or plane, people often feel shame and embarrassment about going into psychotherapy. Even if they think it's okay for someone else, they often resist the idea for themselves—as if this would be an admission of some personal flaw. And the media doesn't help. When we see therapist and client hopping into the sack on television, it's no wonder no one wants to see a "shrink."

In fact, new research found that therapists on TV are generally portrayed either as unethical or as buffoons. And media images of therapy clients are just as bad or worse. Tony Soprano might be a fascinating character, but few of us would trade places with him. Perhaps it's no surprise that viewers who watch TV comedies (like *Frasier*) and dramas (such as *The Sopranos*) on a regular basis assign more stigma to psychotherapy and are less willing to seek it.

Winning the Battle with the Talking Cures

Media misrepresentations and invalid stereotypes about therapy aside, a real person's experience of therapy will depend on what brought him or her there. Just as a physician would treat cancer differently from a cold, a psychotherapist will treat schizophrenia differently from a fear of riding down escalators.

Between these extremes lies a variety of psychological problems that might drive a person to seek help. Some are short-lived but intense, such as a loss or a divorce. Some are mild but persistent and energy draining over time, such as dysthymia or chronic worrying. And some problems are frustratingly repetitive, like realizing you're dating the same loser with a different name. What all these problems have in common is that the person dealing with them feels they exceed his coping skills. For whatever reason, he just can't see the light at the end of the tunnel. And believe me, he's looked and looked for it before he comes in for help.

> **Psychobabble**
>
> While the drop-out rate for face-to-face therapy is nearly 50 percent, less than 8 percent of patients receiving phone therapy for depression dropped out of treatment prematurely.

The SCAT Team to the Rescue

Your mom is driving you batty, so you call your best friend and ask her what to do. You wouldn't dream of making a career move without talking it over with your college mentor. And when you're feeling down, you hang around after church because talking with your minister makes you feel better. These are your informal "counselors," the ones who help you deal with most of your routine frustrations and conflicts.

No matter how good a listener your best friend is, however, there is something to be said for the skills and knowledge that formal psychological training provides. A SWAT team may rescue hostages kidnapped during a bank robbery, but when we are held captive by our problems, we turn to the SCAT team: school workers, counselors, and therapists. These five kinds of mental health professionals most often help us deal with problems when our friends and families can't:

◆ **Counseling psychologists** specialize in the problems of daily living. They often work in community settings such as schools, clinics, and businesses and deal with challenges like relationship conflicts, choosing a vocation, school problems, and stress.

◆ **Clinical psychologists** are trained to treat individuals who suffer from more severe conditions, such as clinical depression, eating disorders, and anxiety.

◆ **Psychiatrists** are medical doctors who specialize in the treatment of emotional and mental disorders. These physicians generally treat more severe conditions and, in these days of managed care, are most likely to prescribe medication for psychiatric disorders.

◆ **Clinical social workers** are mental-health professionals with specialized training in the social context of people's problems. Clinical social workers often work with family problems, like child abuse, and their work often involves entire families in the therapy.

> **Psychobabble**
>
> Psychiatrists are increasingly becoming the medication dispensers, leaving psychologists, social workers, and counselors to do the psychotherapy. In fact, between 1996 and 2007, the number of psychiatrists providing psychotherapy to all their patients decreased from 19.1 percent to 10.8 percent.

◆ **Counselors or therapists** are mental-health professionals covering a wide range of specializations and expertise. Pastoral counselors are members of a religious group or ministry trained to specialize in the treatment of psychological disorders. Marital and family therapists are often master's-degreed professionals who have chosen to focus on family/couple problems, while drug and alcohol counselors often have specialized training in the addictions.

Finding a Partner for the Therapy Dance

A good therapist for you might not be a good therapist for me. In a good therapeutic relationship, a unique and somewhat mysterious chemistry develops between therapist and client. And it's important; in fact, study after study shows that the "fit" between therapist and client is far more valuable than any bag of therapeutic tricks. The ability to trust your therapist, to work as allies on the same team, and to share similar values and goals are the key ingredients to therapy that works. In addition, all good therapists share certain common traits, including the following:

◆ They listen much more than they talk.

◆ They keep their problems to themselves.

◆ They don't answer the phone or nod off while you're spilling your guts.

- They can be completely objective about what you are saying.

- They apologize if they make a mistake.

- They protect your confidences: they wouldn't spill the beans about what the two of you talk about if you dragged them over hot coals.

A good therapist would also make a good friend, but don't make that common mistake. Your therapist is *not* your friend. Friends have needs and agendas of their own that may not always coincide with yours.

Finding Your Therapy Match

Unfortunately, it isn't always easy to find a good therapist. Your first therapy session is like a blind date; you never know for sure what you're going to get. However, there are some guidelines you can use to improve the odds that your "first date" with a therapist will turn into a trusting relationship.

The best approach to finding a good therapist is the same one you'd use when seeking any professional services:

- **Get personal referrals**, particularly from a friend or colleague who has had a problem similar to yours. If you can't find a therapist this way, then check with your doctor or hospital social work department.

- **Interview the therapist over the phone.** Remember, you are hiring this person to be your therapist, and you need to make sure she is qualified.

- **Ask questions.** Be sure to ask what her specialties are, how many people she's seen with the same problem as yours, and what her treatment philosophy is. One person may be a fabulous therapist for substance-abuse problems but have no experience with depression.

- **Trust your instincts.** If you don't like the person or don't feel comfortable after three sessions, switch therapists.

What to Expect When You're Going to Therapy

Much of what you do in therapy will depend upon the problem you're seeking help for, the therapist's style and theoretical orientation, and the nature of the relationship the two of you develop. And no matter what problem brought you to the therapist's office, you can expect to work on the four following goals:

1. **Figuring out what's wrong**. You might think you know what's wrong; after all, that's what brought you to therapy in the first place. And most of the time, you do. However, this can be trickier than you might think. A client who comes in to deal with work conflicts may come to realize that drinking six vodka and tonics a day is a problem. So is the job his problem or is it his drinking? Good therapists will do a thorough clinical interview and ask all kinds of questions that might seem completely irrelevant. This enables the therapist to make a diagnosis that's helpful as a starting point.

Insight

How does your therapist rate? If you're not sure, go to www. cybercouch.com/library/ rati.tag.html and check out Dr. Thomas Grugle's "Rate Your Therapist" quiz.

2. **Figuring out what caused the problem and why you still have it.** Is your problem genetic? Does it run in your family? When did it start? What keeps it going on or coming back again?

3. **Figuring out what's likely to happen in the future.** Therapists try to gauge what or who might take longer to treat and how to keep the problem from happening again. Anorexia, for example, tends to be a long-term problem, and the therapist and client need to be realistic about treatment.

4. **Figuring out how to get rid of it or make it better.** What kind of therapy would work best on the client's particular problem? What does the client's social and professional environment look like? And how can the family or support system help?

Talking It Out

While medications have helped people solve mental problems by acting on the brain, psychotherapy works on the mind. There are four major types of "talk" or psychotherapy: psychodynamic, behavioral, cognitive, and "group" therapies. Though different in approach and process, each has the same goals: to provide people with a rational explanation of their problem; to offer a very real basis for very real hope; and to achieve their success through a positive, one-on-one relationship between the client and her therapist.

The psychotherapist is, in effect, like the patient's driving instructor. He can give advice—talk about how traffic lights work, discuss the importance of a properly executed U-turn, and explain how to merge correctly—but ultimately the patient must drive her own car.

One instructor might concentrate on helping a student unlearn reckless driving habits, while a second might tackle fears of getting behind the wheel. Yet a third might bring new drivers together so that they can support each other. But no matter what, all the "instructors" have the same purpose: to bring forth their patient's inner Dale Earnhardt and point them down the road.

Psychobabble
A recent study found that 60 percent of therapy clients felt their therapy either lasted too long (23 percent) or ended too soon (37 percent). However, clients who reported that termination was on time, i.e., a mutual agreement between both parties, were more satisfied with their therapy. Part of the problem may be that therapists are trained to focus on the emotionally painful aspects of saying goodbye; celebrating the success of the therapeutic relationship and the positive gains in therapy may make a satisfactory ending.

To help you narrow down and understand your options, this table compares and contrasts the four primary types of therapies:

Types of Therapy	Cause of Disorder	Goal	Common Techniques
Psychodynamic (Psychoanalysis, Client-centered therapy, Gestalt therapy)	A childhood during which the person was either forced to disown parts of him- or herself (or his or her feelings); as an adult the person is either in conflict with these hidden parts or has repressed them	Give people a better awareness and understanding of their feelings, motivations, and actions so they will be better adjusted	Interpreting and analyzing one's dreams, role-playing different parts of oneself, working with a therapist who fully accepts all aspects of the client, and mirrors the client's thoughts and feelings

continues

continued

Types of Therapy	Cause of Disorder	Goal	Common Techniques
Behavior	Learning the wrong behavior	Teach people how to behave in a more satisfying way	Rewarding adaptive behavior through behavior contracts, modeling, getting rid of fears through gradual exposure to them
Cognitive	Self-defeating ways of thinking; inaccurate views of the world	Identify and correct erroneous ways of thinking	Consciously replacing negative thoughts with positive, coping thoughts, rationally examining and changing negative or inaccurate thinking
Group	Relationship problems that cause personal distress	To identify ways of relating to others that cause problems and learn to relate more effectively; also to use other people as a motivator/support for behavior change	Family therapy, group therapy, couples therapy, self-help groups

No matter which kind of therapy you choose, always remember you can do numerous things to enhance the odds your therapy will work, including working with your therapist to set clear treatment goals, deciding on how progress will be evaluated, monitoring progress carefully, and revising treatment plans.

Short and Sweet or Long and Slow?

Psychotherapy continues to evolve with the emotional and practical needs of its clients. Many therapists are now utilizing recently developed therapeutic techniques that focus less on the therapeutic process and more on results. They concentrate less on their patient's childhood and more on his current life experiences and relationships. They provide more directive guidance and feedback—and will often even prescribe homework to speed up the process!

For people who don't need more intensive treatment, these sort of "McTherapies" can prove very satisfactory indeed; for example, a review of more than 30 years of short-term (between 7 and 40 sessions) psychodynamic therapies found that 92 percent of the treated adults were better off than similar individuals who received no treatment. Many people, with many common mental-health concerns, will begin experiencing positive gains in therapy in as little as 6 to 12 sessions. At one session per week, that translates into feeling better in between two to three months.

However, according to a recent meta-analysis of 23 studies, longer-duration psycho-therapy (lasting for at least a year or 50 sessions) appears to be more beneficial for treatment of complex mental disorders such as personality, multiple diagnoses, and chronic mental disorders. In this review, long-term psychotherapy was significantly superior to shorter-term methods of psycho-therapy with regard to overall outcome, target problems, and personality functioning. In fact, longer-term therapy patients were better off than 96 percent of the patients in the comparison group, and the differences between the two were even greater over time. Cost-effectiveness, it seems, is much more complicated than the price of therapy sessions.

> **Psychobabble**
>
> For many illnesses, the combination of medication and psychotherapy seems to be more effective than either one used by itself.

Getting Wired

It's only natural that modern technology would influence and modify the work of therapists. These days many of us spend at least as much time communicating via our cell phones and computers as we do face to face. While the use of the Internet and other communication technologies for the purposes of therapeutic counseling is new, it's surely here to stay: already, 70–80 percent of psychologists say they rely on "telephone therapy" for at least some of their patients. Increasingly, therapists are delivering clinical services on the Internet or via satellite.

Insight

How do you know when you have a good alliance with your therapist? You look forward to your sessions; you leave them feeling as if you've done good work and made progress; and you feel like your therapist really *gets* you.

And while the jury is still out on how effective online therapy is, preliminary evidence suggests that "telehealth" may provide new opportunities for effective low-cost treatment, especially for people who are harder to reach by traditional means. A recent study, for example, found that cyber support was extremely useful in helping suicidal teens stay connected to a peer group and in paving the way to a suicide crisis line or local psychotherapist.

Considering the Evidence

In the past, mental health specialists tended to choose a certain theoretical orientation and then treat all patients under this umbrella. So whether you were having marital problems or a panic attack, a psychoanalyst would treat you the same way—by interpreting your dreams, listening to your free associations, and so forth.

Enter the new kid on the block, Evidence Based Therapy (EBT), which says that the kind of treatment you get should be based on the problem you have—not based on the expertise or theoretical bent of your therapist. If research shows that cognitive behavioral therapy works best for anxiety disorders, for example, then that's the kind of therapy your therapist should start with.

But Does It Work?

Of course therapy works! Why else would I be writing this book? Aside from Woody Allen, most of the people I know who have been to therapy know it works. Don't take my word for it, though; thousands of studies have been done, and here's what they have to say:

- ◆ **Psychotherapy works.** About 75 percent to 80 percent of people in therapy show greater improvement than the average person in a control group.

◆ **The outcomes of therapy tend to be maintained**. Numerous follow-up studies have tracked patients after leaving treatment for periods ranging from six months to over five years. These studies are fairly consistent in demonstrating that treatment effects are enduring.

◆ **Some therapies work better for some problems.** Fear and anxiety seem to respond best to behavioral and cognitive therapies, while humanistic therapies do wonders for self-esteem, and psychodynamic therapy can help underachievers.

◆ **Therapy is for better and worse.** Despite overall favorable results, about 5 to 10 percent of patients get worse during treatment, and an additional 15 to 25 percent show no benefit.

So there you have it: the mechanistic (drugs, ECT, psychosurgery) and the idealistic (using therapy to change thoughts, behavior, and feelings). Both can be useful, and both have their pros and cons. Both use different means to get to the same goal—leading a better, happier, and more productive life. In the next chapter we'll go from our general overview of mental-health help to tackling—and treating—two of the most common and most painful disorders that can dampen the light of even the brightest psyche—depression and anxiety.

Straight from the Lab

Combat Trauma Spurs Better Weapons Against PTSD   Prazosin (PRAISE-oh-sin), a generic drug already used by millions of Americans for high blood pressure and prostate problems, has been found to improve sleep and lessen trauma nightmares in veterans with posttraumatic stress disorder (PTSD); the National Institute of Mental Health is currently looking at its usefulness in treating civilian trauma PTSD. In addition, virtual reality exposure therapy, during which soldiers were gradually desensitized to two-minute video clips of scenes depicting the Iraq theater of combat, was effective in reducing the exaggerated startle response so common in traumatized veterans.

Unhappy Kids = Underachieving Adults   Children's mental well-being may affect the types of jobs they eventually get, and thereby, their odds of work-related success and stress, new research findings suggest. In a study of more than 8,000 British adults followed since birth in 1958, researchers found that those excessively sad, anxious, or withdrawn children were more likely to end up with a lower-status job and a stressful working life. These job stressors, in turn, were linked to a greater risk of depression and anxiety once the study participants reached middle-age.

Suicide Risk Consistent Across Cultures   Suicide risk factors are consistent across 17 countries and include having a mental disorder and being female, younger, less educated, and unmarried; additionally, the risk of suicidal thoughts increases sharply during adolescence and young adulthood in every country studied. However, the rate varied from country to country; rates of suicidal thoughts ranged from 3.1 percent of people in China to 15.9 percent in New Zealand. The strongest risk factor associated with suicidal thoughts and behaviors were mood disorders in high-income countries and substance abuse/impulse control disorders in low- and middle-income countries.

The Least You Need to Know

- Psychiatric medications are often a critical part of the treatment for depression, schizophrenia, and bipolar disorder and can also be helpful with anxiety disorders but, especially in children, the rewards should outweigh the risks.

- The techniques used in electroconvulsive treatment and psychosurgery are much safer than they used to be but are still used only when less invasive treatments fail.

- For therapy to be effective, you must have a good relationship with your therapist.

- There are several types of talk therapy, including psychodynamic psychotherapy, behavioral therapy, cognitive therapy, and existential-humanistic therapy.

- A new model for treatment is emerging called Evidence Based Therapy (EBT), which seeks to combine different empirically proven techniques from various psychological disciplines.

Part 6

Between a Rock and a Hard Place

This part is about the major mental illnesses—mood disorders, psychoses, and addictions. You'll learn the difference between a funk and a major depression, find out how normal behavior spirals out of control, and separate the myths and realities of schizophrenia. You'll also learn what treatments give sufferers the best bang for their treatment buck—and how even the most severe diagnoses don't have the gloomy prognoses they used to.

19

Mood Swingers and Scaredy Cats

In This Chapter

- ◆ Exploring the difference between a major funk and a major depression
- ◆ Swinging along with your mood swings
- ◆ Dealing with depression in others
- ◆ Feeling phobic
- ◆ Obsessing compulsively

"I'm afraid the black dog has really got me …. It crouches in the corner of the room, waits for me to make a move. Or lies at the foot of the bed, like a shadow, until I try to get up …."

So begins the prologue of Cathy Kronkite's candid book, *On the Edge of Darkness: Conversations About Conquering Depression*, in which she talks about her own experience with depression as well as other celebrities who've had similar experiences. They're not hard to find: Queen Elizabeth, Elton John, Patti Duke, Tipper Gore—not to mention one out of every 20 of us regular United States citizens.

In this chapter, we explore affective disorders, a family of illnesses in which the main symptom is a disturbance of mood; anxiety and depression are two examples. You'll discover the difference between a bad mood and major depression and learn about the mood swings in manic depression, the low-level sadness of dysthymia, and the gentler ups and downs of cyclothymia. You'll also meet the four anxiety disorders, discover what "panicking" really means, and learn what to do when obsessive thoughts won't go away.

Being Psychologically Correct

You may or may not be politically correct, but *please*, try to be psychologically correct. When you have a bad day and are sharing it with a friend or loved one, say you are "in a funk," "have got the blues," or "are in a bad mood." Please, oh please, don't call it *depression*.

Using the word depression to describe everything from a passing mood to a chronic illness creates confusion for all of us. As long as we use the terms interchangeably, when someone tells you she is suffering from depression, you're likely to think, "So what? I was depressed yesterday, too, and I snapped out of it." But if you were experiencing a major depression, you didn't. Episodes of untreated depression typically last several months and invade every part of your life. Clinical depression can kill you.

In a Major Funk

You don't feel hopeful or happy about anything in your life. You feel like you're moving in slow motion. Nothing tastes good. Getting up in the morning requires a lot of effort. You find yourself crying over nothing, or at something that wouldn't normally bother you; maybe you can't cry at all any more, even if you want to. These are the faces of clinical depression.

Insight

Children of depressed parents are more likely to have medical problems and be depressed themselves.

Major depression, the common term for clinical depression, affects 1 in 20 Americans every year, about twice as many women as men. It's an equal opportunity illness, hitting people at all socioeconomic levels and ethnic backgrounds. It can creep up on you or grab you by the throat. Major depression is debilitating and dangerous—an overwhelming sadness that lasts at least two weeks and is severe enough to interfere with a person's life.

When mental health professionals assess someone for depression, they look for five or more of the following symptoms:

◆ Loss of interest in things you used to enjoy, including sex.

◆ Feeling sad, blue, or down in the dumps.

◆ Feeling either slowed down or so restless you can't sit still.

◆ Changes in appetite.

◆ Thoughts of death or suicide.

◆ Problems with concentrating, remembering, or making decisions.

◆ Loss of energy or feeling tired all the time.

◆ Feeling worthless or guilty.

◆ Trouble sleeping or sleeping all the time.

One of the first two symptoms is mandatory—the depression must cause significant emotional distress or disrupt your daily life. But the first symptom that many people notice, in either themselves or in depressed friends or family members, is a change in sleep patterns.

Of course, a list of clinical symptoms can't capture the personal experience of living with depression. Here are some real-world examples of what a depressed person might say:

"I just don't want to be around anyone. I keep making excuses to my friends. I know I'm hurting their feelings, but I don't want to be a downer to them, and I just can't pretend anymore that I'm up."

"I can't remember the last time I laughed. I have so much to be thankful for, so why can't I just snap out of it?"

"It takes me a week to do what I used to do in a day. Some days I don't get out of bed until noon."

"I feel so bad that sometimes I wish I were dead. Yeah, I guess I've had thoughts of killing myself; anything would be better than this."

> **Psychobabble**
>
> Fifty percent of people with depression report work-related problems, costing the United States 200 million sick days each year.

As you can see, these thoughts and feelings are not typical of being down in the dumps. You might want to pull the covers up over your head when you're in a bad mood, but you don't think about suicide.

Let's take a look at what causes depression and who's likely to get it.

Why Me?

Depression runs in families; more than a fifth of us has a genetic predisposition to depression. However, depression can also occur in people with no family history and, if our life circumstances get bad enough, any of us can develop a clinical case of the blues.

Psychobabble
Twenty one percent of us have the genotype that predisposes us to depression, 26 percent have the genotype with resilience to depression, and 53 percent have a mix of the two.

Insight

Many physical illnesses can mimic psychological problems. If you suddenly find yourself feeling depressed or experiencing unusual emotional symptoms, it is critical that you get a medical check-up. It can save your life.

How our genes and environment interact to predict—or protect us from—a mood disorder is becoming clearer, thanks to new research from the University of South Wales. It turns out that, given similar life circumstances, some of us are more than twice as likely to become depressed as others.

The researchers based their findings on DNA samples of a group of 127 people who they had monitored for over 25 years for depression onset and major life events. They found that individuals with a genetic predisposition for depression had an 80 percent chance of becoming depressed if they experienced three or more negative life events in a year.

Apparently, three is the "magic number" at which most genetically vulnerable individuals are knocked over. One negative life event, such as a health crisis, didn't throw them over the edge; the critical issue seems to be exposure to a series of difficult life events within a relatively short time period.

Those Genes Are Buff!

Some of us, however, are blessed with genes that buffer us from mood disorders. In fact, for the first time in humans, scientists have detected an interaction between genes that may help prevent brain changes that increase vulnerability to depression and those that put us at risk.

A variation on one gene affects how much of the brain chemical serotonin is available to brain cells. This variation raises the risk of depression in people who carry it. But NIMH scientists found that a variation in *another* gene that produces a substance that enables growth and health of brain cells appears to prevent or offset the changes generated by the depression-fostering one.

Using brain imaging in a study of 111 healthy people, the researchers found that those with the depression-promoting gene variation had alterations in their brain's mood-regulating networks. But those who had both the depression-promoting variation *and* the apparently protective variation did not have these alterations in brain-cell networks.

Our genes also set the stage for how we respond to difficult or traumatic events. The stress hormone CRH (corticotropin-releasing hormone) regulates the chemical messages through which our brain cells communicate with each other. Childhood trauma such as abuse tends to hyperactivate the system, increasing the risk of depression in adulthood. Of the people in the study who had a history of child abuse, those with certain genetic variations had only about half the symptoms of moderate to severe depression as those who had more common variations in the same gene.

As you can see, either physical or psychological events can trigger—or prevent—clinical depression. Most commonly, both seem to be involved; remember our diathesis-stress model from Chapter 16? But, however it begins, depression can quickly develop into a set of physical and psychological problems that feed on each other and grow.

How Bad Is Your Mood?

You might think a person would know if he was depressed, but that often isn't true. A person may gradually slip into a clinical depression without fully realizing how far down he's fallen. If you've ever had a cold that gradually turned into bronchitis or pneumonia, you've experienced the medical version of this phenomenon. In fact, you may not have appreciated exactly how bad you felt until you felt better. Depression can be like that, too.

 Insight _____

Switching to or adding cognitive therapy (CT) after a first unsuccessful attempt at treating depression with an antidepressant medication is generally as effective as switching to or adding another medication. Remission tends to take longer, but there are no side effects.

Bad Mood Busters

Whether you're in a really bad mood or a major depression, you can do some things to help ride the situation out. Use these 10 depression buffers as a bad-mood buster or as add-ons to professional help.

◆ Don't hide out in your house or apartment for more than a few hours as depression can worsen when no one else is around.

◆ If possible, don't make major life decisions until you feel better. If you have to make one, talk it over with at least two people you trust.

◆ Structure your mornings. Get up and take a shower every day, even if you don't feel like it.

◆ Avoid drugs and alcohol.

◆ If you've lost your appetite, eat small snacks during the day rather than forcing yourself to eat a big meal.

◆ Take notes and make lists. Concentration problems are common with depression.

◆ If you wake up in the middle of the night, get out of bed and do something (read inspirational material, for example).

◆ At the minimum, go for a 20-minute walk every day. Exercise and exposure to natural sunlight can be helpful in reducing mild depression.

◆ Give yourself a break. Don't expect to do all the things you normally do.

◆ Make a date to get some help. If you've been depressed for two weeks or more, talk to someone—your physician, your minister, or a therapist.

> **Psychobabble**
>
> Severe depression heightens the risk of dying after a heart attack or stroke and reduces the quality of life (and possibly the survival time) for cancer and AIDS patients. And a majority of depressed people who go untreated seriously consider suicide, with up to 17 percent eventually succeeding in killing themselves.

When Someone You Love Is Depressed

When someone you love is depressed, you worry. You probably also feel frustrated, overwhelmed, and confused. You may find yourself asking, "Why can't she just snap out of it?" Or you may think you should be able to do something to cure your loved one's problems.

Sadly, no one can "cure" someone else's depression, but you can say—and do—things that will help. Let them know you care and that you're sorry about their pain. Make sure they know they're not alone; you're there to help! And let them know they aren't "crazy"; depression can hit the smartest and most well-adjusted people.

On the other hand, if you're not careful, you can end up saying things that just make the situation worse. Some good "don'ts" are: don't point out everything they have to be thankful for; it will just make them feel worse. Avoid dismissing comments like, "It's all in your head," or advice like, "Pull yourself together." And don't say, "I know just how you feel!" unless you have really suffered from clinical depression in the past and want to talk about treatments that helped you.

Low-Level Sadness

When I was 25, I started feeling more and more fatigued over a period of six weeks. When I *finally* saw the doctor, she took one look in my ears and diagnosed my ear infection; after a few days of antibiotics, I was back to my energetic self. Dysthymia is like having a low-grade emotional "infection" that saps your mood, drains your energy, and takes a lot of life's pleasure away.

Dysthymic disorder, or dysthymia, is a mild to moderate level of depression that lasts at least two years. It often causes changes in appetite and sleep, low energy, fatigue, and feelings of hopelessness. Even though this type of depression is mild, it's kind of like carrying around a ball and chain; you're still able to do what you have to, but it sure makes it harder.

Up to 3 percent of the United States population suffers from dysthymia, which can begin at any time and seems to affect more women than men. Although the cause is unknown, there may be changes in the brain that involve the neurotransmitter serotonin. In addition, personality problems, medical problems, and chronic life stresses may also play a role.

The Postbaby Plummet

Up to 70 percent of new mothers experience mood swings, tearfulness, and irritability for a few days to a few weeks after birth; in fact, these mild to moderate symptoms are so common that they're considered normal. However, as many as one in five women in the United States suffer from something much worse—postpartum depression.

Symptoms of postpartum depression include extreme fatigue, loss of pleasure in daily life, sleeplessness, sadness, tearfulness, anxiety, hopelessness, feelings of worthlessness and guilt, irritability, appetite change, and poor concentration. In addition, many postpartum depression sufferers describe difficulty bonding with their new baby and may develop fears of harming their infant.

The cause of postpartum depression is unclear and is likely the result of a combination of factors—hormonal vulnerability, lack of sleep, genetic susceptibility, and situational stressors. Some new moms are more at risk than others—women with a low income, young mothers, women with poor social support, and new moms with a prior history of depression. Babies contribute their own two cents; up to ⅓ of new moms with a fussy baby report significant feelings of depression.

> **Psychobabble**
>
> Almost 80 percent of surveyed physicians said they were unlikely to formally screen new moms for depression even though it could be as simple as asking a new mother if her interest in her usual activities has changed and if she feels depressed or hopeless.

Although most postpartum depression starts within two weeks of a child's birth, some women don't experience symptoms right away. In a recent study, more than ¼ of them did not develop high symptom levels of postpartum depression until after three months, and 33 percent had high levels throughout the year.

Riding the Mood Roller Coaster

Bipolar disorder, commonly called manic depression, is a psychological disorder that affects about 1 percent of the population of every country in the world. And unlike major depression, men and women are equally likely to get it.

While all of us have "up" days and "down" days, individuals with bipolar disorder will be severely up sometimes, severely down sometimes, and in the middle some or most of the time. The hallmark of the disorder is the alternation between periods of mania and periods of depression.

> **Insight**
>
> Check out Terri Chaney's *Manic: A Memoir,* a fascinating look at the secret, hopeful, and horrifying illness that almost took her life.

The depressive end of bipolar disorder looks a lot like major depression. For this reason, the manic part of bipolar disorder determines the diagnosis. And when it first starts, it can be productive and fun. Imagine being in a great mood, full of energy and inspiration. The problem is, of course, the person can't stay at that level forever. In a full-blown manic episode, the person may …

◆ Become so restless that he or she can't sit still.

◆ Be unable to concentrate on anything.

◆ Have racing thoughts and rapid, disconnected speech.

◆ Develop paranoid ideas or extremely religious ideas and thoughts.

◆ Be extremely impulsive and put herself at risk through increased sexuality, financial extravagance, or an obsessive interest in some venture or hobby.

◆ Become highly irritable or easily excitable.

◆ Have grandiose delusions.

◆ Suffer profound weight loss.

◆ Stay awake for days and be unable to sleep.

Cyclothymia is similar to bipolar disorder because it is characterized by mood swings from mania to depression. However, a person with cyclothymia experiences symptoms of hypomania but never a full-blown manic episode. Hypomanic symptoms are exactly the same as the symptoms of a manic episode, but milder. A hypomanic episode does not disrupt the person's ability to function, doesn't require hospitalization, and doesn't include hallucinations or delusions.

Likewise, although depression is a part of cyclothymia, the symptoms never reach a clinically depressed level. For cyclothymia to be diagnosed, hypomanic and depressive symptoms must alternate for at least two years. Treatment depends upon the severity of the disorder—mild symptoms may respond to psychotherapy and more severe mood problems may require medications such as lithium or other mood stabilizers.

Moody Children and Terrible Teens

"All children are happy." "Children have nothing to worry about." "Childhood is the best time of your life." These statements reflected the attitudes of the mental health community. Only in the 1980s were mood disorders in children included in the category of diagnosable psychiatric illnesses.

Increasing evidence shows that major depression can develop in children and occurs more often in teenagers than we once thought. Seven to 14 percent of children will experience an episode of major depression before age 15; 20 to 30 percent of adults with bipolar disorder have their first episode before age 20 and an estimated 2,000 teenagers commit suicide each year.

The major ingredients of mood disorders are the same in children and adults. Depressed preschoolers may be frequently tearful or irritable for no apparent reason. They may seem unusually serious and lack the bounce of their peers. And of most concern, they may make frequent negative self-statements ("I hate myself"; "I wish I were dead") and do things that are self-destructive (such as hitting themselves).

However, children may also express their symptoms differently than adults. Because children don't always have the words to accurately describe how they feel, they're more likely to show you their suffering—via behavior problems—than talk about it.

Insight

A teenager who isolates himself in his room and has deteriorating grades and few friends is not just going through a stage; he may be clinically depressed.

Puberty may be a particular period of vulnerability for at-risk children. Certain developmental brain changes may be biomarkers—specific traits—that make the brain more vulnerable to severe mood swings. When a group of bipolar teens were compared to healthy children, the hippocampus (the part of the brain that plays a central role in memory) was smaller in teens with bipolar disorder after puberty, particularly in girls. (Younger [pre-pubescent] children did not show this difference.) These findings suggest that sex hormones may influence how the brains of these vulnerable children develop. Sadly, extreme mood swings aren't something many children grow out of. Bipolar disorder (BD) identified in childhood often persists into adulthood. In the first large follow-up study of its kind, 44 percent of children diagnosed with BD continued to have manic episodes as adults.

Brain Buster

Most people who commit suicide talk about it first. Talking or joking about suicide, acting in a reckless or dangerous manner, giving away possessions, or expressing feelings of hopelessness are common signs of suicidal plans. Recent research also suggests an increase in suicide among middle-age Caucasian men, a new high-risk group.

Insight

Feeling down in the dumps? Go to www.med.nyu.edu/psych/screens/depres.html for a quick online depression assessment.

Playing the Odds: Getting the Best Bang for the Depression Treatment Buck

The treatment of choice for depression depends on the type of depression and how severe it is. For major depression, two options, independently, work about equally well: a type of psychotherapy called cognitive-behavioral therapy (CBT) and anti-depressant medication. Together, CBT and antidepressants are the most effective weapon in the battle against the "black dog" of major depression; they work for 80 to 90 percent of the clients who use them.

CBT is a type of therapy that focuses on the *thinking* that affects our mood. CBT helps individuals with depression challenge the self-defeating thoughts (I'm worthless; I'll never feel better; there's nothing I can do about my situation) that either contribute to, or cause, their depressed mood.

In general, the more severe the depression, the more likely medication will help. Medications most often involve the commonly used serotonin-specific re-uptake inhibitors or SSRIs; think Prozac, Paxil, and Zoloft, among others. (Good news? They are almost impossible to overdose. Bad news? They often involve negative sexual side effects.) There are the tricyclic antidepressants—Elavil, Pamelor, and similar meds—which are cheaper but tend to have yuckier side effects, take longer to kick in, and can be used to overdose. Whatever the medication, the goal is to get the brain chemistry back in balance.

Psychobabble

A neurological pacemaker is a new, last-ditch treatment for severe depression that is unresponsive to psychotropic medication. Preliminary research shows that about ⅓ of treatment-resistant patients respond to it, that it changes the brain much in the same way ECT does, and that it may take up to a year before the antidepressant effect kicks in. The good news is that, for patients who get better, the mood-boosting effects don't wear off.

Mood stabilizers are the treatment of choice for bipolar disorder, a.k.a. manic depression. Newer medications, especially anticonvulsants like Depakote or Tegretol, are showing promising results but are still used primarily when lithium isn't effective.

What about alternative treatments? Well, the bottle of St. John's wort you buy isn't FDA-regulated; that means it could contain a high amount of the active ingredient— or none at all! If it does work, you have to take it three times a day and stay out of the sun. A better choice for an over-the-counter supplement might be DHEA (dehydro-epiandrosterone), but please talk to your physician first!

If ECT sounds too scary, clinical trials are taking place with other nondrug therapies, like transcranial magnetic stimulation (TMS), magnetic stimulation therapy (MST), and vagus nerve stimulation (VNS). The first two involve magnetic fields; the last one involves stimulation of an important nerve. Again, the final goal is to somehow "knock" an out-of-whack brain back into balance.

I'm Always Anxious About *Everything*

If you've ever found yourself unable to relax or get to sleep at night because of worries, you know some of the toll anxiety can take. Everyone experiences anxiety or fear in certain life situations, but 15 percent of the population has, at some point in their lives, experienced so much anxiety it disrupted their lives.

> **Psychobabble**
>
> Although suicide is most commonly associated with depression, studies show that severe anxiety, especially when accompanied by panic attacks, often leads to suicidal thoughts.

> **Insight**
>
> New research suggests that difficulty identifying and managing emotions may contribute to a person's ongoing vulnerability to panic attacks.

When a person feels anxious or worried most of the time for a period of at least six months, she is suffering from generalized anxiety disorder. The anxiety might focus on a specific circumstance, such as unrealistic money worries or an inexplicable fear that a loved one will die or be injured. Or it might be a general apprehension that something bad is about to happen. For example, a person suffering from generalized anxiety disorder might start calling the emergency rooms if her spouse was late coming home from work.

In addition to the emotional discomfort, a person with generalized anxiety disorder is often tense, is easily startled, is unusually attentive to the cause or source of the anxiety, and may lie awake at night worrying. You can imagine what an energy drain this would be over time, and people who suffer from generalized anxiety disorder often report fatigue and tiredness. They literally wear themselves out with worry.

Hit-and-Run Fear

With generalized anxiety disorder, a person worries about everything. With panic disorder, on the other hand, the person never knows when an attack will occur. Panic disorder, an anxiety disorder during which the person experiences recurrent episodes of intense anxiety and physical arousal that last up to 10 minutes, is one of the most confusing and terrifying psychological disorders.

In the Path of an Onrushing Train

People who've had panic attacks often say it feels like a train is bearing down on them at top speed and they can't move out of the way. They *know* there's no train, but their body responds as if there is; their hearts race, their mouths get dry, their blood pressure rises, and they feel as if they're going to die—or at the very least, lose their minds.

Sufferers of panic disorder experience unexpected but severe bouts of anxiety, from out of the blue, at least several times a month. They can happen anywhere—during a romantic dinner with your spouse, at the grocery store, or in the middle of an aerobics class. And, wham! There you go again.

Panic-Attack Pile-Up

As you might imagine, it wouldn't take too many of these emotional whacks upside the head before you started worrying about when the next one will happen. It's impossible to relax because they never know when the next terrifying jolt will hit them. One coping strategy is to avoid any place where they've had an attack, in hopes that this will cut down the odds of having another one. But as you'll see later in this chapter, this can lead to even worse problems.

Panic disorder has a strong biological component. For some reason, the normal "fight-or-flight" response begins misfiring. And the disorder tends to run in families. Once it starts, the frightening physical symptoms snowball into a psychological nightmare, characterized by constant worry ("When will it happen again?"), catastrophic thinking ("What if I go crazy?"), and self-doubt ("I can't handle another one").

Stuck in the House All Day

To look at Kim Basinger, it's hard to imagine she has a care in the world. She's beautiful. She's smart. She's an Academy Award winner. And she's a recovering agoraphobic.

Individuals with agoraphobia experience anxiety in public places where escape might be difficult or embarrassing. They are controlled by the fear that if they panic or become frightened outside the home, they'll either embarrass themselves or become paralyzed with their fear. As a result, they may gradually narrow their world until they literally become prisoners in their own homes. Agoraphobia often starts out with panic attacks that are terrifying and random. Maybe someone is shopping at the mall and has a panic attack. She leaves immediately and feels better. But the next time she needs to go to the mall for something, she starts to feel a little anxious. "What if it happens again?" a little voice whispers. The mere thought of going through another panic attack—or the fear of public humiliation—sends chills up her spine. Maybe she decides go to a different mall, just in case. Everything is fine, but a few weeks later she has a panic attack there, too.

Over time, you can see how a person might become more and more afraid to venture out. After all, if a panic attack could happen anywhere, no place is 100 percent safe. At least at home no one will see it happen.

Meet the Phobia Family

If your house is on fire or you're being mugged, fear is a rational reaction. In contrast, a person with a phobia suffers from an ongoing, irrational fear of something that is so strong it creates a compelling desire to avoid it. Common phobias include the fear of heights (acrophobia), the fear of cramped spaces (claustrophobia), and the fear of snakes (ophidiophobia).

The Five Most Common Phobias

Name	Percentage of Phobias
Agoraphobia (fear of crowds or public places)	10–50%
Social phobia (fear of embarrassing oneself in public)	10%
Fear of inanimate objects (heights, storms, closed spaces)	20%
Illness-injury (death, cancer)	15–25%
Animals (snakes, dogs, insects)	5–15%

In addition to phobias that center on places or things, there's also social phobia, a pervasive and ongoing fear of social or performance situations in which the person might either be under scrutiny from others (public speaking, speaking to authority figures) or around strangers (going to parties, striking up conversations, dating). The sufferer will generally experience a lot of anxiety in these situations, and the fear of embarrassment and humiliation can lead him to avoid having to face such situations.

One out of every eight Americans will develop a phobia at some point in his or her life. Some of those phobias gradually go away by themselves, and some of us just live with them unless they begin to disrupt our lives. For example, if you were considering a run for public office or up for a promotion that involved giving presentations, a fear of public speaking (one form of social phobia) would be a real drag. On the other hand, if you're a computer programmer, the fear of public speaking might be annoying but it wouldn't necessarily kill your career. My fear of insects is a lot less cumbersome now that I live in California than it was living with those Texas-size cockroaches in Dallas.

> **Insight**
>
> Okay, you movie fans, check out Jack Nicholson in *As Good As It Gets*. For once, the person with a psychiatric disorder is not portrayed as "crazy or violent." He isn't cured by the love of a good woman although she does inspire him to get help. And, at the end of the movie, he's taken charge of his obsessive-compulsive disorder—and gets the girl, to boot! Hooray for Hollywood!

This Can't Be as Good as It Gets

You've just locked the door and gotten into your car to head to the movie. You're running late, and you don't want to miss the beginning. But just as you're backing out of the driveway, a thought pops up. "Did I turn off the stove?" You mentally retrace your movements, and you're 95 percent sure you did. But horrible images of your house in flames still dance through your head. Are you *sure?* What if your house burns down while you're watching *The Dark Knight?* Odds are you'll give up and run back in the house to check—or spend much of the movie wishing you had.

> **Insight**
>
> Intensive therapy may speed up progress for OCD patients. A recent study found that adaptive changes in activity in certain regions of the brain can be produced with as little as four weeks of daily cognitive-behavioral therapy in OCD patients.

Moments like this are normal. But what if you ran back into the house, saw you'd turned off the stove, got back into your car—and had the exact same level of doubt and fear about burning the house down? And what if that fear surfaced every single time you left the house, even though you knew it was irrational and illogical? Welcome to obsessive-compulsive disorder (OCD).

My Obsessions Made Me Do It!

Obsessive-compulsive disorder is an illness that traps people in endless cycles of repetitive thoughts (obsessions) and behaviors (compulsions). This could mean checking 100 times to make sure that the stove is off before leaving for work or washing your hands for hours after using a public toilet because of a profound fear of germs.

> **Insight**
>
> Helping fearful children face their individual fears may be the most effective strategy in reducing their overall anxiety. And for children who already have an anxiety disorder, cognitive behavioral treatment combined with antidepressant medication is most likely to help children with anxiety disorders, but each of the treatments alone is also effective.

These behaviors are prompted by obsessive thoughts—unwanted and intrusive ideas, images, and impulses that run through your mind over and over again. You might perform these compulsive behaviors—often called rituals—according to "rules" you make up to try to control the nervous feelings that come along with the obsessive thoughts. Rituals like this do make the nervous feelings go away but usually only for a short while. Then fear and discomfort return, and you find yourself repeating the routine all over again.

Playing the Odds: Overcoming Anxiety and OCD

Simple phobias are the easiest phobias to treat. The systematic desensitization technique discussed in Chapter 7 usually works in a few hair-raising sessions.

With generalized anxiety disorder, agoraphobia, panic attacks, and obsessive-compulsive disorder, cognitive-behavioral therapy and medication are the first lines of defense. In addition to CBT, self-calming talk can be particularly effective with panic attacks, while behavior therapy aimed at reducing compulsive acts can be really helpful in OCD. Relaxation training is useful with all anxiety disorders.

The SSRI drugs are often used with OCD, but so are medications like Anafranil. Benzodiazapines like Klonopin and Xanax will help treat anxiety in the short run, but in the long run they can be dangerously addictive. Generally, they are used in conjunction with psychotherapy.

For simple phobias, the odds are almost 100 percent if you stick with the treatment. The success rate for anxiety disorders is about 80–90 percent with full treatment. And OCD? About 60 percent respond to medications; the response rate is higher with psychotherapy added in. Of course, these impressive therapy stats are meaningless unless a person doesn't bail when the going gets tough!

I Can't Throw It Away!

For actress Delta Burke, it was antique furniture and porcelain dolls enough to fill 27 climate-controlled storage units. For Roger Gorman's father-in-law, it was over 2,000 books, newspapers, plastic grocery bags, and leisure magazines. Three to six million Americans suffer from the an overwhelming desire to acquire, save, and compulsively collect so much stuff that it literally takes over their lives. But thanks to new research, the cluttered, confusing world of the compulsive hoarder may finally be starting to sort itself out.

PET scans of hoarders were found to have lower activity in a specific part of the brain that's involved in decision-making, focused attention, and the regulation of emotion. These findings may pave the way for future studies on medication and other treatments that can increase the activity in this particular part of the brain and regulate the impulses that make hoarders save and acquire excessively. In the meantime, therapy offers hope on another front. Following 7 to 12 months of treatment, 50 percent of compulsive hoarders were well on their way to recovery.

While most of us haven't been clinically depressed or anxious, we all know what it feels like to have the blues or to feel nervous so we can relate to mood disorders. But in the next chapter, we'll take a look at a mental illness whose symptoms—hallucinations, disorganization, delusions—most of us will never experience as we explore the fascinating, complex, and misunderstood condition known as schizophrenia.

> **Psychobabble**
>
> Compulsive hoarders are different from die-hard collectors or "clutter bugs" in that they *can't stop* acquiring things or make themselves throw anything away. According to a new study, 8 to 12 percent of hoarders have been evicted or threatened with eviction and many suffer from health problems like asthma, arthritis, high blood pressure, diabetes, and obesity.

Straight from the Lab

The Learning Drug D-cycloserine, an antibiotic used to treat tuberculosis, is being used to enhance the emotional learning process that takes place in psychotherapy and hopefully make these new emotional memories more robust. Taken just before an exposure therapy session, D-cycloserine–enhanced psychotherapy has been found effective for social phobia and OCD.

Give Kids' Brains a Self-Esteem Boost First-graders who are already performing poorly in school are at risk of being depressed by the time they reach junior high. Therefore, researchers say, focusing early on what such youngsters are doing well— whether it's art, sports, or helping others—may help build self-esteem and guard against a downward spiral.

Hopelessness Holds On People taking antidepressants typically feel a lot better during the first few months, but a sense of hope may not appear until several weeks, or even months, after other depressive symptoms have lifted. This finding is troubling because hopelessness is a strong risk factor for suicide.

"Antidepressants Can't Swing It for People with Bipolar Disorder" The swings in mood from depression to mania that afflict people with bipolar disorder can be tempered with drugs such as lithium, but adding an antidepressant drug to ease the depression component is not helpful, new research suggests.

The Least You Need to Know

♦ Clinical depression lasts for at least two weeks, causes significant emotional distress, and interferes with a person's ability to conduct normal activities.

♦ The best treatments for depression are a combination of antidepressant medication and psychotherapy.

♦ Dysthymia is a low-grade sadness that lasts for at least two years and responds well to antidepressants.

♦ Bipolar disorder—commonly called manic depression—is characterized by extreme mood swings of highs and lows; cyclothymia is a milder version of the disorder.

♦ Depressed children are more likely to show their illness through behavioral problems and a declining school performance.

♦ Anxiety disorders generally respond to cognitive behavioral psychotherapy or medication.

20

Postcards from the Edge of Reality

In This Chapter

- ◆ Symptoms of schizophrenia
- ◆ Hallucinations, delusions, and other strange things
- ◆ Causes for our brains to go over the edge
- ◆ A perspective on paranoia

More than 30 years ago, Frederick Frese was locked up inside an Ohio mental hospital. A college graduate and Marine, Frese had been guarding atomic weapons in Jacksonville, Florida, when he developed the belief that enemy nations had hypnotized American leaders in a plot to take over the United States supply. He was diagnosed with paranoid schizophrenia.

Twelve years later, Frese was the chief psychologist for the same mental-health system that had once confined him. He was also happily married and had four children. Despite 10 further hospitalizations, Frese earned a Master's degree and a Doctorate. The moral of the story is: a mental illness is not a death sentence.

def•i•ni•tion

Schizophrenia is a severe mental disorder characterized by a breakdown in perceptual and thought processes, often including hallucinations and delusions.

This chapter presents one of the most challenging, elusive, and maligned mental illnesses: *schizophrenia*. We discuss the different types, their symptoms and causes, and new groundbreaking treatments for this difficult condition. And you learn about paranoia in all its forms and why you can't just talk someone out of his or her suspicious beliefs. Finally, you see why anatomy is never destiny: someone with a biological vulnerability to schizophrenia can take steps to minimize the risk of getting it.

The General Scoop on Schizophrenia

Schizophrenia is the disorder people usually mean when they talk about "crazy," "psychotic," or "insane." It is probably the most conspicuous mental illness, or at least it runs a close second to dissociative identity disorder, discussed in Chapter 13. It's also not very well understood by the general public; when portrayed in the media, it's often linked to a violent crime. Although violence by a mentally ill person is rare, it is most likely to happen with someone with a diagnosis of paranoid schizophrenia.

It is also the most costly of all mental illnesses. People with this illness make up the majority of all patients hospitalized with mental disorders. It strikes approximately 1 percent of the world's population, generally in adolescence and young adulthood.

Schizophrenia is not a rare mental disorder. In the United States alone, there are as many people with schizophrenia as the combined populations of Wyoming, Vermont, Delaware, and Hawaii. It is equally common in men and women, although, for some reason, it tends to strike men earlier (between the ages of 18 and 25) and women later (26 to 45). It can hit as early as childhood but almost never after age 50.

Insight

Watch—or rewatch—*A Beautiful Mind*, a movie inspired by Nobel prize winner and schizophrenia sufferer John Nash, to get an up-close-and-personal look at this devastating disorder.

It is also a scary diagnosis to receive. While the treatment for schizophrenia has improved dramatically over the past few decades, no one thinks we've won the battle. Mental-health professionals often talk about the "one-third" prognosis for schizophrenia: one-third go on to lead normal lives; one-third make a partial recovery; and one-third face a slow, downhill spiral of the disease throughout the rest of their life.

The Split Personality

Much of what is known about schizophrenia comes from the Swiss psychiatrist who "discovered" it: Eugen Bleuler. He was the first person to use the label schizophrenia to describe the devastating symptoms he saw in the people who suffered from this illness. The term schizophrenia comes from the Greek words *schizo*, which means split, and *phrenum*, which means mind. Bleuler observed that patients with schizophrenia often acted as if different parts of their minds were split off from each other.

This splitting of the various functions of the brain can lead to bizarre and disorganized thoughts and actions. For example, patients with schizophrenia might be listening to auditory hallucinations and thus be unable to attend to anything going on around them. Or they might talk about the recent death of a loved one—but smile or laugh as they're doing so. As you can see, our ability to function effectively depends on our attention, emotions, thoughts, behaviors, perceptions, and motivations all working in harmony with each other—or at least being on the same page.

Brain Buster

Don't believe what you see in the media! You're not likely to get ambushed by a homicidal stranger suffering from schizophrenia. When violence does occur, it's most often self-directed (40 percent attempt suicide) and when directed elsewhere, is much more likely to involve a family member rather than a stranger.

Unfortunately, while many of Bleuler's insights still apply today, his choice of names leaves a lot to be desired. Many of us commonly confuse schizophrenia with dissociative identity disorder (DID), although the two have little in common. Someone in the acute stages of schizophrenia has one mind that may not be in touch with reality. A person with DID, on the other hand, sees reality pretty clearly but has at least two distinct personalities that compete for dominance.

Blurred Boundaries

While schizophrenia and dissociative disorder have little in common, schizophrenia and bipolar disorder are kissing cousins. In fact, in spite of our classy diagnoses, the distinction between the two is far from clear. We know now that symptoms of bipolar disorder are often seen in patients with schizophrenia, and the reverse is also true.

Further, there is growing evidence that both disorders emerge, in part, from the cumulative impact of a large number of risk genes, each of which contributes a relatively small component of the vulnerability to these disorders. Recently a Scots medical research team has identified a new gene linked to major mental illness that links back to a previously discovered gene, Disrupted in Schizophrenia 1 (DISC-1), which significantly increases the chances of schizophrenia, bipolar, and depression. PDE4B is another gene that helps regulate mood, cognition, and behavior.

Schizophrenia from the Inside Out

Schizophrenia can literally put a person in another world. In the acute stage of the illness, the differences in thinking, altered sensory experiences, and disruptions in the ability to relate to others gives the person a drastically different experience of the world than you or I have. The essence of schizophrenia is impaired reality testing: the person is unable to tell the difference between fact and imagination or fantasy.

What's Real?

Most of us evaluate the reality of our inner worlds against the outer one. You notice that, despite your fond daydreams of office romance, your co-worker is merely cordial and polite to you, and frequently talks about her fabulous husband. Or you wake up in your bed with no sunburn and can easily calculate the odds against the likelihood that you traveled to and from Tahiti overnight.

Someone with schizophrenia reverses this procedure. Inner experiences are the criteria against which he tests the validity of his outer world. So for example, if a person with schizophrenia hears a voice within his head, it is more real to him than any lack of confirming evidence. And if that voice orders him to go out into the street and alert people that enemy missiles are about to strike the city, he will do so. To him, this voice is as real as your boss's voice on Monday morning.

To receive a diagnosis of schizophrenia, a person has to have a serious, long-lasting decline in his ability to work, care for himself, and connect with other people. In addition, he must have at least two of the five following symptoms: delusions, hallucinations, disorganized speech, extremely disorganized behavior, and what clinicians call "negative" signs. Let's take a look at each of these.

Delusions

Delusions are basically false ideas that a person believes to be true. These ideas cannot be verified objectively, but the person suffering from schizophrenia believes them in the face of all reason. Delusional beliefs can be outlandish (such as believing that you can control the space shuttle) or they might just be unrealistic or untrue (such as believing that your partner is being unfaithful to you even though she is home every night and has given you absolutely no reason to think this). If you've ever been extremely jealous, you can see how easy it might be to slide down the slippery slope into delusion.

Some common types of delusions in schizophrenia are …

◆ **Delusions of persecution.** These are beliefs that others are plotting against you or that you are being watched, followed, persecuted, or attacked.

◆ **Delusions of grandeur.** These are beliefs in one's own extraordinary importance. If you think you're Jesus Christ or the Queen of England, then you're suffering from a delusion of grandeur. Sometimes delusions are based on something going on in the person's real life: it is not unusual for a schizophrenic who is also HIV-positive to believe that he knows the cure for AIDS.

◆ **Delusions of being controlled.** These are beliefs that your thoughts or movements are being controlled by radio waves or by invisible wires, like a puppet.

Hallucinations

As explained in Chapter 6, hallucinations are imagined sensory perceptions thought to be real. The most common hallucinations with schizophrenia are auditory—the hearing of voices. For example, a person might hear a running commentary on her behavior or several voices having a conversation.

Hallucinations and delusions can occur together as can several different *types* of delusions. For example, a person who believes she's the Queen of England might also "overhear" others plotting to overthrow the throne. Or a man who has delusions of persecution may also hear the voice of his imagined persecutor threatening or insulting him. Clearly, these symptoms severely impair a person's ability to function in the day-to-day world and are what psychologists call symptoms of *psychosis*.

def•i•ni•tion

Psychosis (also called "psychotic disorder") is a general term for a severe mental disorder that prevents an accurate understanding of and interaction with reality due to impaired thoughts, inappropriate emotions, and distorted perceptions.

Sufferers of schizophrenia can be pretty creative in their battle against hallucinations and often develop elaborate rituals to control them. Some can stop the voices by humming to themselves, counting, or holding their mouth in a certain way.

Mental health professionals may use rituals to help. For instance, in one mental health hospital, the psychiatrist convinced a man with hallucinations to wear a towel on his head to "block" the radio signals he was convinced were being beamed at him. It worked, and the man learned to arrange the towel creatively so it appeared to be a turban!

> **Psychobabble**
>
> Contrary to what Hollywood would have you believe, visual hallucinations (seeing something that isn't there) are not usually part of schizophrenia. Visual hallucinations are usually related to medication problems, diseases of the brain, or street-drug use.

Interestingly enough, auditory hallucinations in schizophrenia occur through the same mechanism that produces vividly imagined speech sounds in everyone. For example, if you "rehearse" an argument before you face the person you're angry with or if you imagine how your boss's voice will sound after you ask her to double your salary, you're generating the imagined sound by the same means that is used to create auditory hallucinations.

Disorganized Speech

The speech of people with schizophrenia often reflects the level of disorganization in their thinking. They may jump wildly and illogically from one idea to another, a phenomenon known as a flight of ideas. Or they may suddenly start rhyming. For example, a person may begin talking about the school bell ringing and suddenly jump to "sing, fling, wing, ding, the school bells always ring." Such speech patterns represent a disturbance in the logical thought processes.

Grossly Disorganized Behavior

We're not talking about something as minor as wearing messy clothes or forgetting to write things down so that you'll remember them. Grossly disorganized behavior is behavior that is completely inappropriate for the situation, such as wearing layers of wool clothes on a hot day or behaving in a silly manner at a funeral. Other examples of grossly disorganized behavior are the failure or inability to prepare a simple meal or to dress oneself.

Changes in Emotions

The earliest emotional changes seen in schizophrenia are rapid changes in mood and an exaggeration of normal feelings, particularly of guilt and fear. As the schizophrenia gets worse, the person may exhibit strange or bizarrely inappropriate emotions. For example, he might burst into laughter at news of a death or burst into tears at a joke. Or the person may seem to lack emotions at all and gradually become more detached and apathetic toward other people.

Insight

Sometimes a person in the midst of psychosis needs to be hospitalized until her symptoms are under control. While people can be hospitalized against their will, they must present a clear danger to themselves or to others and refuse voluntary admission before involuntary commitment is considered.

Negatively Speaking

Psychologists often talk about "positive" and "negative" signs of schizophrenia, but don't confuse these terms with "good" and "bad." In this case, positive means a sign that is present that shouldn't be; delusions, hallucinations, and disorganized speech and behavior are all positive signs of schizophrenia. When they are present, the illness is said to be in the acute (or psychotic) phase. When such symptoms subside, the illness is said to be in the residual phase.

Negative is a sign that should be there, but isn't. People suffering from schizophrenia lack certain behaviors, thoughts, feelings, and drives that most people have. They may move more slowly than their peers do. Their speech may lack spontaneity and their range of emotional expression may be restricted. They may lose touch with basic drives, such as hunger or thirst, and lose the normal pleasure that comes from satisfying them. For the person with schizophrenia, these symptoms cause real problems in coping with day-to-day life.

The Faces of Schizophrenia

One of schizophrenia's challenges for psychologists is that it appears in many different guises. Two people with the same diagnosis may share very few of the same symptoms. One might hear taunting voices and attribute them to a specific (delusional) source. Another may just seem to indulge in silly and inappropriate behavior and not make a lot of sense. Researchers have tried to determine which symptoms are most likely to go together and have come up with three different clusters of symptoms:

◆ Clusters of positive symptoms—usually a combination of delusions and hallucinations

◆ Clusters of disorganized symptoms—for example, a combination of illogical speech and disorganized behaviors

◆ Clusters of negative symptoms

According to the *Diagnostic and Statistical Manual of Mental Disorders* (*DSM-IV-TR*), here's how mental health professionals classify the diverse symptoms of schizophrenia:

The Many Faces of Schizophrenia

The Type of Symptoms	What It Looks Like
Disorganized	Inappropriate behavior and emotions, incoherent speech, random delusions or hallucinations.
Catatonic	Bizarre movements, either a frozen or rigid posture or very excitable movements.
Paranoid	Behavior is more organized, delusions and hallucinations centered around a theme of persecution or grandiosity.
Undifferentiated	A grab-bag category, mixed set of symptoms, unusual thinking with features from other categories.
Residual	No positive symptoms appear, but the person still shows some signs like flattened affect and social withdrawal.

What Causes Schizophrenia?

Because of its seriousness, schizophrenia has been studied more than any other mental disorder. But while we've ruled out some possible causes—for instance, we know that poor family communication does *not* cause the disorder, which means we've quit blaming mothers—we still haven't gotten to the root of the problem, probably because there's more than one root.

The Biological Connection

One thing we know for certain is that schizophrenia is as much a medical illness as diabetes, multiple sclerosis, and cancer. On PET scans and other brain images, the brain of a person with severe schizophrenia looks significantly different. But what causes this?

In the early 1970s, neuroscientists thought schizophrenia might be caused by having too much of the neurotransmitter dopamine in the brain. Alas, while dopamine is involved in schizophrenia, neuroscientists now know it's not simply a matter of how much or how little one has—in fact, the way dopamine is distributed and what it does are far more important factors. Unusual patterns of dopamine activity, perhaps including overactivity in some areas and underactivity in others, may be partly responsible for schizophrenia (For a refresher on the role of neurotransmitters, see Chapter 2.).

Other researchers argued that glutamate, a chemical that's part of another brain-signaling system, contributes to psychosis, thought disorder, and schizophrenia. While the "dopamine hypothesis" and "glutamate hypothesis" were once hotly debated, new research suggests the two neurotransmitters interact and work together and medications that target either one may be effective.

So like cancer, schizophrenia probably has more than one cause. Let's take a look at the extent to which four other factors play a role in the onset of schizophrenia:

> **Psychobabble**
>
> Approximately one-third of the 600,000 homeless people in the United States have been diagnosed with a serious mental illness, including schizophrenia and other psychotic disorders.

- Genes
- Prenatal development
- Home life
- Cultural influences

Gene Links

If someone in your family has schizophrenia, you're four times more likely to get it than someone whose family doesn't have it lurking in the gene pool. If one identical twin has schizophrenia, the other twin has a 50-50 chance of getting it, too. The siblings of a nontwin or a fraternal twin with the disease have a 9 percent chance of developing the illness, while the child of one parent with schizophrenia has a 13 percent chance. And a child whose parents both suffer from the disease has a 46 percent chance of developing it.

Research conducted at Mount Sinai School of Medicine has linked variations of a gene related to brain development and function—OLIG2—to the development of schizophrenia. In addition, OLIG2 also showed a genetic association with schizophrenia when examined together with two other genes previously associated with schizophrenia—CNP and ERBB 4. All of these are active in the development of myelin, the fatty substance or white matter in the brain that coats nerve fibers and is critical for the brain to function properly. Several other genes have also been implicated, suggesting that schizophrenia is—or can be—caused through multiple avenues.

However, the fact that even people with the exact same genes (identical twins) share it only half the time also points out the obvious fact that our genes don't necessarily "make" us get schizophrenia. If the disease were completely genetic in origin, both twins would always get the disease. Also, some people with no family history at all develop it. Obviously, therefore, other factors must be involved.

Genetic vulnerabilities for these illnesses may not necessarily be inherited from parents, at least in the sense that these vulnerabilities were not present in the parental genome. It turns out that individuals with no family history who develop schizophrenia harbor eight times more spontaneous mutations—most in pathways affecting brain development—than healthy controls, suggesting that rare, spontaneous mutations are likely to contribute to vulnerability in cases of schizophrenia from previously unaffected families.

Prenatal Effects

Prenatal or birth trauma also may stack the deck against someone with a genetic vulnerability to schizophrenia. When one identical twin develops schizophrenia, it's more likely to be the one who had the more difficult birth. Prenatal viral infections or lack of nutrition also put a baby at risk. But even here, the sequence of cause and effect isn't completely straightforward—trauma alone is not enough to cause the problem. According to one long-term study, prenatal and birth traumas were related to the later development of schizophrenia in babies whose mothers had schizophrenia but *not* in the babies who weren't genetically at risk.

Oddly enough, two risk factors for schizophrenia are place and season of birth. Babies born in February and March have a 10 percent above-average risk for schizophrenia, while babies born in August and September have a 10 percent lower risk than average. And here's a reason to move out of the city—an urban birth puts a child at twice the risk for schizophrenia, compared with babies born in rural areas.

Teenage Brains Run Amok

No matter what gets the schizophrenia ball rolling earlier, it really ramps up in adolescence. In fact, new research findings add to evidence that changes in brain development which lead to schizophrenia aren't limited to the prenatal stage and early childhood but also occur during the late-teen and young-adult years—the ages when symptoms usually begin to appear.

Specifically, recent studies suggest that schizophrenia may occur, in part, because brain development goes awry during adolescence and young adulthood when the brain is eliminating some connections between cells as a normal part of maturation. Comparing a group of schizophrenic adolescents and young adults who had recently had their first psychotic break with a group of healthy peers, researchers found that this loss of tissue began around the same time and occurred in the same brain areas. However, the rate of loss in the prefrontal lobes—which control higher functions like thinking, judgment, and memory—and parietal lobes was more pronounced and covered a greater area of the brain's surface in the youth with schizophrenia.

Effects of the Home Environment

A chaotic family environment can contribute to schizophrenia, but it doesn't cause the disease. A study of adopted children in Finland found that when high-risk children (whose biological mothers had schizophrenia) were adopted by parents with poor communication skills, they had more bizarre or unusual thoughts than did high-risk children whose parents communicated in a calmer, more organized fashion. No such difference was found for low-risk children, however, so communication styles alone can't account for the onset of schizophrenia.

Other research has focused on the effects of criticism and negative attitudes or feelings expressed about and toward a person with schizophrenia by his or her family members. Other things being equal, the greater the expressed anger and hostility toward someone with schizophrenia, the more likely his symptoms will worsen and he will require hospitalization. So these factors can intensify the symptoms of the disease, but once again, they don't appear to be the cause of it.

> **Psychobabble**
>
> Schizophrenic patients who were abused as children often develop hallucinations or voices that bully them as their abuser did, thus causing paranoia and a mistrust of people close to them.

Cultural Influences

We can't blame American culture for causing schizophrenia—the disease looks remarkably the same across cultures. The prevalence of symptoms, the average age of onset, and the sex difference in age of onset (men getting it earlier than women) are similar despite wide variations in the ways people live.

However, Western culture may make it harder to get well. Patients in developing countries get better much faster than those do in developed countries like the United States, and this holds true for every category of schizophrenia, using every measure of recovery. In fact, in one study of 1,379 patients across 10 countries, 63 percent of the patients in developing countries, compared with only 37 percent in the developed countries, showed a full recovery within a two-year period.

One possible explanation for this difference in recovery patterns is the different cultural attitudes toward mental illness. Family members in developing countries are more accepting of a family member with schizophrenia—and so is the culture in which the family lives. They are much less likely to label the person as "sick" or to think of schizophrenia as a permanent condition. They may call it "a case of nerves," which sounds more benign, and they may be more likely to tie it to experiences that everyone has had.

> **Insight**
>
> After reviewing 35 studies evaluating the link between drugs and psychosis, researchers have found that marijuana users had a 41 percent increased chance of developing psychosis marked by symptoms of hallucinations or delusions later in life than those who never used the drug. The risk rose with heavier consumption. This is some of the strongest evidence yet linking the drug to a mental disorder.

Perhaps more important, the social organization common to non-Western cultures provides more support for a person suffering from schizophrenia and for his or her family. Extended families provide more resources and care, which helps caregivers be more nurturing and tolerant. And nonindustrialized, more agriculturally based cultures can be more flexible in allowing a person with schizophrenia to play a useful role in the family economy by performing chores on the family farm. These social factors are generally unavailable in highly individualistic, nonagricultural societies like the United States.

When Schizophrenia Happens in Childhood

The appearance of schizophrenia before age 12 is rare—less than $\frac{1}{60}$ as common as adult-onset schizophrenia. Some children who develop the illness seem to be different from their peers at an early age; about 30 percent have on-and-off symptoms in the first years of life. As a group, they are more anxious and disruptive than their peers and are more likely to exhibit behaviors frequently seen in pervasive developmental disorders such as autism—rocking, arm flapping, or other unusual, repetitive behaviors. Most of them also show delays in learning language and other skills.

Childhood schizophrenia tends to develop gradually, without the sudden onset of psychotic symptoms—called a psychotic break—that we see in adults and adolescents. Hallucinations, delusions, and disorganized thinking almost always occur after age seven. Once the schizophrenia starts, its symptoms often parallel those seen in adults and older adolescents.

A significant drop in I.Q. during early childhood (between ages four and seven) may signal an increased risk of psychotic symptoms in adulthood. The *American Journal of Psychiatry* reported a study of 547 Americans born between 1959 and 1966. A decline in I.Q. between ages four and seven was associated with psychotic symptoms 16 years later. This was seven times higher than for individuals whose childhood I.Q. did not decline.

> **Psychobabble**
>
> "Nervous breakdown" is a vague term for any acute mental problem. In fact, the term has been used to describe emotional problems ranging from a severe stress reaction (like post-traumatic stress disorder) to debilitating depression or psychosis.

Who Gets Better?

One thing should be clear by now: the human spirit is stronger than any psychiatric illness. But as a clinician I know that some people with a serious mental illness get better; some coast along; and some get worse. My job is to push my clients into the first category as hard as I can.

Studies of the outcome of treatment suggest some things that make a good recovery more—or less likely. A person with little or no family history of schizophrenia—as was true for Mr. Frese—is more likely to have a better treatment outcome than someone whose family genes are stacked against him. Another good sign is having lived a normal and productive life before the onset of schizophrenia. And early intervention is critical: the sooner someone gets help for his first psychotic episode, the more likely he is to avoid future crashes.

On the downside, if schizophrenia strikes at an early age, the person may have a tougher road to recovery. The gender of the patient makes a difference, too; for some reason, men tend to do worse than women. In addition, patients who have a lot of *negative* signs—such as apathy and withdrawal from others—often have a harder time than those who do not. Last but not least, the greater the number of relapses a patient suffers, the lower his chances for complete recovery.

Psychobabble

Preliminary research suggests that different variations in the same gene influence how well different ethnic groups, and people within the same ethnic group, respond to various antipsychotic medications. Looking at how over 350 diverse schizophrenic patients responded to five different medications, researchers found that variations on the gene RGS3 reliably predicted what medication was likely to be most effective. If confirmed, their findings could one day help clinicians predict which medication is most likely to help a patient, based on his genetic makeup.

Playing the Odds: Schizophrenia

What's the treatment of choice? Medication is the first line of defense. When schizophrenia is treated right from the start, remission rates are as high as 80 to 85 percent. As with diabetes, we use medication to control the symptoms, not to cure the disease itself. But when the symptoms are under control, a person with schizophrenia can lead a normal life. These medications, called antipsychotic or neuroleptic drugs, help restore the function of the brain to normal levels. And they have an encouragingly high success rate: on average, a person with schizophrenia who takes medication has a 60 percent chance of not being rehospitalized. Without medication, those odds drop to 20 percent.

Treatment of schizophrenia improved drastically in the 1990s, with the advent of new antipsychotic medications called atypical antipsychotics. Some of the commonly used ones include Clozaril, Zyprexa, Seroquel, and Risperdal. For patients who don't respond to these medications, new research suggests that topiramate, a drug that blocks glutamate, can be an effective add-on.

The biggest problem with antipsychotics is that people don't want to take them. A common cycle is a full-blown psychotic episode, resulting in a trip to the emergency room or the psych hospital. The person gets medication, improves, and is released. And eventually she either (1) feels so good that she decides she doesn't need the medications anymore or (2) has unpleasant side effects and therefore stops taking the meds. In both cases, the person stops the medications. Gradually the symptoms come back, and the cycle starts again.

Unfortunately, recent research indicates that the newer antipsychotics may be different but not necessarily better. They aren't more effective at treating childhood and adolescent schizophrenia than the older ones. They don't seem to reduce the risk of violence better than the older ones. And a recent study following 114 patients who had quit taking the older drug perphanzine and been randomly assigned to one of the atypicals found that most quit taking the new drug, too.

Because psychotherapy doesn't work when someone is out of touch with reality, it traditionally hasn't been considered an important part of the treatment for schizophrenia. However, that may be about to change. Recent research suggests that cognitive rehabilitation techniques, such as teaching memorization strategies commonly used by healthy individuals, is very effective in addressing some of the cognitive changes (difficulty learning new information, memory problems, poor attention span) associated with schizophrenia. Cognitive-behavioral therapy that focuses on medication adherence (consistently and correctly taking the drugs) can be a crucial part of treatment, and family and group support can also be very effective. Psychodynamic therapy, however, can actually make the condition worse!

> **Insight**
>
> One benefit of the availability of more antipsychotic meds is that it offers patients more choices when one fails. Recent research suggests that asking a patient *why* she discontinued a medication (either because of the side effects or because it wasn't working) can be useful in picking the most effective medication next.

Clearing Up Any Remaining Confusion

We've already cleared up the confusion between schizophrenia and multiple-personality disorder. However, because of the common use of generic words like *nervous breakdown* and *psychotic break*, schizophrenia is often confused with a number of other, very different mental illnesses. Let's clear up the confusion once and for all.

Schizophrenia is *not* …

- ◆ **Bipolar disorder (manic depression).** This is a periodic, recurrent mood disorder of extreme highs and lows interspersed with periods of complete normalcy. It does not involve negative signs or fixed delusions.

- ◆ **Schizoaffective disorder.** This disorder has symptoms of schizophrenia and bipolar disorder. It involves a disturbance of mood (depression, anxiety) on top of the usual signs of schizophrenia.

◆ **Brief reactive psychosis.** While this disorder has symptoms similar to schizophrenia, it lasts for less than two weeks and is generally brought on by extreme stress. An example is postpartum psychosis.

◆ **Personality disorders.** Schizoid and schizotypal personality disorders share some of the odd behaviors and impaired relationships found in schizophrenia, but there are no breaks with reality and the person can still function more or less competently in society.

◆ **Creativity.** Extremely creative people may have unusual thoughts and views and eccentric behavior, but the creative person remains in control of his thought processes.

◆ **Brain disease.** A brain infection or a tumor can cause hallucinations or delusions, but once the infection is treated or the tumor removed, these symptoms will end.

The Perils of Paranoia

One of my all-time favorite bumper stickers says, "Just because I'm paranoid doesn't mean they're not out to get me." This humorous bumper sticker illustrates how often (although certainly not always) there can be a grain of truth in the most irrational beliefs.

Dealing with Distress

Suppose Mr. Smith has worked for a national pharmacy chain for 30 years, has been an exemplary employee, and has never missed a day's work. One day he comes to work to discover the pharmacy chain has been bought out and he's abruptly laid off from work. Understandably, he feels hurt and betrayed. He spends hours thinking about what's happened to him and how, after all his years of service to the company, something like this could have happened to him.

From Distress to Delusion

So far, Mr. Smith's reactions are perfectly normal. But what if, after a while, his thoughts take a stranger turn? Unemployed and isolated in his apartment, he begins to believe that his layoff has nothing to do with the company buyout and begins to wonder if his former employer was engaged in a systematic plot to destroy his life and take away his sanity. He begins believing company agents are tampering with his mail, following him, and even tapping his phone.

Mr. Smith has developed a paranoid delusion. This is a serious psychological diagnosis—not what most people mean when they use the term paranoid casually, to refer to simple suspiciousness. When a person is suspicious based on past personal experience or observation, it is inappropriate to call him paranoid. In fact, mental-health clinicians only use the term when a person's suspiciousness or mistrust is either highly exaggerated or completely unwarranted.

Because paranoia is common in many psychiatric disorders, it can be difficult to fit the symptoms to the right diagnosis. We've already explored one diagnosis in which paranoia plays a part—paranoid schizophrenia. Now let's talk about another disorder in which paranoia reaches delusional proportions.

> **Psychobabble**
>
> More than one condition has paranoid symptoms. Paranoid schizophrenia, paranoid delusional disorder, and paranoid personality disorder each is a different condition, with different preferred treatments.

> **Brain Buster**
>
> "Uppers" such as cocaine and amphetamines can greatly increase the symptoms of schizophrenia in people who already have them and, at high doses, can induce those symptoms in people who do not. And the abuse of drugs like amphetamines, LSD, and PCP can also cause paranoid thinking and behavior.

Paranoid Delusional Disorder

Someone with a paranoid *personality* might frequently suspect colleagues of making jokes at his expense. But a person with paranoid *delusions*, on the other hand, might believe that her colleagues are poisoning her, drugging her, spying on her, or plotting a grand conspiracy to smear her name. There's a big difference between the two.

The Green-Eyed Monster

Not all people who suffer paranoid delusions are convinced they're going to be harmed or killed. Jealousy can become delusional. I once knew a man who truly believed his wife had deliberately gotten into an automobile accident to cover up her rendezvous with her lover. This man took *everything* as a sign that his partner was unfaithful. Although his beliefs might sound almost comical, the genuine emotional distress his delusion caused both him and his partner was no laughing matter.

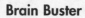

Brain Buster

Don't confuse paranoid schizophrenia with paranoid delusional disorder. The latter is not accompanied by hallucinations or generally disorganized behavior. In fact, except for actions and thoughts that center around the specific delusion, the person with paranoid delusional disorder can often function normally.

The Strange Psyche of the Stalker

On rare occasions, you read about a celebrity whose life is plagued by a stalker. Late-night talk-show host David Letterman was stalked for years by such a woman. She phoned him, wrote him love letters, and became a constant and unwelcome presence in his life. Despite Letterman's consistent failure to respond to her proclamations of love, she continued to believe he really loved her. She was arrested, hospitalized, and eventually killed herself.

This woman was in the grip of a powerful form of paranoia—an erotic delusion. No amount of external evidence could shake her belief that Letterman returned her love. A paranoid delusion like hers is an extreme example of the power that our beliefs can hold over our entire lives.

The Origins of Paranoid Delusions

Families of people with paranoid delusional disorder do not have higher than normal rates of schizophrenia or depression. A person suffering from the disorder, however, is more likely to come from a family in which other members have the same problem: twins are more likely to share paranoia than regular siblings, and paranoid disorders are more common among relatives. Although we don't know exactly what causes paranoia, we do know that certain drugs make it worse. And there's bad news for *all* of us these days—some studies show that paranoia has increasingly become more common over the past 100 years.

Other factors are at work as well. Stress, for example, can trigger paranoia or make it worse. Prisoners of war, immigrants, and other people living under extreme stress all show a higher likelihood of developing paranoid delusions. Even "normal" people can suffer from a short-lived form of paranoia, called acute paranoia, when thrust into highly stressful new situations. The relationship between stress and paranoia is complex, but it appears that a person can be genetically predisposed to paranoia and that stress is likely to trigger it.

Playing the Odds: Delusional Disorders

Delusional disorders can actually be one of several types: erotomanic (like Letterman's stalker), grandiose, jealous, persecutory (the fictitious Mr. Smith), or somatic (odd beliefs about bodily function). Unlike schizophrenia, these disorders commonly occur later in life—middle age and beyond. Delusional disorders are generally less disruptive to day-to-day living than is schizophrenia. They are also less prevalent: most estimates say perhaps less than ⅓ of 1 percent of the population has a delusional disorder.

Treatment prognosis, however, may be worse. Paranoia, by its very nature, involves the belief that the problem is *out there* rather than inside oneself. As a result, many people with these disorders refuse treatment, and, unless they are a clear and present danger to themselves or others, treatment cannot be forced upon them. Both medications (from antidepressants to antipsychotics) and psychotherapy (usually psychodynamic) have been used with some success, but many people with the disorders simply drop out of treatment early. In the next chapter, we'll take a look at another group of diagnoses that present their own treatment challenges—the addictions.

Straight from the Lab

Public Paranoia Alive and Well   A virtual reality Underground ride used by researchers to reveal the extent that paranoia occurs in the general public demonstrates that suspicious or paranoid thoughts are much more common than was previously thought and, in fact, are almost as common as anxiety and depression.

Wearing virtual reality headsets, 200 volunteers walked around a virtual London underground carriage in a four-minute journey between station stops. The carriage contained neutral computer people (avatars) that breathed, looked around, and sometimes met the gaze of the participants. Participants interpreted the same computer characters very differently, with almost 40 percent of the participants experiencing at least one paranoid thought. Participants who, prior to the experiment, were anxious, worried, reported bad experiences from others in the past, and had low self-esteem were the most likely to have paranoid thoughts.

Fitness May Fight Schizophrenia Free-Fall   Dr. Anthony Hannan from Melbourne's Howard Florey Institute has already shown that an environment rich with mental and physical exercise can slow the onset and progression of devastating brain disorders such as Huntingdon's disease. He's now taking the same approach to schizophrenia in the hope that it will improve behavioral deficits in schizophrenia and repair damaged chemical transmitter pathways in the brain. His approach has already been successful with a genetically altered mouse with schizophrenic-like behaviors; by putting running wheels in its cage along with interesting items to smell, see, and touch, the mouse's schizophrenia-like symptoms eased and a specific chemical transmitter pathway found to be abnormal in the cerebral cortex of the mice was selectively rescued.

Poor Social Skills May Signal Schizophrenia   But some studies have shown that when the school records of adults with schizophrenia are examined, the individuals showed poor social skills early on. Once they develop the illness, new research is finding significant deficits in the ability to detect false notes in music or read social cues (facial expressions or tone of voice). Brain scans suggest these sensory abnormalities are driven by disconnections between the brain stem and the auditory cortex, helping to explain why people with schizophrenia often have poor social skills even before they begin to show symptoms of the disease. Hopefully, identifying these deficits before full-blown symptoms show up may help devise early interventions that can prevent the worst from happening; at-risk interventions could range from musical training to social skills education.

The Least You Need to Know

- Schizophrenia is a serious medical illness that affects about 1 percent of the global population.

- Common symptoms of schizophrenia are delusions, hallucinations, disorganized speech, disorganized behavior, and inappropriate emotions.

- Schizophrenia is a disease of the brain—much as diabetes or cancer are diseases of the body—and its symptoms can be controlled with medication.

- The odds of getting schizophrenia are greater if one or more members of a family have it; prenatal birth trauma and living in a chaotic home may also contribute.

- Paranoia is a symptom found in many psychiatric disorders, including paranoid schizophrenia, paranoid delusional disorder, and paranoid personality disorder.

- Paranoid delusional disorder is characterized by a highly exaggerated and unwarranted mistrust and suspicion of others, but it does not involve hallucinations or other psychotic symptoms.

Chapter 21

Outta Control!

In This Chapter

- Normal behavior goes haywire
- Food fights: dealing with eating disorders
- The trouble with booze
- Dangerous impulses: pyromania, kleptomania, and compulsive gambling

In August 2006, Luisal Ramos, a 22-year-old Uruguayan model, suffered an anorexia-related heart attack after living on lettuce leaves and diet Coke for 3 months; she was the second model to die from this disease in 2006. Six months later, her 18-year-old model sister collapsed and died from malnutrition.

Why do young, talented, beautiful women starve themselves? And why would a fashion industry require a model to share the waist size of an average eight-year-old?

Back in 1983 we didn't understand the seriousness of anorexia nervosa or what caused it. Today, the news of another death from anorexia still saddens us, but isn't such a shock. Eating disorders in general (especially anorexia) are the deadliest of the psychiatric disorders. Without treatment, a serious eating disorder will kill 20 percent of its victims.

In this chapter, we look at a group of disorders which all start out with normal or common behaviors. Most of us have dieted, consumed alcohol, or gambled—without developing an eating disorder or an addiction to alcohol or gambling. Similarly, although young children are often fascinated by fire and, at least once, might take something that doesn't belong to them, they rarely grow up to become fire setters or kleptomaniacs. So let's explore when, why, and how these behaviors get out of control, what can be done to prevent them, and how people with addictions or impulse control disorders can kick the habit.

What's Eating You?

You might be surprised to know that *eating disorders* are not about vanity and not really about weight. They are complex psychological illnesses in which people try to control the conflict and stress in their lives by controlling their food intake. The food, weight, and body-image issues are obvious symptoms of deeper problems.

def•i•ni•tion

A person with an **eating disorder** develops a pathological relationship with food—she may eat extreme amounts of food in a single sitting, starve herself, or prevent her body from digesting her food by purging or using laxatives.

Typically, people who develop an eating disorder are at a difficult time in their lives. Let's use a fictitious person, whom we'll call Suzanne, as an example of how the eating disorder ball gets rolling. Suzanne came from a family in which a slim physique was a prized attribute. Luckily, she never had to worry about her weight—until she graduated from college.

Her first job required a move to a new city, where she was cut off from her family and old friends. Because she had to work long hours, she had little chance to make new friends and no time to exercise. At 23, Suzanne was lonely, homesick, and terrified of failing at her job. After six months, she was horrified to learn she'd gained 10 pounds. Her life already felt out of control; now her weight was out of control, too!

Over time, all her anxiety, self-doubt, and feelings of failure and inadequacy became tied to her weight. She began making herself vomit after her business dinners and started bingeing as a way to comfort herself in her lonely apartment on weekends. What would have been a difficult time in anyone's life gradually turned into an anorexic nightmare. If it had lasted long enough, Suzanne could have died.

Wasting Away to Nothing

Think back to a time when you were on a diet. Maybe you crash dieted to get ready for the senior prom, or shed a few pounds for your tenth high school reunion. Remember how hard it was? Most of us have sympathy for anyone who had trouble sticking to a diet, but we're dumbfounded that it could be hard to *quit* one!

Anorexia is a lot more complicated than an out-of-control diet. With anorexia, the strong desire to be thin, which plagues most American women, turns into an obsession. Someone with this disorder is terrified of becoming obese.

The problem is compounded by the fact that people with anorexia have lost their ability to see themselves objectively. People with anorexia feel fat no matter what their actual weight is; even when they're close to death, they'll point out areas of their bodies where they "need" to lose weight.

There's also new evidence that individuals with anorexia process taste in a different way than those without the disorder. Brain images from recovering anorexics showed significantly reduced response in the insula and related brain regions that recognize taste and judge how rewarding that taste is. In addition, while the controls showed a strong relationship between the pleasantness of the taste and the activity of the insula, this relationship was not seen in those recovering from anorexia. This suggests that, in anorexics, this region of the brain perceives food as aversive, rather than rewarding.

In addition to the physical findings, we have plenty of psychological ones to add to the mix. For example, a person with anorexia may also be trying to cope with feelings of powerlessness: she may feel that if she can't control what is happening around her, at least she can control her weight. Each morning, the number on the bathroom scale determines whether she has succeeded or failed in her goal for thinness. She feels powerful and in control when she can make herself lose weight.

And sometimes, focusing on calories and losing weight is a way of blocking out feelings and emotions. It's easier to diet than to deal with problems directly. In addition, a person with anorexia usually has low self-esteem and sometimes feels she doesn't deserve to eat.

Insight

Anorexia is a pattern of self-starvation that occurs primarily in young girls in Western cultures from middle and upper socioeconomic classes; in fact, anorexia and bulimia are extremely rare in non-Western countries.

If you try to get a person with anorexia help, he'll fight you because he's likely to see therapy as a way to force him to eat. A person with an eating disorder can do some significant damage to himself—in ways you might never have imagined. About 300,000 people with anorexia and bulimia use ipecac, a drug often kept around the house in case of accidental poisoning because it causes immediate vomiting, to get rid of unwanted food. Some physicians believe that many mysterious heart failures in patients with anorexia and bulimia may actually be due to ipecac abuse.

The Food Roller Coaster

Have you ever overeaten because you were stressed? Then consumed with guilt, you pulled yourself up by your bootstraps and dieted like crazy the next day? Maybe you even consciously added up the extra calories you ate the day before and made sure you deprived yourself of the same amount. Welcome to food games. These are mini-versions of the big eating-disorder roller coaster, bulimia nervosa. Bulimia takes the splurging and cutting back to extremes.

Bulimia nervosa is a cycle of binge eating followed by some method of trying to rid the body of unwanted calories—through fasting, vomiting, laxatives, diuretics, diet pills, or excessive exercise. People with bulimia are amazingly different in how they define a binge; although most of us have the image of a young woman locking herself in her apartment and eating her way through her entire refrigerator, another person may define a binge as eating foods that are normally prohibited from her diet.

The psychological dynamics of bulimia nervosa are different from those associated with anorexia. In bulimia, food often becomes a person's only source of comfort and a way to hide or suppress uncomfortable feelings. Unlike many people suffering from anorexia, people with bulimia are often well aware they have a problem, but may be too ashamed or scared to get help.

Psychobabble

Currently, bulimia and anorexia nervosa are the only officially recognized eating disorders in the DSM-IV-TR. A third, known as "binge eating disorder," is listed in the Appendix as needing more follow-up although compulsive overeating is the most common problem seen in treatment centers.

I Just Can't Quit Eating

Compulsive overeating or as professionals call it, binge-eating disorder, is the other side of the eating-disorder coin and is characterized by uncontrollable eating and consequent weight gain. A person who compulsively overeats uses food as a way to cope with stress, emotional conflicts, and daily problems. The food blocks out feelings and emotions, but at a price—a compulsive overeater usually feels out of control and, like people with bulimia, recognizes she has a problem but is often too ashamed of her "lack of discipline" with regard to food to seek help with the problem.

"Comfort" Food Gone Wrong

Compulsive overeating usually starts in early childhood when eating patterns are formed. Perhaps a child watches a parent overeat in response to stress. When he falls and skins his knee, he is treated to an ice cream sundae. When he feels mad, a grandparent suggests he "treat himself" to a special food. Over time, the child learns that food can soothe hurt feelings, melt away loneliness, and push down unpleasant feelings.

Most people who become compulsive eaters have never learned the proper way to deal with stressful situations and so use food as a way of coping. In addition, whereas a person with bulimia is terrified of getting fat, people who compulsively overeat often find comfort in their excess weight, using fat as a barrier that protects them from other people getting too close. This is especially common in people who have been victims of sexual abuse.

Insight

New research is also making a case for a new eating disorder—purging disorder. Unlike the large, out-of-control binge eating episodes associated with bulimia, some women eat normal or even small amounts of food and then purge, often by vomiting. They use purging to control their weight or shape rather than compensate for overeating, or to lose weight, as with anorexia.

The Vicious Binge-Diet Cycle

But no matter how much emotional protection a large body size may provide for someone who compulsively overeats, she's likely to be disgusted by her excess weight and undisciplined eating habits. So her binges are usually followed by feelings of powerlessness, guilt, shame, and failure. The more weight she gains, the harder she diets, and her drastic dieting usually leads to the next binge. This vicious cycle can go on and on—unless she gets help or begins to address the underlying emotional issues that trigger her out-of-control eating.

> **Psychobabble**
>
> While heterosexual men are at relatively low risk for eating disorders (90 percent of eating disordered clients are female), homosexual men are at higher risk as the gay male culture in many countries places especially strong emphasis on looking attractive. On the other hand, men are 5 times more likely to develop an alcohol addiction.

Most people who have an overeating problem are directed to diet centers and health spas, where they lose weight and then regain it. However, that only addresses a part of the problem; it does nothing to help them overcome the emotional issues underlying the overeating in the first place. As far as I'm concerned, the studies are in. Although most eating-disorder fatalities are due to starvation, bingeing itself can be fatal. A 23-year-old model, who had starved herself down to 84 pounds, died after gaining 19 pounds in a single binge. In fact, people with bulimia as well as those with binge eating disorder have been known to binge so severely that the abdominal wall ruptures; they literally split open from the inside out from massive amounts of food.

We Might Look Different, But We Have a Lot in Common

A woman who weighs 210 pounds looks dramatically different from a woman who weighs 75 pounds—on the outside, at least. But if you put these two women in a dark room and listen to them talk, you might not be able to tell them apart. They share a pathological relationship with food and eating, no matter which eating disorder they're struggling with. And anorexia, bulimia, and binge-eating disorder share other common circumstances and risk factors …

- ◆ Family problems or a troubled home life

- ◆ Major life changes (divorce, death of a loved one, a move)

- ◆ Romantic or social problems

- ◆ Abuse or trauma (especially physical or sexual)

These disorders are also similar in the kinds of physical dangers they can cause for their sufferers. These include disruptions in blood sugar levels, kidney infection and failure, liver failure, poor circulation, heart problems, vitamin and mineral deficiencies, weakness, fertility problems, impaired digestion, and osteoporosis or arthritis. Dental problems are also common, particularly in bulimia, as the stomach acids produced by repeated vomiting eat away the tooth enamel.

An Ounce of Prevention Is Worth a Pound of Cure

An environmental factor plays a role in the development of eating disorders: family attitudes toward food and eating. If one or both parents are stressed about how to deal with their own anxieties about their body or weight, they can unintentionally pass them along to their children.

If you're committed to teaching healthy eating habits and a positive *body image* to your children, you're swimming upstream. By the time your child is six, she will have formed a definite prejudice against obesity and a clear idea that thin is in. Throw in a few fashion magazines and, by the time she reaches adolescence, she's a lucky girl indeed if she's managed to escape our culture's beauty obsession unscathed.

def•i•ni•tion

Your **body image** is the subjective way you view your physical appearance. It consists of a complex array of thoughts, feelings, and behaviors.

Ten Seeds That Grow Healthy Eaters

You can do some things, though, to at least buffer your children against this culture's bondage to beauty and to decrease the risk that they'll develop eating disorders. But here's a warning: these tips are not for the fainthearted and may require you to do a little body-image work of your own!

◆ **Don't** make disparaging comments about your child's weight or body size—they play a direct role in the number of times a child tries to diet, their self-esteem, and their concern about weight gain.

◆ **Don't** soothe your child with food. If he's hurt, let him cry, put a Band-Aid on it, or give him a punching bag to work his feelings out on. Just don't give him a cookie!

Psychobabble

New research suggests that family meals may provide a strong protective influence against disordered eating. Teenage girls who ate five or more meals a week with their families were significantly less likely to binge, purge, or use laxatives five years later—regardless of their body size.

♦ **Don't** use food as a regular reward. If your children do something good, give them hugs, kisses, and praise, or spend special time with them.

♦ **Don't** withhold food as punishment or force your children to eat when they're not hungry. This teaches them not to trust their own bodily cues for hunger and fullness.

♦ **Do** engage in fun physical activity as a family, and limit the amount of television your family watches.

♦ **Do** provide structure for your child's eating. Eat around the same time each day and provide a well-balanced meal.

> **Psychobabble**
>
> New research suggests that eating disorder symptoms are only temporary for many adolescents. In fact, teens who were anxious at the time their eating problems began were 20 times more likely to have disordered eating a year later.

♦ **Don't** forbid any foods. Completely restricting sweets from your children's diet will backfire and make them want them more, especially as they start school and see other children eating and enjoying them.

♦ **Do** set an example. Kids learn their lifestyles from the people around them.

♦ **Don't** *ever* put your child on a diet unless it is for medical reasons. If your child is complaining about feeling "fat," then encourage her to become more physically active and to feel better about her body image.

Playing the Odds: Battling Eating Disorders

The recommended team consists of a physician, a psychiatrist or psychologist, and a nutritionist, at the minimum. Outpatient treatment can work if the disorder is not life threatening, but hospitalization or inpatient psychiatric treatment may be necessary if the person's weight is dangerously low or if he just can't stop the self-destructive behaviors on his own.

Psychotherapy is a critical component of treatment. Two types of therapy appear particularly beneficial: cognitive-behavioral therapy (CBT), which we discussed in previous chapters, and interpersonal therapy. Interpersonal psychotherapy focuses on a person's relationships with other people, a core issue for many people with eating disorders. While some professionals advocate hard-core behavior therapy (eat this much, get this reward), others criticize this as keeping the focus on eating as a control issue.

In the past, preliminary studies suggested that the SSRI medications used in the treatment of depression and anxiety (such as Prozac or Zoloft) appeared to work well in some people with anorexia, as did some of the tricyclic antidepressants. However, while antidepressants may help address a co-existing mood disorder, a recent NIMH-funded study following 93 recovering anorexics found that Prozac was no more effective than a placebo in preventing relapse or in helping them maintain a medically healthy weight.

What's the prognosis? With extensive treatment, about 60 percent of people with eating disorders recover. While we're working to get this number higher, there is hope; the earlier the treatment begins, the better!

When Someone You Love Has an Eating Disorder

Eating disorders don't just hurt the people who have them. Family members spend a lot of time worrying, trying to get their loved one help, and, oftentimes, getting into energy-draining food battles in an attempt to "fix" their loved one's eating problem. When someone has an eating disorder, it can be hard to know when to step in and where to draw the line.

And if you *do* step in to help a family member with an eating disorder, your help is often unappreciated. That doesn't mean, however, that you shouldn't try. Silence can be deadly, and a compassionate talk with your troubled loved one about worrisome behaviors can at least plant seeds that could later blossom into the recognition of the need for treatment. Here are eight ways to help someone with an eating disorder and still keep your sanity:

- ◆ Know your limits. You can be supportive and encourage the person to get help. But you cannot *make* the person get help before she is ready.

- ◆ Provide information about treatment, and offer to go along for the first visit to a therapist or doctor.

- ◆ Refrain from weight-related comments like "you're too thin" or "you don't have to worry about your weight." Do not talk about weight loss. And *never* say, "I'm glad you've put on a few pounds."

- ◆ Do not ignore behavior that concerns you. If you see clear signs that someone has been purging (for example, she always heads to the bathroom right after a meal), tell her in a nonjudgmental way and express your concern.

- ◆ Avoid power struggles over food—you will never win.

◆ Do not let the person control when, where, or what *you* eat. For example, if you live together, don't quit buying certain foods or changing your eating schedule in the hope that she will eat more.

◆ No matter how tempting it is, don't nag, beg, bribe, threaten, or manipulate.

◆ Get support for yourself. Being in a relationship with someone who has an eating disorder can take its toll.

Eat, Drink, and Be ... Addicted?

"First the man takes the drink, then the drink takes a drink, and then the drink takes the man." This Japanese proverb applies to at least 1 out of every 10 people in the United States. Odds are, you personally know someone who is addicted to alcohol—a friend, a family member, or a co-worker. Although thousands of people attend Alcoholics Anonymous every week, many more alcoholics are secretly drinking their lives away.

Of course, not all drinking is problem drinking. The National Institute on Alcohol Abuse and Alcoholism defines moderate drinking as an average of two drinks a day or less. But 15 million Americans exceed this drinking limit. And the 15 percent of men and 3 percent of women who drink more than four drinks a day are on the slippery slope to alcohol dependence.

The Road to Alcoholism

Some people drink till they're drunk from the time they take their first drink. Others start with acceptable social drinking that gradually spirals out of control. But no matter how they start, alcoholics end up at the same place—with their lives revolving around booze.

Alcoholism is not always progressive, although it usually is. And it generally follows some remarkably predictable steps:

◆ **Step One.** The drinker comes to depend upon alcohol to perk him up, relieve anxiety and stress, make special occasions more fun, and temporarily take away the blues. The drinking might still be under control, but the amount of alcohol consumed gradually increases.

◆ **Step Two.** The drinker's life starts to revolve around alcohol. The urge to drink starts earlier in the day, and the person begins to prefer alcohol-related activities. An increasing tolerance for alcohol is accompanied by *blackouts* and an increasing loss of control.

◆ **Step Three.** The later stages of alcoholism are often characterized by an obsession with alcohol—to the exclusion of relationships and financial responsibilities. The person in the late stages of alcoholism may drink around the clock. Without help, the alcoholic may eventually drink herself to death.

def•i•ni•tion

Blackouts are a type of amnesia in which the person can still function (drive or make dinner) but later can't remember what happened. A blackout is always a symptom that should be taken *very* seriously.

Psychobabble

During the middle stages of alcoholism, some drinkers may try to monitor their alcohol consumption, switch brands, or limit drinking to a certain time of day. As their strategies fail, they may begin to deny their powerlessness and rationalize that they could quit if they "really wanted to."

Are You Hitting the Booze Too Hard?

Alcohol abuse can sneak up on anyone. You can be a problem drinker and still not drink more than the people you hang out with. You can be the life of the party and let no one know you keep drinking when you go home. You can have a problem with alcohol and still get up and go to work the next day.

Assessing Your Intake

Because of the misguided stereotypes we have of what alcoholics are like, it can be difficult to identify the point at which "normal" social drinking becomes problem drinking. The following quiz may help you assess your own alcohol use or abuse.

Respond to the following questions using the number key below:

1 = never	4 = often
2 = rarely	5 = almost always
3 = sometimes	

1. Have you ever awakened the next day after partying the night before and not been able to remember part of the evening? _____

2. Is it hard to stop drinking after you've had one or two drinks? _____

3. Does someone you care about worry or complain about your drinking? _____

4. Do you ever feel guilty about your drinking? _____

5. Have you ever gotten in trouble at work because of your drinking? _____

6. Has your drinking caused problems between you and your spouse, parent, or other friend/relative? _____

7. Have you ever blown off your responsibilities for two or more days in a row because you were drinking? _____

8. Do you drink before noon? _____

9. Do people close to you say you have a problem with alcohol? _____

10. Do you drink more than most people you know? _____

Now, total up your answers. Here's how to assess your score:

10–15: We all have problems, but alcohol probably isn't one of yours. When it comes to booze, you can usually take it or leave it.

16–20: It might surprise you that, despite your relatively low score, I'm urging you to take a look at the role alcohol plays in your life. Even if it "rarely" causes blackouts or arguments, the numbers show that you're experiencing negative consequences from drinking.

21–30: Consider the red flag truly raised. If your score is over 25, you are at least at the "drink takes a drink" stage half of the time you use alcohol.

31 or higher: I am worried about your alcohol use. And judging by your answers, so are you. Why not err on the side of caution and talk to a professional—or attend an AA meeting just to see what's it's like?

Why Can't I Handle My Liquor?

Some people can drink like a fish and never develop a drinking problem. For others, alcohol is like a hypnotic poison—it quickly puts them under its spell, dramatically changes their behavior, and causes blackouts and other physical problems. Why can some of us handle liquor so much better than others?

There's no question that some of us inherit a predisposition for alcoholism. Identical twins reared apart are more likely to share alcoholism than fraternal twins living in the same family. A child of an alcoholic has four times the risk of becoming an alcoholic than a child of a nonalcoholic—even when raised by teetotalers.

However, new research suggests that it's not just our genes that set us up. Young rats exposed to alcohol (ethanol) in the womb drank significantly more alcohol than non-exposed rats. This suggests that a biologically instilled preference for alcohol's taste and smell can make young people much more likely to abuse alcohol, especially in light of social pressures, risk-taking tendencies, and alcohol's addicting qualities.

Alcohol dependence is also more prevalent in some cultures. Have you ever heard the saying, "God invented whiskey to keep the Irish from taking over the world?" People with this Anglo-Saxon ancestry do, in fact, seem to have higher rates of alcoholism, as do many people of Native American ancestry. Conversely, many Asian groups appear to have relatively low rates of alcoholism.

Alcoholism is not like a cold, however; you can't catch it from your family. Most people who develop an addiction to alcohol start out with a genetic predisposition, but the actual progression of a drinking problem is triggered by stressful life events. Developing effective stress-management strategies is one way to buffer yourself against life's tornadoes. And there are no two ways around it: it pays to stay away from the booze. No matter how many studies you read touting the heart benefits of a glass of wine a day, you're better off exercising regularly than risking addiction.

> **Psychobabble**
>
> Currently one in four children (under the age of 18) grow up in a household affected by alcoholism, according to the National Association of Children of Alcoholics.

> **Insight**
>
> The best way to find out if you're hitting the booze too hard is to ask friends, family members, or co-workers. It can be hard to objectively evaluate a behavior that's enjoyable or that you've used to cope with problems in your life.

Researchers who followed 160 teens referred to AA or NA following rehab found that teens who attended three meetings a week were abstinent during an eight-year period. This stands in contrast to the "90 meetings in 90 days" typically recommended for adults and implies that adolescents may not need to attend as frequently as adults to obtain similar outcomes.

Playing the Odds: Overcoming Alcohol Dependence

The treatment of choice for addiction is the self-help support group. While there are different types of these, the best known is Alcoholics Anonymous (AA).

AA, a worldwide self-help support group of individuals recovering from alcohol addiction, was started in 1935 by two alcoholics, Bill W. and Dr. Bob, after all their professional treatment programs had failed. Neither one of them ever drank again.

In an informal survey of AA members, 29 percent said they had remained sober for more than five years, 38 percent for one to five years, and 33 percent for less than a year. Overall recovery rates suggest that between 20 percent and 35 percent of alcohol-dependent adults will completely recover, another third of them will struggle, and the rest are likely to die prematurely or remain alcohol-dependent.

Like eating disorders' treatment, however, a treatment team can significantly boost the odds of recovery. Physical withdrawal from alcohol can be fatal if not closely supervised, so some professionals routinely recommend inpatient treatment for detoxification (detox). Psychotherapy can be an important part of treatment, especially when used in conjunction with a support group.

Brain Buster

Depression and alcohol don't mix. Although most people with alcohol problems are not clinically depressed, the substantial minority who suffer from depression are much more likely to relapse if they don't get treatment for both. And substance abusers who are depressed are much more likely to commit suicide.

And what about medications? The old treatment rule was the three "A's"—abstinence, AA, and Antabuse. While the first two are still recommended, the medication Antabuse, which made you vomit violently if you consumed alcohol, has been largely replaced by new medications aimed at reducing the cravings. Perhaps the most promising of these drugs is naltraxone. It can't stop someone from picking up that bottle, but it can help reduce the urge to.

Helping a Loved One with a Drinking Problem

Most people have heard about 12-step programs—there's one for just about every compulsive behavior out there, from narcotics abuse to gambling to shoplifting. And of course, there's the granddaddy of all 12-step programs: the one AA introduced. Here's my own recommended 12 steps for coping when someone you love has a drinking problem:

1. Don't try to control your loved one's drinking. Don't hide or get rid of the booze; she will only replace it and feel justified in her anger.

2. Don't bail your loved one out of trouble or lie for him to cover up his drinking. Let him suffer the consequences.

3. Don't blame yourself. You didn't cause your loved one to start drinking, and you can't make her stop.

4. Don't make threats unless you've thought them through and are willing to carry them out.

5. Don't try to be your loved one's therapist. Express your concern about his alcohol use in terms of the problems it creates, not by labeling him with the term *alcoholic*.

6. Don't nag, preach, or lecture.

7. Take care of yourself. Read as much as you can about alcoholism and the traps that family members can fall into.

8. Don't drink with your loved one in the hope that he will drink less.

9. Support any and every attempt your loved one makes to get help—even if it's not the method you would choose.

10. Offer as much love and support as you can without sacrificing yourself or neglecting your own needs.

11. Give Al-Anon a try. It's a self-help group for the friends and families of alcoholics. You'll find that it's helpful to be around other people who are dealing with the same issues you are.

12. Don't give up. Contrary to popular belief, not everyone with an alcohol problem has to hit bottom and lose everything before she sees the light.

I Can't Control My Impulses

Okay, let's admit it. At some time in our lives, we've all behaved impulsively. Most of us have said or done something in our lives that, looking back, seems completely out of character, something we regret. Maybe we blamed our behavior on the full moon or our first love. However we tried to explain it to ourselves, the fact is that we all commit impulsive actions once in a while.

People suffering from impulse-control disorders, however, have to live with the consequences of their rash actions *all the time*. They repeatedly fail in their attempts to resist temptation and wind up doing something that could be harmful to themselves or others.

The immediate payoff for impulsive behavior is usually a release of tension: by acting impulsively, you can "blow off steam" or feel an immediate sense of pleasure and gratification. Later, however, you're likely to feel regret or guilt or, if the behavior has gone on over time, you may find yourself constantly having to rationalize or justify your actions. The long-term consequences, whether it's jail or financial ruin, are much harder to escape.

Let's take a look at three impulse-control disorders that can get people into a lot of trouble: kleptomania, pyromania, and compulsive gambling.

I Just Had to Take It!

Kleptomania is a psychological disorder whereby a person literally cannot resist the impulse to steal objects that are not needed for personal use or for their monetary value. We're not talking about a plain old shoplifter or common criminal. In fact, the stolen objects are often discarded or given away or, if the person suffers enough remorse, returned surreptitiously at a later date. It is the act of stealing that is the goal, not the object that is stolen.

For people with kleptomania, stealing provides a relief of tension. They'll report feeling increasingly tense before the theft and an immediate sense of relief or pleasure after they commit the act. They don't really want to steal—they know that stealing is wrong and senseless, and they often feel depressed and guilty afterward. However, when tension builds, they can't resist.

> **Psychobabble**
>
> Winona Ryder isn't the only star-studded shoplifter. Miss America 1945, Bess Myerson, and actress Hedy Lamarr were both arrested for taking store items they didn't need and could easily afford to pay for.

Pyromania

Pyromania is characterized by well-planned fire-setting on at least more than one occasion. In addition to setting actual fires, people with pyromania often set off false alarms, hang out around fire stations, follow fire trucks, and watch neighborhood fires. Like all impulse-control disorders, the fire-setting is a response to emotional tension and serves as a way for the person to find relief; individuals who set fires for financial gain, revenge, or to hide other criminal activity are arsonists, not pyromaniacs. In fact, while arson is relatively common, true pyromania accounts for less than 2 percent of all fire-setting.

Pathological Gambling

There's a big difference between taking an occasional trip to Las Vegas and rolling the dice every day. Social gambling typically occurs with friends or colleagues, lasts for a fixed amount of time, and results in affordable (although unwelcome) financial losses.

Compulsive gambling, on the other hand, is out of control. Compulsive gamblers gamble with money they can't afford to lose, and use gambling either to escape from problems or to get a "high." People who compulsively gamble truly feel compelled to roll the dice. They'll lie to friends, family members, or therapists to conceal the extent to which their behavior is affecting their job or their relationships.

Unlike other addictive disorders, this one is very likely to hit in older age. Many retirees become addicted and lose a lifetime of savings before they seek treatment or before family members realize what's going on.

Not only does problem gambling run in families, a recent study found that general chaos does, too. The study consisted of interviews of 31 pathological gamblers and 31 controls and their respective first-degree relatives (parents, siblings, and children). Families with pathological gamblers had an excess of alcoholism, drug disorders, and antisocial personality disorder. In addition, more than half the pathological gamblers interviewed were either single, divorced, or widowed, which was not true of the control group.

Something is being passed along in these families that tilts them toward impulsive and ultimately self-destructive behavior. In some persons, it manifests as substance abuse, in others as antisocial behavior, and in others gambling, and often the three are combined.

Playing the Odds: Getting Control Over Impulse Disorders

While it may not seem like drinking too much, setting fires, or spending each week's paycheck at the casino could be treated the same way, they are. The first line of defense is always abstinence—staying away from the temptation! Avoid the first drink that leads to the tenth one, avoid the casino, and don't touch the matches.

Next, the self-help support groups, or 12-step groups, exist for gambling as well. People with pyromania or kleptomania are more likely to have to rely on individual or group psychotherapy.

Antidepressants may be helpful if there is an underlying depression, which there often is. What's the prognosis? Truthfully, it's not really known for pyromania and klep-tomania. For compulsive gambling, the prognosis appears similar to that of alcohol dependence—possibly with more financial consequences and fewer physical ones.

We've explored a number of behaviors that, when taken to excess, can become serious psychological disorders. Whether the addiction is food, alcohol, or setting fires, these disorders can have serious psychological, physical, and, sometimes, legal consequences. But with the right treatment, people with one of these disorders can also get better.

Straight from the Lab

The State of Our Addictions   Vermont leads the United States in marijuana use and underage drinking, while Utah has the highest number of people reporting men-tal health problems (Hawaii had the lowest, at 8.8 percent). Cocaine use was highest in the District of Columbia during the combined survey years of 2005–2006 at 2.4 percent of those 12 and older. These results indicate that, while all states struggle with substance abuse and mental health issues, prevention and intervention may be most effective if targeted to the specific patterns of the state in which they are provided.

Internet, Alcohol, and Sleep: The Triple Threat of Teen Weight Gain   U.S. researchers asked more than 5,000 teen girls to reflect on their weekly habits over the past year and report: (1) hours of sleep per night; (2) leisure time spent on the Internet; (3) number of alcoholic and coffee beverages consumed. Girls aged 18 years or older who consumed two or more alcoholic beverages a week or slept less than six hours a night gained more weight than other study participants. In fact, when combined with Internet use, girls in this group have the potential to gain four extra pounds a year.

Teenage Wasteland Starts Before 15   A recent study found that adolescents who were exposed to drugs and alcohol before the age of 15 were two to three times more likely to become dependent on substances, contract STDs, drop out of school, and have criminal records. In addition, teen pregnancy rates were higher among females who used drugs and alcohol before the age of 15 compared to those who did not use illicit substances at a young age. Interestingly, the researchers discovered that 50 per-cent of the adolescents exposed to drugs and alcohol before age 15 had no prior his-tory of negative behavioral problems suggesting that, as opposed to the popular "bad kids do drugs" theory, drug use creates bad kids.

The Least You Need to Know

◆ Eating disorders are complex psychological disorders in which eating is used to cope with other problems.

◆ The three eating disorders are anorexia nervosa, bulimia nervosa, and binge-eating disorder.

◆ All eating-disorder sufferers have a lot in common and are all at risk for a number of life-threatening medical problems.

◆ Alcoholism can start out slowly or quickly, but its downward spiral is surprisingly predictable.

◆ Kleptomania (compulsive stealing), pyromania (compulsive fire-setting), and compulsive gambling are all impulse-control disorders that can have serious emotional, social, and legal consequences.

Glossary

affective disorders A family of illnesses in which the primary symptom is a disturbance of mood, also called mood disorders.

alienist A specialist who treated mental and nervous disorders before the science of psychology was developed.

amnesia The partial or complete loss of memory; psychologically based amnesia can be triggered by a traumatic event; memory almost always returns after a few days.

anorexia nervosa A pattern of self-starvation that occurs primarily in young girls in Western cultures from middle and upper socioeconomic classes.

appetizer effect Hunger that is stimulated by external stimuli, such as the smell or sight of food or food advertisements.

archetype In Jungian theory, a universal symbol of human experience that is stored in the collective unconscious, the storehouse of ideas and forces shared by every human being who has ever lived.

aspirational groups Social groups we don't yet belong to but in which we would like to be accepted.

attention A state of focused awareness coupled with a readiness to respond.

attribution theory   A system of explanations for the causes of individual and social behavior.

behavior modification   The application of principles of operant and classical conditioning to change a person's behavior in a more adaptive direction.

binge-eating disorder   The official diagnosis given a person who eats a large amount of food within two hours, at least two days a week for six months, without purging in any way to lose or maintain her weight. This disorder is commonly called compulsive overeating.

bipedalism   The ability to walk upright on two legs.

bipolar disorder   (Commonly called manic depression.) A psychological disorder characterized by extreme mood swings of highs and lows.

blackout   A type of amnesia in which the person can still function (drive or make dinner) but later can't remember what happened.

body dysmorphia disorder   The severe preoccupation with slight or imaginary defects of the body, an obsession with body image.

body image   A complex array of thoughts, feelings, and behaviors that make up the subjective way a person views his physical appearance.

bulimia nervosa   A disorder in which a person binges (overeats) and purges (attempts to get rid of the food).

burnout   A unique pattern of emotional symptoms often found in professionals who have high-intensity contact with others on a daily basis; it is characterized by exhaustion, a sense of failure, and a tendency to relate to others in a depersonalized and detached manner.

cingulotomy   A form of psychosurgery that uses radio frequency current to destroy the cingulum, a small structure in the brain known to be involved in emotionality.

circadian rhythm   The clock that regulates your sleep/wake cycle.

classical conditioning   When two stimuli become so closely associated that one of them can elicit the same reactive behavior as the other.

cognitive dissonance   The inner conflict we experience when we do something that is counter to our prior values, beliefs, and feelings.

cognitive model   A hypothetical representation of how cognitive processes work.

cognitive processes   The mental abilities that enable us to know and understand the things around us; they include attending, thinking, remembering, and reasoning.

collective unconscious   The storehouse of ideas and forces shared by every human being who has ever lived.

consciousness   Our awareness of ourselves and all things we think, feel, and do.

contingency management   A technique designed to change behavior by modifying the consequences.

counterconditioning   A behavioral modification technique in which a new response is substituted for an unwanted or ineffective one.

cyclothymia   A disorder in which a person experiences the symptoms of bipolar disorder but in a milder form. The symptoms are not severe enough to disrupt normal functioning and don't include hallucinations or delusions.

declarative memory   The portion of memory that stores information and facts.

defense mechanism   A mental process of self-deception that reduces an individual's awareness of threatening or anxiety-producing thoughts, wishes, or memories.

demand characteristics   Situational cues that influence our perceptions and our behaviors. For example, most of us would automatically obey the directions of a police officer or the advice of our physician because we have been taught to do so.

diathesis-stress model   The psychological theory that says predisposing biological factors interact with life stressors in the environment to cause illness.

diffusion of responsibility   A weakening of each person's sense of personal responsibility and obligation to help. It happens when one person perceives that the responsibility is shared with other group members.

dissociative disorder   A psychological disorder characterized by a disturbance in the integration of identity, memory, or consciousness.

dissociative identity disorder   (Better known as multiple personality disorder.) A psychological disorder in which two or more distinct personalities coexist in the same person at different times.

dual diagnosis   A term used to describe a person with two or more simultaneous mental-health problems, such as a person suffering from alcohol dependence and major depression. It is also referred to as coexisting disorders.

dysthymia   A psychological disorder in which the feelings of depression are less severe than those in major depression but last for at least a two-year period.

eating disorder   A psychological disorder during which a person develops a pathological relationship with food, using it to meet needs other than physical hunger.

ego   Freud's term for the part of our personality that focuses on self-preservation and the appropriate channeling of our basic instincts.

emotional intelligence   The ability to successfully understand and use emotions. It involves a group of skills, including the ability to motivate ourselves, regulate our moods, control our impulses, and empathize with others.

encephalization   The development of a larger brain during the course of evolution.

event-related potential (ERP)   The measurable change in brain waves in response to a particular stimulus.

explicit memory   The ability to retain information we've put real effort into learning.

false memory syndrome   A pattern of thoughts, feelings, and actions based on a mistaken or inaccurate memory for traumatic experiences that a person claims to have previously repressed.

flow   The sense of effortless action we feel when we are totally absorbed in a task.

Freudian slip   A mistake or substitution of either spoken or written words. Freud believed that such slips come from subconscious wishes that pop up unexpectedly through unintentional words. By analyzing these slips, a person might get some clues into her inner thoughts or real intent or wishes.

fundamental attribution error   A tendency to overestimate the influence of personality or other internal traits and to underestimate situational factors in explaining other people's behavior.

gender dysphoria   A clinical illness characterized by a desire to be, or insistence that one is, of the opposite sex; men have this disorder two to three times more often than women.

General Adaptation Response (GAS)   A pattern of general physical responses triggered by any stressors, no matter what kind.

genome   The full complement of an organism's genetic material, in other words, a blueprint for building all the structures and directing all the processes for the lifetime of that organism.

habituation   The process whereby a person becomes so accustomed to a stimulus that he ignores it and attends instead to less familiar stimuli.

hypnotizability   A measure of how susceptible a person is to entering a hypnotic state.

hypothesis   An answer to a question, based on theoretical assumptions, that can be tested to see if the answer can be proven wrong.

id   Freud's term for the uninhibited pleasure-seeker in one's personality.

implicit memory   The ability to remember information we haven't deliberately tried to learn.

impression management   All the ways in which people try to control the perceptions other people have of us.

judgment   The process of using available information to form opinions, draw conclusions, and evaluate people and situations.

Kleptomania   An impulse-control disorder during which a person feels an uncontrollable urge to steal regardless of economic need.

language acquisition devices (LADs)   The preprogrammed instructions for learning a language that some linguists believe all infants are born with.

language acquisition support system (LASS)   The circumstances that facilitate the efficient acquisition of language.

latent content (of a dream)   The meaning that lies hidden underneath the dream—its symbols, images, and actions.

learning   Any process through which experience at one time can change our behavior at another.

locus of control   A person's perception of the usual source of control over rewards; an internal locus of control means we believe our behavior determines our fate; an external locus of control means we think external forces (destiny, luck, or the gods) control our fate.

manifest content (of a dream)   The literal story told by a dream.

maturation   The process of growth typical of all members of a species who are reared in the usual environment of the species.

mental retardation   A condition in which a person has significantly impaired intelligence in combination with problems in living (taking care of oneself, getting along with others, and doing other age-appropriate tasks).

mnemonics   Short verbal strategies that improve and expand our ability to remember new information by storing it with familiar and previously encoded information.

morality   A system of beliefs, values, and underlying judgments about the rightness of human acts.

motivation   The physical and psychological process that drives us toward a certain goal.

natural selection   The Darwinian principle that says the best-adapted traits are the ones that will be passed along from one generation to another in a species. Creatures with less well-adapted traits will die out before they can reproduce, so their poorly adapted traits will eventually disappear from the population.

nerve   A bundle of sensory or motor neurons that exist anywhere outside the central nervous system. We have 43 pairs of them—12 pairs from the brain and 31 pairs from the spinal cord.

neuron   A nerve that specializes in information processing.

neuropsychologist   A psychologist specially trained in identification, assessment, and possible rehabilitation of brain damage.

neurotransmitter   Biochemical substances that stimulate other neurons. More than 60 substances have been identified as neurotransmitters, including dopamine, norepinephrine, and serotonin.

off-labeling   The process of prescribing a medication not yet approved or extensively studied for safety and/or efficacy.

operant conditioning   Encouraging voluntary behavior that attempts to influence control over the environment. When a rat learns that pressing a lever gets more food, it has been operant conditioned to push the lever.

panic disorder   An anxiety disorder during which a person experiences recurrent episodes of intense anxiety and physical arousal that last up to 10 minutes.

pathological gambling   Also known as compulsive or addictive gambling. A behavioral addiction during which a person gambles to the extent that it has a severe negative impact on job, relationships, mental health, or other important aspects of life.

paresis   A disease of the brain contracted by a syphilis-caused infection of the central nervous system characterized by dementia and paralysis.

personality   The unique bundle of all the psychological qualities that consistently influence an individual's usual behavior across situations and time.

personality disorder   A long-standing, inflexible, and maladaptive pattern of thinking, perceiving, or behaving that usually causes serious problems in a person's social or work environment.

postpartum depression   Depression after childbirth which lasts more than two weeks and interferes with the mother's ability to function.

prejudice   A learned negative attitude toward a person based on his membership in a particular group.

procedural memory   The long-term memory of how things are done.

psychoanalysis   The field of psychology that specializes in applying Freudian principles to the treatment of psychological disorders.

psychoanalyst   Specialist in Freud's school of psychological treatment; one must complete an intensive post-graduate training program, specializing in psychoanalytic theory and practice (including undergoing one's own analysis).

psychodynamic personality theory   A model of personality that assumes that inner forces (needs, drives, motives) shape personality and influence behavior.

psychological diagnosis   A label used to identify and describe a mental disorder, based on information collected by observation, testing, and analysis. It is also a judgment about a person's current level of functioning.

psychoneuroimmunology   The study of the interactions between the brain, the body, the emotions, and the immune system.

psychopathology   The clinical term for an abnormality or disorder in thought, emotion, or behavior.

psychophysics   The study of psychological reactions to physical stimuli.

psychosis   (Also called psychotic disorder.) A general term for a severe mental disorder that prevents an accurate understanding and interaction with reality due to impaired thoughts, inappropriate emotions, and distorted perceptions.

pyromania   A psychological disorder in which a person feels an uncontrollable urge to start fires. The motive behind the fire-setting is to relieve tension, and the person typically feels relief or gratification afterward.

reasoning   A process of realistic, goal-directed thinking in which conclusions are drawn from a set of facts.

reference group   Any group that a person uses to compare and evaluate himself against, from age-related peers to supermodels on the covers of fashion magazines.

reinforcement   A consequence that increases the occurrence of a particular behavior over time. Reinforcement can be either positive (a hug, a raise in pay) or negative (a punishment).

REM sleep   Sleep characterized by rapid eye movement, brain activity close to that of wakefulness, and a complete absence of muscle tone. Most dreaming takes place during REM sleep.

reference group   A group to whom a person looks to get information about what attitudes and behaviors are acceptable or appropriate. It can be a formal group (church or club) or an informal group (peers or family).

repressed memory   The memory of a traumatic event retained in the unconscious mind, where it is said to affect conscious thoughts, feelings, and behaviors even though one has no conscious memory of the alleged trauma.

resilience   The ability to thrive, mature, and increase competence in the face of risk and adversity.

retrieval cues   Mental or environmental aids that help us retrieve information from long-term memory.

savant ability   An exceptional skill in a narrow area, such as doing calculations or composing music, that is significantly higher than the person's overall level of functioning.

schizophrenia   A severe mental disorder characterized by a breakdown in perceptual and thought processes, often including hallucinations and delusions.

scientific method   A way of answering questions that helps remove bias from the study. First you form your question into a statement that can be proven false, and then you test it against observable facts. Other researchers who doubt your findings can duplicate your test and see if they get the same results.

self-actualization   The constant striving to realize one's full potential.

self-concept   A person's awareness of his identity as a distinct and unique individual.

self-fulfilling prophecies   Predictions about a behavior or event that actually shape its outcome in the expected direction.

self-monitoring   The degree to which we vary our self-presentation to match the people we're with.

self-serving bias   A tendency to accept credit when things turn out well and to blame the situation or other people when things go badly.

shaping   A process of rewarding small steps in the direction of the desired behavior.

signal detection theory   The assumption that both physical and psychological factors influence the ability to perceive environmental stimuli.

situationism   The assumption that situational factors can have subtle and powerful effects on our thoughts, feelings, and actions.

social comparison   The process of comparing ourselves with others to identify our own unique abilities.

social psychology   The study of how people are influenced by their interactions and relationships with other people.

somatization   The tendency to channel emotions into physical complaints; instead of feeling angry, one might get a headache. A hypochondriac is an extreme example of somatization.

somatoform disorder   A mental disorder in which a person experiences symptoms of physical illness but has no medical disease that could cause them.

state   A temporary emotional condition.

stimulus generalization   When an individual who has become conditioned to respond to one stimulus in a certain way will also respond in that same way to any similar stimuli.

stress   A general term that includes all the physical, behavioral, emotional, and cognitive responses we make to a disruptive internal or external event.

stressors   The events that trigger a stress response.

superego   Freud's term for an individual's social conscience.

tardive dyskinesia   An unusual disturbance in motor control (especially of the facial muscles) that can be caused by long-term use of antipsychotic medication.

theory   A set of assumptions about a question.

think-aloud protocols   A research method during which subjects are asked to describe their problem-solving strategy at the time that they are actually trying to solve a real-life problem.

trait   A stable characteristic that influences an individual's thoughts, feelings, and behavior.

Psychology Resources

Mental Health Advocacy Groups

National Mental Health Association
1021 Prince Street
Alexandria, VA 22314-2971
www.nmha.org.index/cfm

National Alliance for the Mentally Ill
www.nami.org

National Mental Health Consumer's Self-Help Clearinghouse
www.libertynet.org/mha/cl_housc.html

General Online Psychology Resources

American Psychological Association
www.apa.org

American Psychological Society
www.psychologicalscience.org

Self-Help and Psychology Magazine
www.shpm.com

Internet Mental Health
www.mentalhealth.com

Health Touch
www.healthtouch.com

KEN Consumer Information
www.mentalhealth.org/consumer/index.html

Psych Central
www.psychcentral.com

Psych Watch
www.psychwatch.com

Psych Web
www.psywww.com

PsychRef
www.maple.lemoyne.edu/~hevern/psychref.html

Psychology Today
www.PsychologyToday.com

Mental Health Net
www.cmhc.com

Mental Health Infosource
www.mhsource.com

Sites That Have Lists of Psychology Links and Online Resources

Amoebaweb: Psychology on the Web
www.vanguard.edu/faculty/ddegelman/amoebaweb

Cyber Psych
www.cyber.psych.com

Encyclopedia of Psychology
www.psychology.org/links/resources/MetaSites/index/html

Psych Central
www.psychcentral.com

Resources for Specific Problems

Alcohol Resources

Alcoholics Anonymous
www.alcoholics-anonymous.org

Depression Resources

Depression and Related Affective Disorders Association (DRADA)
Meyer 3-181
600 N. Wolfe Street
Baltimore, MD 21287-7381
Online contact: drada@welchink.welch.jhu.edu

Depressive and Bipolar Support Alliance (formerly National Depressive and Manic
Depressive Association)
730 North Franklin Street, Suite 501
Chicago, IL 60610-3526
1-800-826-3632
312-642-7243
www.dbsalliance.org

National Organization for Seasonal Affective Disorder (NOSAD)
P.O. Box 40190
Washington, D.C. 20016

Depression After Delivery
P.O. Box 1282
Morrisville, PA 19067
1-800-944-4773
www.beharenet.com/dadinc

Postpartum Support International
927 North Kellog Avenue
Santa Barbara, CA 93111
805-967-7376
Online contact: THONIKMAN@compuserve.com

Wing of Madness: A Depression Guide
www.wingofmadness.com

Dr. Ivan's Depression Central
www.psycom.net/depression.central.html

Bipolar Resources

Moodswing.org
www.moodswing.org

Pendulum
www.pendulum.org

Anxiety Resources

Anxiety Disorders Association of America
11900 Parklawn Drive, Suite 1200
Rockville, MD 20852
www.adaa.org

Anxiety Disorders Education Program
www.nimh.nih.gov/anxiety

Obsessive-Compulsive Foundation, Inc.
P.O. Box 70
Milford, CT 06460-0070
203-878-5669
Online contact: JPHS28A@prodigy.com
www.pages.prodigy.com/alwillen.ocf.html

Eating Disorders Resources

American Anorexia Bulimia Association
www.abainc.org

Anorexia Nervosa and Related Disorders, Inc.
www.anred.com

National Eating Disorders Association (NEDO)
6655 South Yale Avenue
Tulsa, OK 74136
918-481-4044
www.laureate.com/nedo/nedointro.asp

Overeater's Anonymous World Service Office
6075 Zenith Court NE
Rio Rancho, NM 87124
505-891-2664
www.recovery.hiway.net

The Something Fishy Website on Eating Disorders
www.something-fishy.org/top/html

Schizophrenia

Schizophrenia Home Page
www.scizophrenia.com

Mental Wellness
www.mentalwellness.com

NAMI Consumer and Family Guide to Schizophrenia Treatment
www.nami.org/disordcrs/trcatmcnt/html

Therapy Resources

California Board of Psychology: A Consumer Guide to the Mental Health Professions
www.psychboard.ca.gov/pubs/consumer.html

Counselling Resource
www.counsellingresource.com

Finding a Therapist
1-800-THERAPIST

Psychology Today magazine's FREE Find-a-Therapist database
www.PsychologyToday.com

Rating a Therapist
www.cybercouch.com/library/rati.tag.html

Personality and I.Q. Self-Assessment

Personality Psychology Links
www.wesleyan.edu/spn/person.html#online

Personality and I.Q. Tests
members.aol.com/HOON4R/personality.html

ABC's Personal Growth
www.helpself.com

Online I.Q., Personality, Political Tests, and Novelty Games
www.universityoflife.com/serious.html

Positive Psychology Websites

Authentic Happiness Website
www.authentichappiness.org

Positive Psychology Center
www.positivepsychology.org

Quality of Life Research Center
www.qlrc.cgu.edu

Values in Action Institute
www.viastrengths.org

Questions About Psychiatric Medicine

Medications—Health Center's Pharmacy Page
www.health-center.com/english/pharmacy/meds/default/html

Index

D

E

F

I

J–K

L

N

U–V

W–X–Y–Z

CHECK OUT THESE BEST-SELLERS

More than 450 titles available at booksellers and online retailers everywhere!

978-1-59257-115-4

978-1-59257-900-6

978-1-59257-855-9

978-1-59257-222-9

978-1-59257-957-0

978-1-59257-785-9

978-1-59257-471-1

978-1-59257-483-4

978-1-59257-883-2

978-1-59257-966-2

978-1-59257-908-2

978-1-59257-786-6

978-1-59257-954-9

978-1-59257-437-7

978-1-59257-888-7

ALPHA   idiotsguides.com